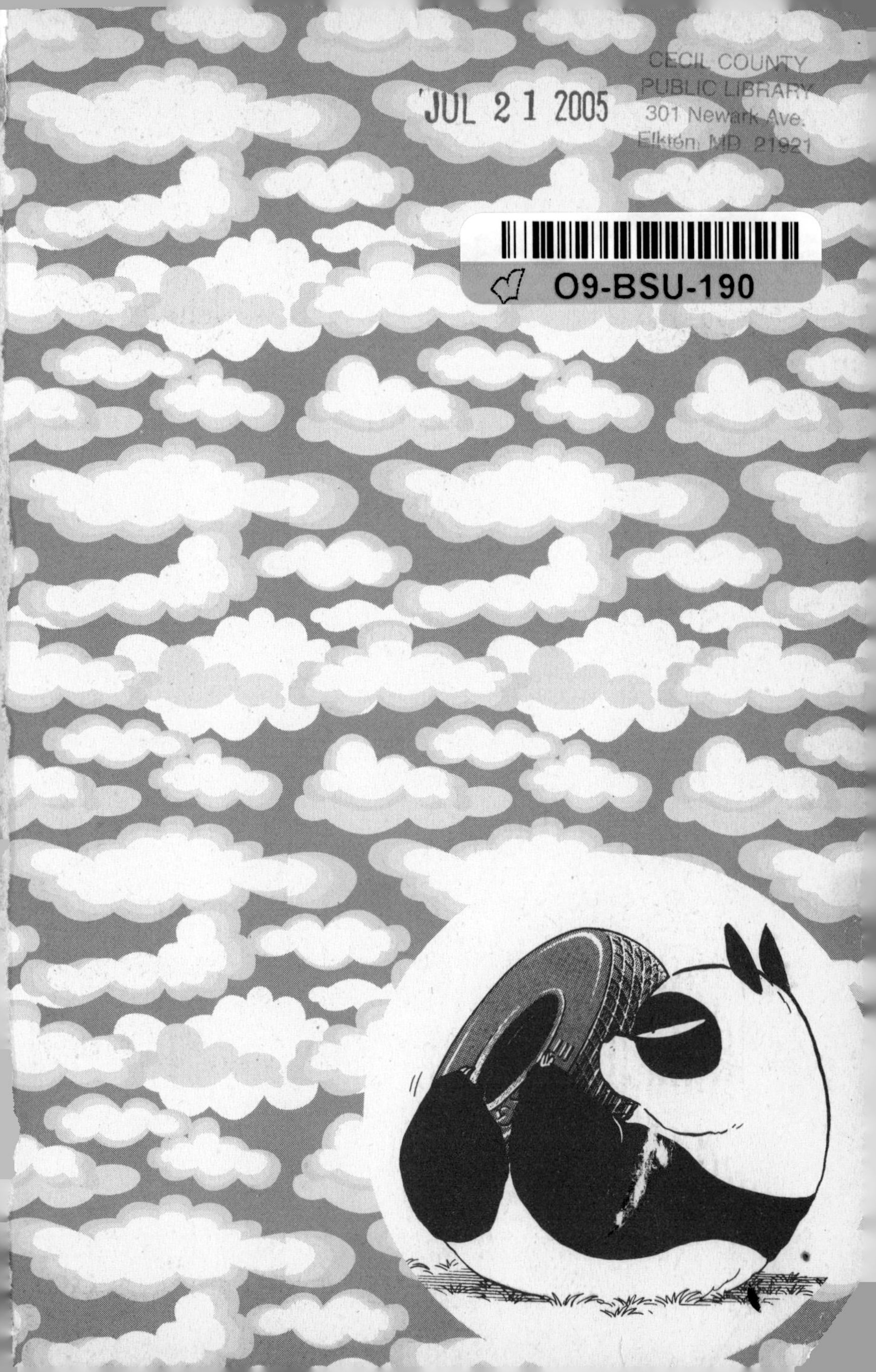

VOL. 5
Action Edition (2nd Edition)

Story and Art by
RUMIKO TAKAHASHI

English Adaptation by Gerard Jones and Toshifumi Yoshida and Matt Thorn
Touch-Up Art & Lettering/Wayne Truman
Cover Design/Yuki Ameda
Graphics & Design/Sean Lee
Editor (1st Edition)/Trish Ledoux
Editor (Action Edition)/Julie Davis

Production Manager/Noboru Watanabe
Managing Editor/Annette Roman
Editor in Chief/William Flanagan
Dir. of Licensing & Acquisitions/Rika Inouye
Sr. VP of Sales & Marketing/Liza Coppola
Sr. VP of Editorial/Hyoe Narita
Publisher/Seiji Horibuchi

RANMA 1/2 is rated "T+" for Older Teens. It may contain violence, language, alcohol or tobacco use, or suggestive situations.

© 1988 Rumiko Takahashi/Shogakukan. First published by Shogakukan, Inc. in Japan as "Ranma 1/2."

RANMA 1/2 is a trademark of VIZ, LLC. © 2003 VIZ, LLC. All rights reserved. No unauthorized reproduction allowed.

New and adapted artwork and text
© 2003 VIZ, LLC

All rights reserved.

The stories, characters and incidents mentioned in this publication are entirely fictional. For the purposes of publication in English, the artwork in this publication is printed in reverse from the original Japanese version.

Printed in Canada.

Published by VIZ, LLC
P.O. Box 77010
San Francisco, CA 94107

1st Edition published 1995

Action Edition (2nd Edition)
10 9 8 7 6 5 4 3 2
First printing, October 2003
Second printing, October 2003

www.viz.com

store.viz.com

Ranma 1/2™

VOL. 5 **Action Edition**

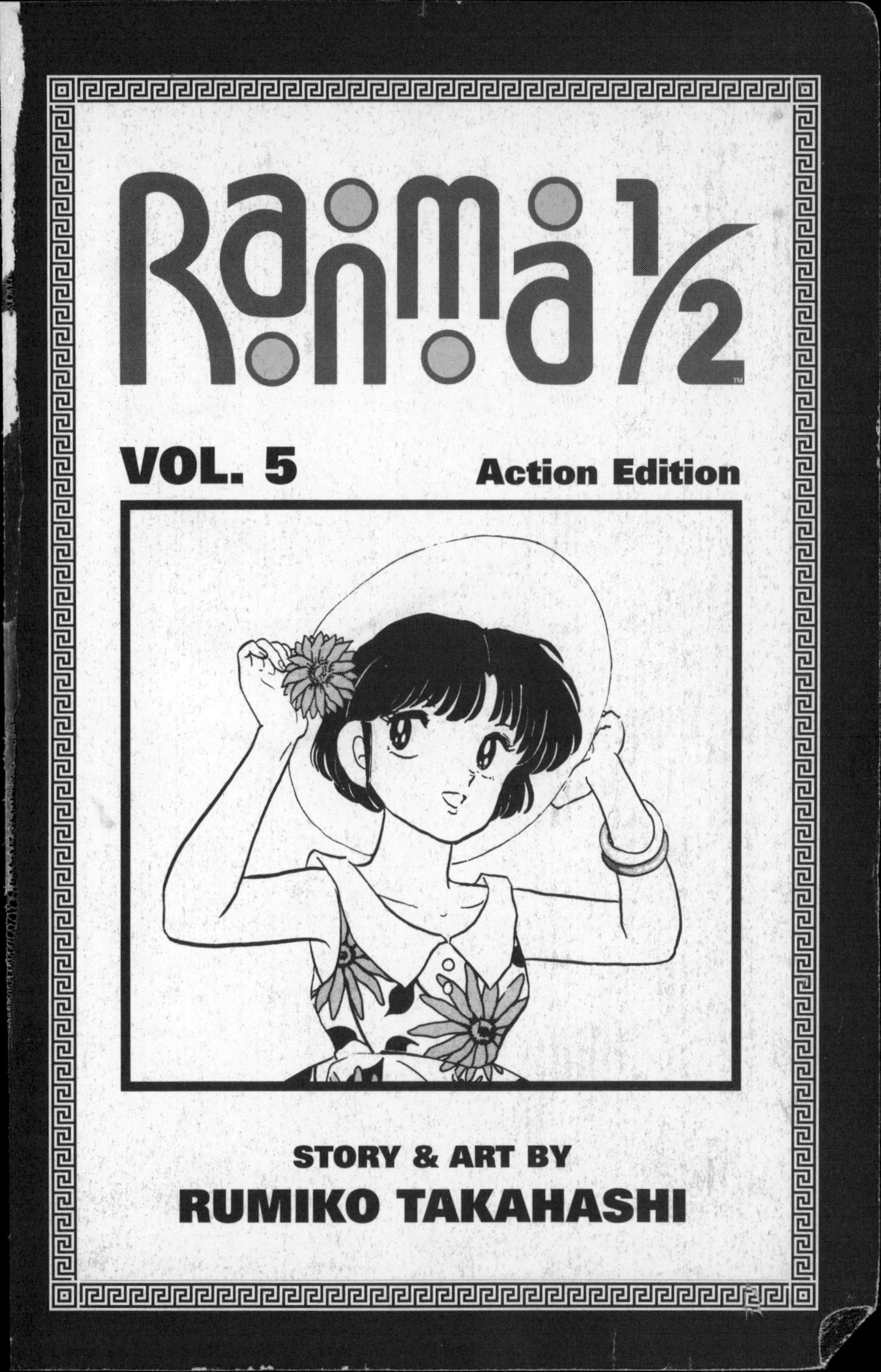

STORY & ART BY

RUMIKO TAKAHASHI

STORY THUS FAR

The Tendos are an average, run-of-the-mill Japanese family—at least on the surface, that is. Soun Tendo is the owner and proprietor of the Tendo Dojo, where "Anything-Goes Martial Arts" is practiced. Like the name says, anything goes, and usually does.

When Soun's old friend Genma Saotome comes to visit, Soun's three lovely young daughters—Akane, Nabiki, and Kasumi—are told that it's time for one of them to become the fiancée of Genma's teenage son, as per an agreement made between the two fathers years ago. Youngest daughter Akane—who says she hates boys—is quickly nominated for bridal duty by her sisters.

Unfortunately, Ranma and his father have suffered a strange accident. While training in China, both plunged into one of many "accursed" springs at the legendary martial arts training ground of Jusenkyo. These springs transform the unlucky dunkee into whoever—or whatever—drowned there hundreds of years ago.

From now on, a splash of cold water turns Ranma's father into a giant panda, and Ranma becomes a beautiful, busty young woman. Hot water reverses the effect...but only until next time.

Ranma and Genma weren't the only ones to take the Jusenkyo plunge—it isn't long before they meet several other members of the "cursed." And although their parents are still determined to see Ranma and Akane marry and carry on the training hall, Ranma seems to have a strange talent for accumulating extra fiancées, and Akane has a few suitors of her own. Will the two ever work out their differences, get rid of all these extra people, or just call the whole thing off? And will Ranma ever get rid of his curse?

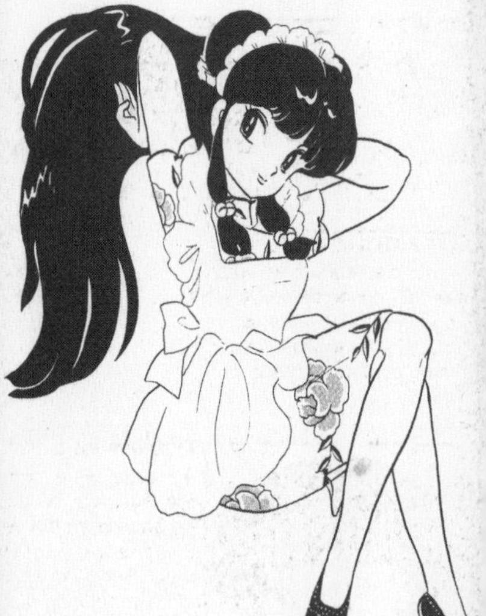

CAST OF CHARACTERS

RANMA SAOTOME
Martial artist with far too many finacées, and an ego that won't let him take defeat easily. He changes into a girl when splashed with cold water.

SHAMPOO
A Chinese Amazon warrior who has changed her mind from wanting to kill Ranma to wanting to marry him.

GENMA SAOTOME
Ranma's lazy father, who left his home and wife years ago with his young son to train in the martial arts. He changes into a panda.

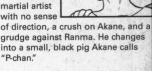

RYOGA HIBIKI
A melancholy martial artist with no sense of direction, a crush on Akane, and a grudge against Ranma. He changes into a small, black pig Akane calls "P-chan."

AKANE TENDO
A martial artist, tomboy, and Ranma's fiancée by parental arrangement. She has no clue how much Ryoga likes her, or what relation he has to her pet black pig, P-chan.

MOUSSE
A nearsighted martial artist and Shampoo's childhood suitor, Mousse's specialty is the art of hidden weapons.

TATEWAKI KUNO
A kendo expert who loves both Akane and "the pigtailed girl" (i.e., Ranma).

COLOGNE
Shampoo's great-grandmother, a martial artist and matchmaker

CONTENTS

Part 1

KITTEN OF THE SEA

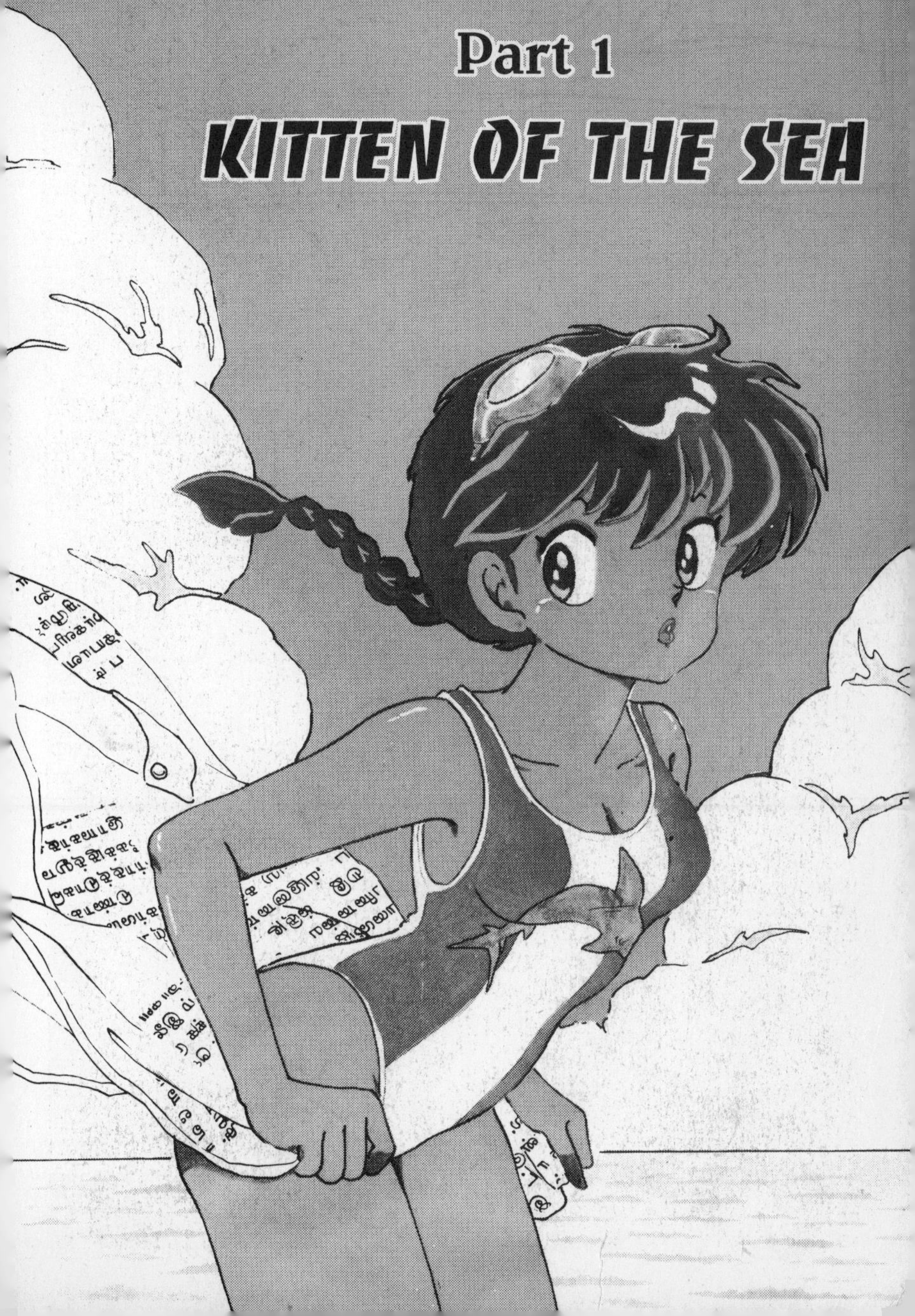

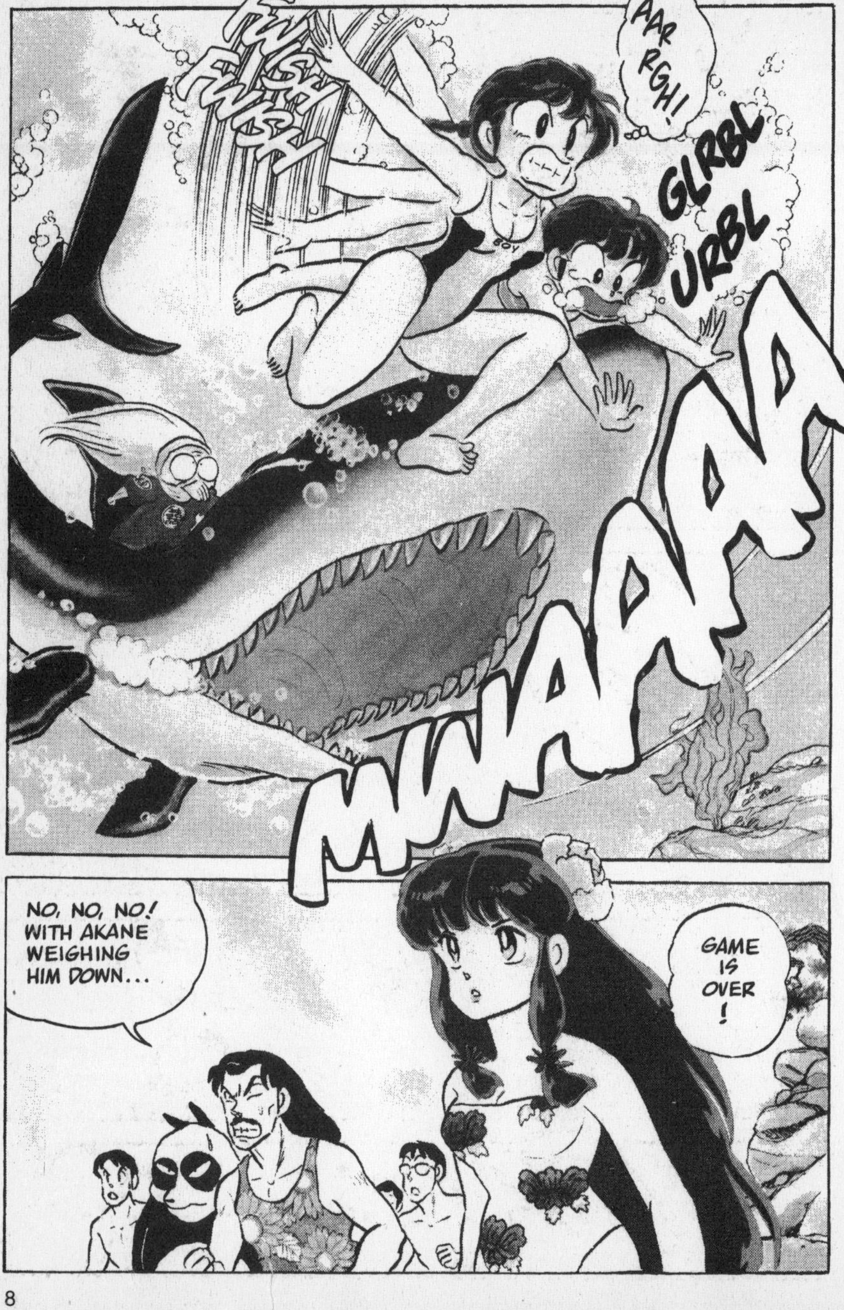
FWISH FWISH
AAR RGH!
GLRBL URBL
MUNAAAA
NO, NO, NO! WITH AKANE WEIGHING HIM DOWN...
GAME IS OVER!

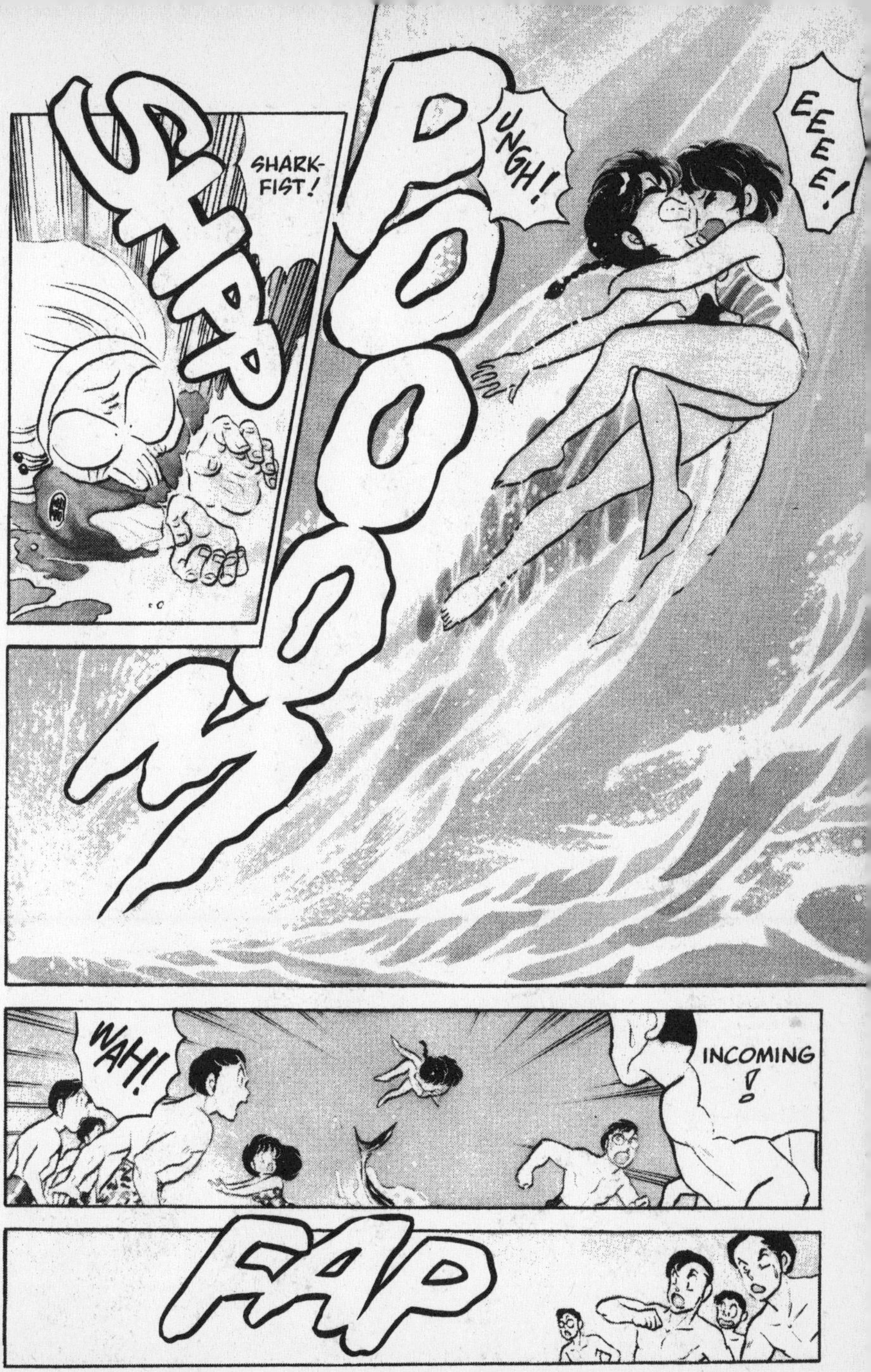
SHIPP
SHARK-FIST!
POOOOM
UNGH!
EEEEE!
WAH!
INCOMING!
FAP

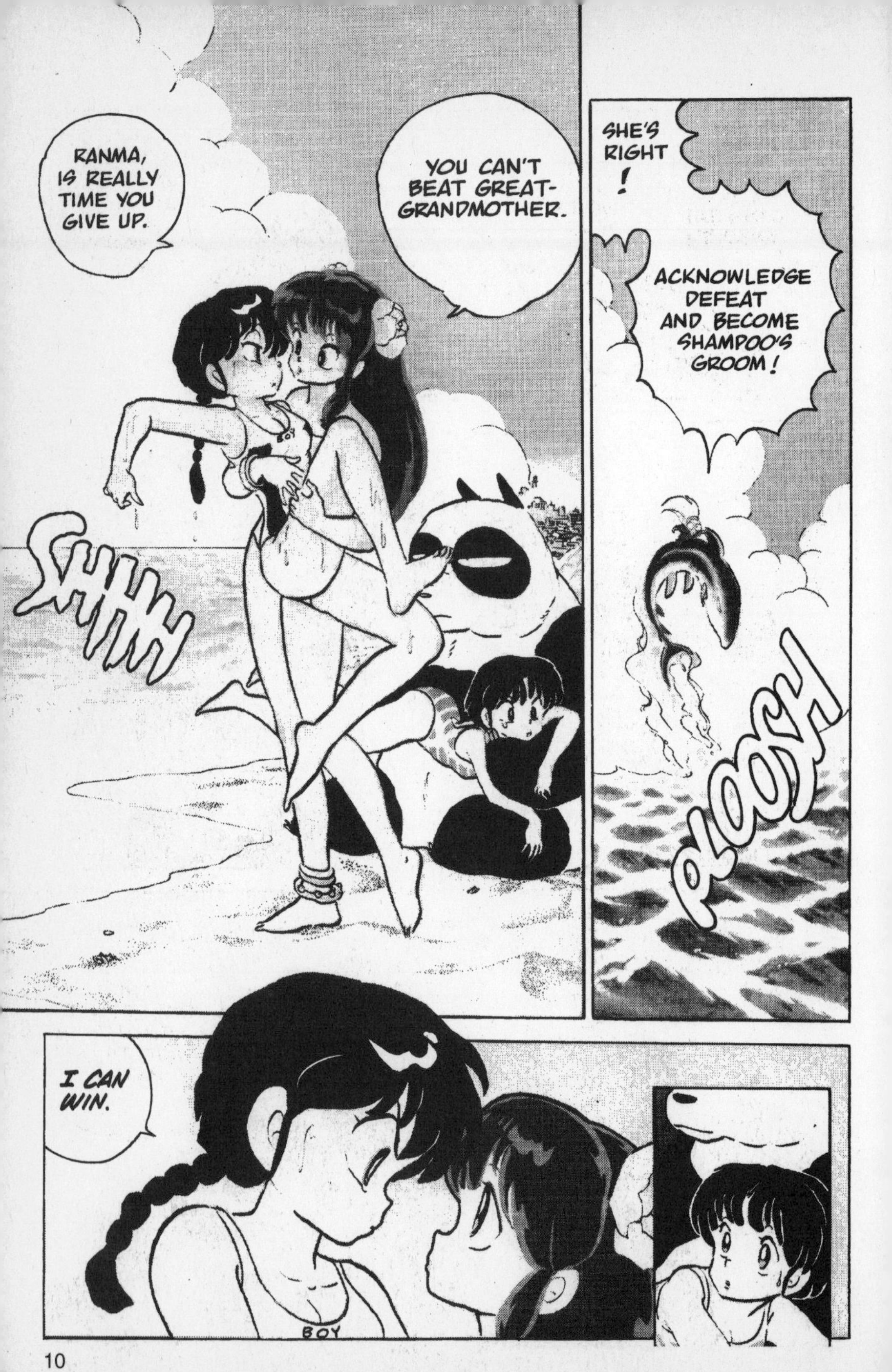
RANMA, IS REALLY TIME YOU GIVE UP.
YOU CAN'T BEAT GREAT-GRANDMOTHER.
SHHHH
SHE'S RIGHT !
ACKNOWLEDGE DEFEAT AND BECOME SHAMPOO'S GROOM!
PLOOSH
I CAN WIN.
BOY

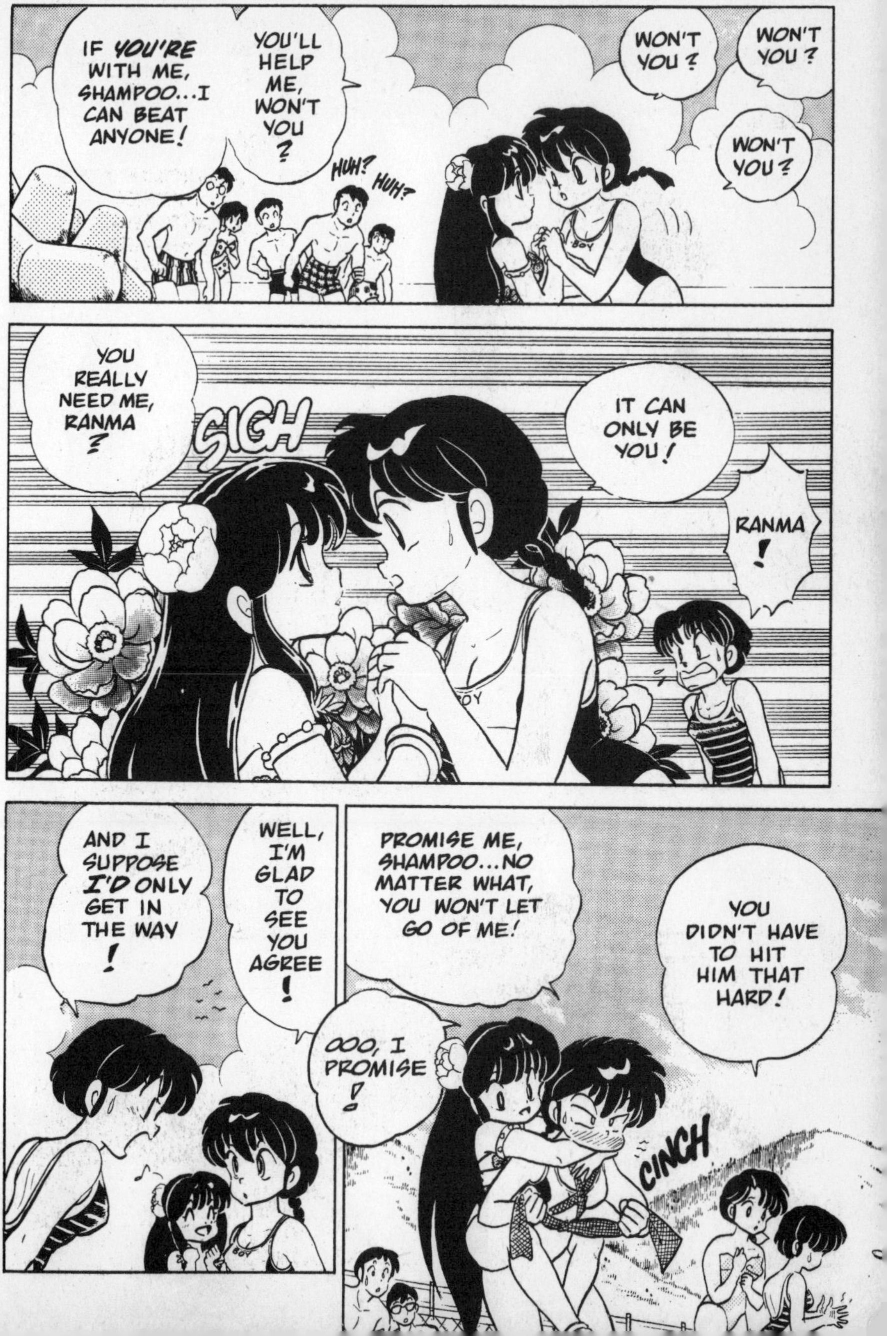
IF YOU'RE WITH ME, SHAMPOO...I CAN BEAT ANYONE!
YOU'LL HELP ME, WON'T YOU?
HUH? HUH?
WON'T YOU?
WON'T YOU?
WON'T YOU?
YOU REALLY NEED ME, RANMA?
SIGH
IT CAN ONLY BE YOU!
RANMA!
AND I SUPPOSE I'D ONLY GET IN THE WAY!
WELL, I'M GLAD TO SEE YOU AGREE!
PROMISE ME, SHAMPOO...NO MATTER WHAT, YOU WON'T LET GO OF ME!
OOO, I PROMISE!
YOU DIDN'T HAVE TO HIT HIM THAT HARD!
CINCH

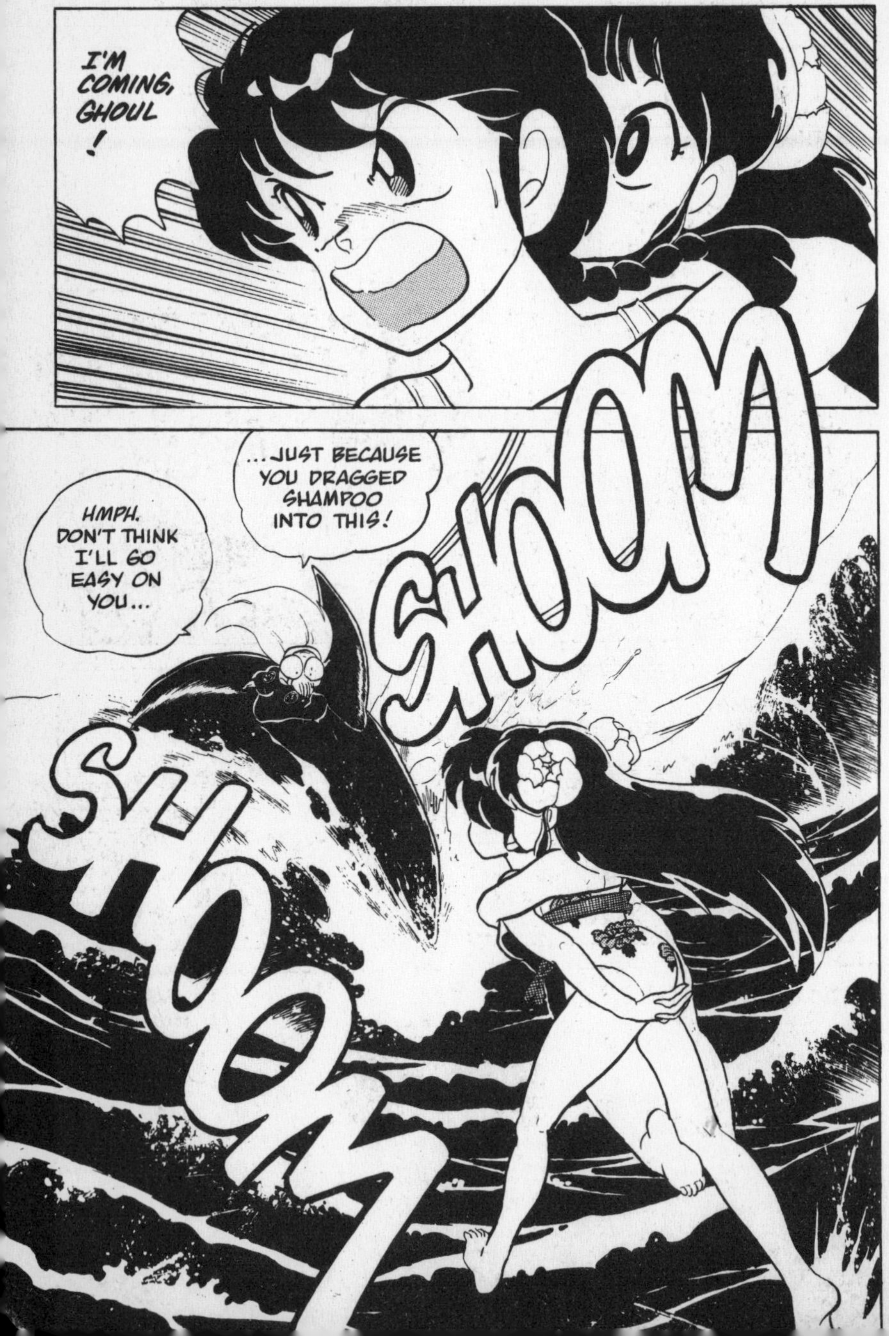
I'M COMING, GHOUL!
HMPH. DON'T THINK I'LL GO EASY ON YOU...
...JUST BECAUSE YOU DRAGGED SHAMPOO INTO THIS!
SHOOM
SHOOM

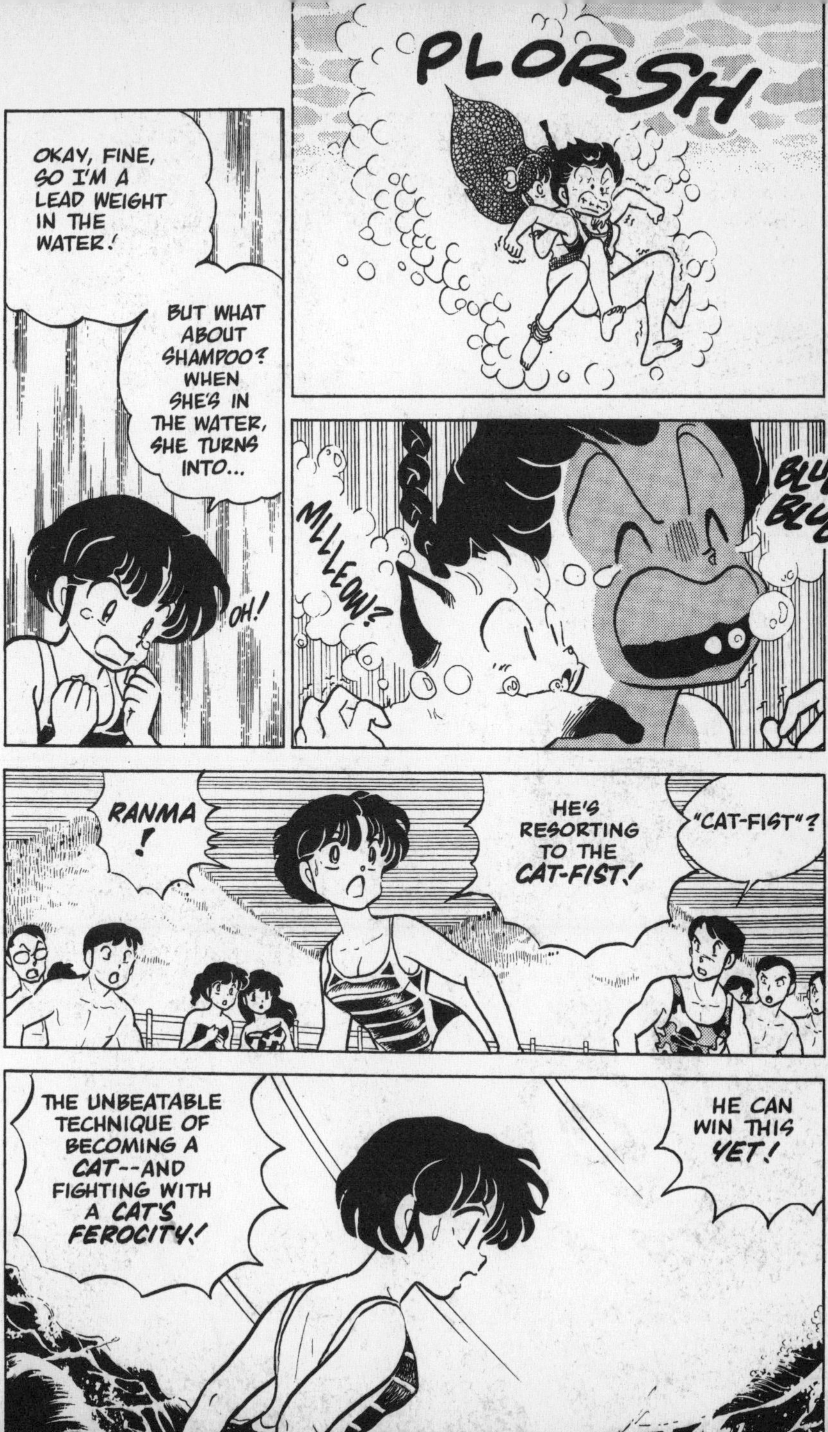
OKAY, FINE, SO I'M A LEAD WEIGHT IN THE WATER!
BUT WHAT ABOUT SHAMPOO? WHEN SHE'S IN THE WATER, SHE TURNS INTO...
OH!
PLORSH
MLLEOW?
BLUB BLUB
RANMA!
HE'S RESORTING TO THE CAT-FIST!
"CAT-FIST"?
THE UNBEATABLE TECHNIQUE OF BECOMING A CAT--AND FIGHTING WITH A CAT'S FEROCITY!
HE CAN WIN THIS YET!

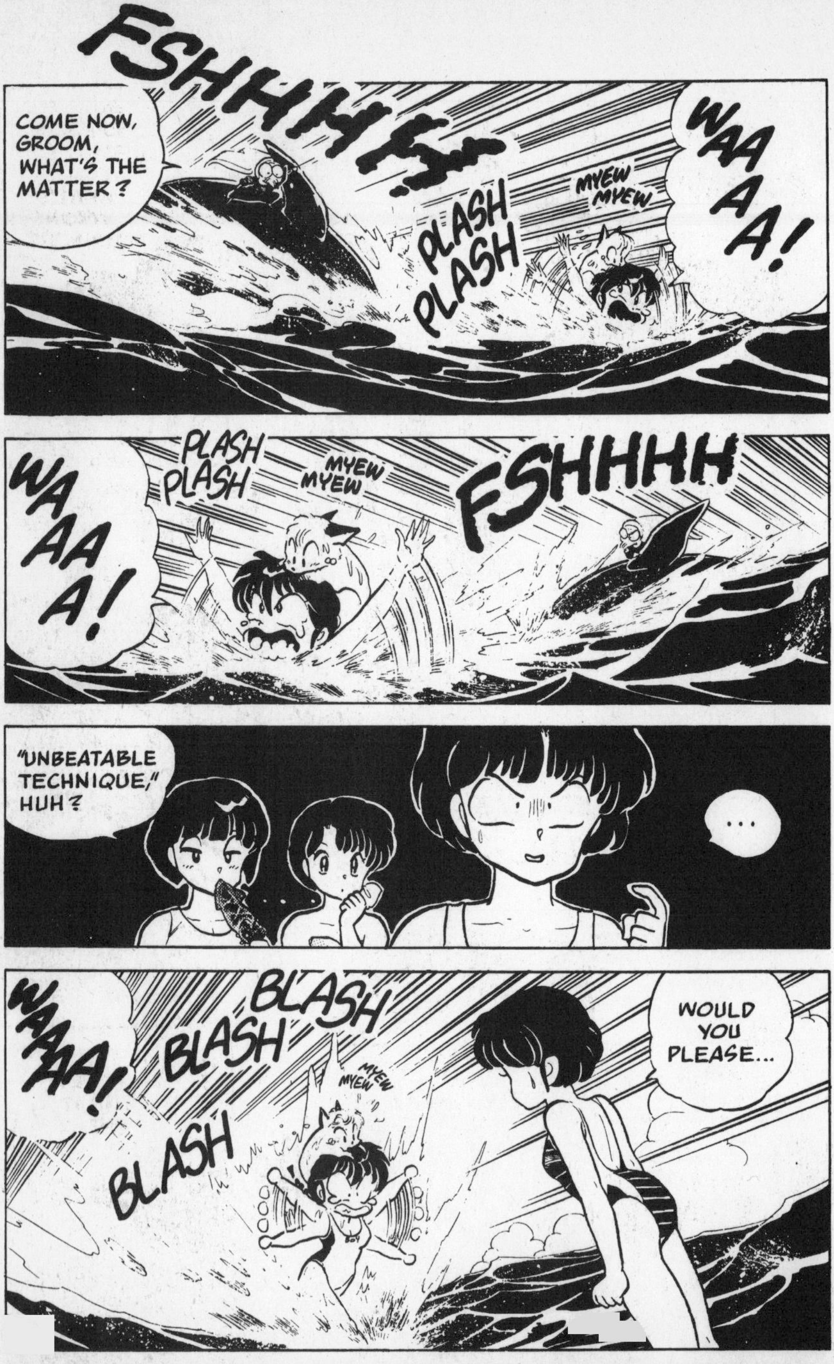
FSHHHH
COME NOW, GROOM, WHAT'S THE MATTER?
PLASH PLASH
MYEW MYEW
WAAAAA!
WAAAAA!
PLASH PLASH
MYEW MYEW
FSHHHH
"UNBEATABLE TECHNIQUE," HUH?
...
WAAAAA!
BLASH
BLASH
BLASH
MYEW MYEW
WOULD YOU PLEASE...

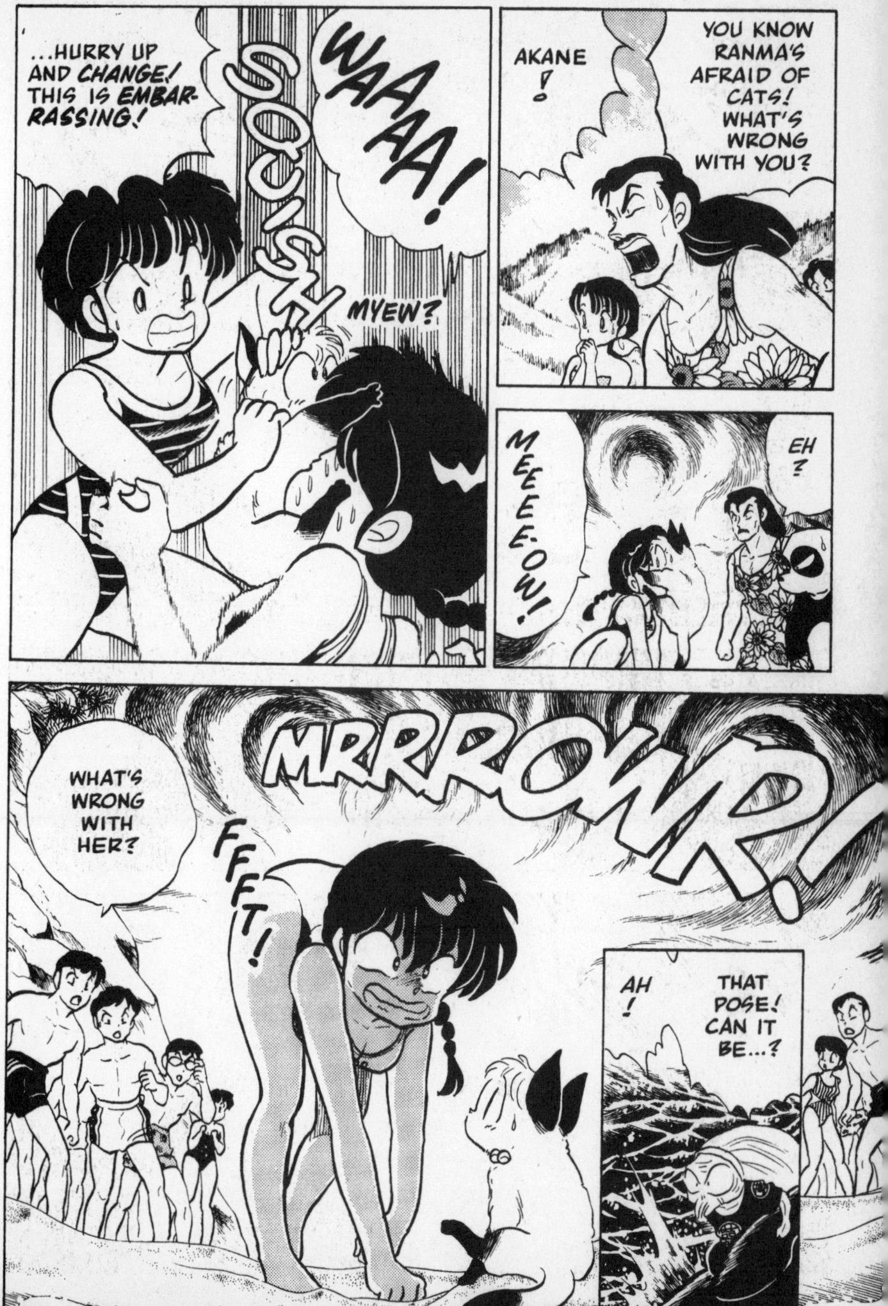
...HURRY UP AND CHANGE! THIS IS EMBARRASSING!
SQUISH
WAAAAA!
MYEW?
AKANE!
YOU KNOW RANMA'S AFRAID OF CATS! WHAT'S WRONG WITH YOU?
MEEEEOW!
EH?
WHAT'S WRONG WITH HER?
FFFT!
MRRROWR!
AH!
THAT POSE! CAN IT BE...?

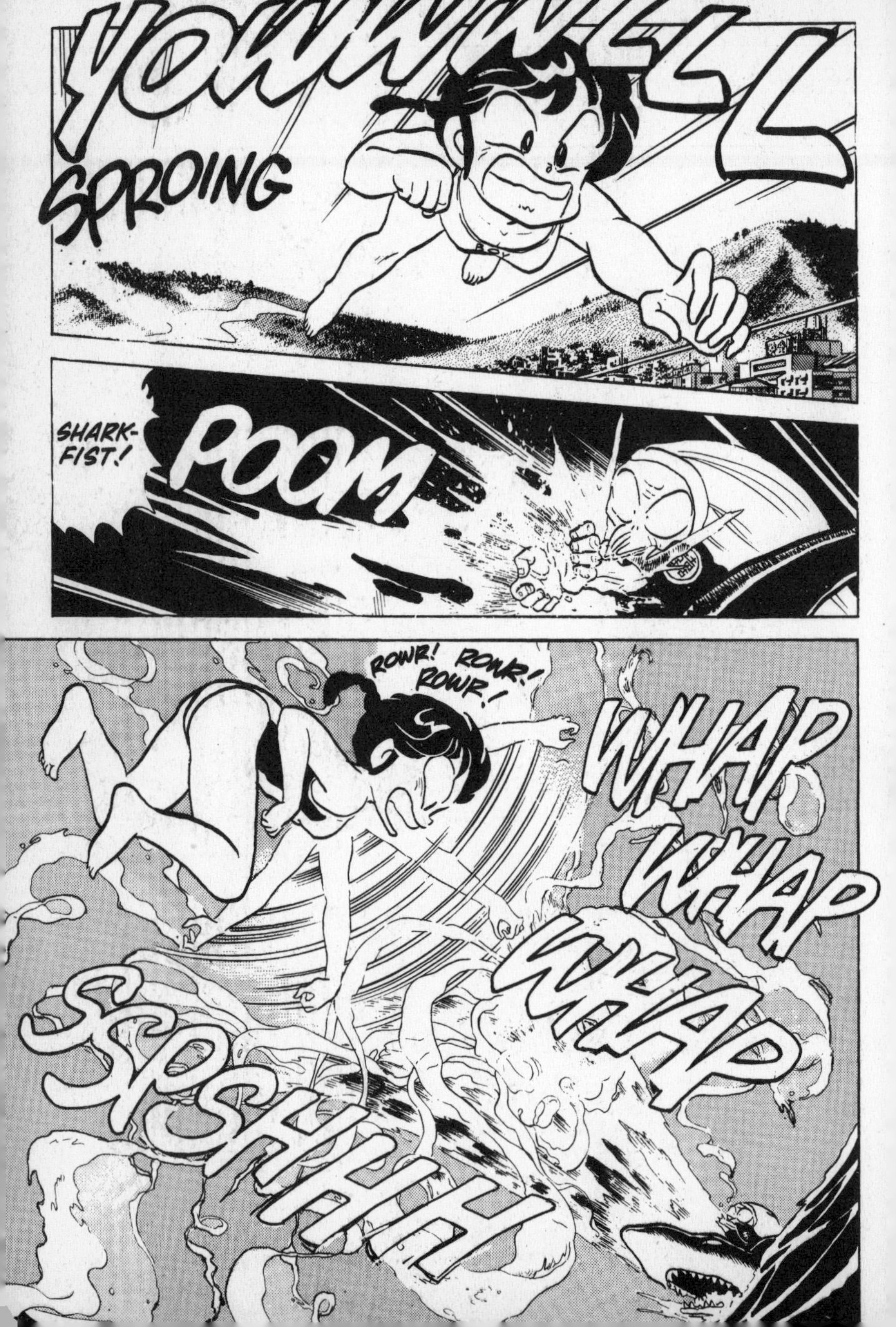
YOWWWLLL
SPROING
SHARK-FIST!
POOM
ROWR! ROWR! ROWR!
WHAP
WHAP
WHAP
SPSHHH

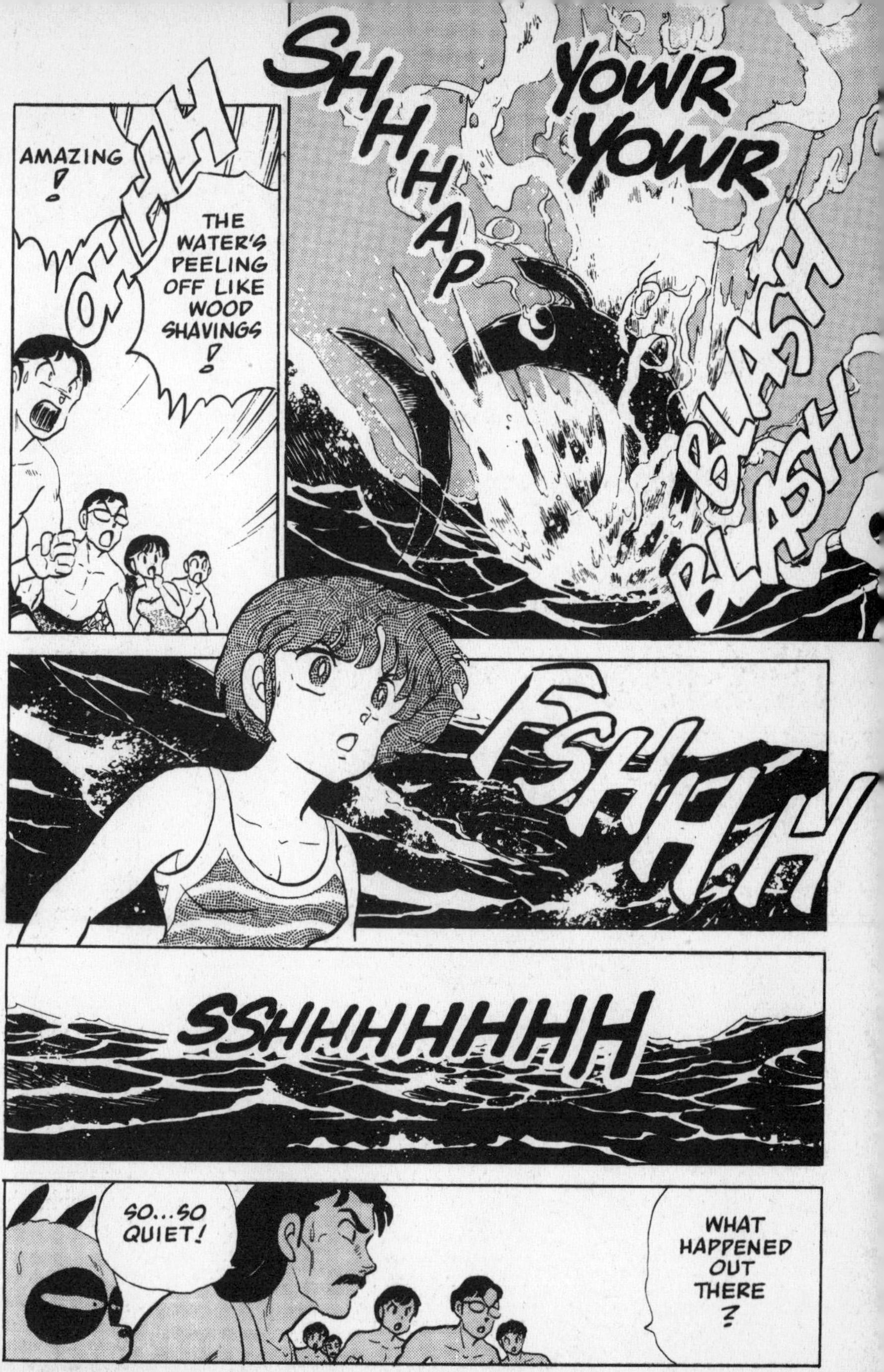
AMAZING!
OHHH
THE WATER'S PEELING OFF LIKE WOOD SHAVINGS!
SHHHAP
YOWR YOWR
BLASH
BLASH
FSHHHH
SSHHHHHHH
SO...SO QUIET!
WHAT HAPPENED OUT THERE?

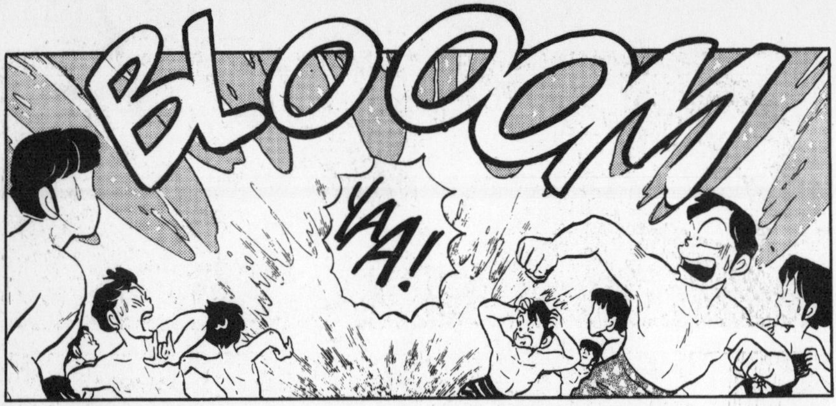
BLOOOM
YAAA!
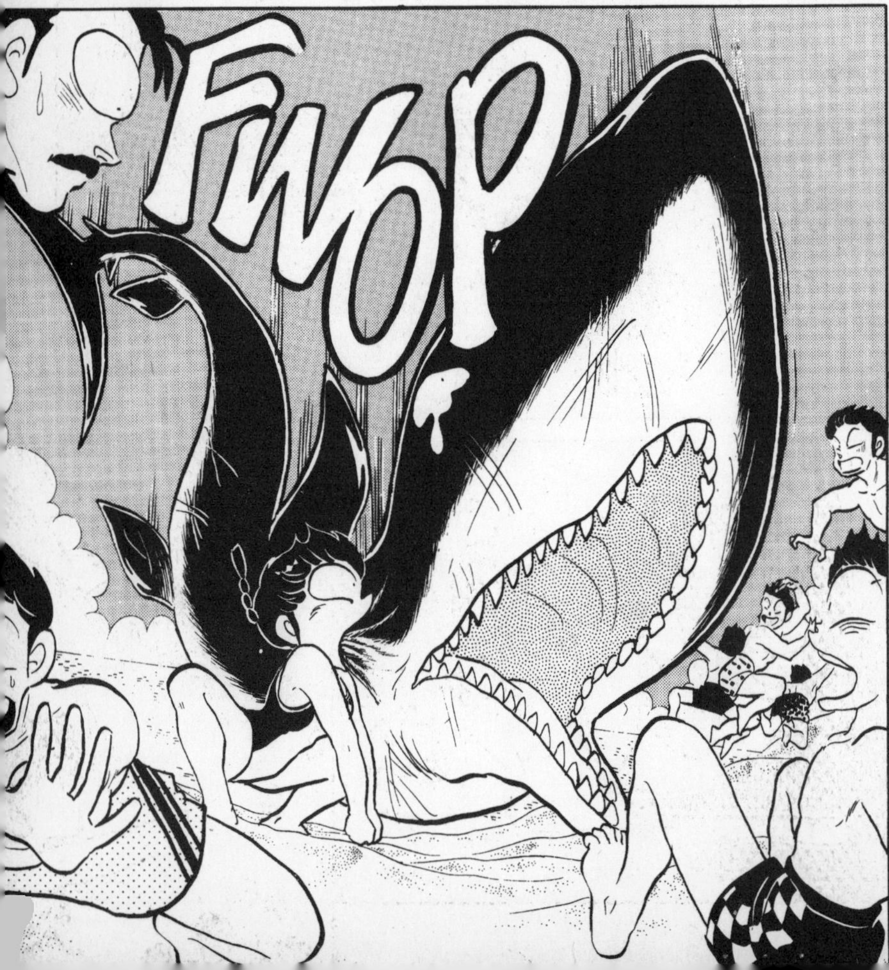
FWOP

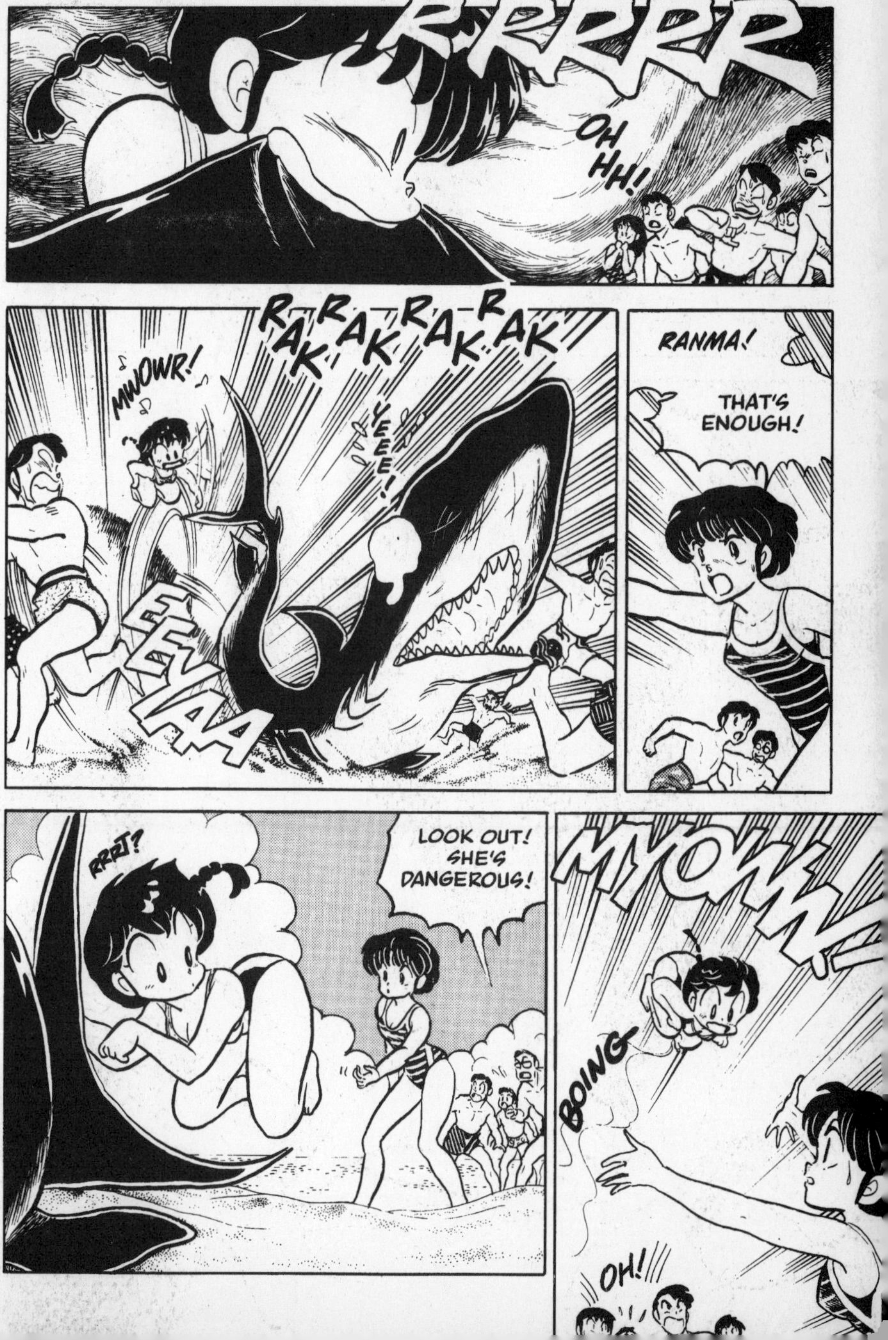
RRRRRR
OHHH!
R-R-R-R
AK AK AK AK
MWOWR!
YEEEE!
EEYAA
RANMA!
THAT'S ENOUGH!
RRRT?
LOOK OUT! SHE'S DANGEROUS!
MYOW!
BOING
OH!!

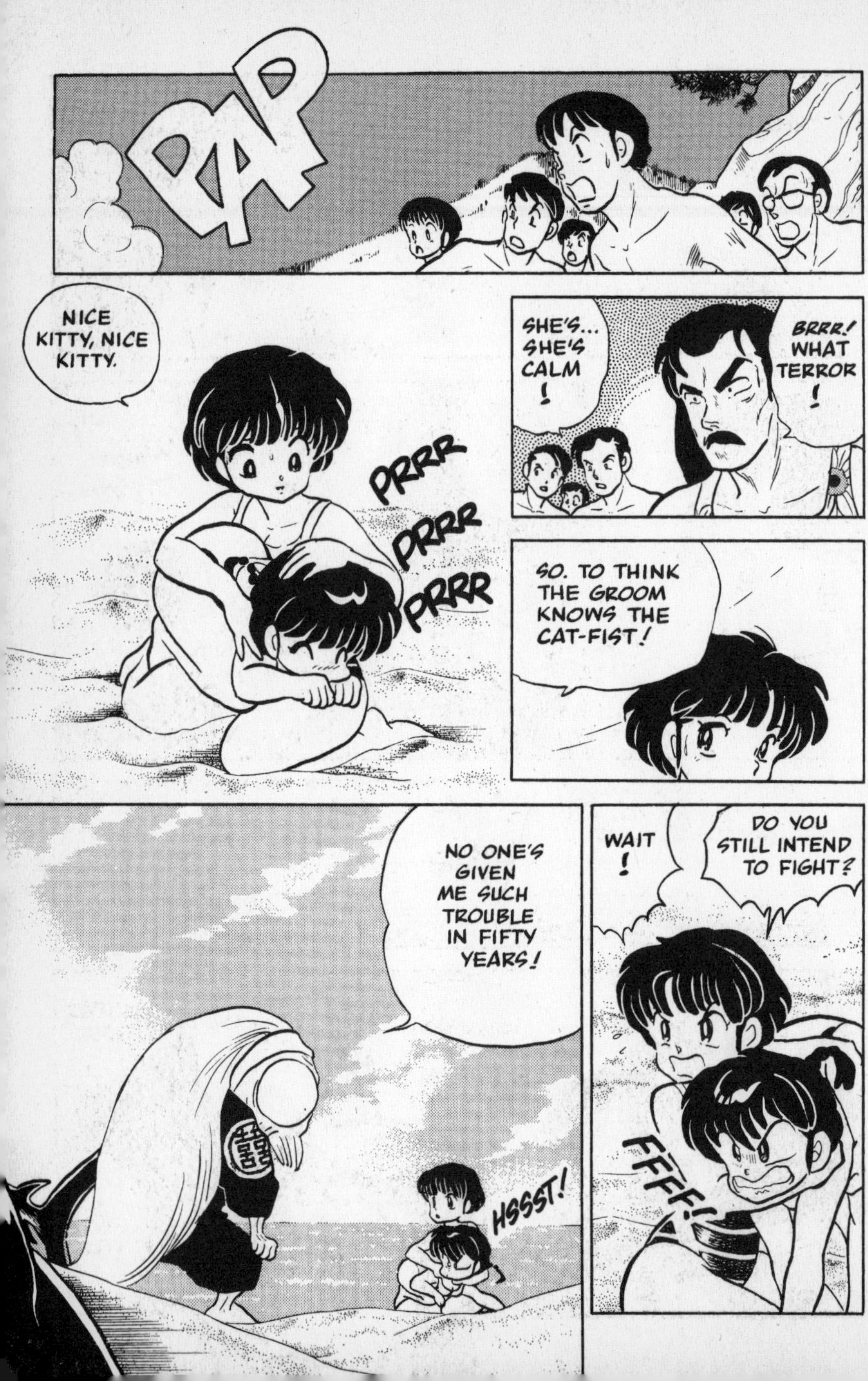
PAP
NICE KITTY, NICE KITTY.
PRRR PRRR PRRR
SHE'S... SHE'S CALM!
BRRR! WHAT TERROR!
SO. TO THINK THE GROOM KNOWS THE CAT-FIST!
NO ONE'S GIVEN ME SUCH TROUBLE IN FIFTY YEARS!
HSSST!
WAIT!
DO YOU STILL INTEND TO FIGHT?
FFFF!

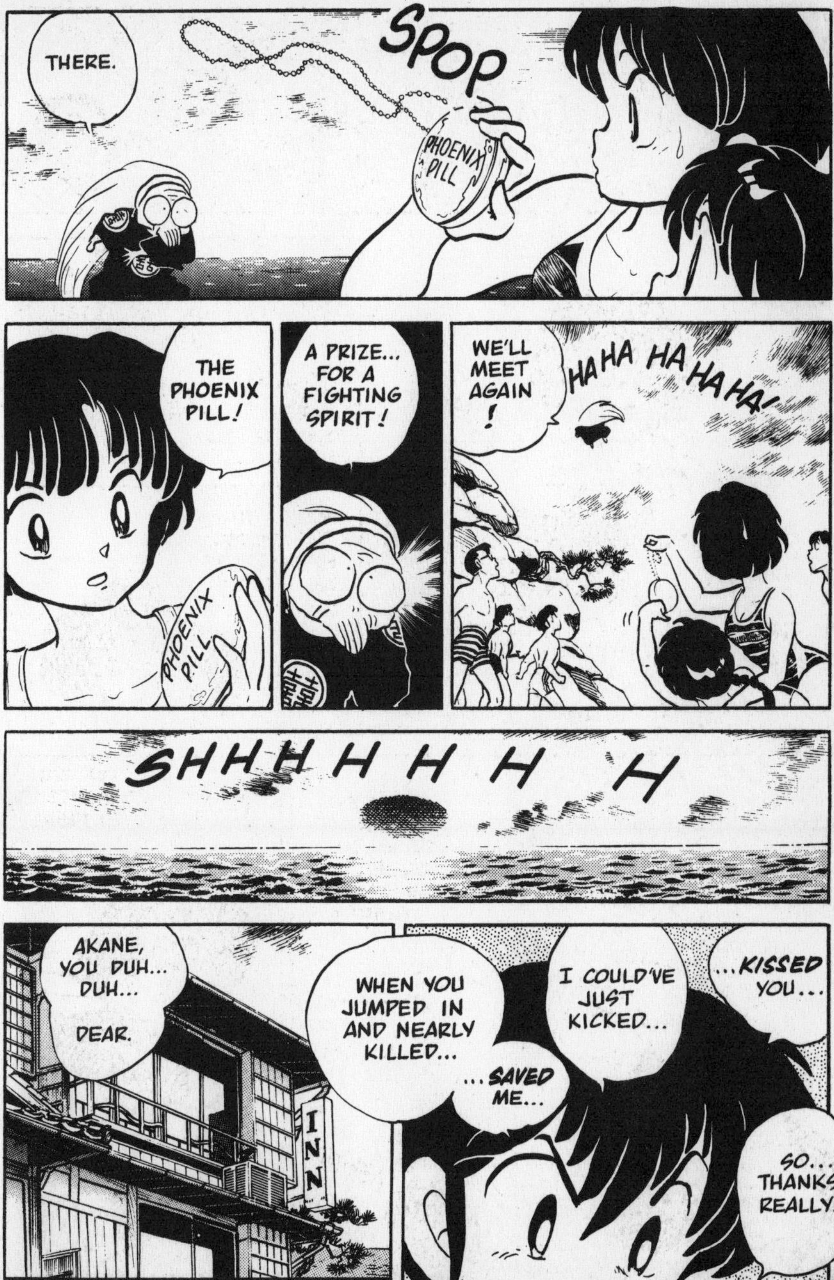
THERE.
SPOP
PHOENIX PILL
THE PHOENIX PILL!
PHOENIX PILL
A PRIZE... FOR A FIGHTING SPIRIT!
WE'LL MEET AGAIN!
HA HA HA HA HA HA!
SHHHHHH H
AKANE, YOU DUH... DUH...
DEAR.
INN
WHEN YOU JUMPED IN AND NEARLY KILLED...
...SAVED ME...
I COULD'VE JUST KICKED...
...KISSED YOU...
SO... THANKS. REALLY.

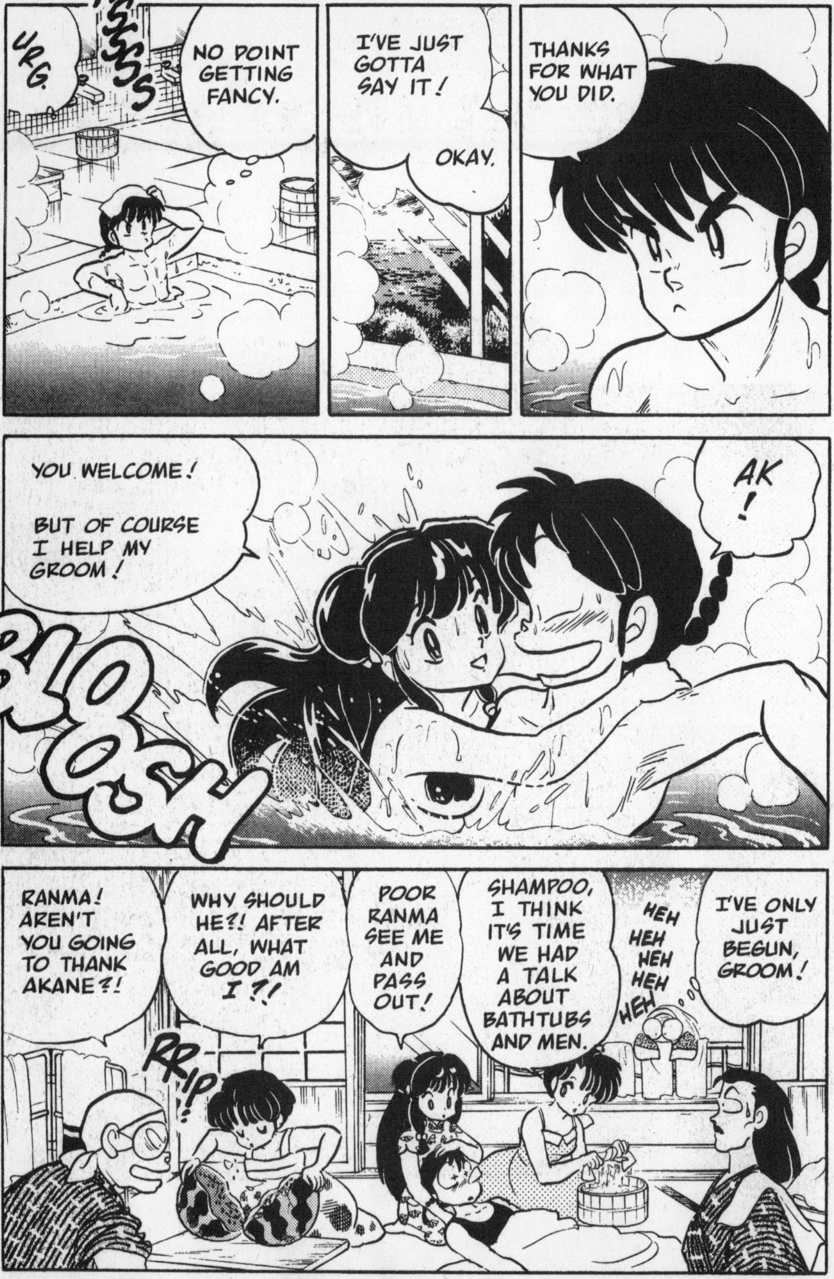
URG.
HSSSSS
NO POINT GETTING FANCY.
I'VE JUST GOTTA SAY IT!
OKAY.
THANKS FOR WHAT YOU DID.
YOU WELCOME!
BUT OF COURSE I HELP MY GROOM!
BLOOSH
AK!
RANMA! AREN'T YOU GOING TO THANK AKANE?!
WHY SHOULD HE?! AFTER ALL, WHAT GOOD AM I?!
RRIP!
POOR RANMA SEE ME AND PASS OUT!
SHAMPOO, I THINK IT'S TIME WE HAD A TALK ABOUT BATHTUBS AND MEN.
HEH HEH HEH HEH HEH
I'VE ONLY JUST BEGUN, GROOM!

Part 2

CARE TO JOIN ME?

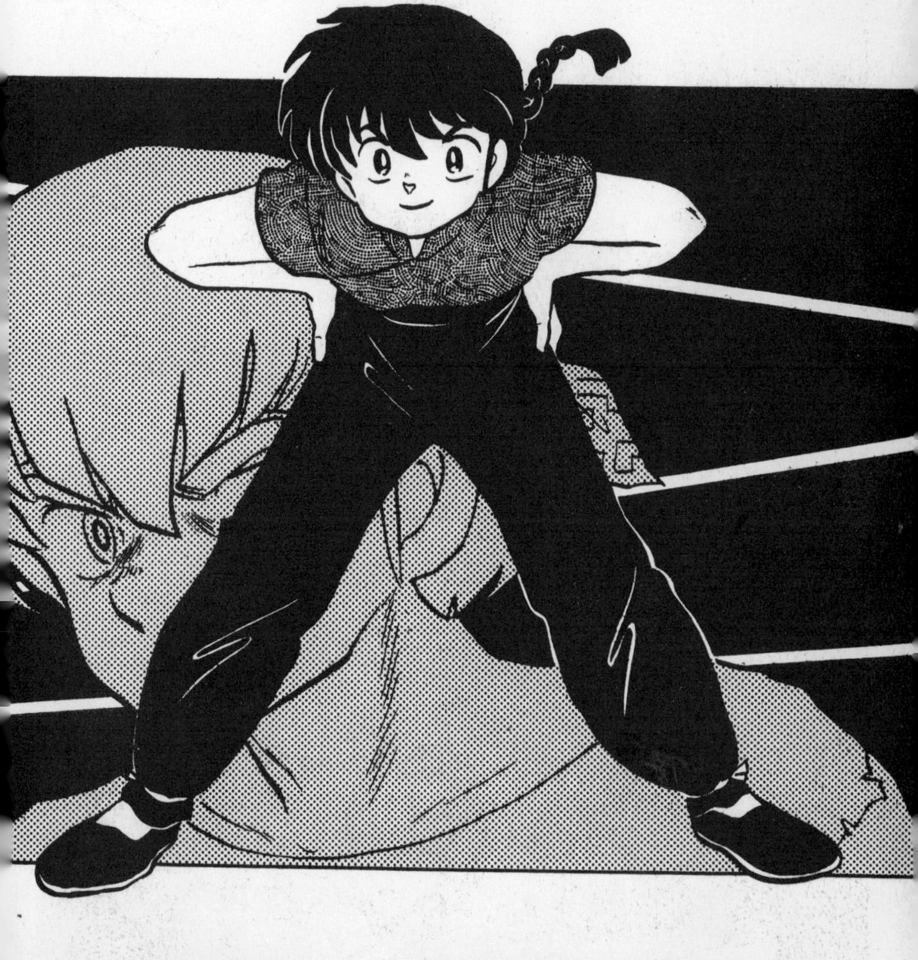

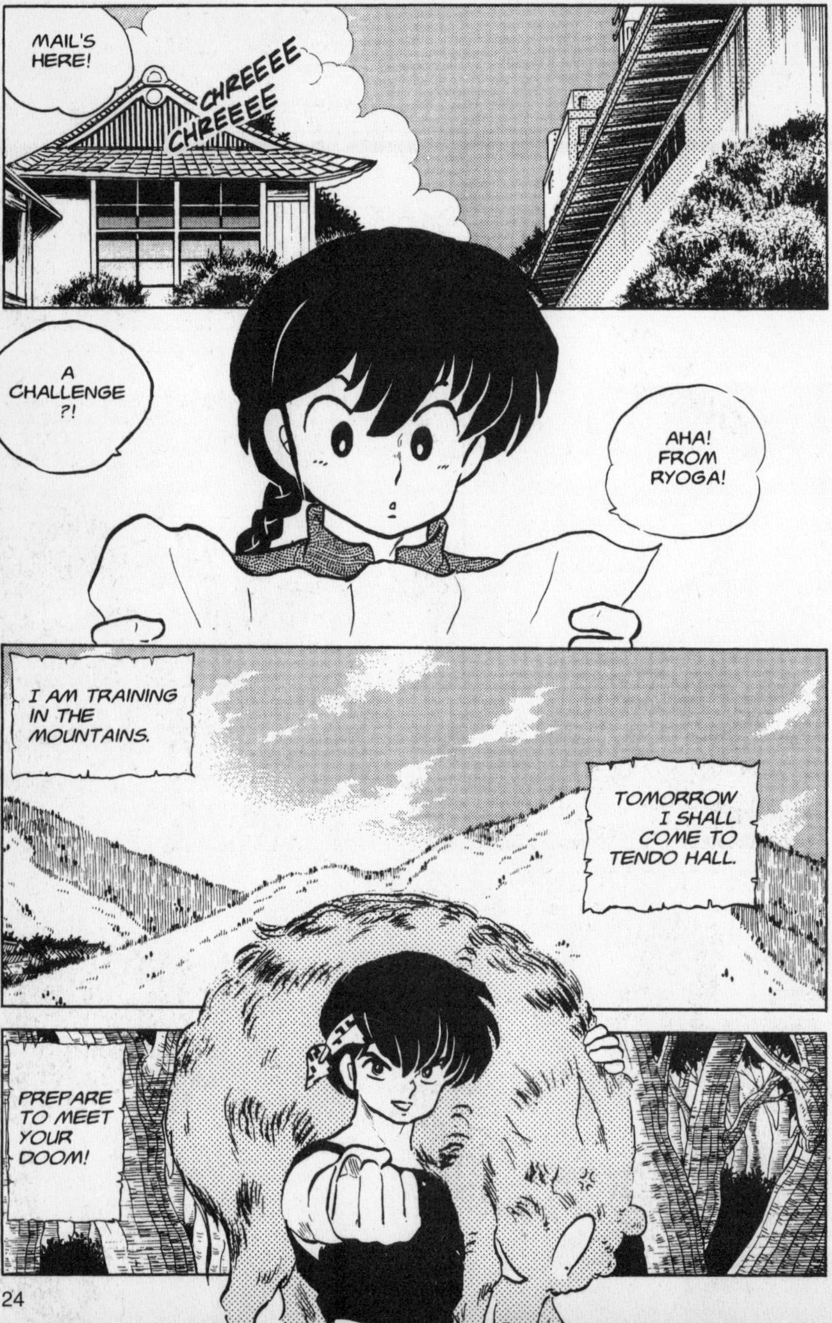
MAIL'S HERE!
CHREEEE CHREEEE
A CHALLENGE ?!
AHA! FROM RYOGA!
I AM TRAINING IN THE MOUNTAINS.
TOMORROW I SHALL COME TO TENDO HALL.
PREPARE TO MEET YOUR DOOM!

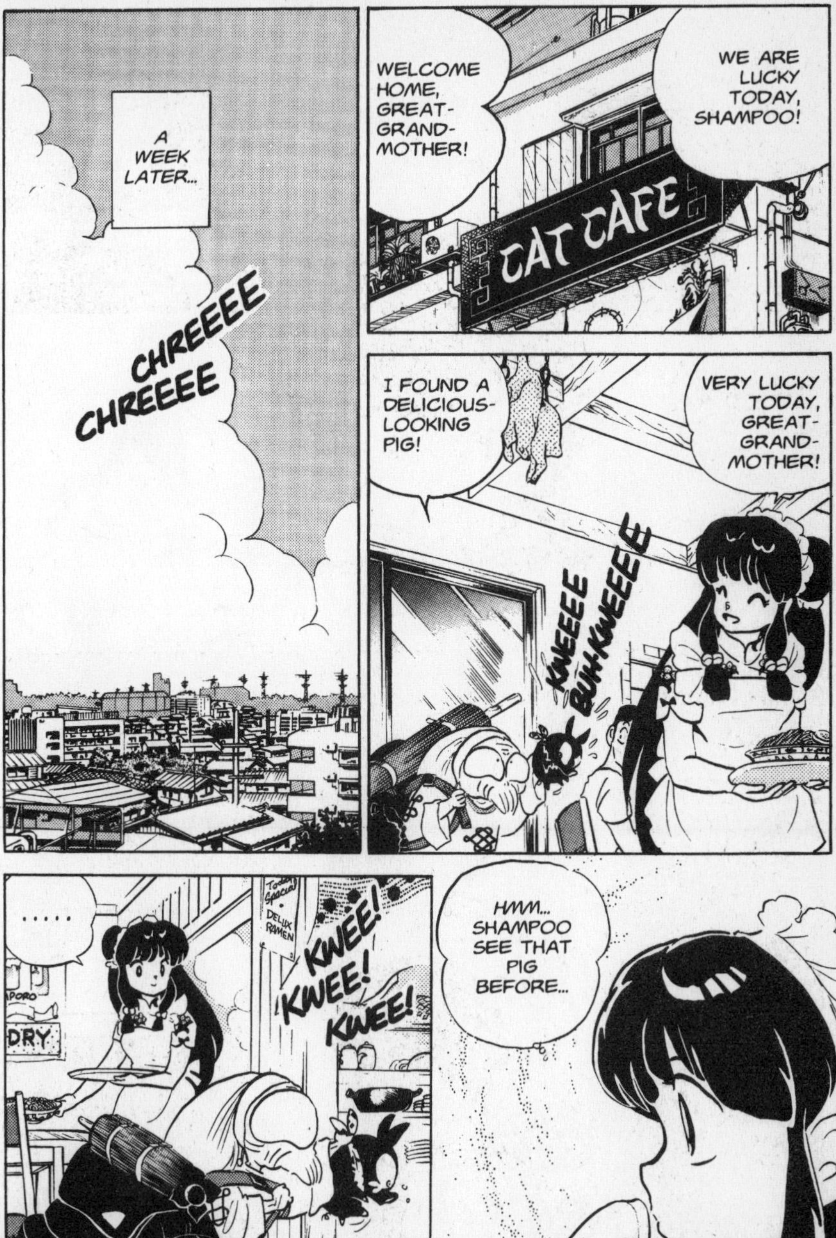
A WEEK LATER...
CHREEEEE CHREEEEE
WELCOME HOME, GREAT-GRAND-MOTHER!
WE ARE LUCKY TODAY, SHAMPOO!
CAT CAFE
I FOUND A DELICIOUS-LOOKING PIG!
VERY LUCKY TODAY, GREAT-GRAND-MOTHER!
KWEEEE BUH-KWEEEE
.....
KWEE! KWEE! KWEE!
HMM... SHAMPOO SEE THAT PIG BEFORE...

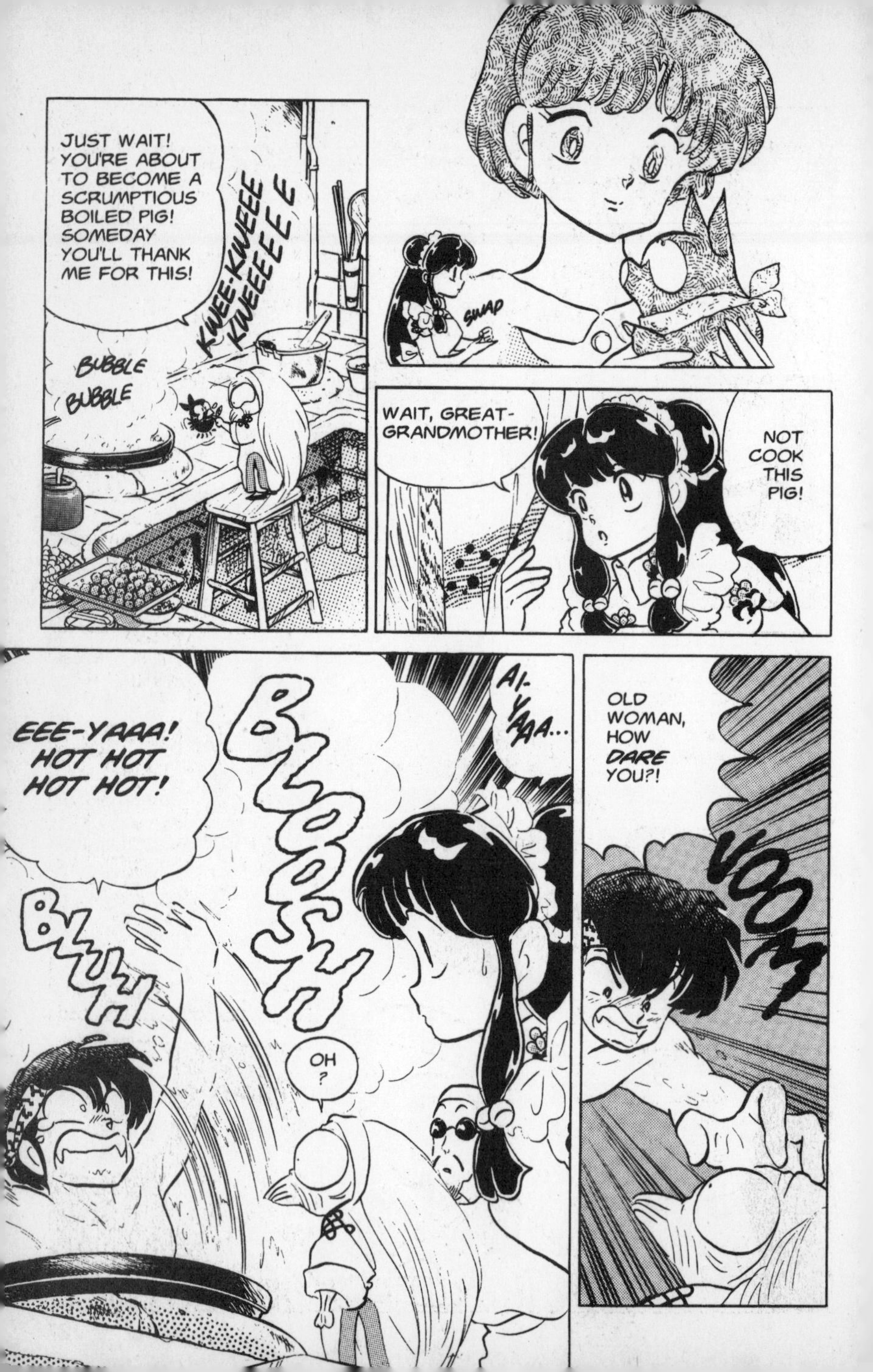
JUST WAIT! YOU'RE ABOUT TO BECOME A SCRUMPTIOUS BOILED PIG! SOMEDAY YOU'LL THANK ME FOR THIS!
KWEE-KWEEE KWEEEEEEE E
BUBBLE
BUBBLE
SWAP
WAIT, GREAT-GRANDMOTHER!
NOT COOK THIS PIG!
EEE-YAAA! HOT HOT HOT HOT!
BLOOSH
AI-YAAA...
BLUSH
OH ?
OLD WOMAN, HOW DARE YOU?!
VOOM

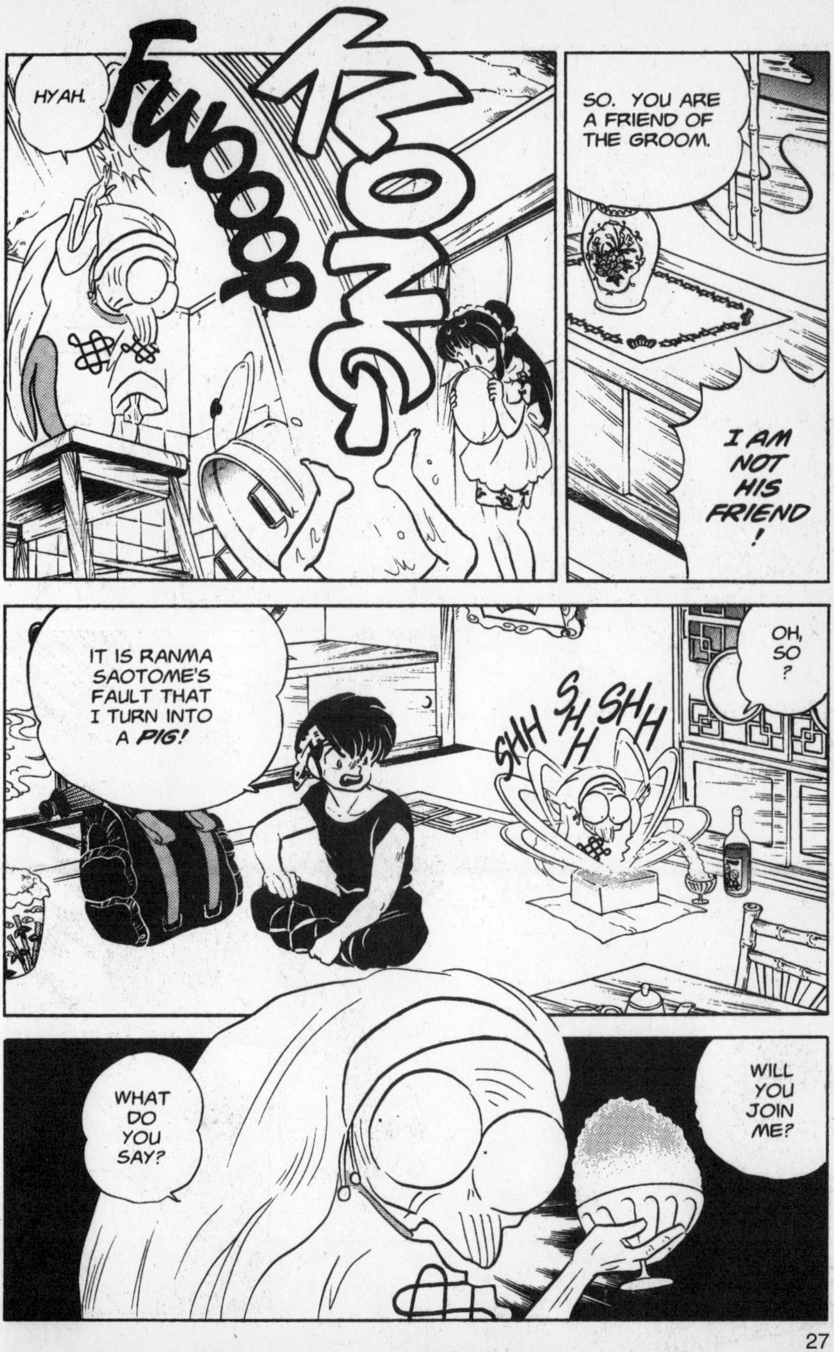
HYAH.
FWOOOP
KLONG
SO. YOU ARE A FRIEND OF THE GROOM.
I AM NOT HIS FRIEND!
IT IS RANMA SAOTOME'S FAULT THAT I TURN INTO A *PIG*!
SHH SHH SHH
OH, SO?
WHAT DO YOU SAY?
WILL YOU JOIN ME?

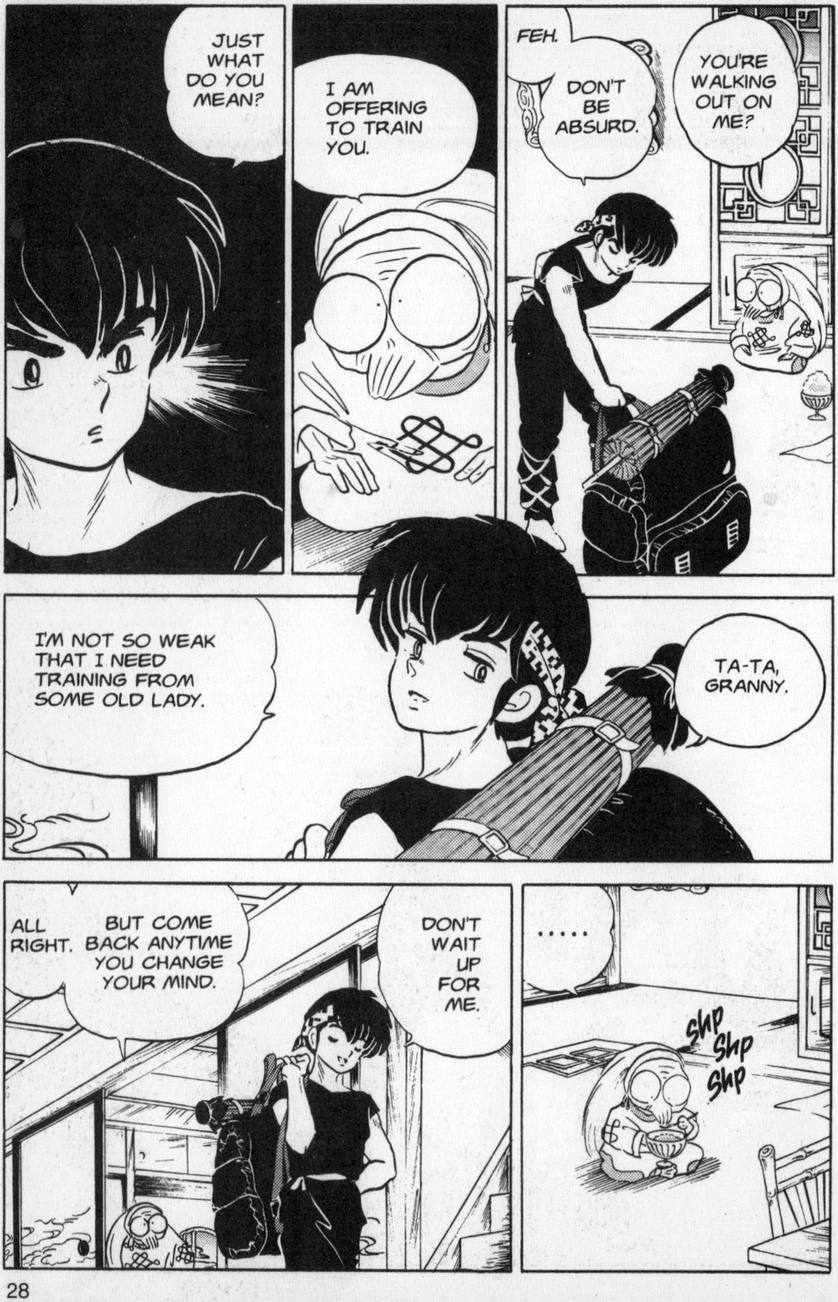
JUST WHAT DO YOU MEAN?
I AM OFFERING TO TRAIN YOU.
FEH.
DON'T BE ABSURD.
YOU'RE WALKING OUT ON ME?
I'M NOT SO WEAK THAT I NEED TRAINING FROM SOME OLD LADY.
TA-TA, GRANNY.
ALL RIGHT.
BUT COME BACK ANYTIME YOU CHANGE YOUR MIND.
DON'T WAIT UP FOR ME.
.....
SHP SHP SHP

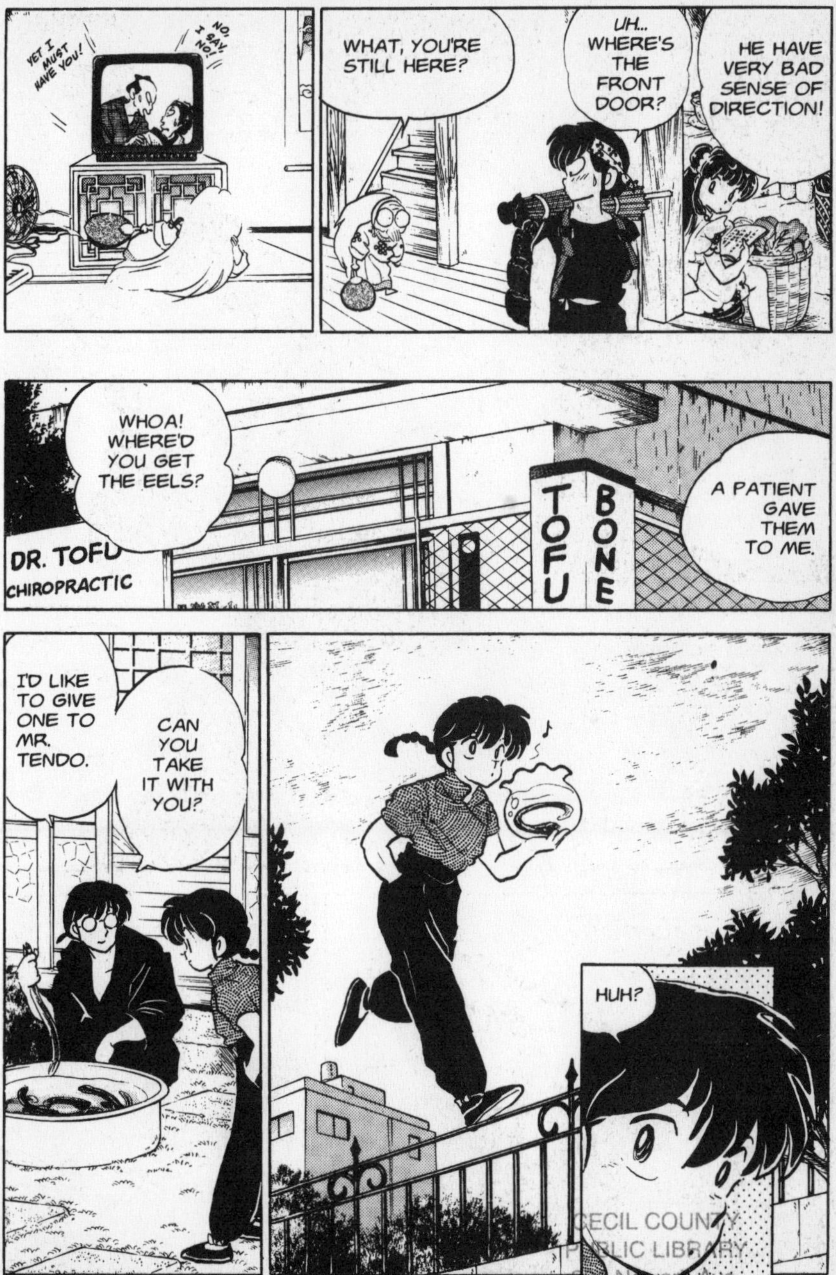

YET I MUST HAVE YOU!
NO, I SAY, NO!
WHAT, YOU'RE STILL HERE?
UH... WHERE'S THE FRONT DOOR?
HE HAVE VERY BAD SENSE OF DIRECTION!
WHOA! WHERE'D YOU GET THE EELS?
DR. TOFU CHIROPRACTIC
TOFU
BONE
A PATIENT GAVE THEM TO ME.
I'D LIKE TO GIVE ONE TO MR. TENDO.
CAN YOU TAKE IT WITH YOU?
HUH?

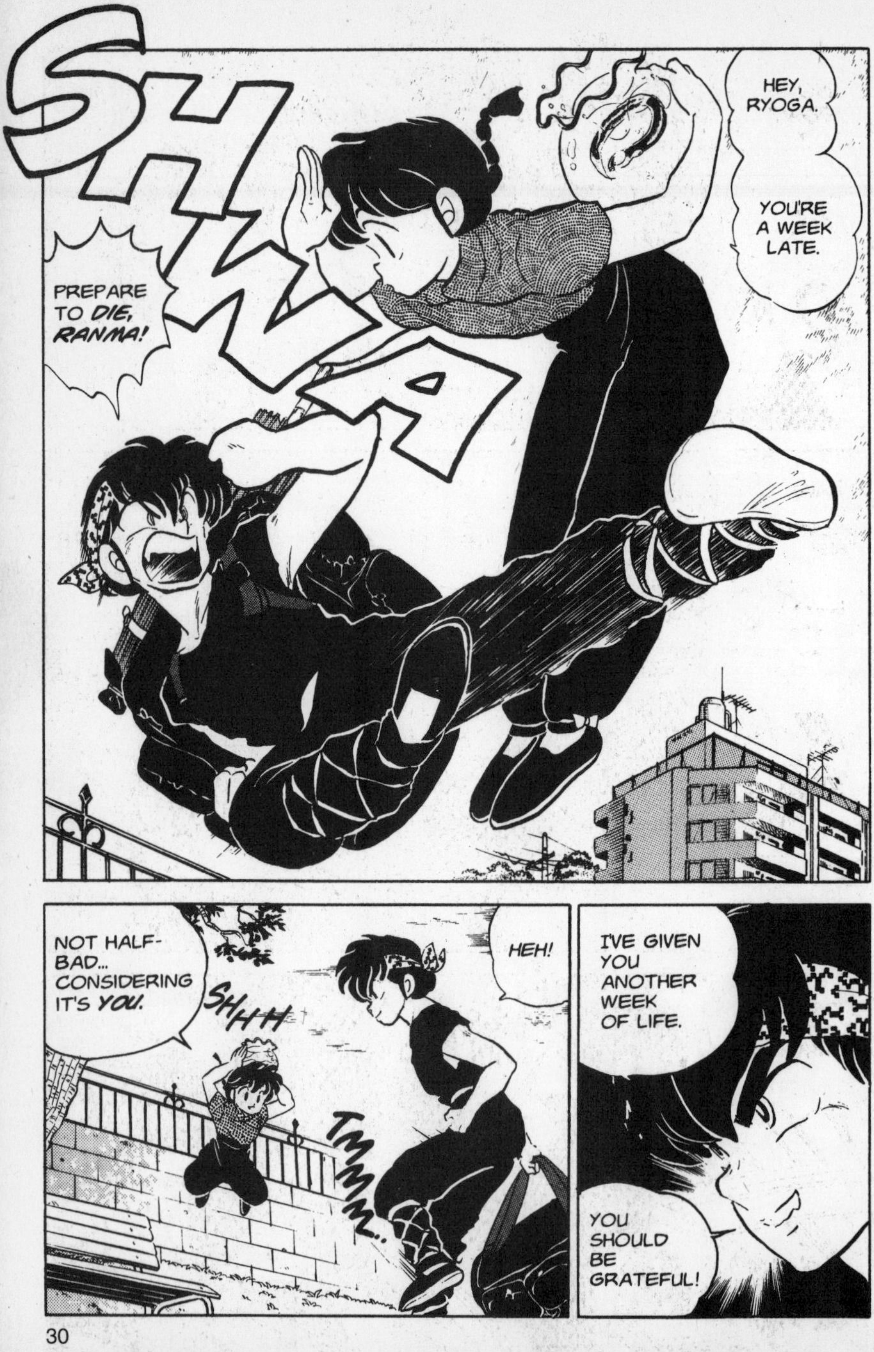

SHWA
PREPARE TO *DIE, RANMA!*
HEY, RYOGA.
YOU'RE A WEEK LATE.
NOT HALF-BAD... CONSIDERING IT'S *YOU.*
SHHH
HEH!
TMMM..
I'VE GIVEN YOU ANOTHER WEEK OF LIFE.
YOU SHOULD BE GRATEFUL!

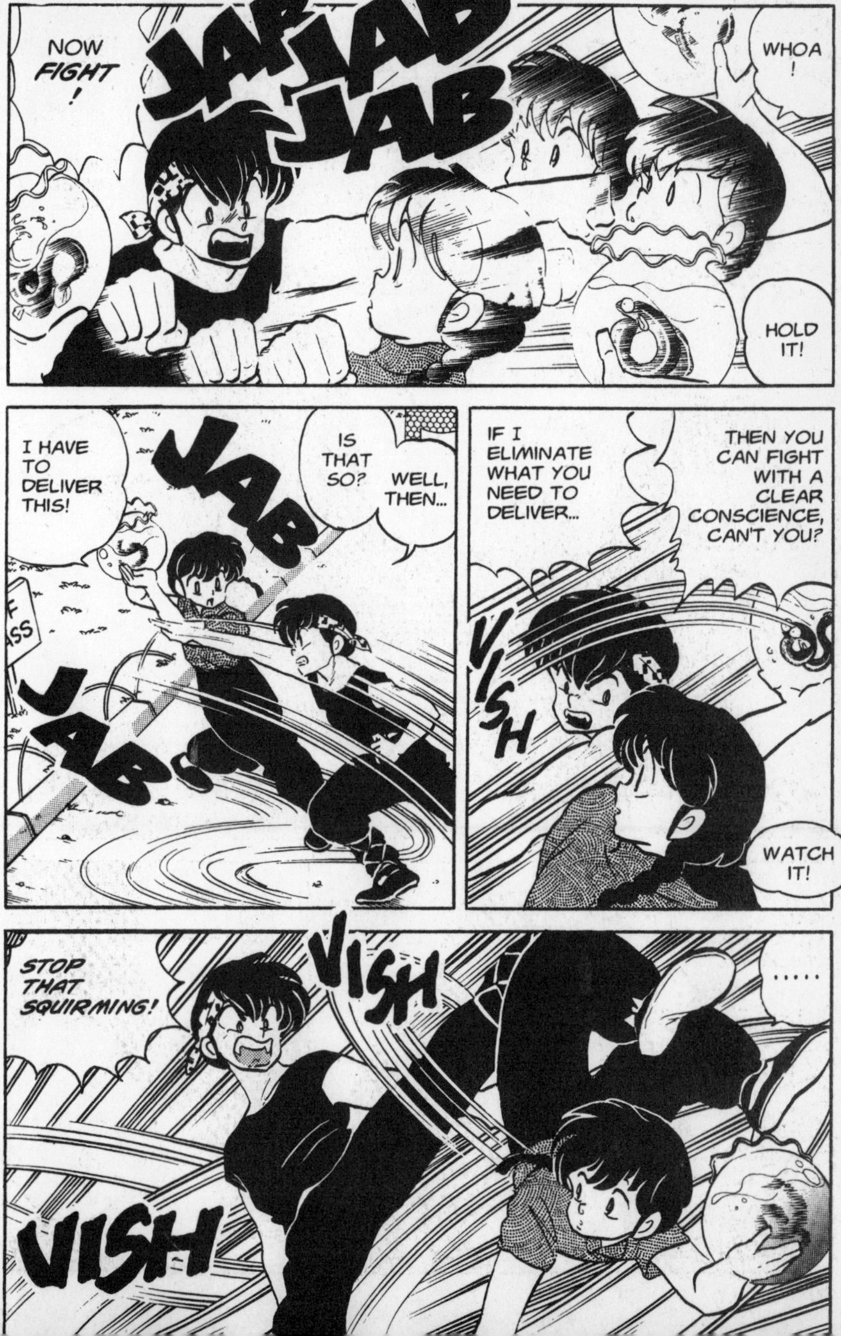
NOW FIGHT!
JAB JAB JAB JAB
WHOA!
HOLD IT!
I HAVE TO DELIVER THIS!
JAB
IS THAT SO?
WELL, THEN...
JAB
IF I ELIMINATE WHAT YOU NEED TO DELIVER...
THEN YOU CAN FIGHT WITH A CLEAR CONSCIENCE, CAN'T YOU?
VISH
WATCH IT!
STOP THAT SQUIRMING!
VISH
.....
VISH

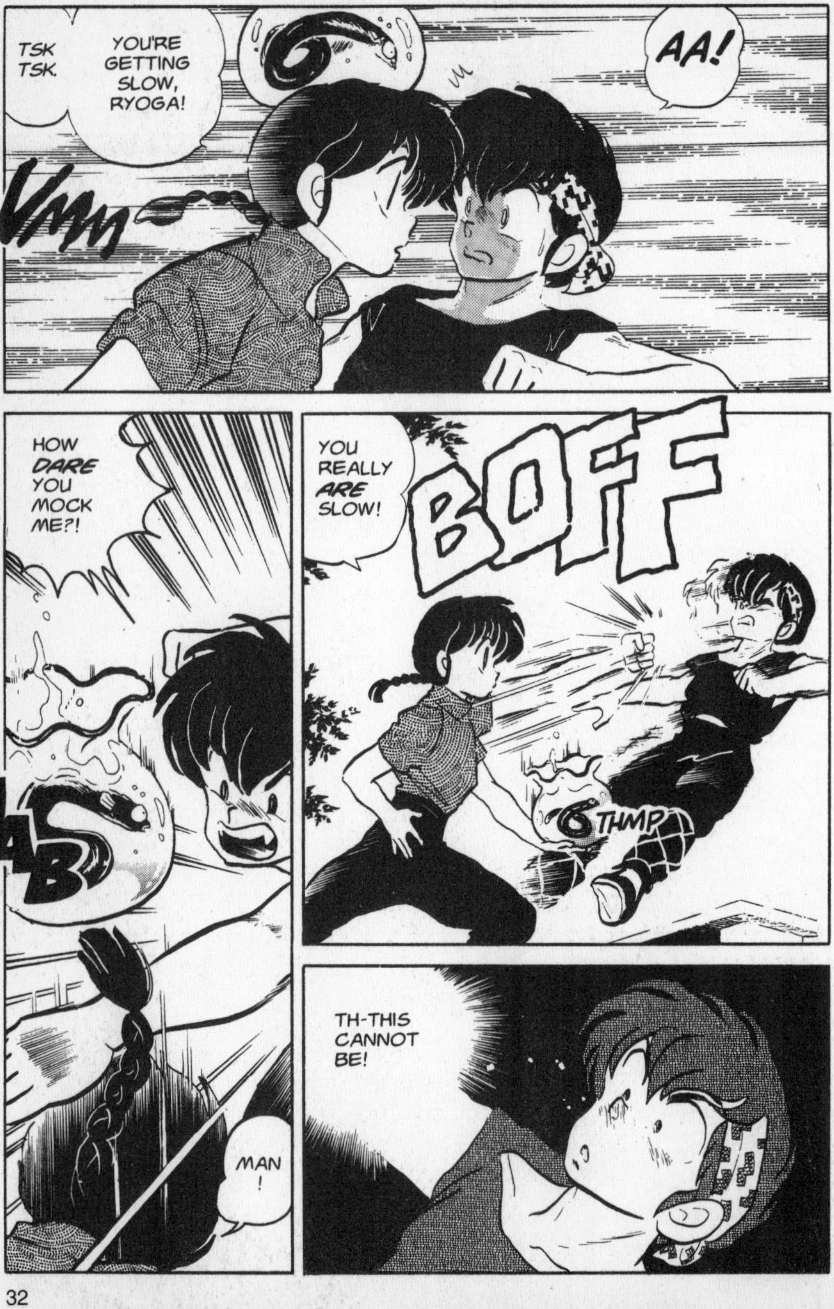
TSK TSK.
YOU'RE GETTING SLOW, RYOGA!
AA!
VMM
HOW DARE YOU MOCK ME?!
JAB
MAN!
YOU REALLY ARE SLOW!
BOFF
THMP
TH-THIS CANNOT BE!

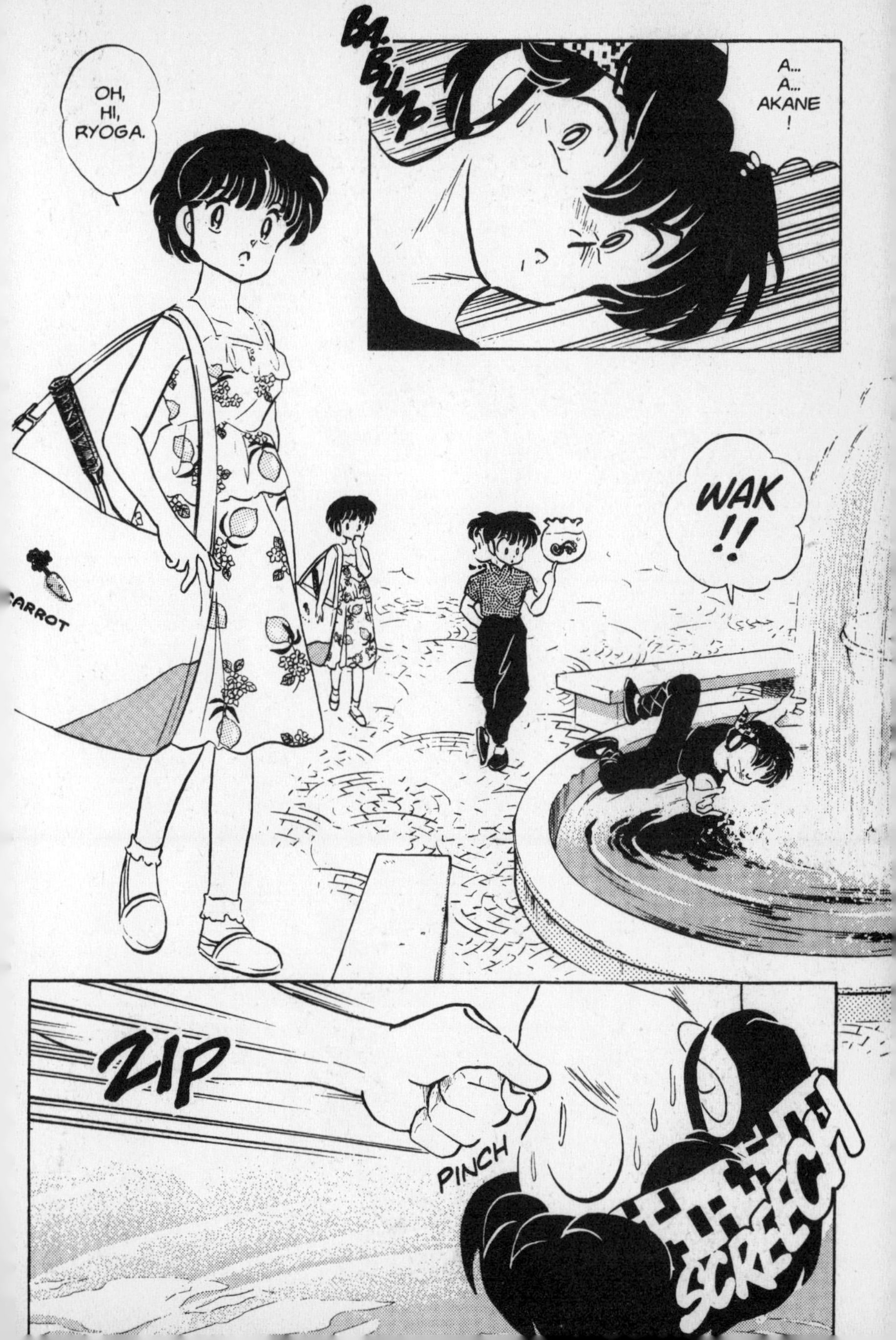
BA-BUMP
A... A... AKANE!
OH, HI, RYOGA.
CARROT
WAK!!
ZIP
PINCH
SCREECH

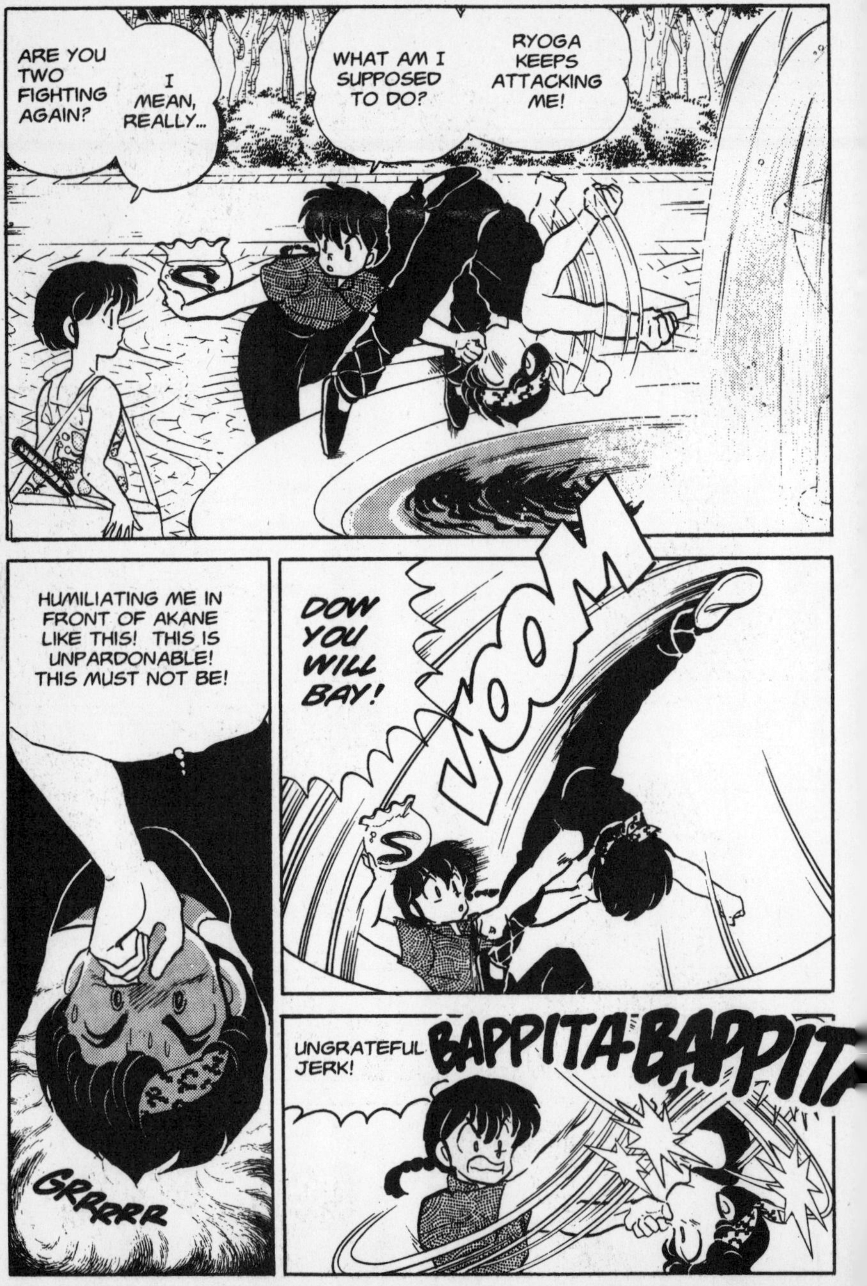
ARE YOU TWO FIGHTING AGAIN?
I MEAN, REALLY...
WHAT AM I SUPPOSED TO DO?
RYOGA KEEPS ATTACKING ME!
HUMILIATING ME IN FRONT OF AKANE LIKE THIS! THIS IS UNPARDONABLE! THIS MUST NOT BE!
GRRRRR
DOW YOU WILL BAY!
VOOM
UNGRATEFUL JERK!
BAPPITA BAPPITA

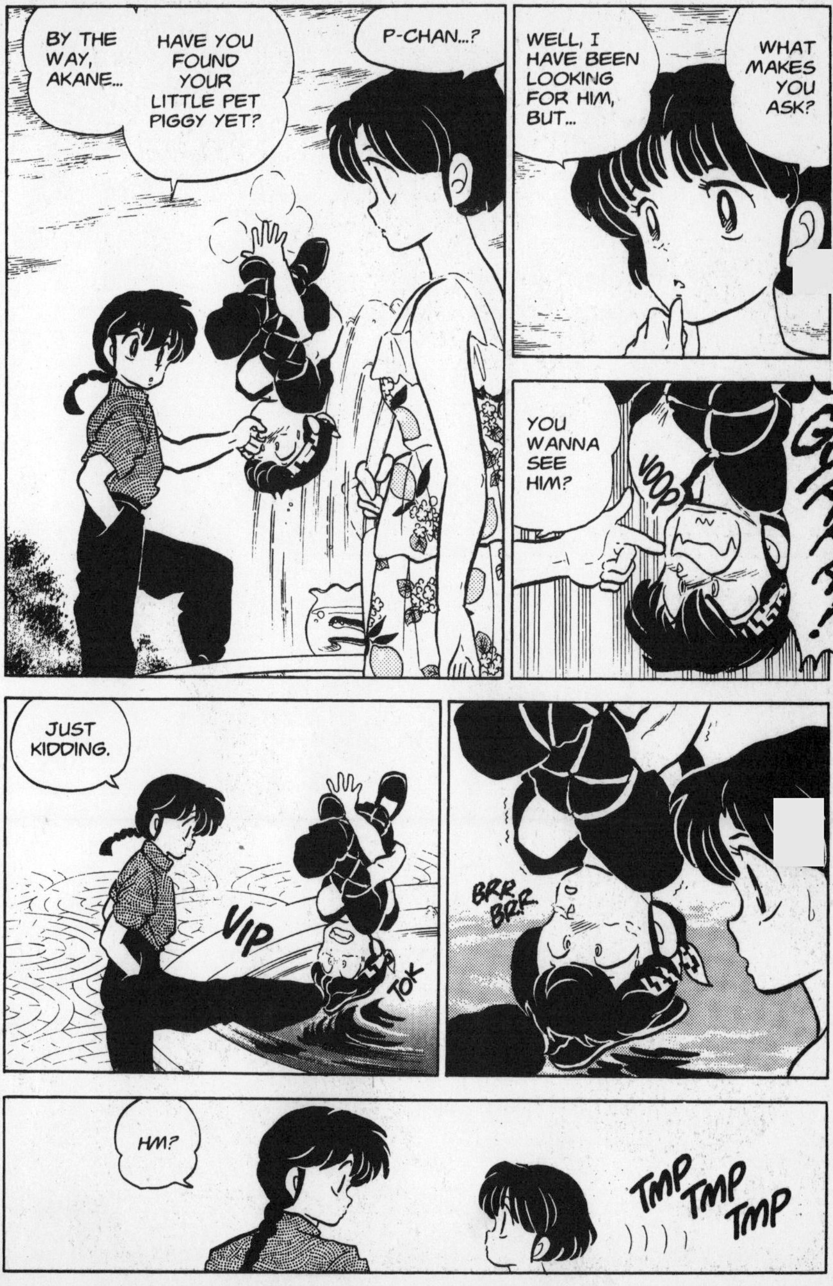
BY THE WAY, AKANE...
HAVE YOU FOUND YOUR LITTLE PET PIGGY YET?
P-CHAN...?
WELL, I HAVE BEEN LOOKING FOR HIM, BUT...
WHAT MAKES YOU ASK?
YOU WANNA SEE HIM?
VOOP
GYAAAA!
JUST KIDDING.
VIP
TOK
BRR BRR
HM?
TMP TMP TMP

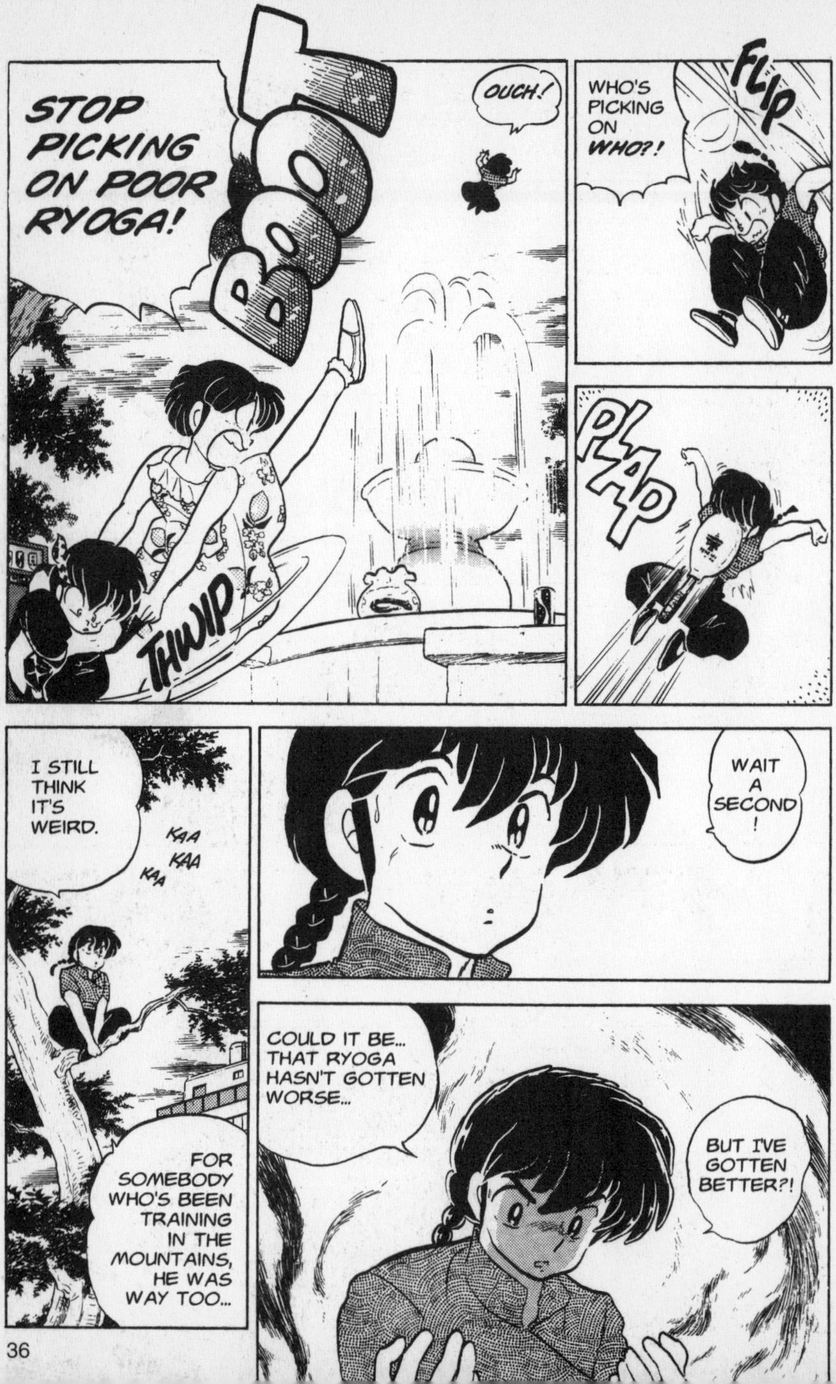
STOP PICKING ON POOR RYOGA!
BOOT
OUCH!
THWIP
WHO'S PICKING ON WHO?!
FLIP
PLAP
I STILL THINK IT'S WEIRD.
KAA KAA KAA
FOR SOMEBODY WHO'S BEEN TRAINING IN THE MOUNTAINS, HE WAS WAY TOO...
WAIT A SECOND!
COULD IT BE... THAT RYOGA HASN'T GOTTEN WORSE...
BUT I'VE GOTTEN BETTER?!

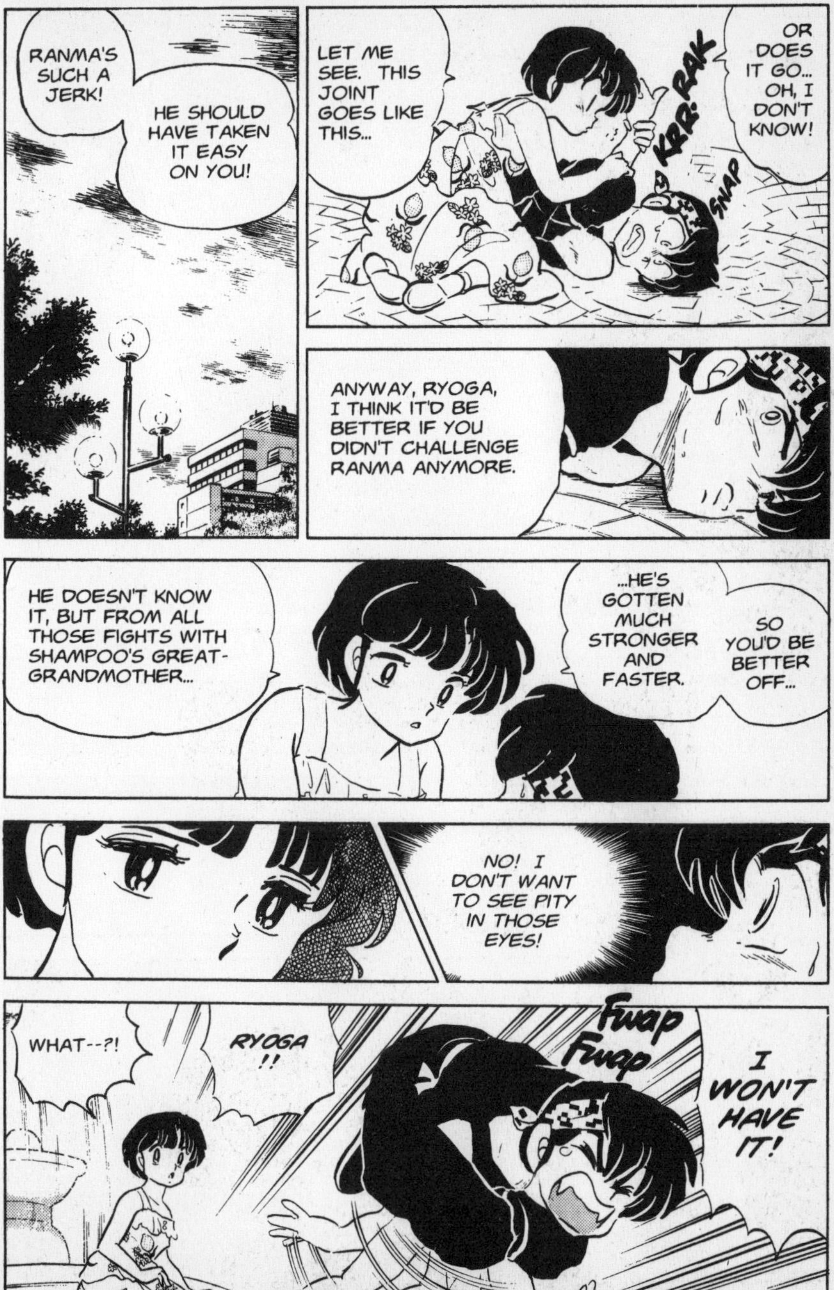
RANMA'S SUCH A JERK!
HE SHOULD HAVE TAKEN IT EASY ON YOU!
LET ME SEE. THIS JOINT GOES LIKE THIS...
KRR-RAK
SNAP
OR DOES IT GO... OH, I DON'T KNOW!
ANYWAY, RYOGA, I THINK IT'D BE BETTER IF YOU DIDN'T CHALLENGE RANMA ANYMORE.
HE DOESN'T KNOW IT, BUT FROM ALL THOSE FIGHTS WITH SHAMPOO'S GREAT-GRANDMOTHER...
...HE'S GOTTEN MUCH STRONGER AND FASTER.
SO YOU'D BE BETTER OFF...
NO! I DON'T WANT TO SEE PITY IN THOSE EYES!
WHAT--?!
RYOGA !!
Fwap Fwap
I WON'T HAVE IT!
Fwap

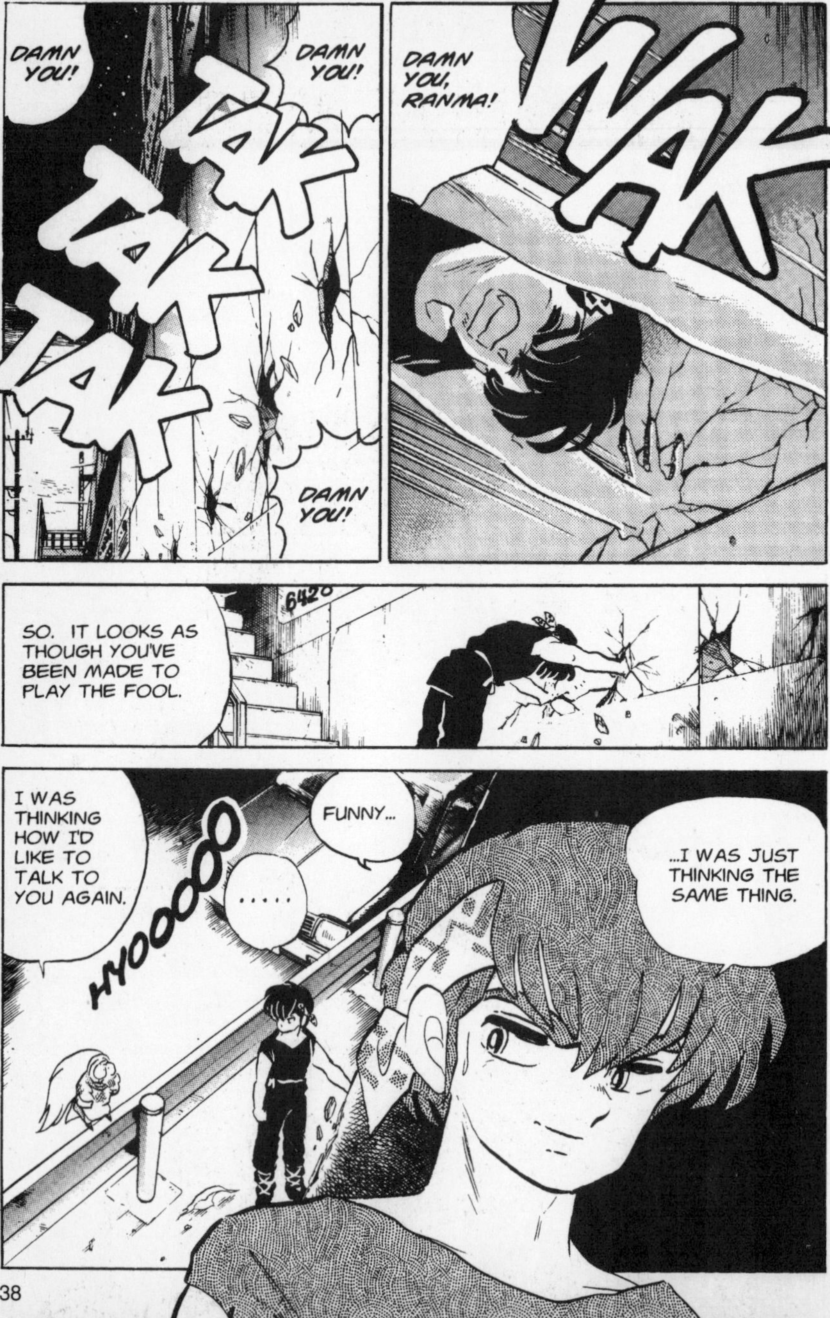
DAMN YOU!
TAK
TAK
TAK
TAK
DAMN YOU!
DAMN YOU!
DAMN YOU, RANMA!
WAK
SO. IT LOOKS AS THOUGH YOU'VE BEEN MADE TO PLAY THE FOOL.
I WAS THINKING HOW I'D LIKE TO TALK TO YOU AGAIN.
HYOOOOO
FUNNY...
.....
...I WAS JUST THINKING THE SAME THING.

Part 3
TRAINING MEALS

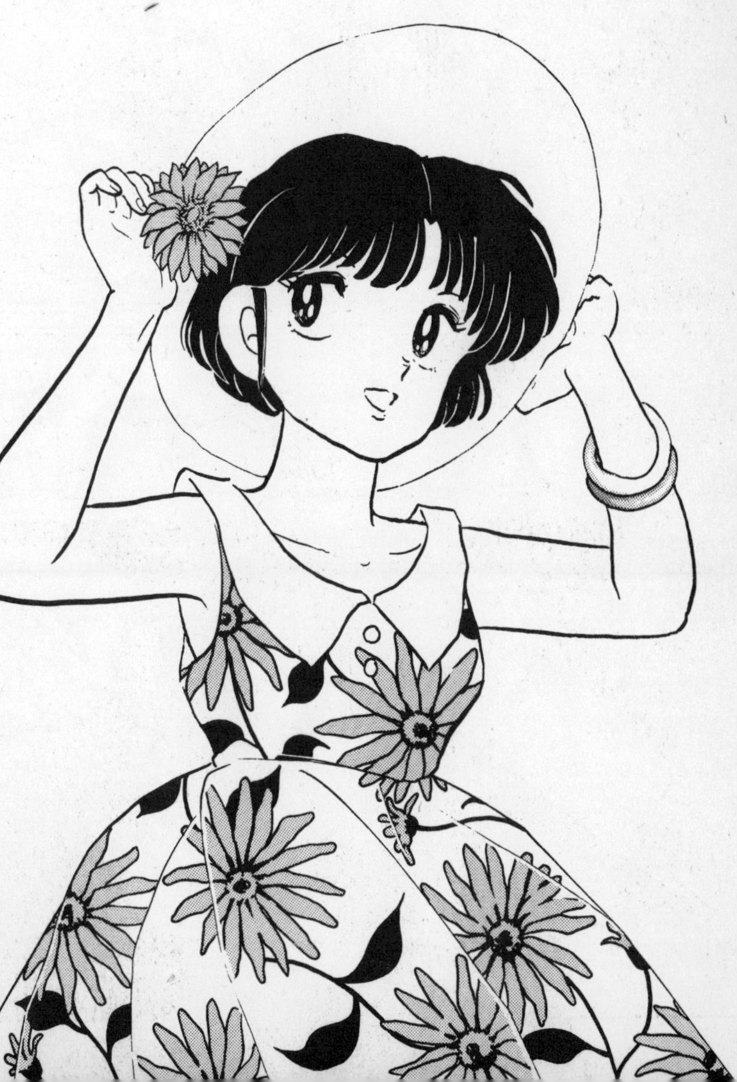

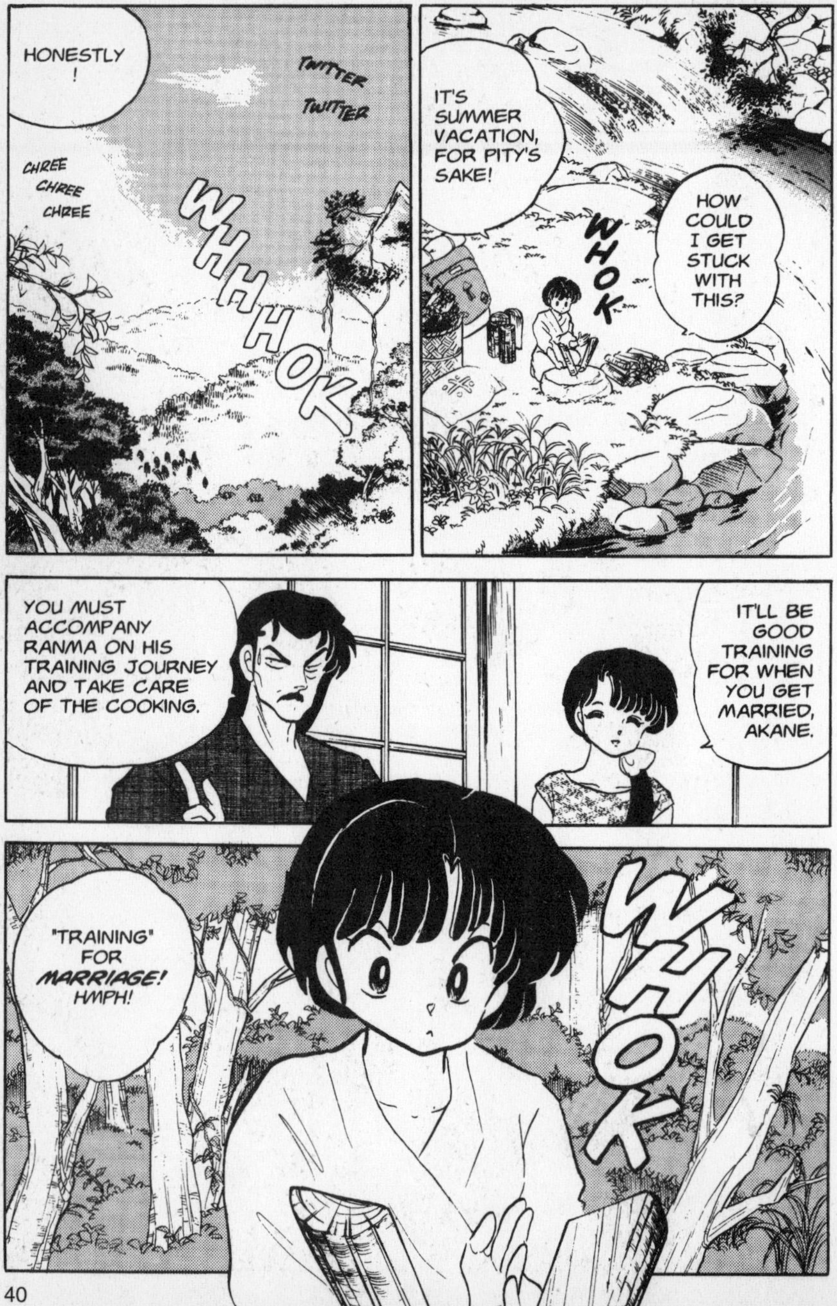
HONESTLY!
TWITTER TWITTER
CHREE CHREE CHREE
WHHHOK
IT'S SUMMER VACATION, FOR PITY'S SAKE!
WHOK
HOW COULD I GET STUCK WITH THIS?
YOU MUST ACCOMPANY RANMA ON HIS TRAINING JOURNEY AND TAKE CARE OF THE COOKING.
IT'LL BE GOOD TRAINING FOR WHEN YOU GET MARRIED, AKANE.
"TRAINING" FOR MARRIAGE! HMPH!
WHHOK

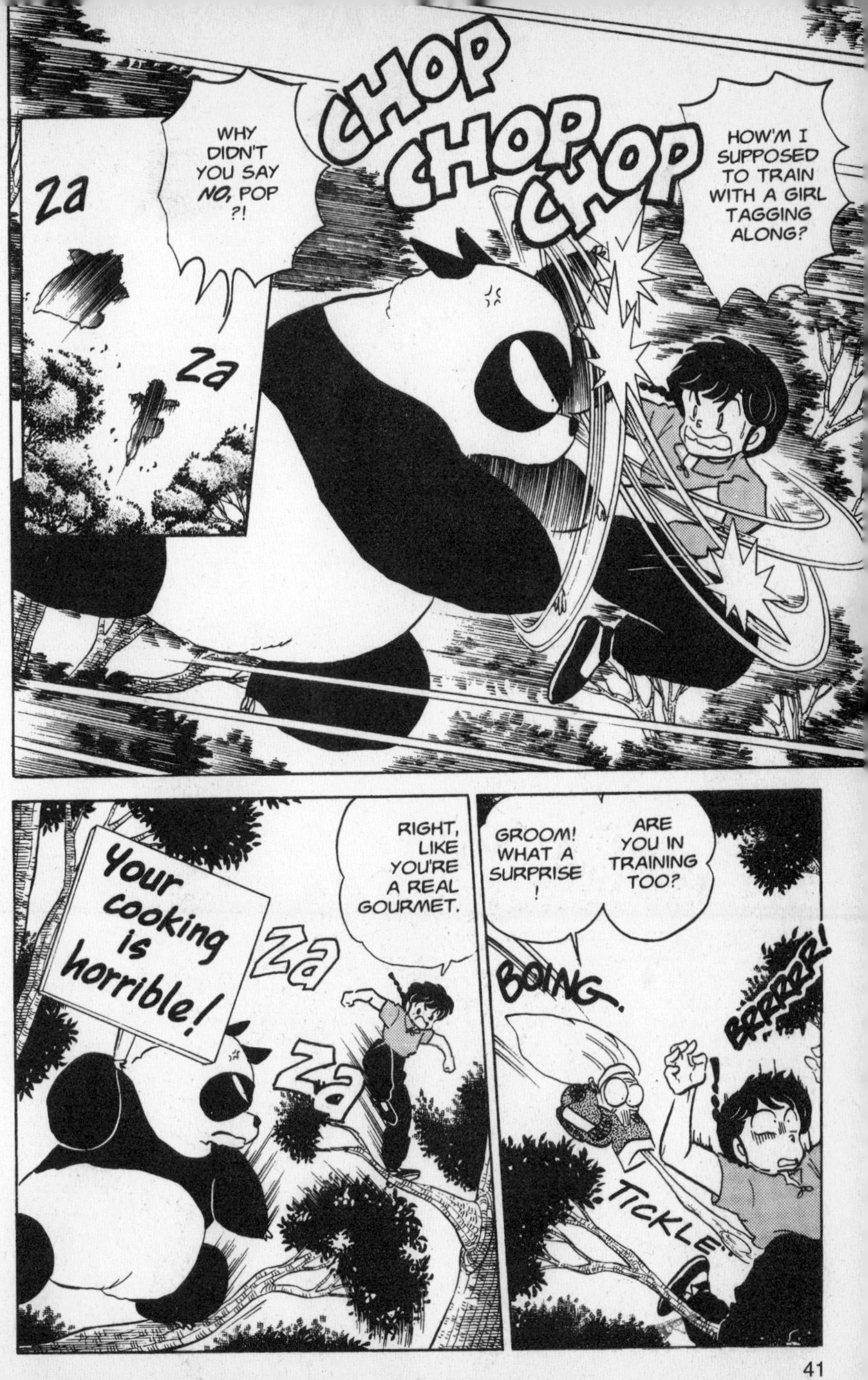
Za
Za
WHY DIDN'T YOU SAY NO, POP ?!
CHOP CHOP CHOP
HOW'M I SUPPOSED TO TRAIN WITH A GIRL TAGGING ALONG?
Your cooking is horrible!
RIGHT, LIKE YOU'RE A REAL GOURMET.
Za
Za
GROOM! WHAT A SURPRISE!
ARE YOU IN TRAINING TOO?
BOING
BRRRRR!
TICKLE

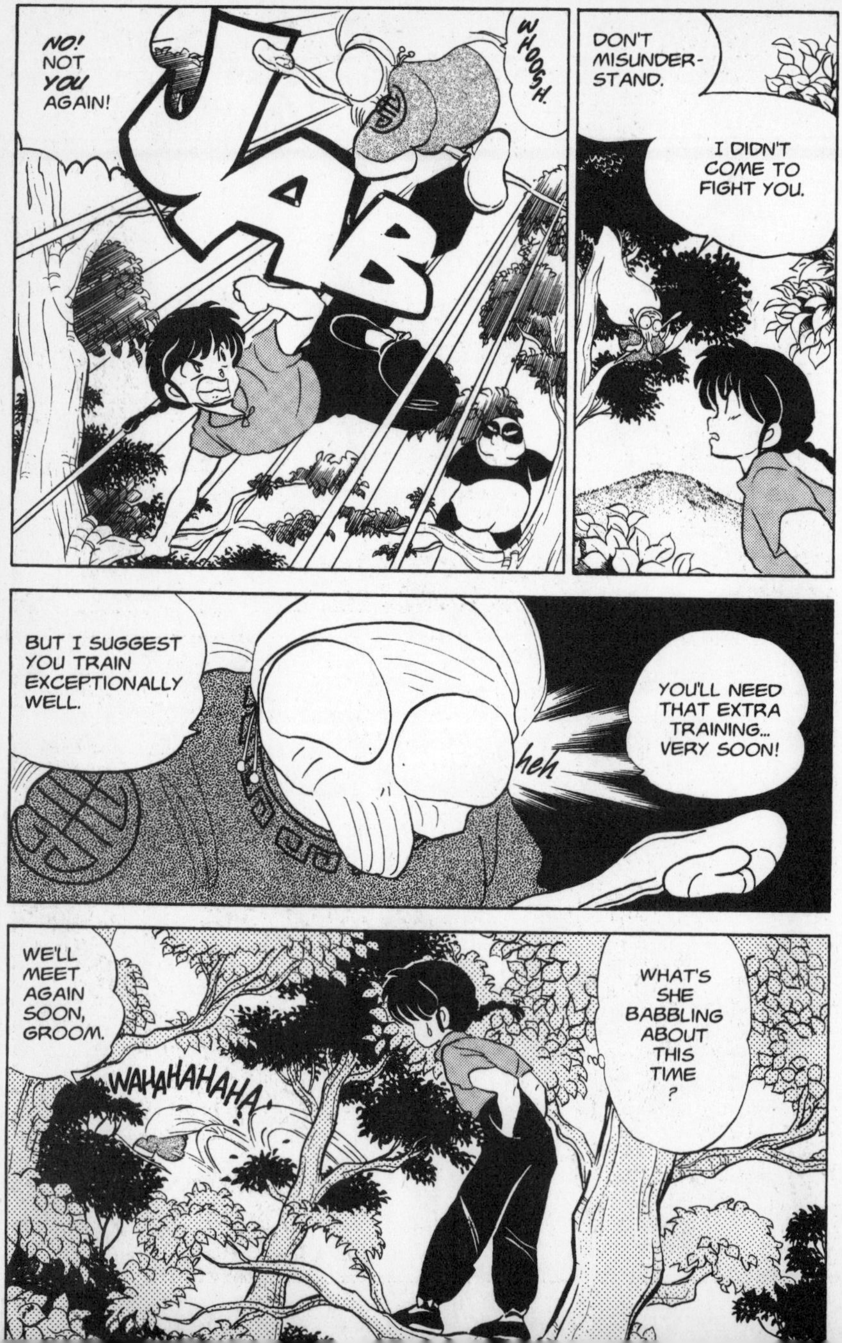

NO! NOT YOU AGAIN!
JAB
WHOOSH.
DON'T MISUNDER-STAND.
I DIDN'T COME TO FIGHT YOU.
BUT I SUGGEST YOU TRAIN EXCEPTIONALLY WELL.
heh
YOU'LL NEED THAT EXTRA TRAINING... VERY SOON!
WE'LL MEET AGAIN SOON, GROOM.
WAHAHAHAHA!
WHAT'S SHE BABBLING ABOUT THIS TIME?

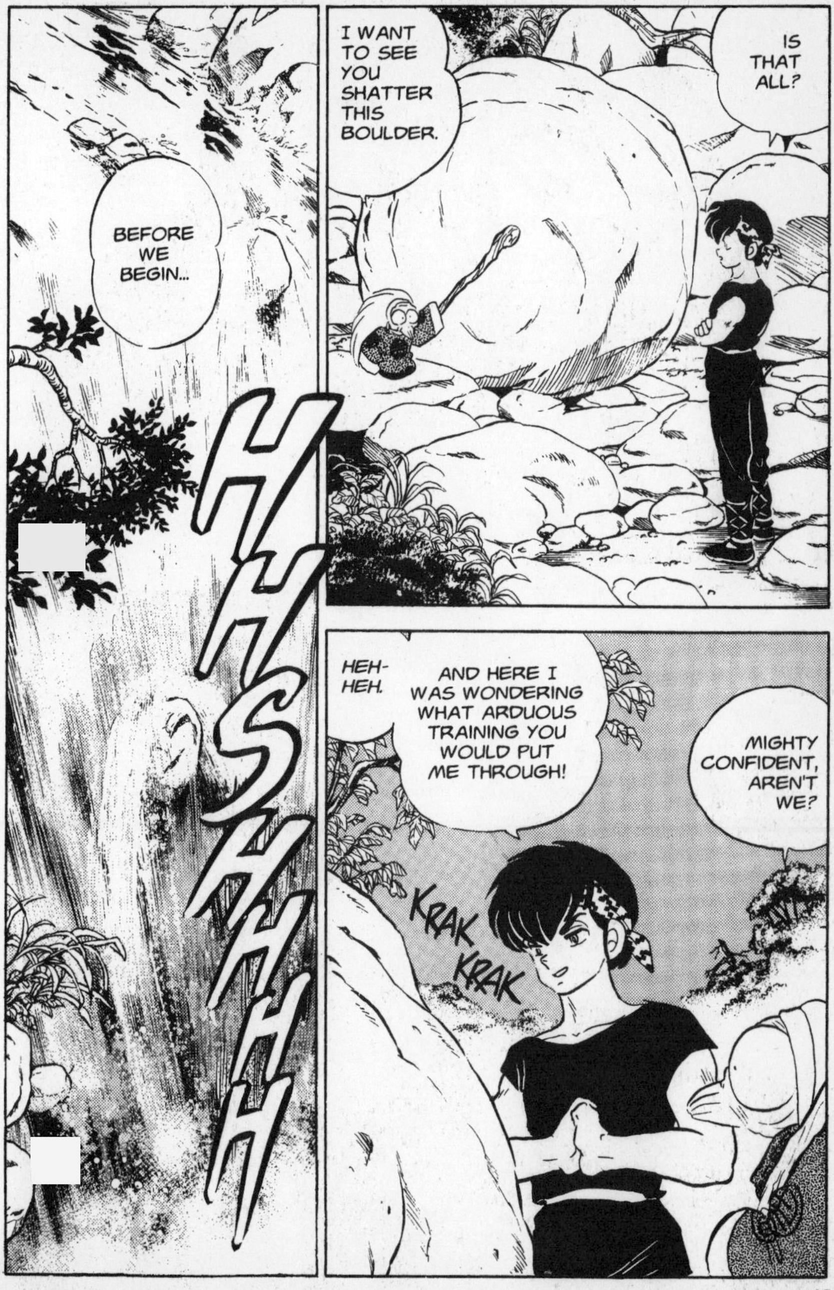
BEFORE WE BEGIN...
HHHSHHHHH
I WANT TO SEE YOU SHATTER THIS BOULDER.
IS THAT ALL?
HEH-HEH.
AND HERE I WAS WONDERING WHAT ARDUOUS TRAINING YOU WOULD PUT ME THROUGH!
MIGHTY CONFIDENT, AREN'T WE?
KRAK KRAK

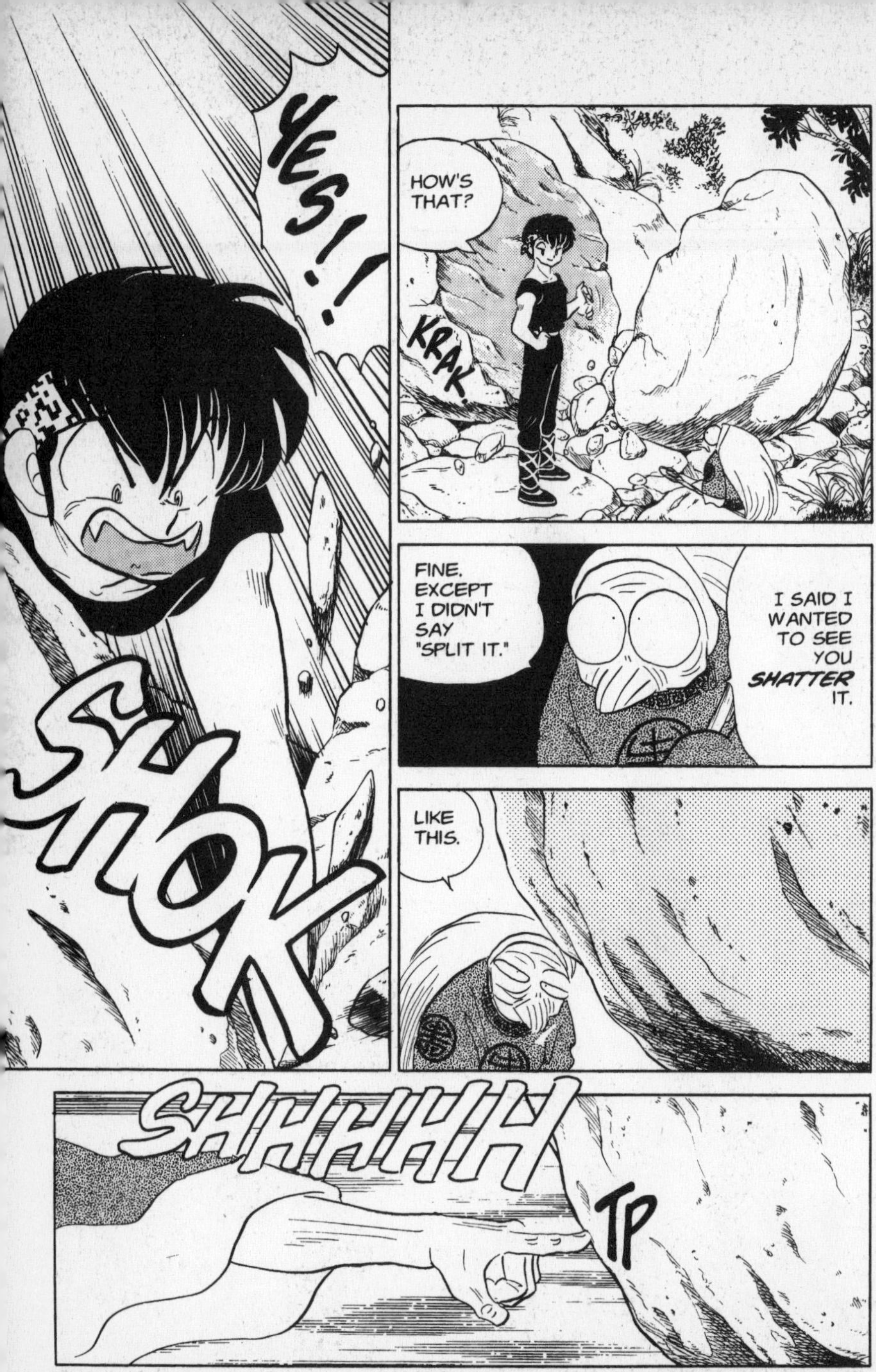
YES!!
SHOK
HOW'S THAT?
KRAK
FINE. EXCEPT I DIDN'T SAY "SPLIT IT."
I SAID I WANTED TO SEE YOU *SHATTER* IT.
LIKE THIS.
SHHHHHH
TP

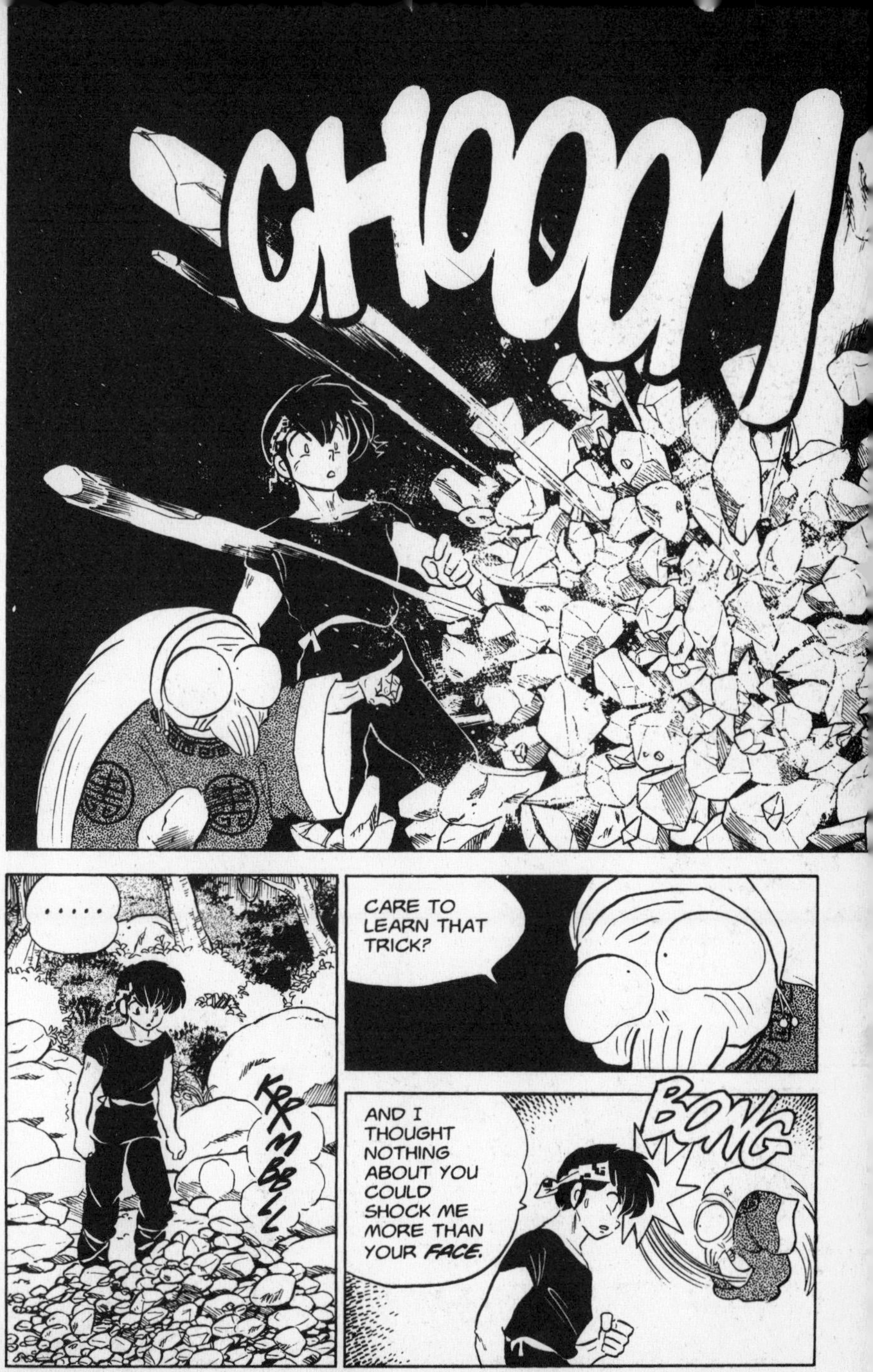
CHOOOM
.....
KRRMBBLL
CARE TO LEARN THAT TRICK?
BONG
AND I THOUGHT NOTHING ABOUT YOU COULD SHOCK ME MORE THAN YOUR *FACE*.

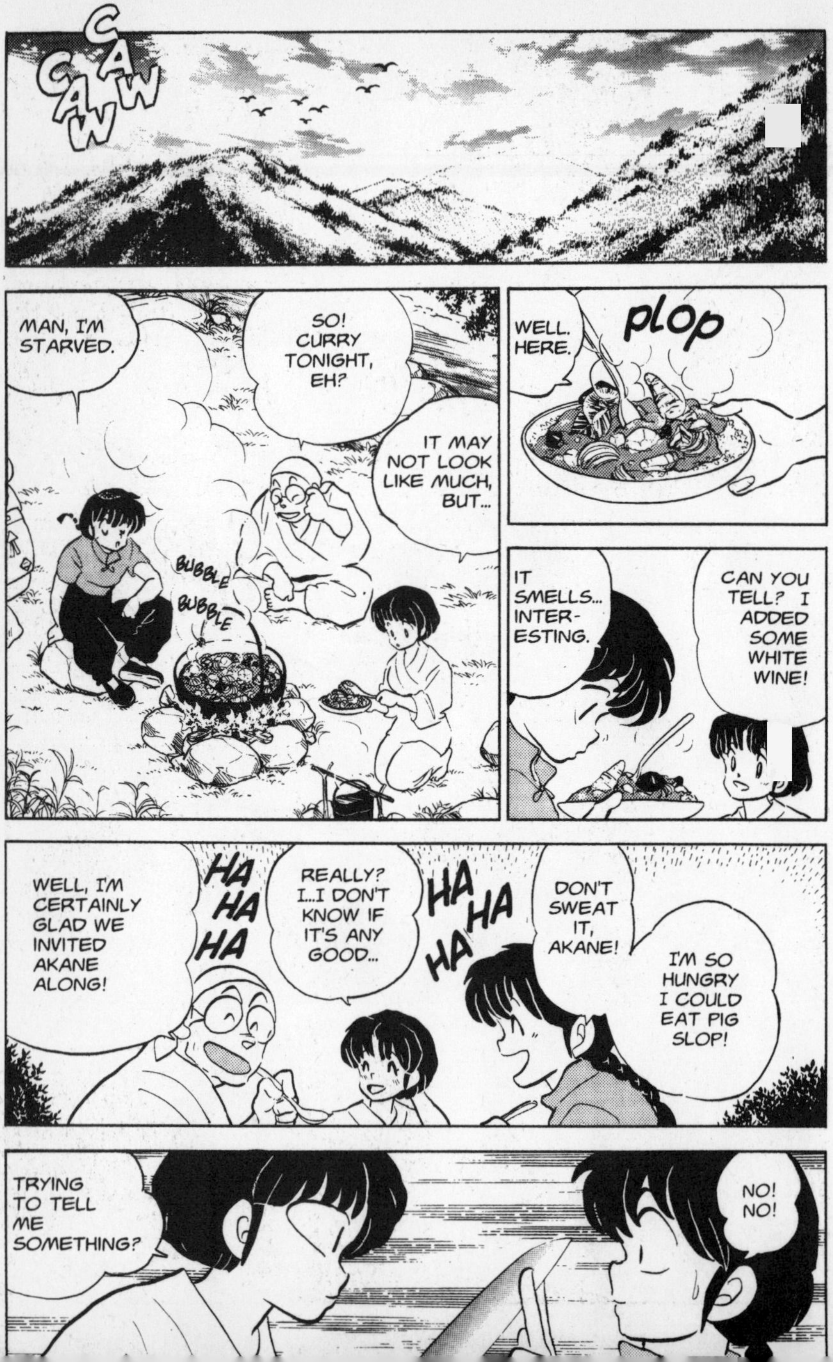
CAW CAW
MAN, I'M STARVED.
SO! CURRY TONIGHT, EH?
IT MAY NOT LOOK LIKE MUCH, BUT...
BUBBLE BUBBLE
WELL. HERE.
PLOP
IT SMELLS... INTER-ESTING.
CAN YOU TELL? I ADDED SOME WHITE WINE!
WELL, I'M CERTAINLY GLAD WE INVITED AKANE ALONG!
HA HA HA
REALLY? I...I DON'T KNOW IF IT'S ANY GOOD...
HA HA HA HA
DON'T SWEAT IT, AKANE!
I'M SO HUNGRY I COULD EAT PIG SLOP!
TRYING TO TELL ME SOMETHING?
NO! NO!

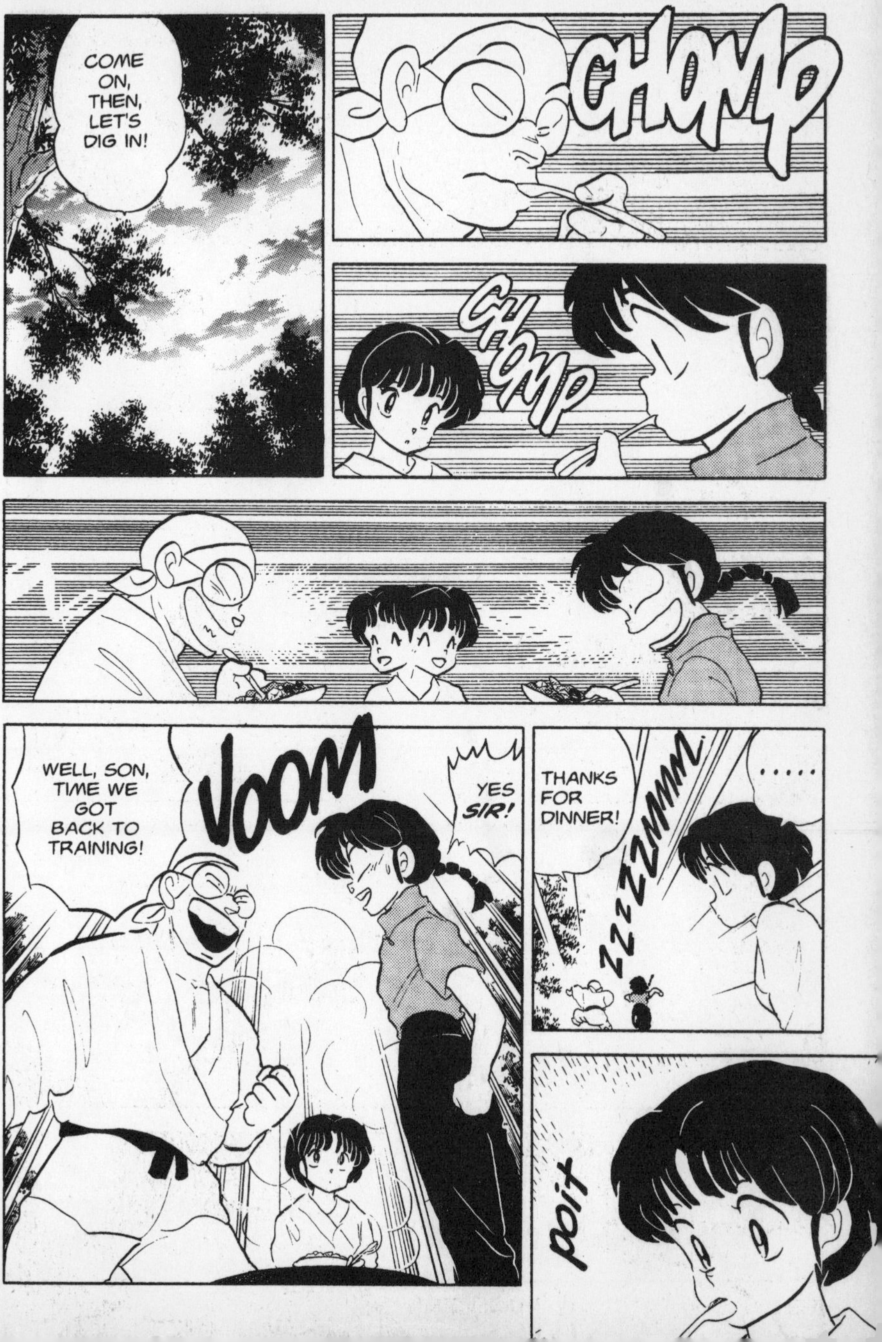
COME ON, THEN, LET'S DIG IN!
CHOMP
CHOMP
WELL, SON, TIME WE GOT BACK TO TRAINING!
VOOM
YES SIR!
THANKS FOR DINNER!
ZZZZZMMMM
.....
poit

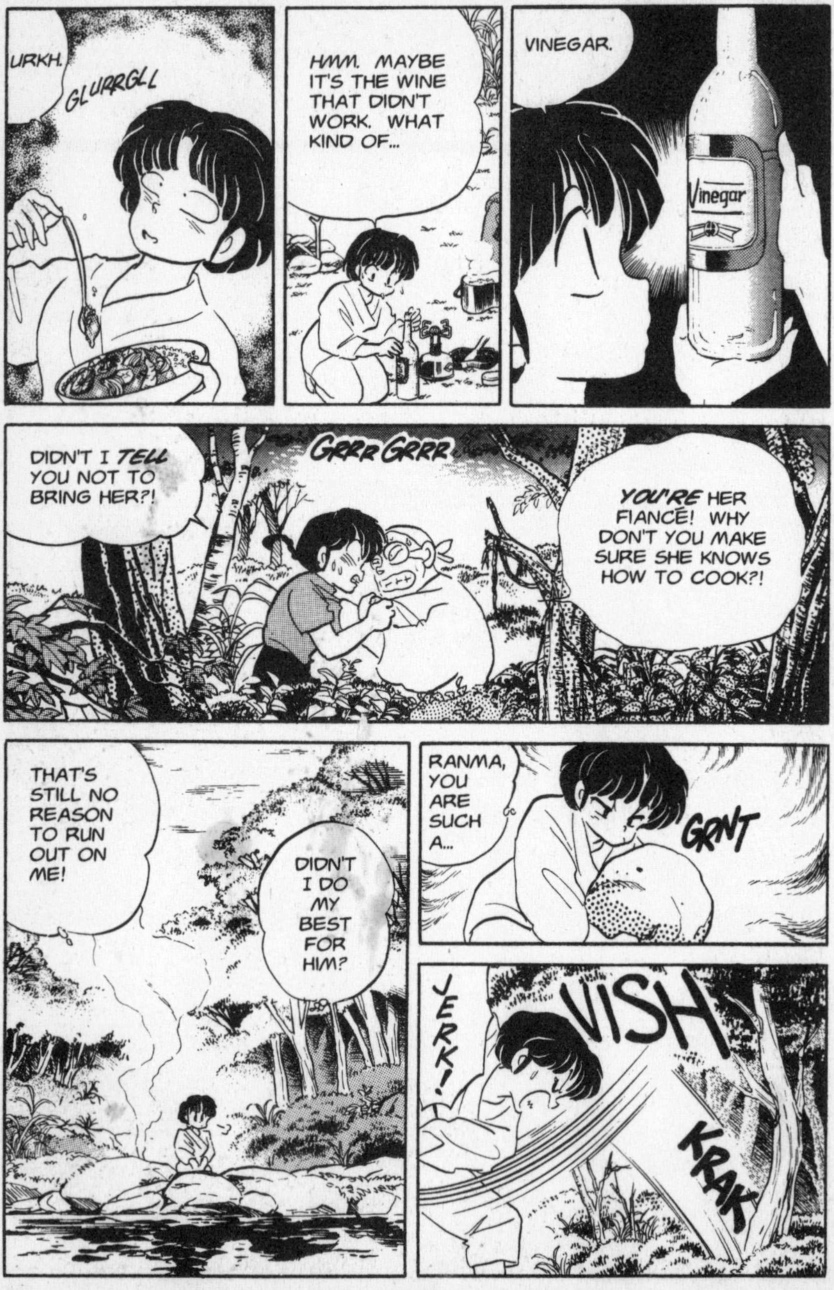
URKH.
GLURRGLL
HMM. MAYBE IT'S THE WINE THAT DIDN'T WORK. WHAT KIND OF...
VINEGAR.
Vinegar
DIDN'T I TELL YOU NOT TO BRING HER?!
GRRR GRRR
YOU'RE HER FIANCÉ! WHY DON'T YOU MAKE SURE SHE KNOWS HOW TO COOK?!
THAT'S STILL NO REASON TO RUN OUT ON ME!
DIDN'T I DO MY BEST FOR HIM?
RANMA, YOU ARE SUCH A...
GRNT
JERK!
VISH
KRAK

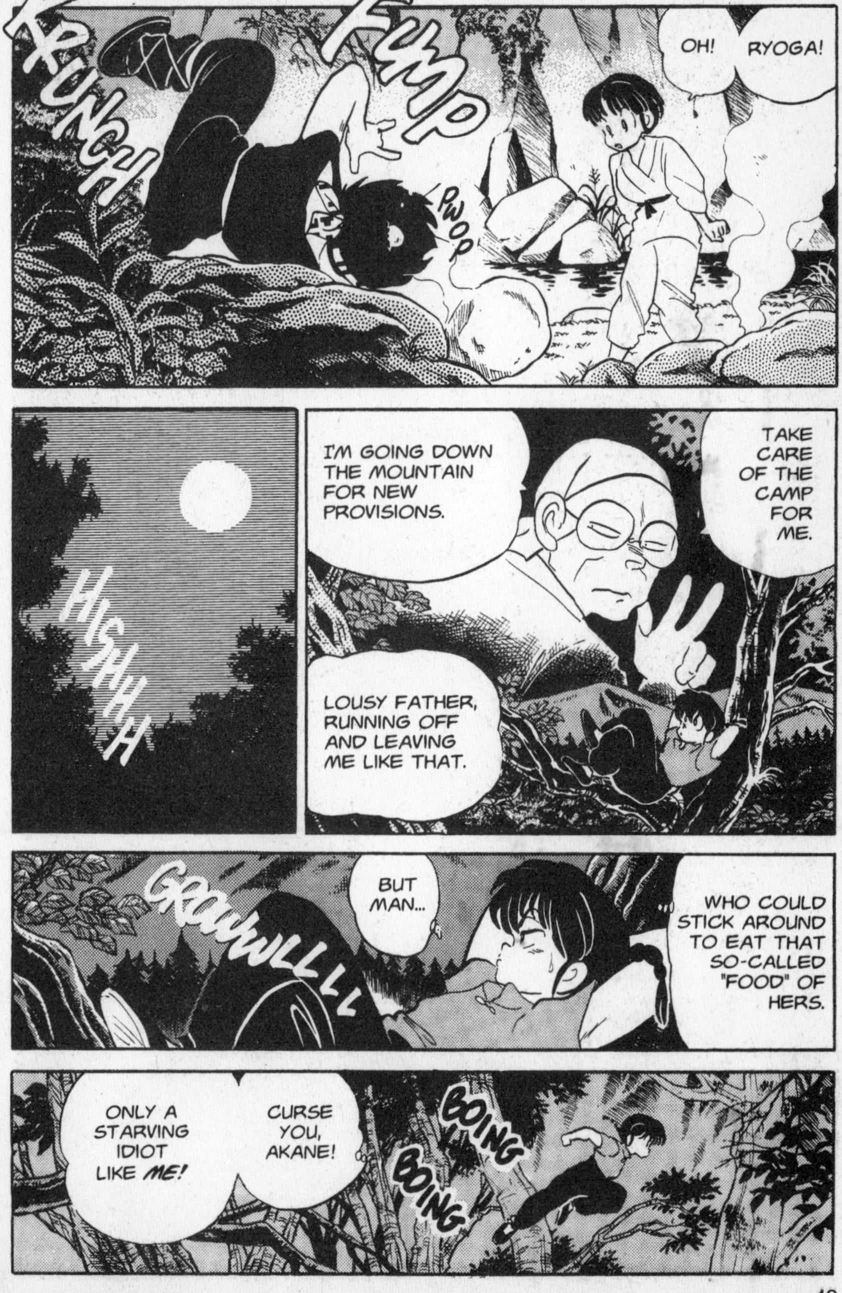
KRUNCH
FUMP
PWOP
OH!
RYOGA!
HISHHH
I'M GOING DOWN THE MOUNTAIN FOR NEW PROVISIONS.
TAKE CARE OF THE CAMP FOR ME.
LOUSY FATHER, RUNNING OFF AND LEAVING ME LIKE THAT.
GROWWLLLL
BUT MAN...
WHO COULD STICK AROUND TO EAT THAT SO-CALLED "FOOD" OF HERS.
ONLY A STARVING IDIOT LIKE *ME!*
CURSE YOU, AKANE!
BOING
BOING

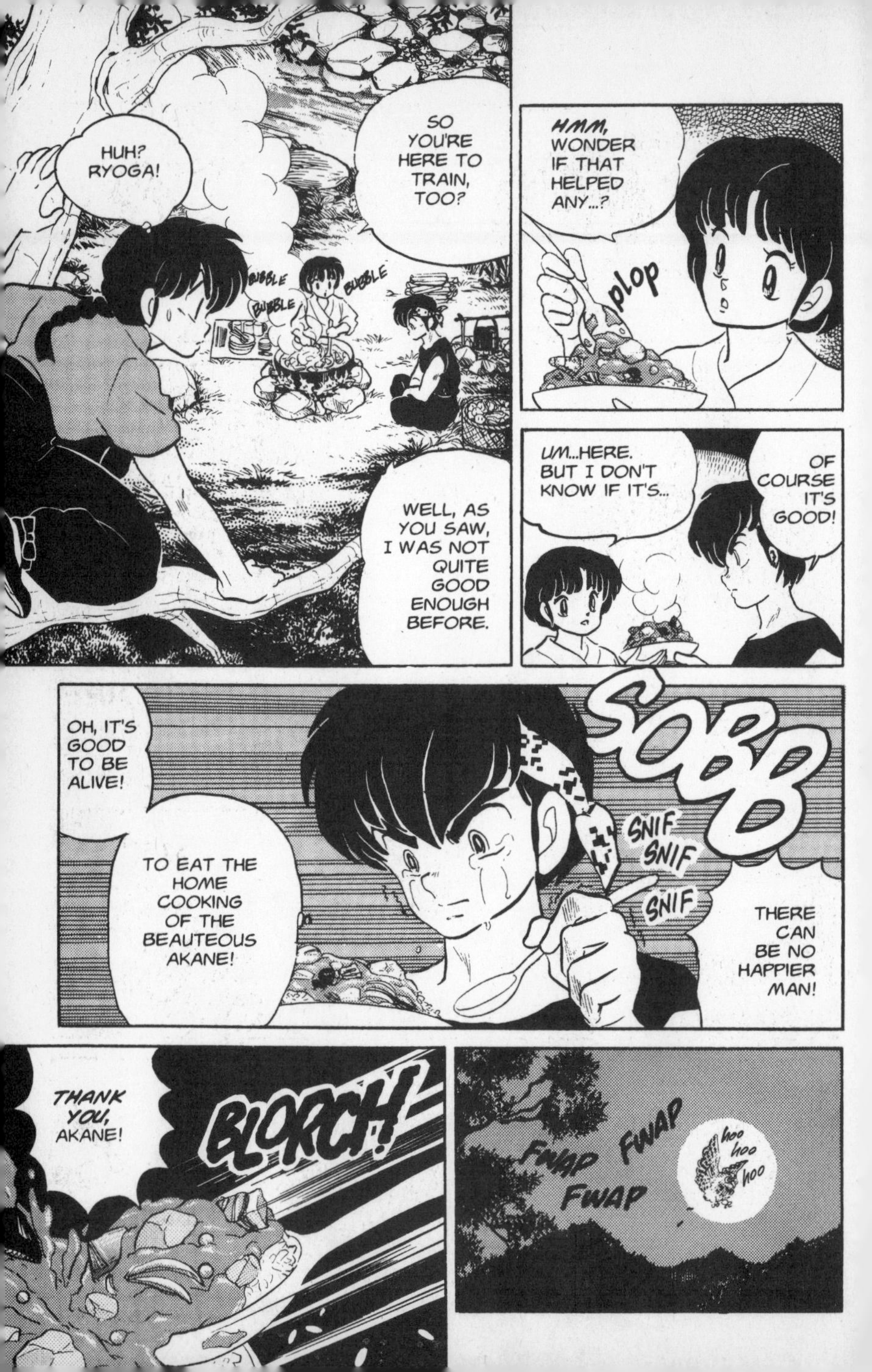
HUH? RYOGA!
SO YOU'RE HERE TO TRAIN, TOO?
BUBBLE BUBBLE BUBBLE
WELL, AS YOU SAW, I WAS NOT QUITE GOOD ENOUGH BEFORE.
HMM, WONDER IF THAT HELPED ANY...?
plop
UM...HERE. BUT I DON'T KNOW IF IT'S...
OF COURSE IT'S GOOD!
OH, IT'S GOOD TO BE ALIVE!
TO EAT THE HOME COOKING OF THE BEAUTEOUS AKANE!
SOB
SNIF SNIF SNIF
THERE CAN BE NO HAPPIER MAN!
THANK YOU, AKANE!
BLORCH!
FWAP FWAP FWAP
hoo hoo hoo

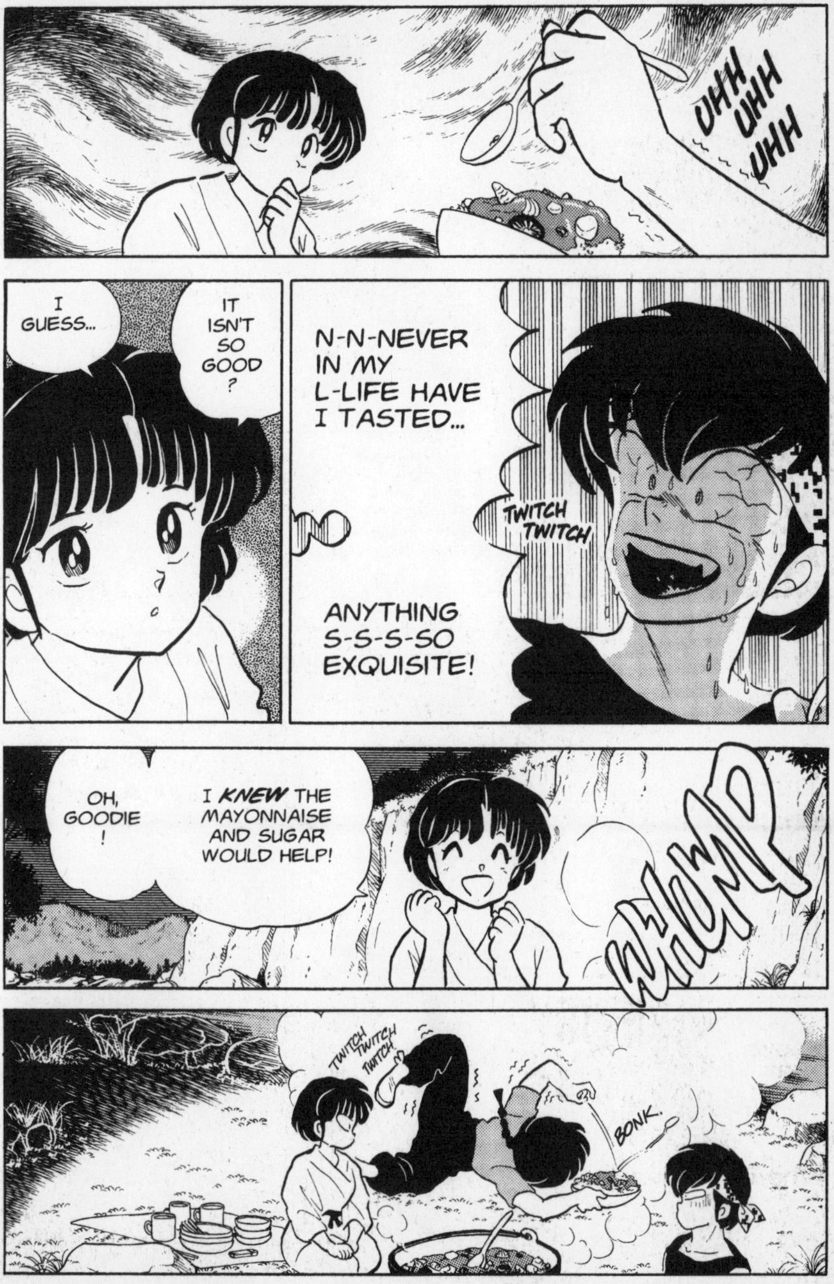
UHH UHH UHH
I GUESS...
IT ISN'T SO GOOD?
N-N-NEVER IN MY L-LIFE HAVE I TASTED...
TWITCH TWITCH
ANYTHING S-S-S-SO EXQUISITE!
OH, GOODIE!
I *KNEW* THE MAYONNAISE AND SUGAR WOULD HELP!
WHUMP
TWITCH TWITCH TWITCH
BONK.

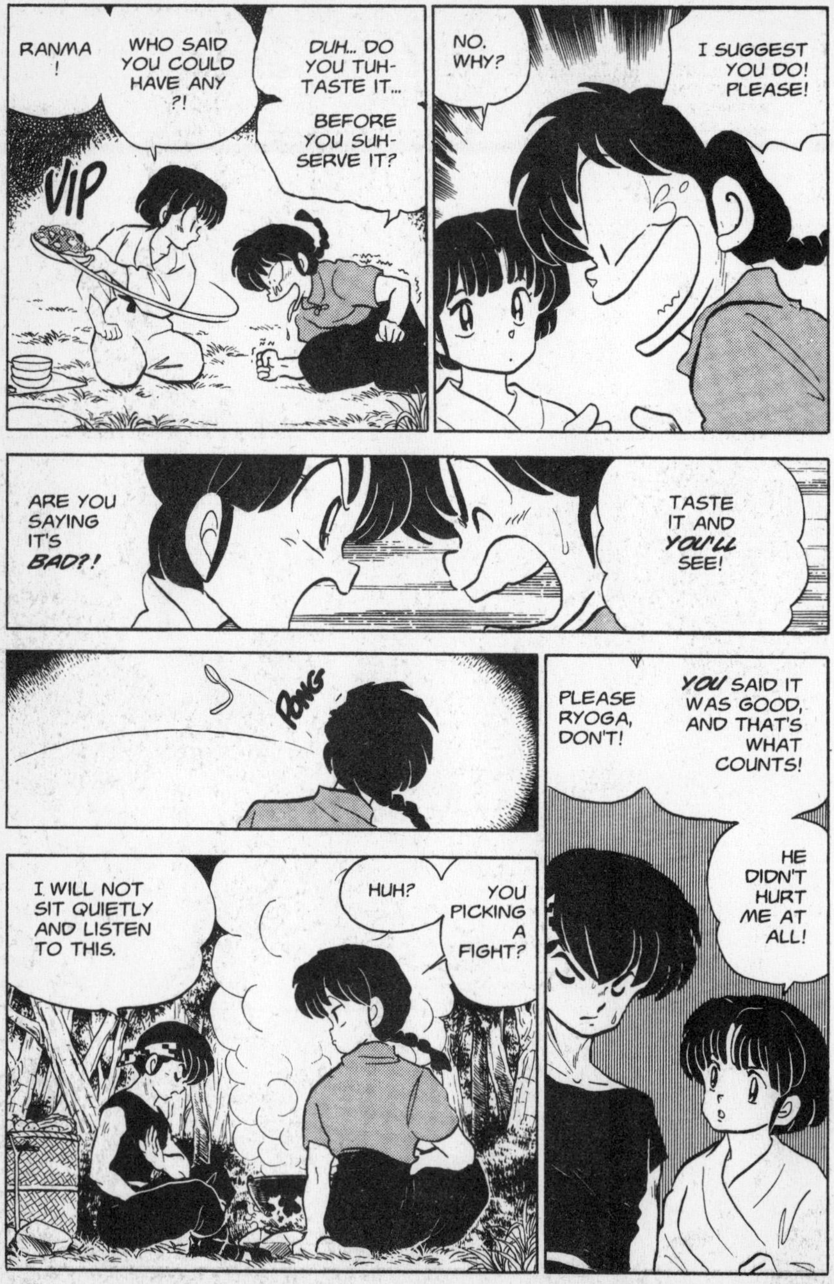
RANMA !
WHO SAID YOU COULD HAVE ANY ?!
VIP
DUH... DO YOU TUH-TASTE IT... BEFORE YOU SUH-SERVE IT?
NO. WHY?
I SUGGEST YOU DO! PLEASE!
ARE YOU SAYING IT'S *BAD?!*
TASTE IT AND *YOU'LL* SEE!
PONG
I WILL NOT SIT QUIETLY AND LISTEN TO THIS.
HUH?
YOU PICKING A FIGHT?
PLEASE RYOGA, DON'T!
YOU SAID IT WAS GOOD, AND THAT'S WHAT COUNTS!
HE DIDN'T HURT ME AT ALL!

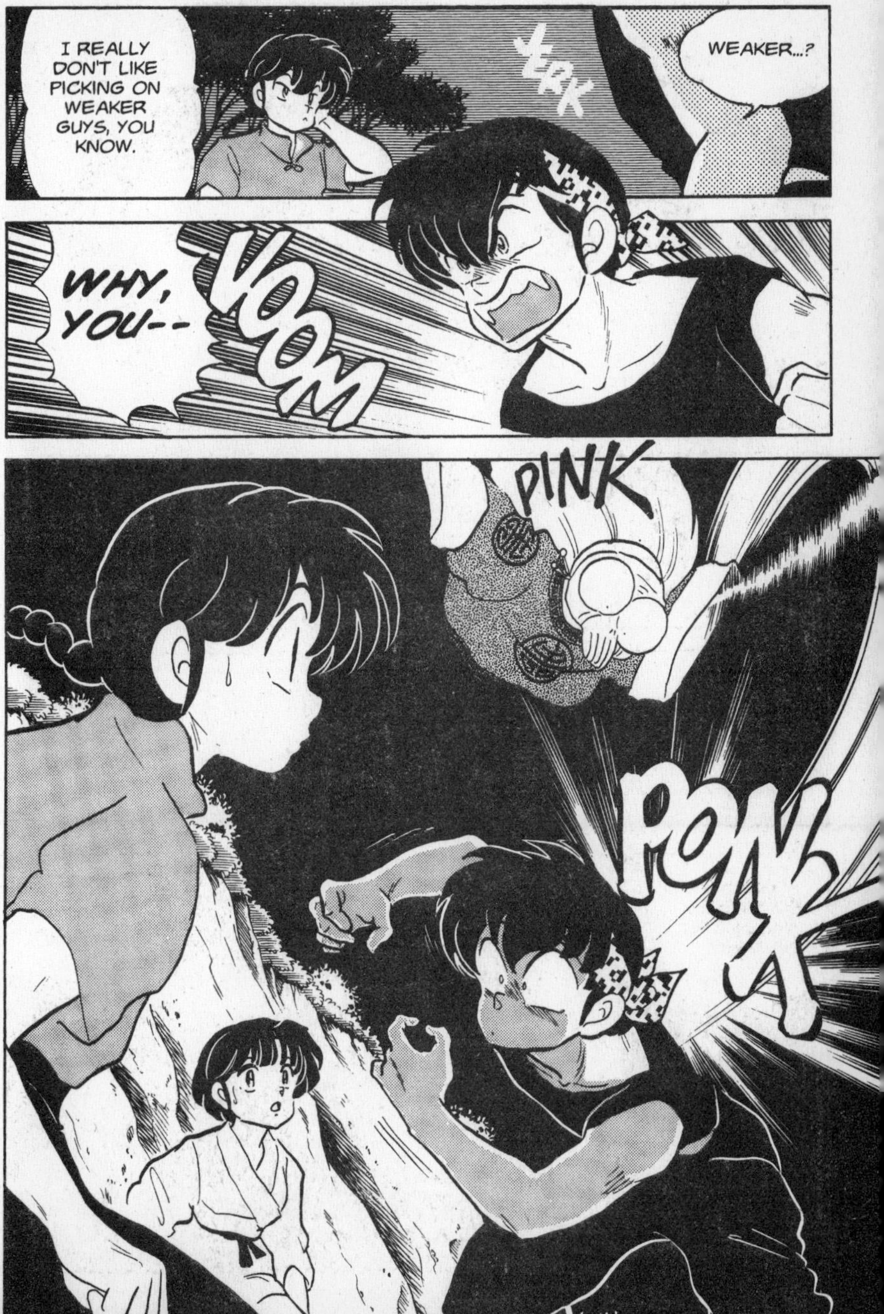
I REALLY DON'T LIKE PICKING ON WEAKER GUYS, YOU KNOW.
JERK
WEAKER...?
WHY, YOU--
VOOM
PINK
PON

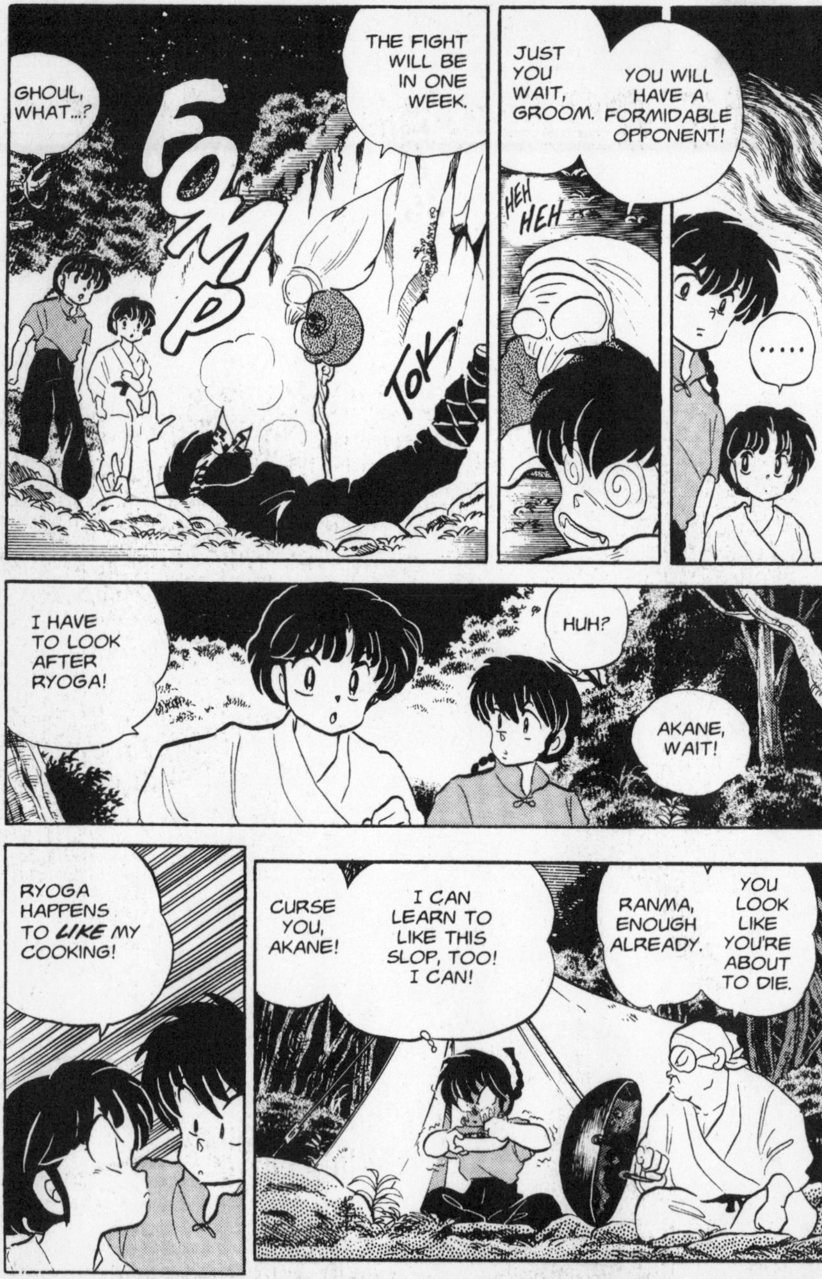
GHOUL, WHAT...?
THE FIGHT WILL BE IN ONE WEEK.
FOMP
TOK
JUST YOU WAIT, GROOM.
HEH HEH
YOU WILL HAVE A FORMIDABLE OPPONENT!
......
I HAVE TO LOOK AFTER RYOGA!
HUH?
AKANE, WAIT!
RYOGA HAPPENS TO LIKE MY COOKING!
CURSE YOU, AKANE!
I CAN LEARN TO LIKE THIS SLOP, TOO! I CAN!
RANMA, ENOUGH ALREADY.
YOU LOOK LIKE YOU'RE ABOUT TO DIE.

Part 4

THE BREAKING POINT

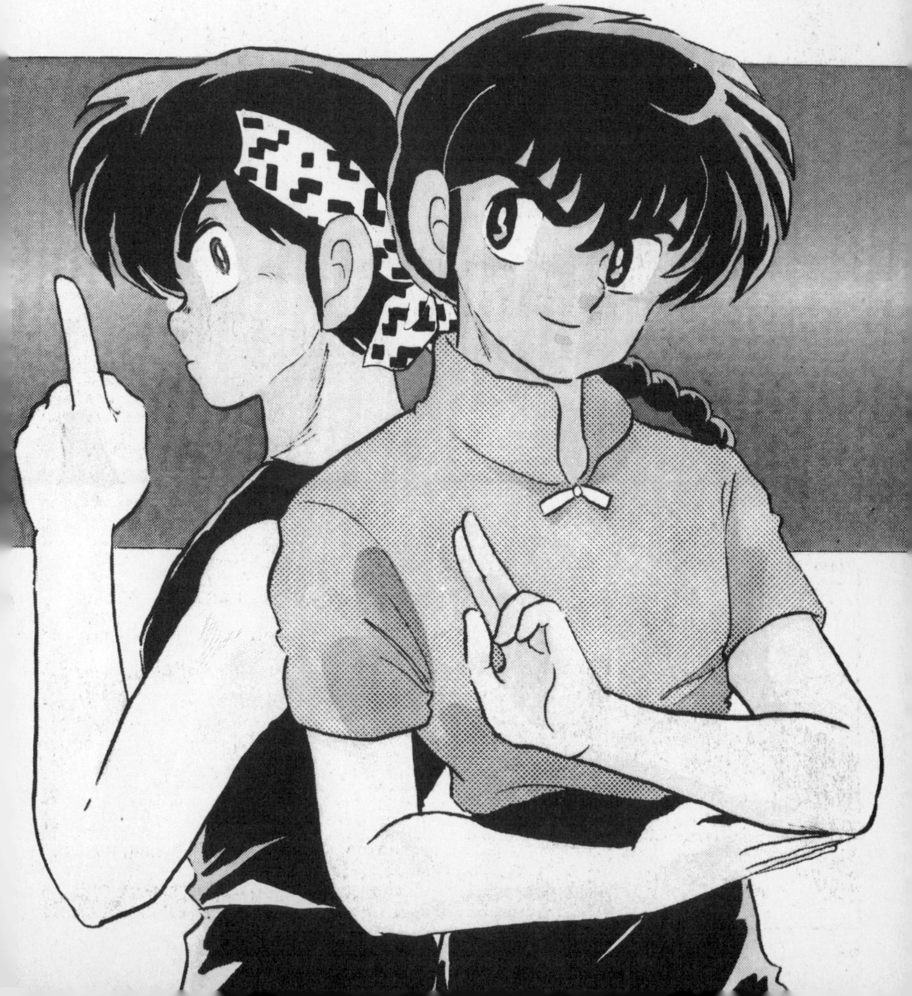

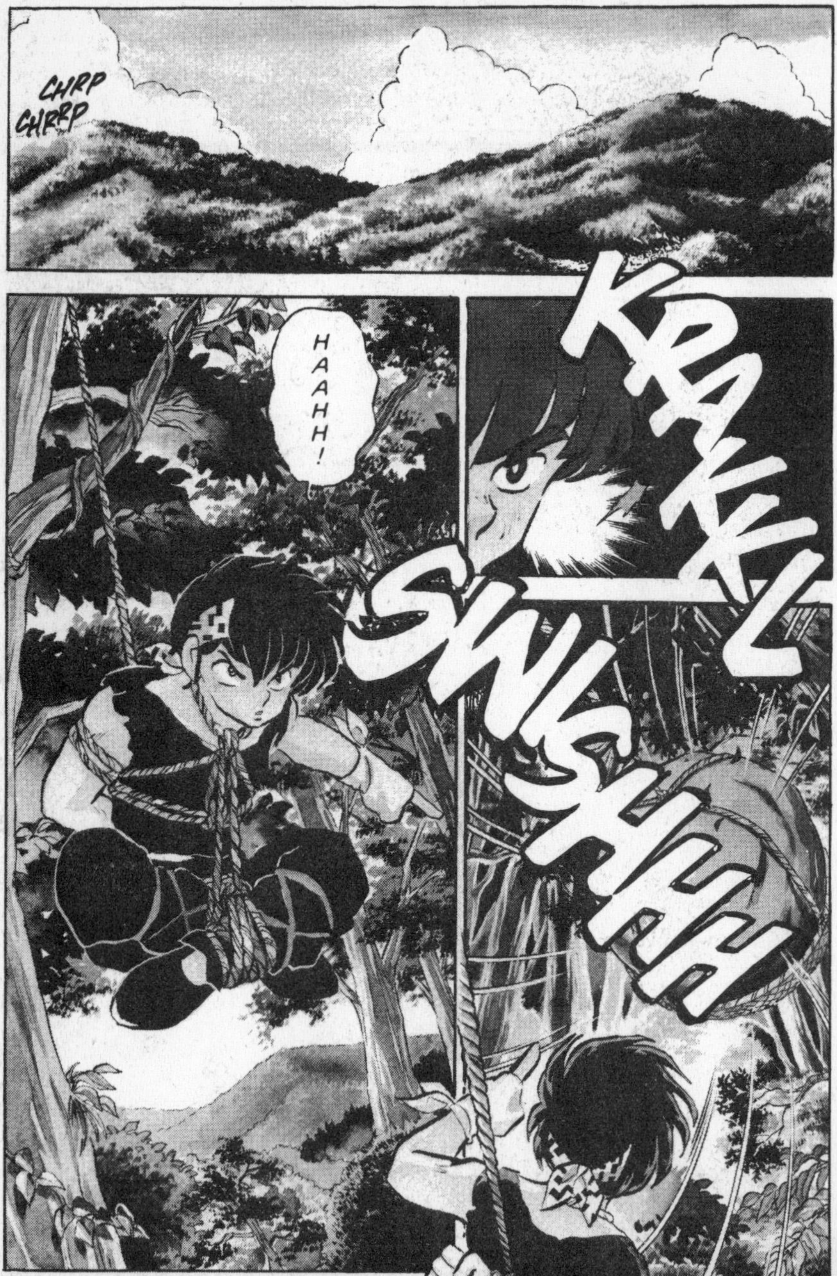
CHRP
CHRRP
HAAAHH!
KRAKKL
SWISHHH

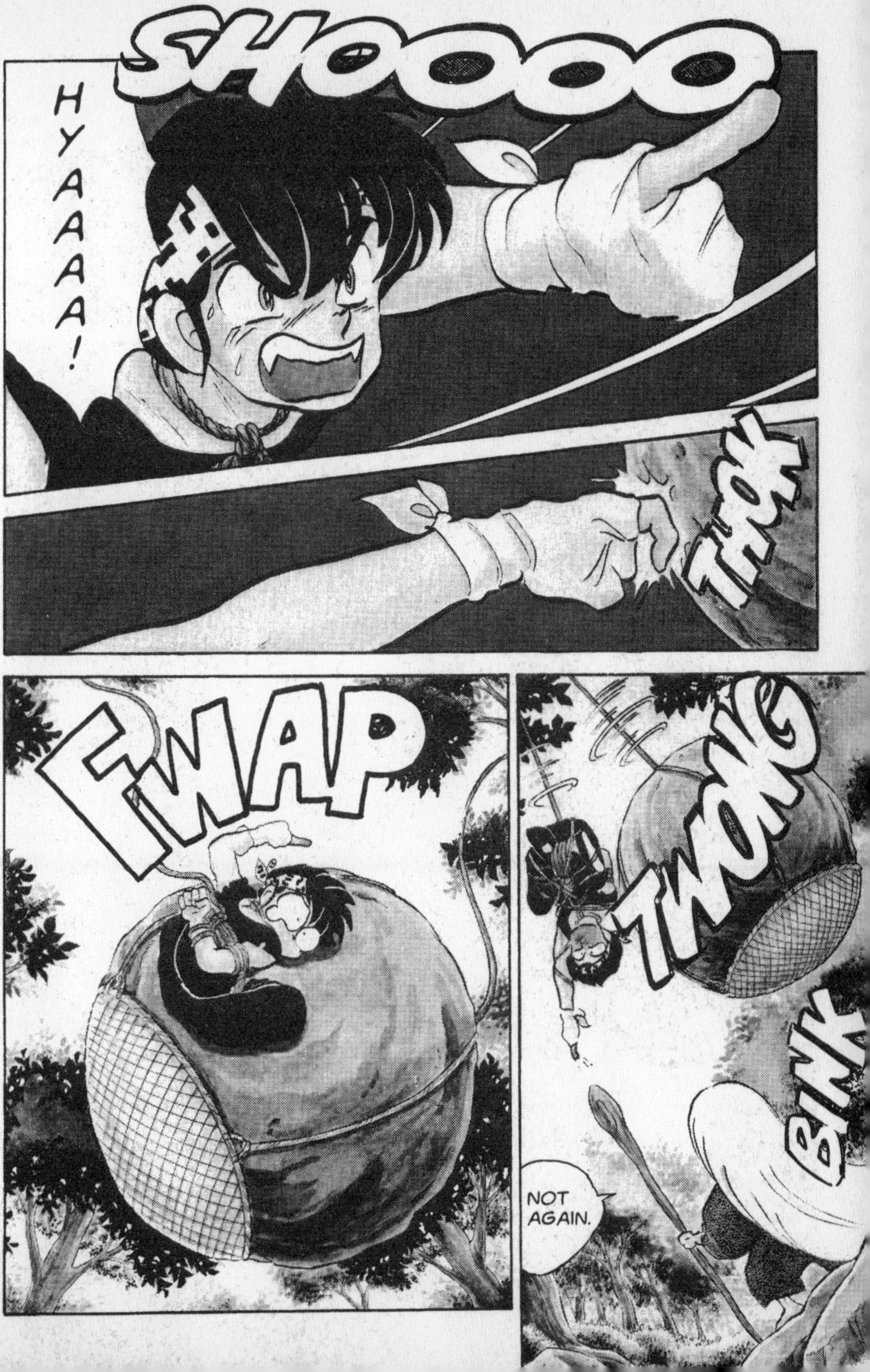
SHOOOO
HYAAAAA!
THOK
FWAP
TWONG
BINK
NOT AGAIN.

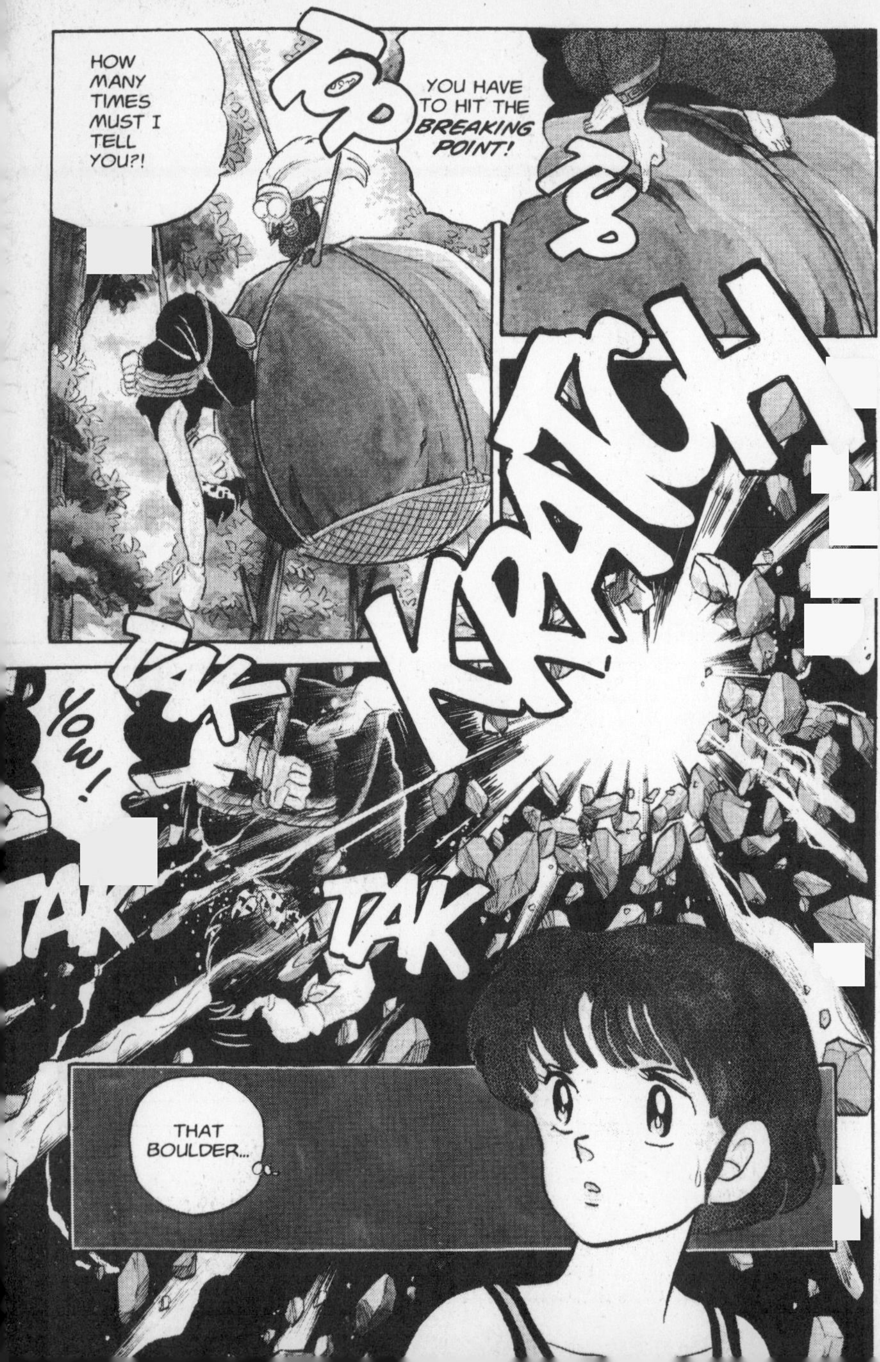
HOW MANY TIMES MUST I TELL YOU?!
TOP
YOU HAVE TO HIT THE BREAKING POINT!
TUP
KRACH
TAK
YOW!
TAK
TAK
THAT BOULDER...

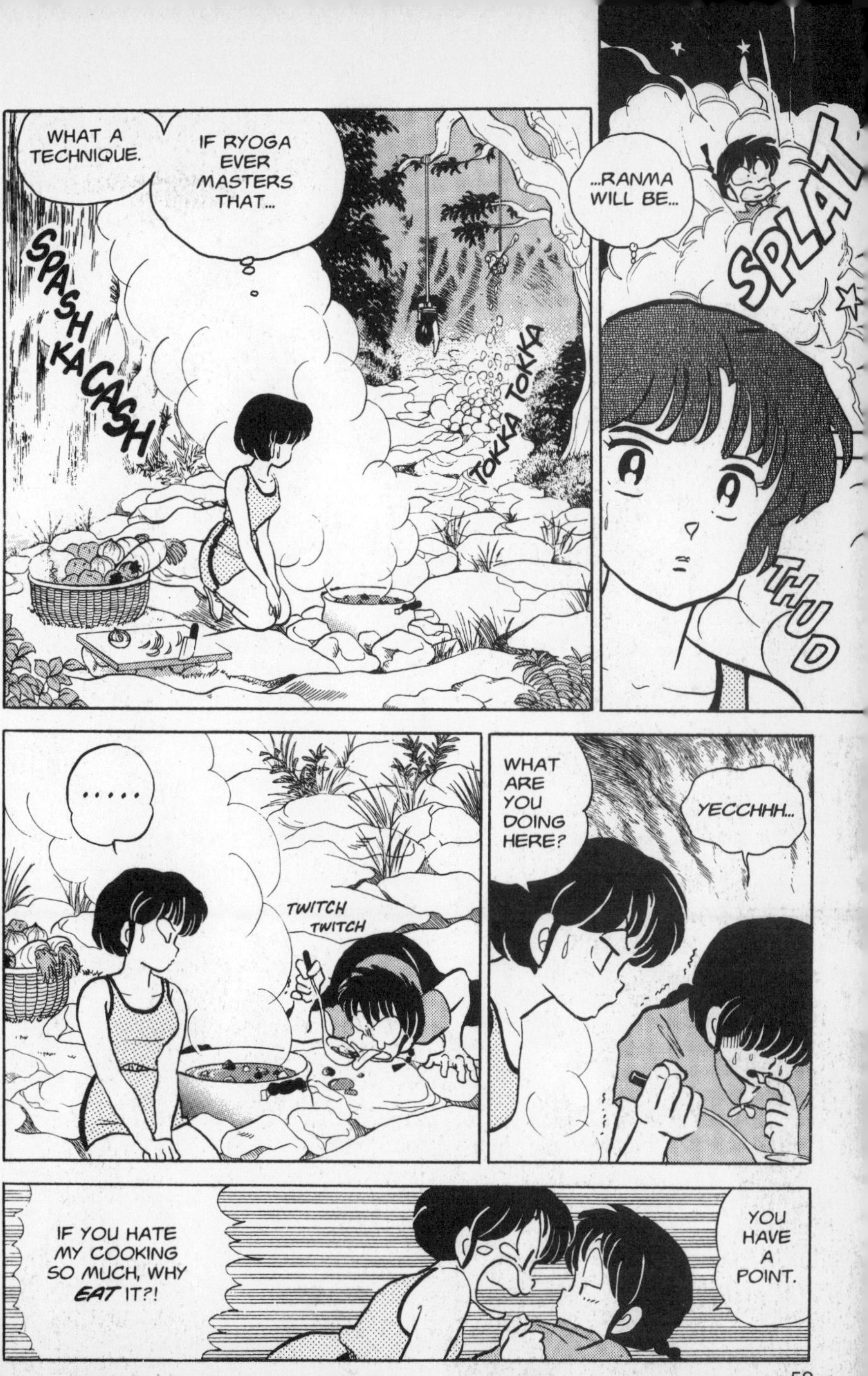
WHAT A TECHNIQUE.
IF RYOGA EVER MASTERS THAT...
SPASH KA CASH
TOKKA TOKKA
...RANMA WILL BE...
SPLAT
THUD
.....
TWITCH TWITCH
WHAT ARE YOU DOING HERE?
YECCHHH...
IF YOU HATE MY COOKING SO MUCH, WHY *EAT* IT?!
YOU HAVE A POINT.

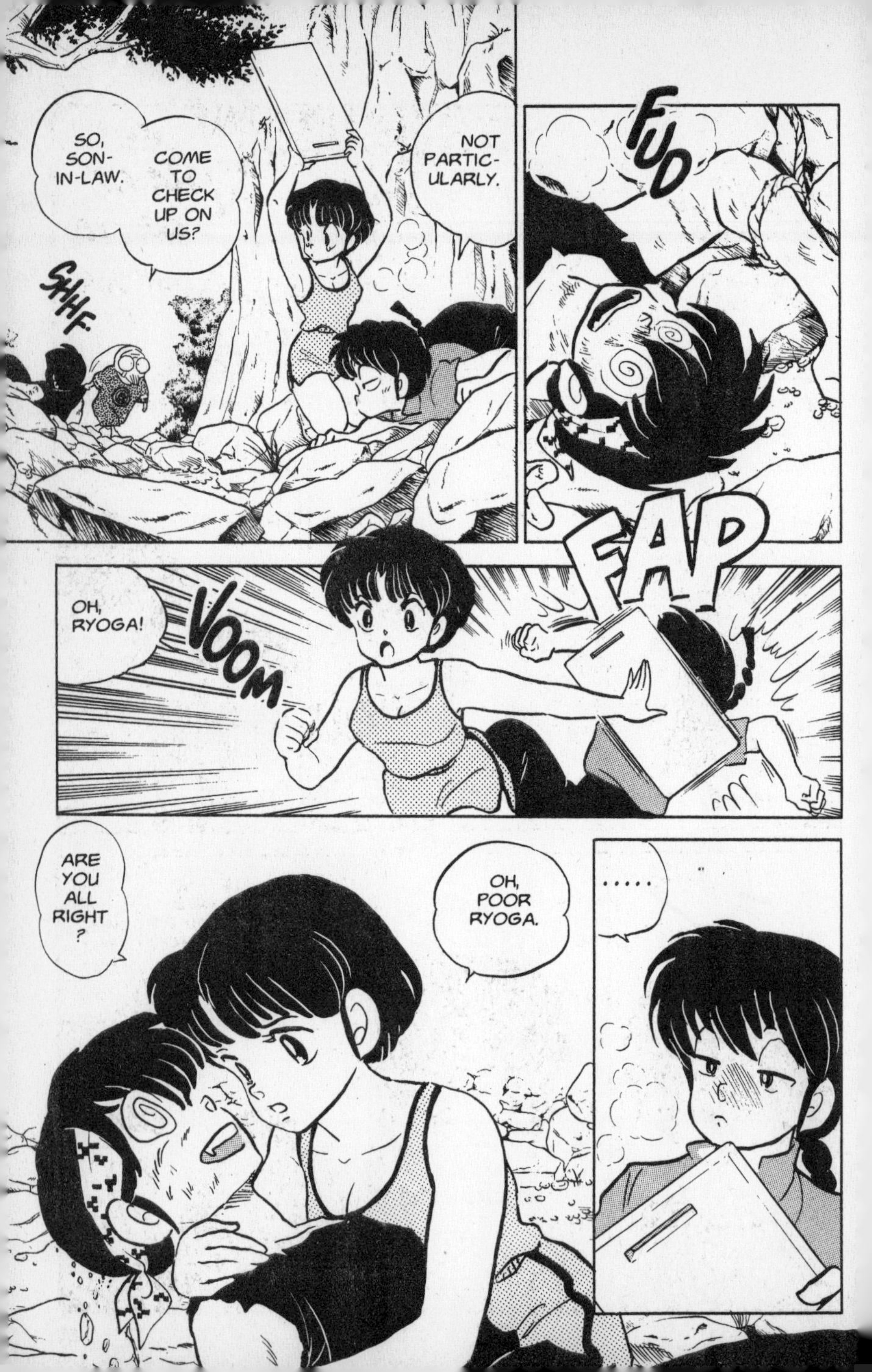
SO, SON-IN-LAW.
COME TO CHECK UP ON US?
SHHF
NOT PARTIC-ULARLY.
FUD
FAP
OH, RYOGA!
VOOM
ARE YOU ALL RIGHT?
OH, POOR RYOGA.
.....

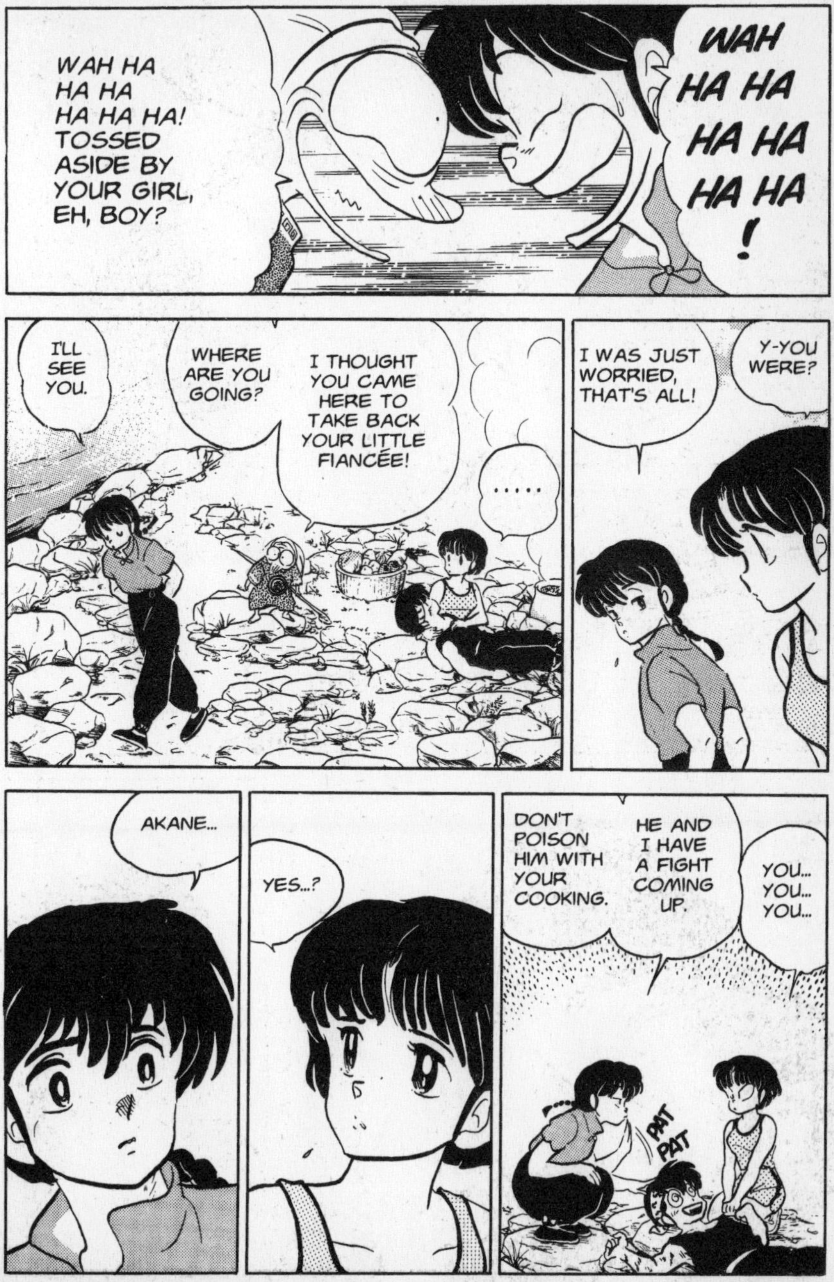
WAH HA HA HA HA HA HA! TOSSED ASIDE BY YOUR GIRL, EH, BOY?
WAH HA HA HA HA HA HA !
I'LL SEE YOU.
WHERE ARE YOU GOING?
I THOUGHT YOU CAME HERE TO TAKE BACK YOUR LITTLE FIANCÉE!
.....
I WAS JUST WORRIED, THAT'S ALL!
Y-YOU WERE?
AKANE...
YES...?
DON'T POISON HIM WITH YOUR COOKING.
HE AND I HAVE A FIGHT COMING UP.
YOU... YOU... YOU...
PAT PAT

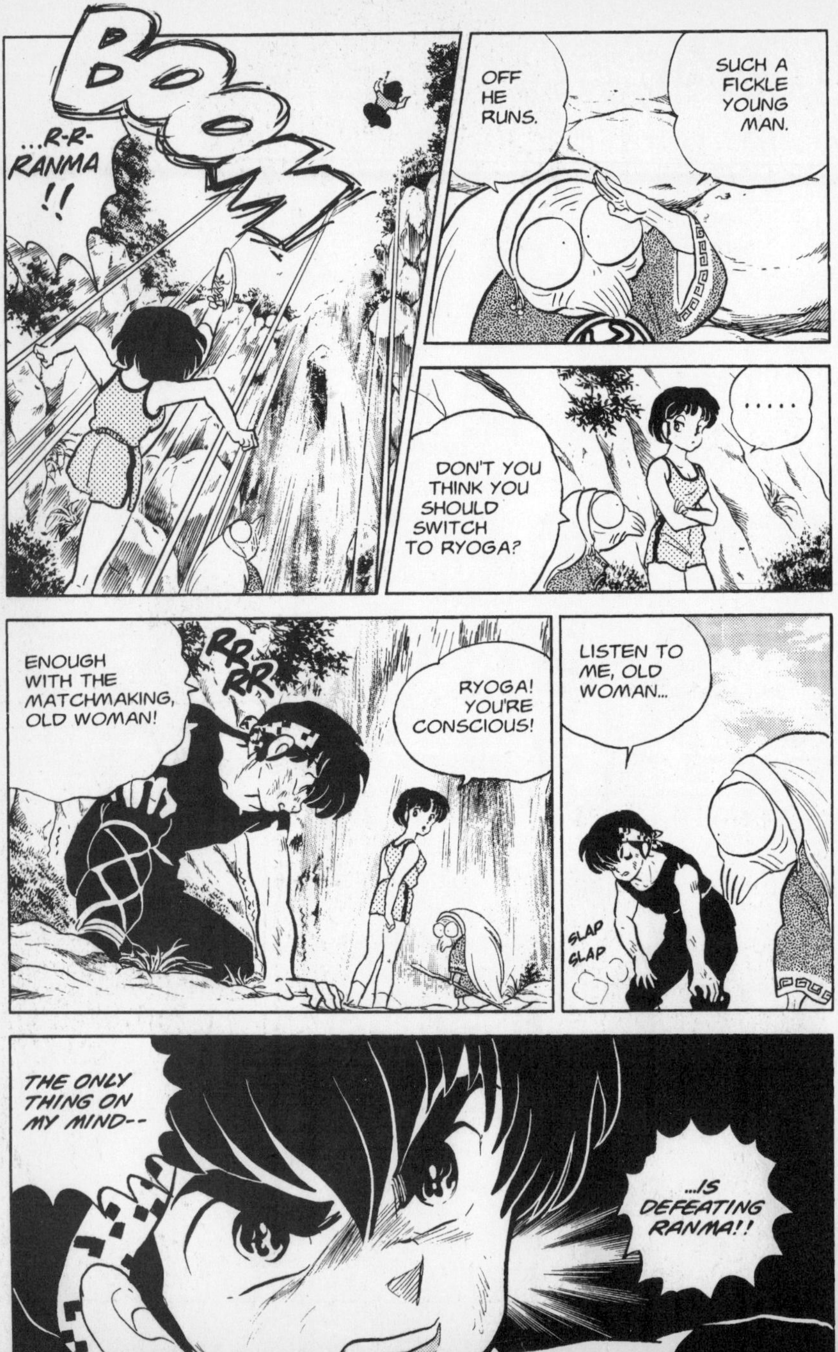
BOOM
...R-R-RANMA!!
OFF HE RUNS.
SUCH A FICKLE YOUNG MAN.
DON'T YOU THINK YOU SHOULD SWITCH TO RYOGA?
......
ENOUGH WITH THE MATCHMAKING, OLD WOMAN!
RRRR
RYOGA! YOU'RE CONSCIOUS!
LISTEN TO ME, OLD WOMAN...
SLAP SLAP
THE ONLY THING ON MY MIND--
...IS DEFEATING RANMA!!

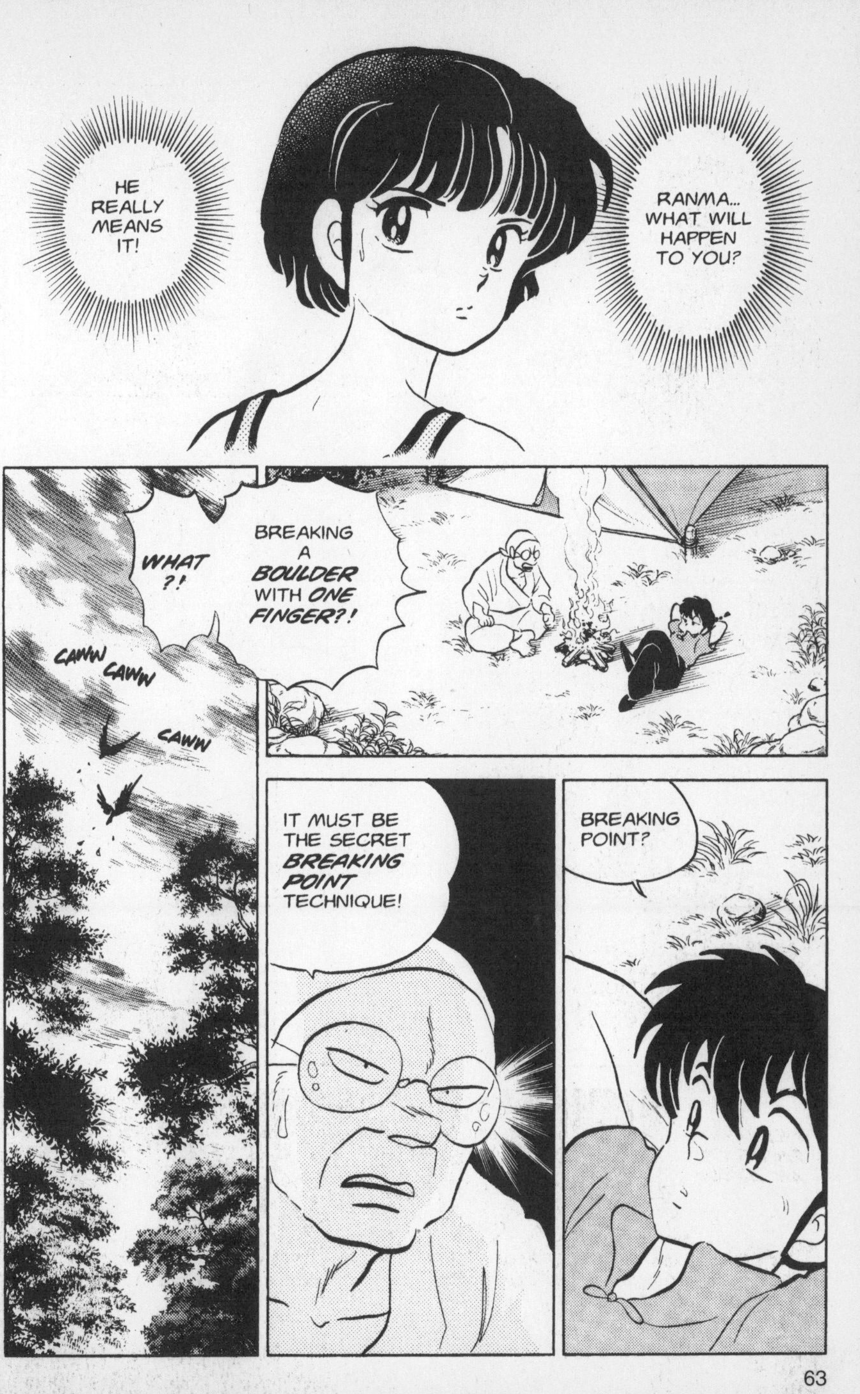
HE REALLY MEANS IT!
RANMA... WHAT WILL HAPPEN TO YOU?
WHAT?!
CAWW CAWW
CAWW
BREAKING A BOULDER WITH ONE FINGER?!
IT MUST BE THE SECRET BREAKING POINT TECHNIQUE!
BREAKING POINT?

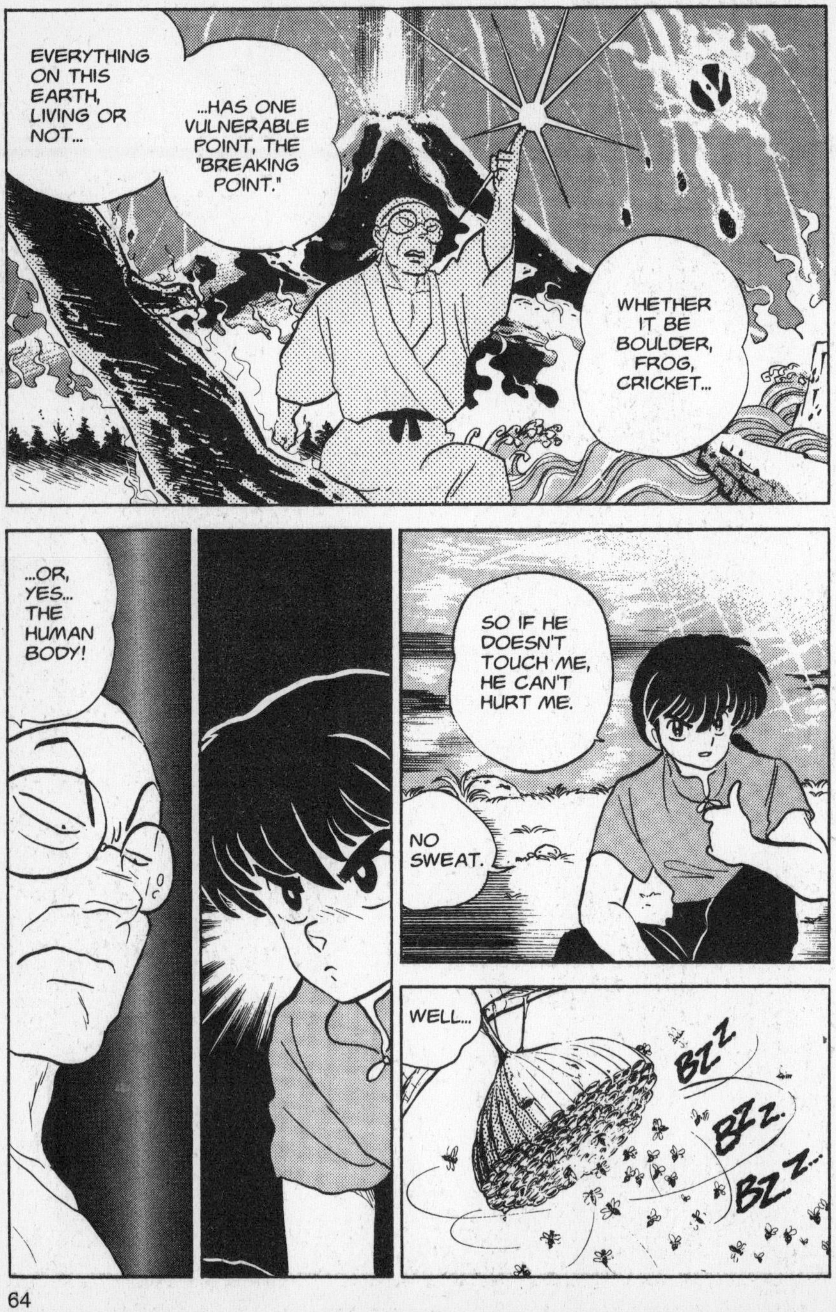
EVERYTHING ON THIS EARTH, LIVING OR NOT...
...HAS ONE VULNERABLE POINT, THE "BREAKING POINT."
WHETHER IT BE BOULDER, FROG, CRICKET...
...OR, YES... THE HUMAN BODY!
SO IF HE DOESN'T TOUCH ME, HE CAN'T HURT ME.
NO SWEAT.
WELL...
BZZ
BZZ.
BZZ...

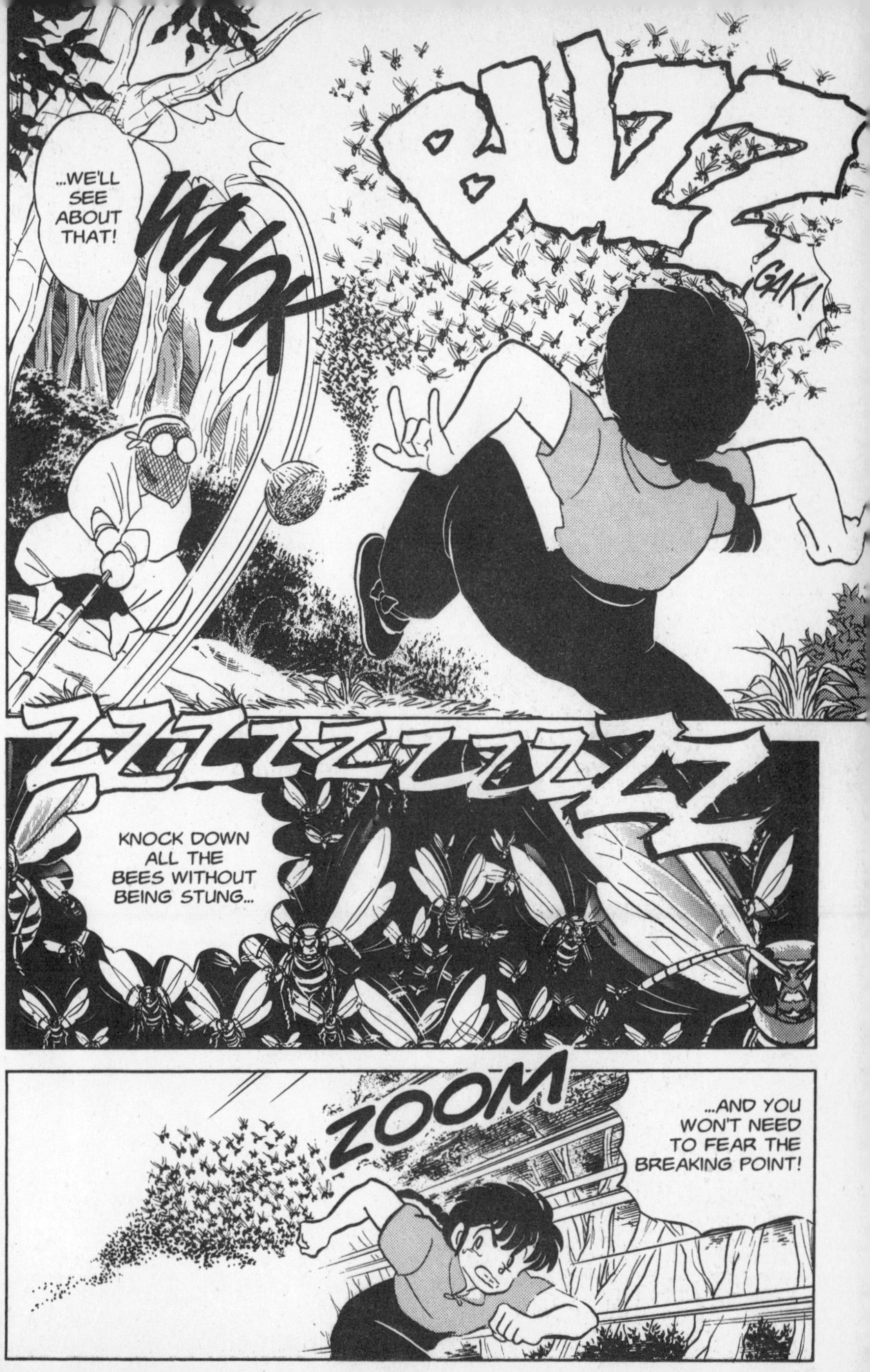

...WE'LL SEE ABOUT THAT!
WHOK
BUZZ
¡GAK!
ZZZZZZZZZ
KNOCK DOWN ALL THE BEES WITHOUT BEING STUNG...
ZOOM
...AND YOU WON'T NEED TO FEAR THE BREAKING POINT!

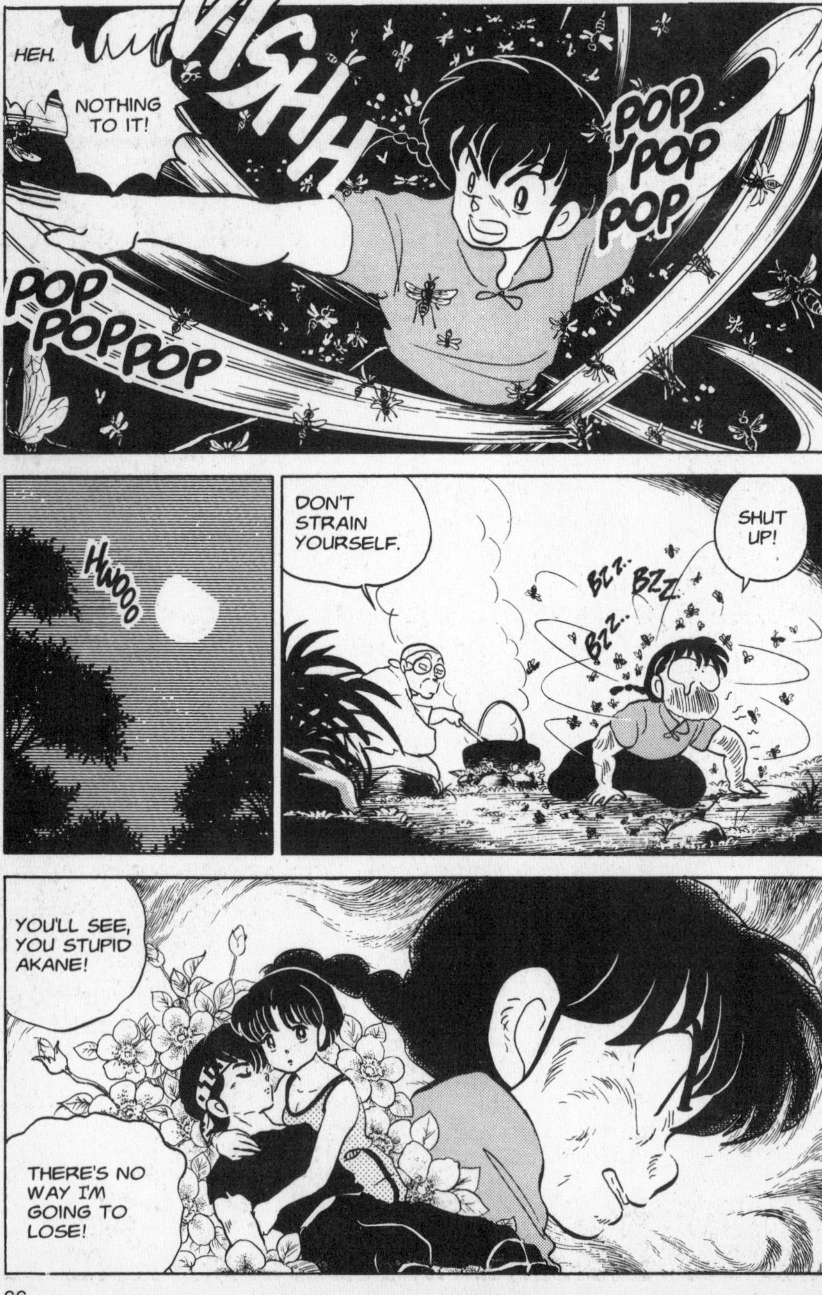
HEH.
VISHH
NOTHING TO IT!
POP POP POP
POP POP POP
HWOOO
DON'T STRAIN YOURSELF.
BZZ.. BZZ.. BZZ..
SHUT UP!
YOU'LL SEE, YOU STUPID AKANE!
THERE'S NO WAY I'M GOING TO LOSE!

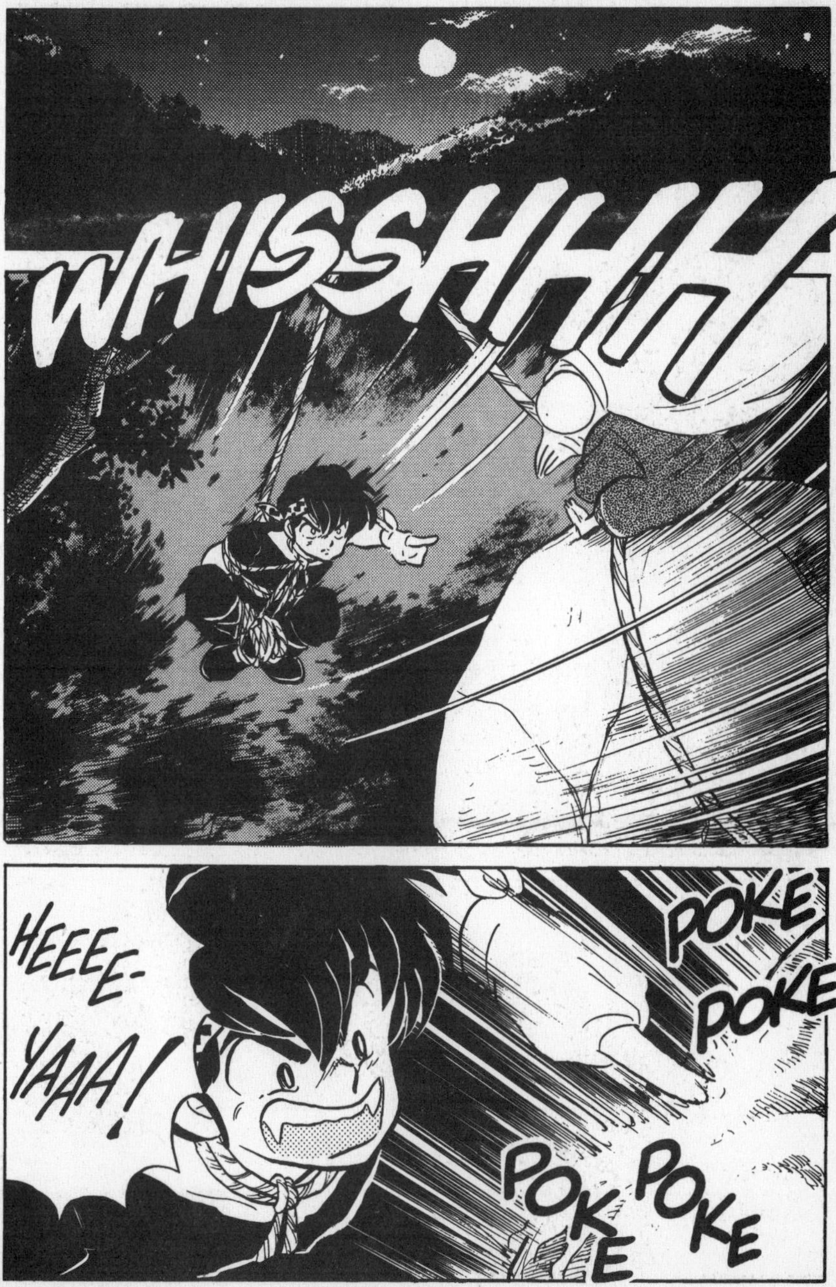
WHISSHHH
HEEEE-
E-
YAAA!
POKE
POKE
POKE
POKE

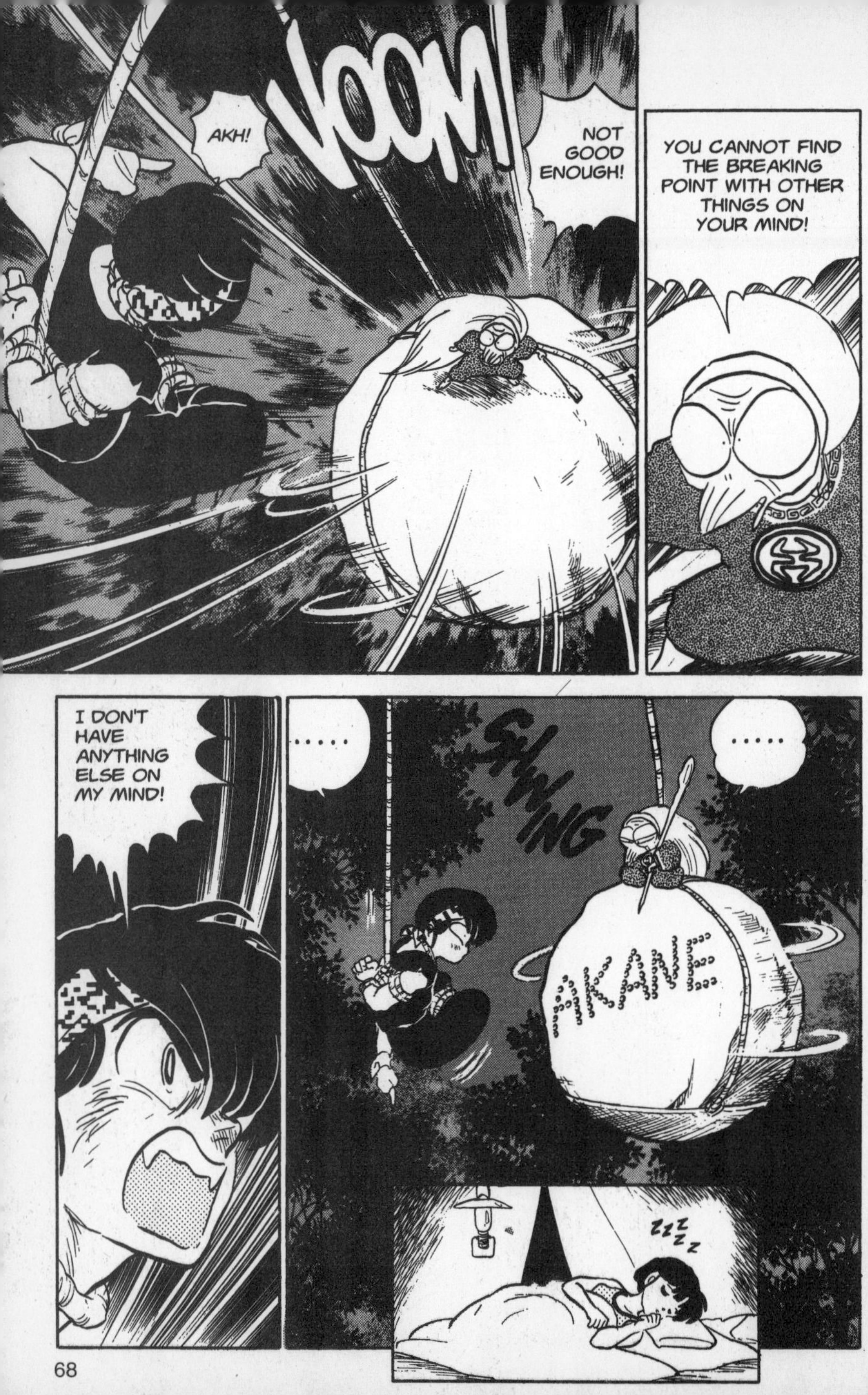
AKH!
VOOM!
NOT GOOD ENOUGH!
YOU CANNOT FIND THE BREAKING POINT WITH OTHER THINGS ON YOUR MIND!
I DON'T HAVE ANYTHING ELSE ON MY MIND!
.....
SHWING
.....
AKANE
ZZZZZ

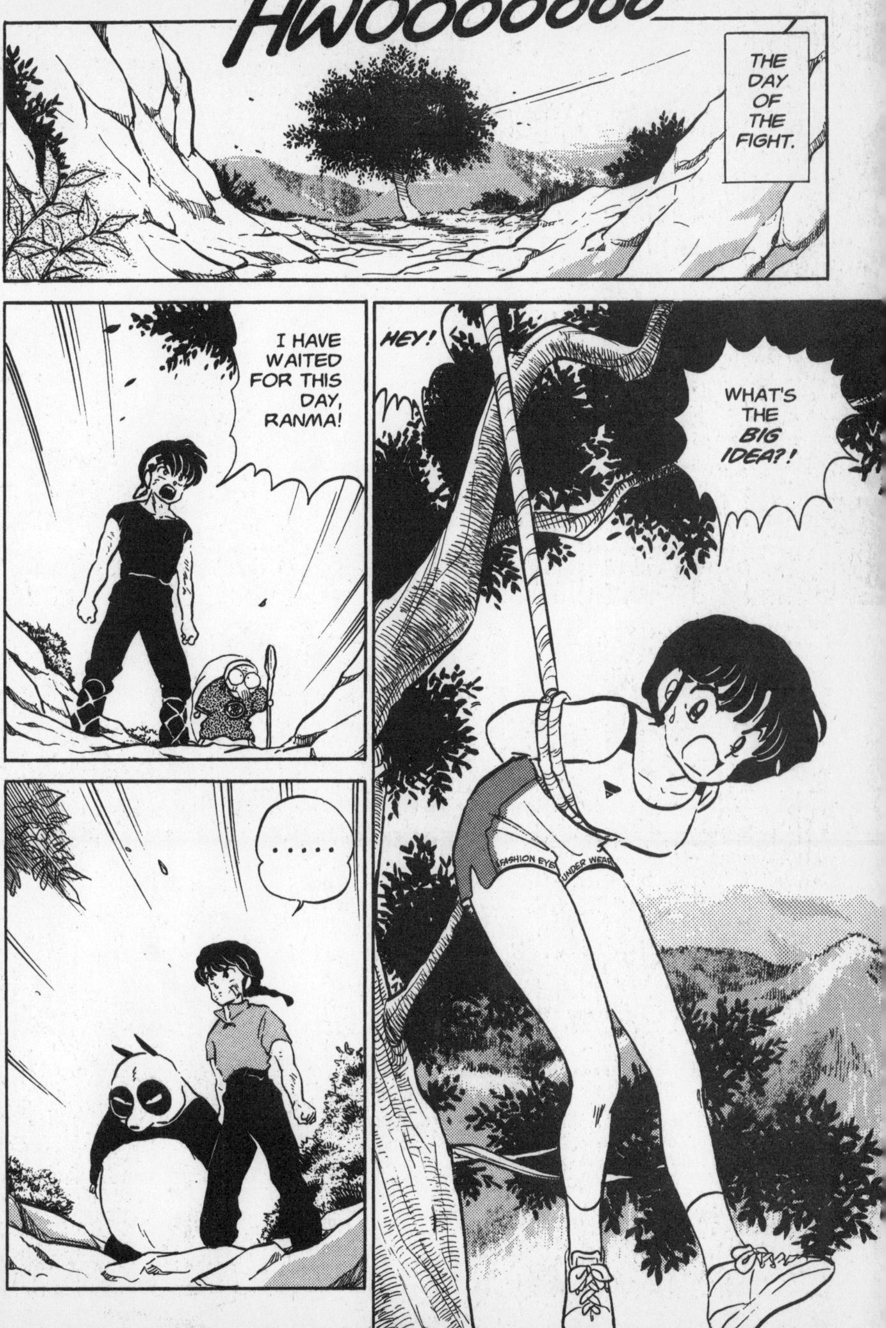
HWOOOOOOO
THE DAY OF THE FIGHT.
I HAVE WAITED FOR THIS DAY, RANMA!
.....
HEY!
WHAT'S THE BIG IDEA?!
FASHION EYE UNDER WEAR

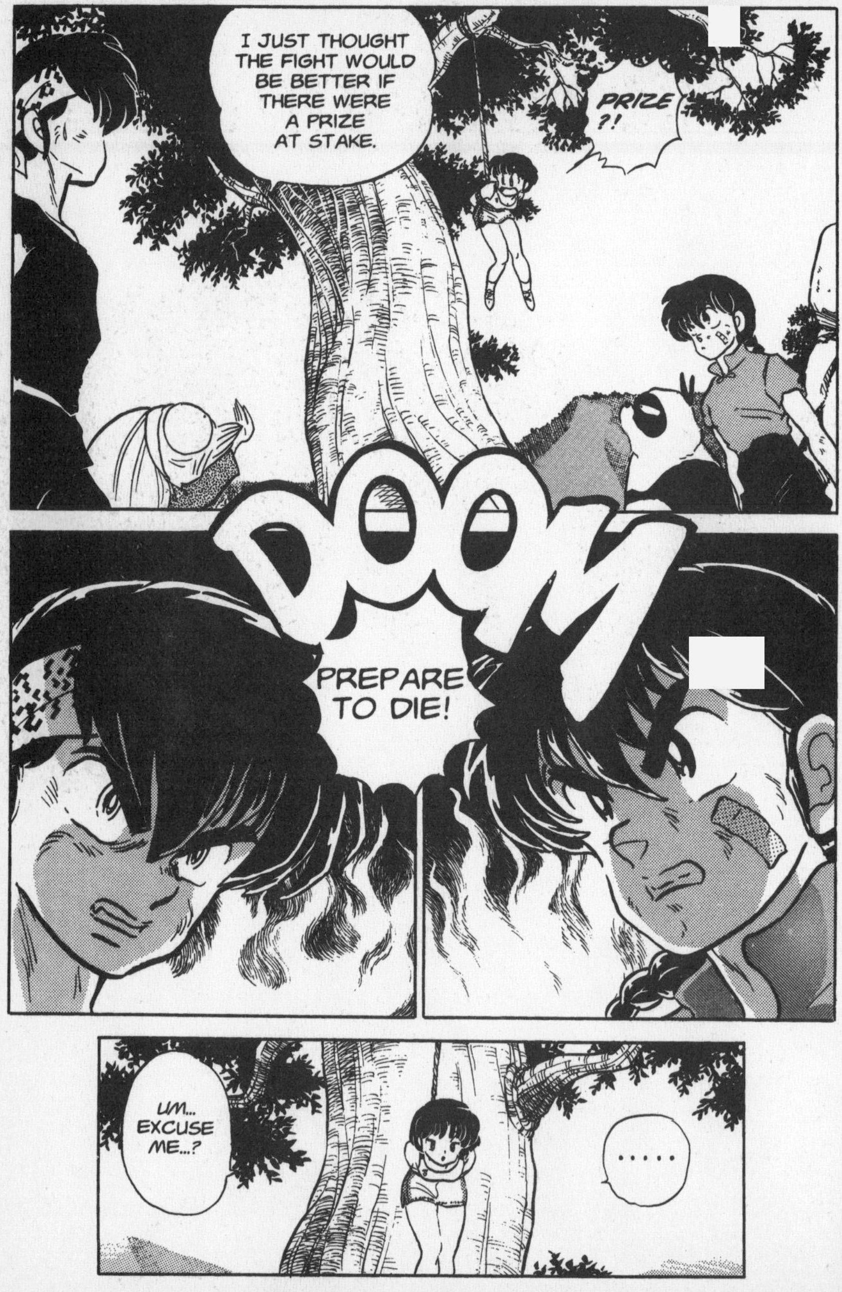
I JUST THOUGHT THE FIGHT WOULD BE BETTER IF THERE WERE A PRIZE AT STAKE.
PRIZE ?!
DOOM
PREPARE TO DIE!
UM... EXCUSE ME...?
.....

Part 5
THE IMMORTAL MAN

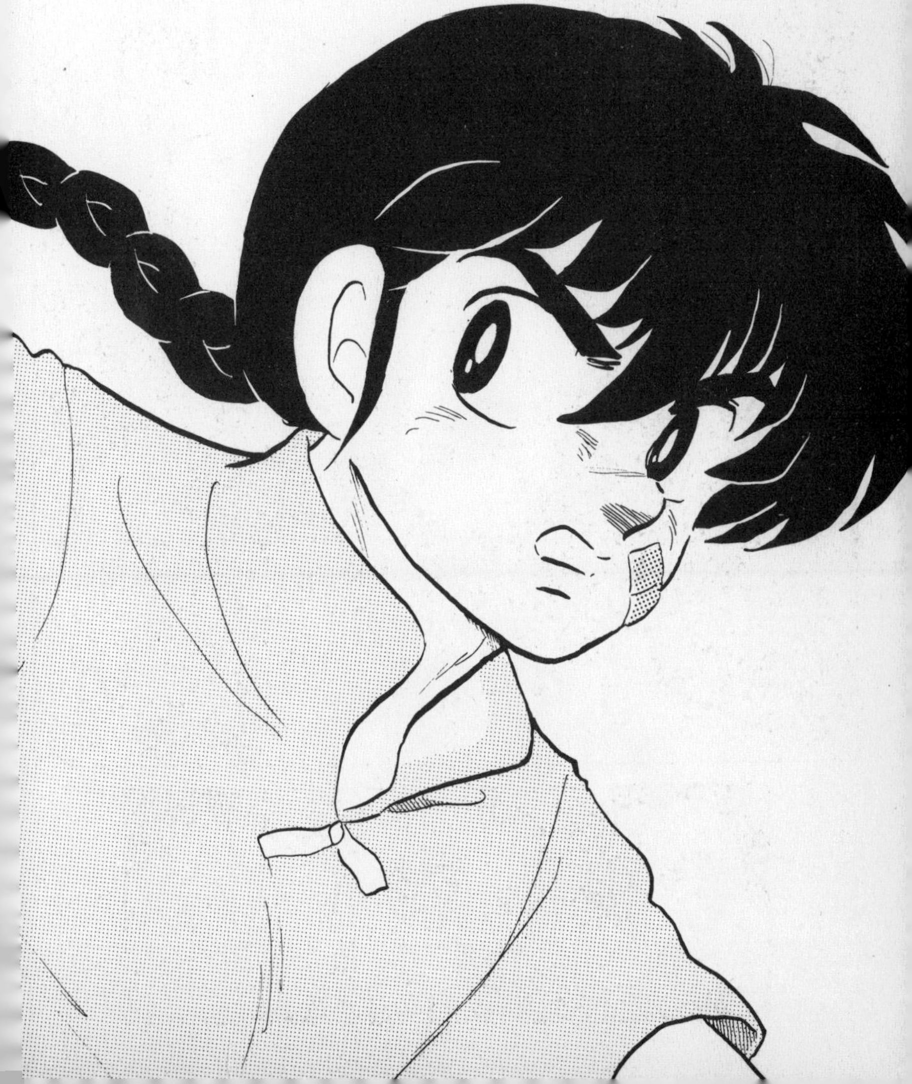

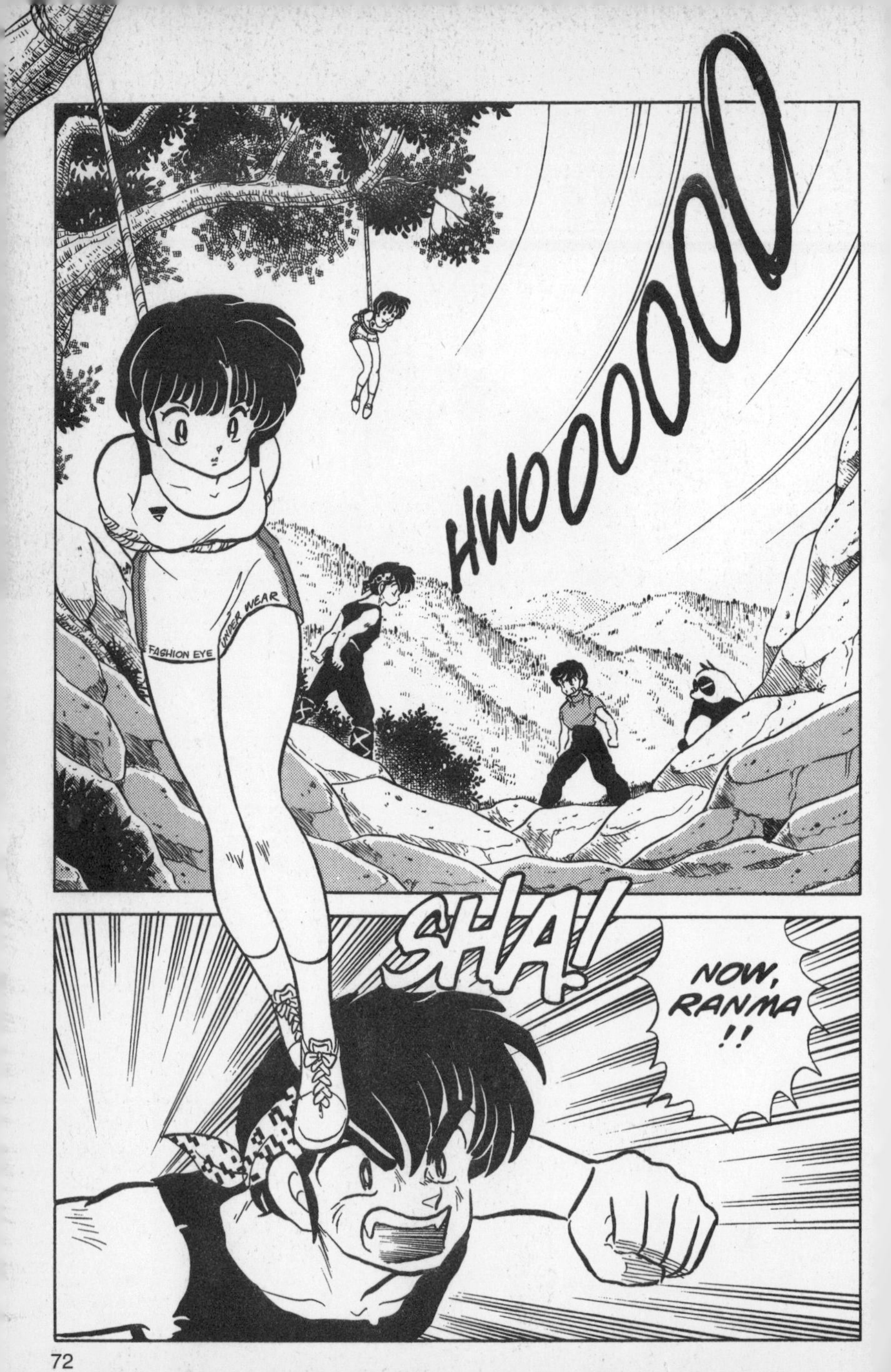
HWOOOOOO
FASHION EYE
UNDER WEAR
SHA!
NOW, RANMA !!

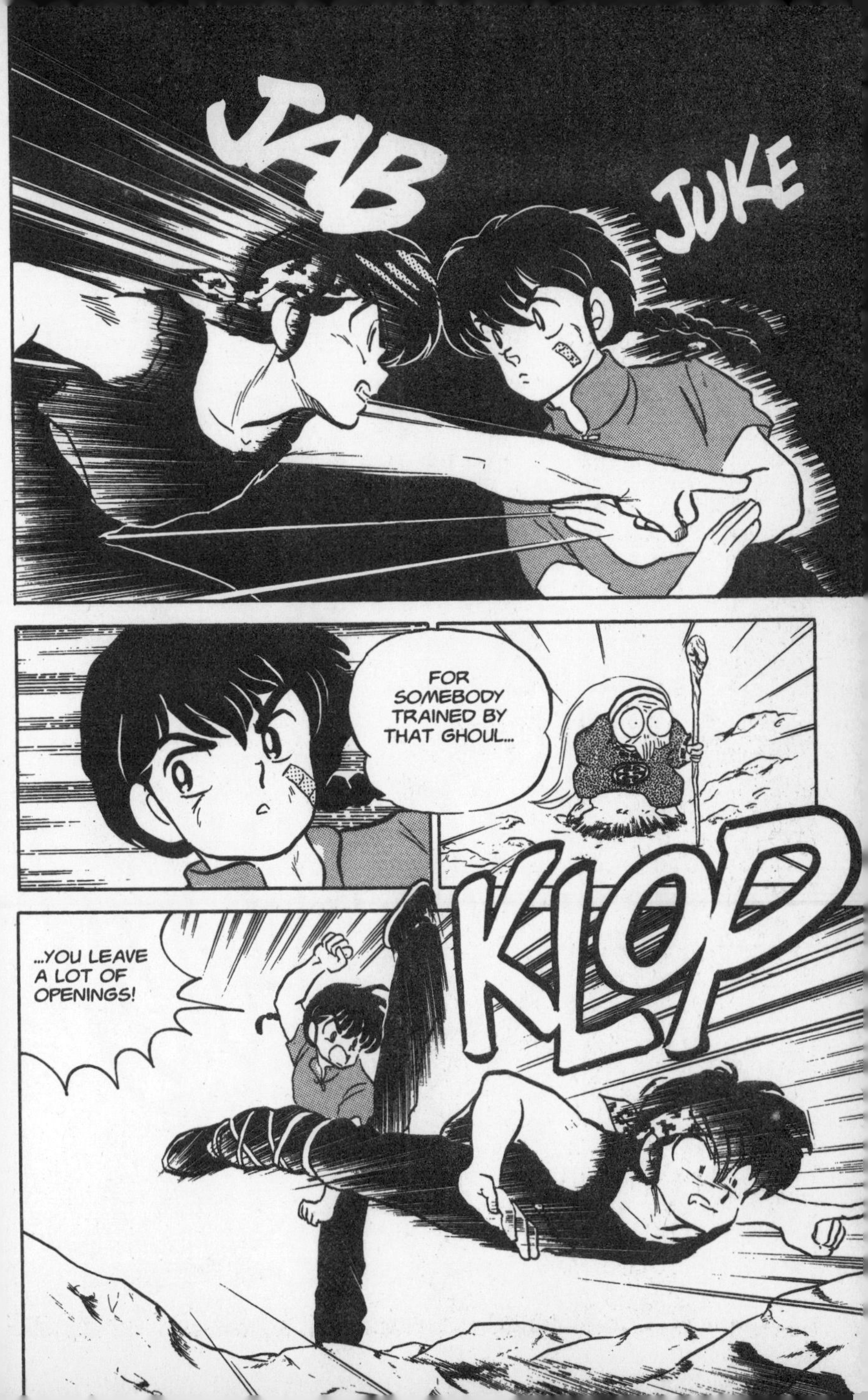
JAB
JUKE
FOR SOMEBODY TRAINED BY THAT GHOUL...
KLOP
...YOU LEAVE A LOT OF OPENINGS!

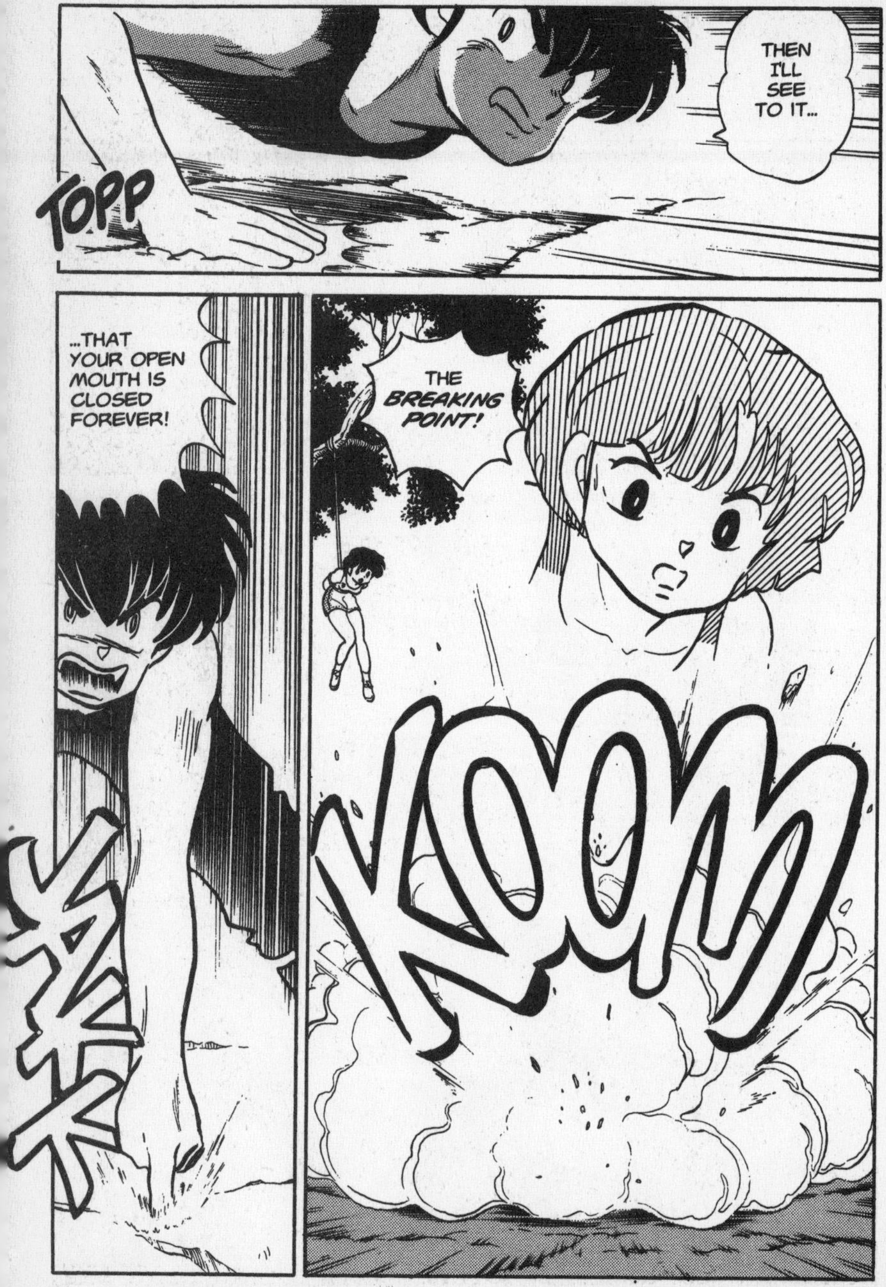
TOPP
THEN I'LL SEE TO IT...
...THAT YOUR OPEN MOUTH IS CLOSED FOREVER!
THE BREAKING POINT!
KOOM

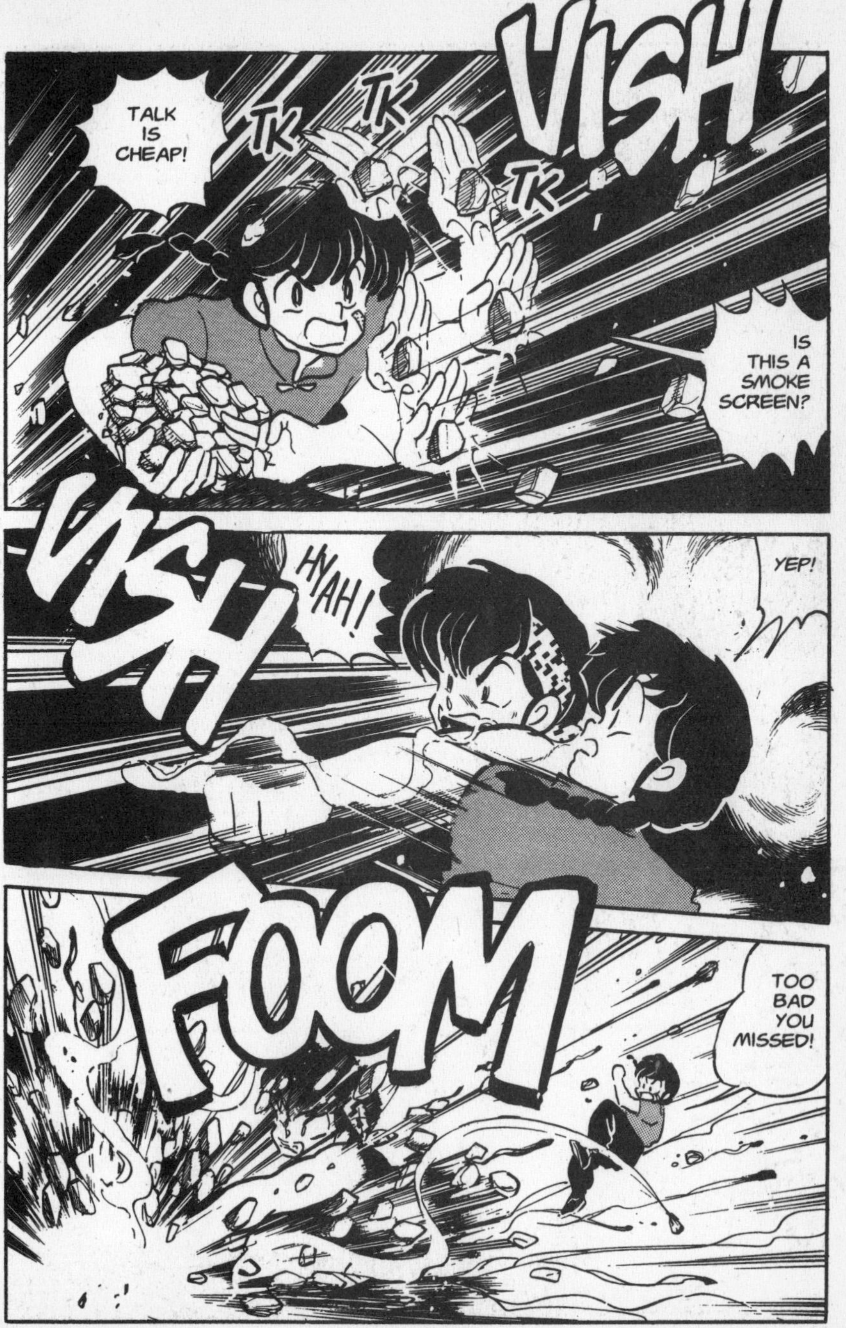
TALK IS CHEAP!
TK TK
VISH
TK
IS THIS A SMOKE SCREEN?
VISH
HYAH!
YEP!
FOOM
TOO BAD YOU MISSED!

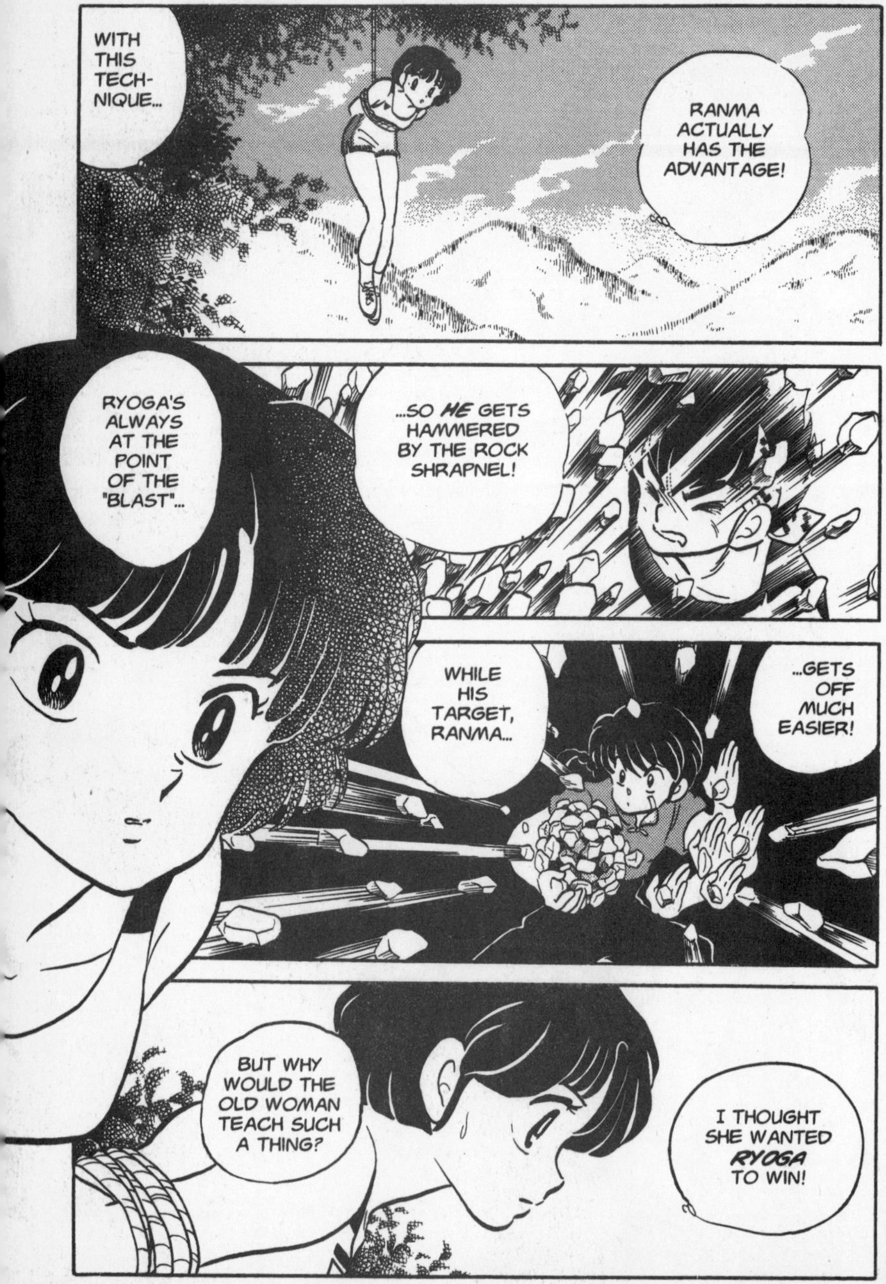
WITH THIS TECH-NIQUE...
RANMA ACTUALLY HAS THE ADVANTAGE!
RYOGA'S ALWAYS AT THE POINT OF THE "BLAST"...
...SO *HE* GETS HAMMERED BY THE ROCK SHRAPNEL!
WHILE HIS TARGET, RANMA...
...GETS OFF MUCH EASIER!
BUT WHY WOULD THE OLD WOMAN TEACH SUCH A THING?
I THOUGHT SHE WANTED *RYOGA* TO WIN!

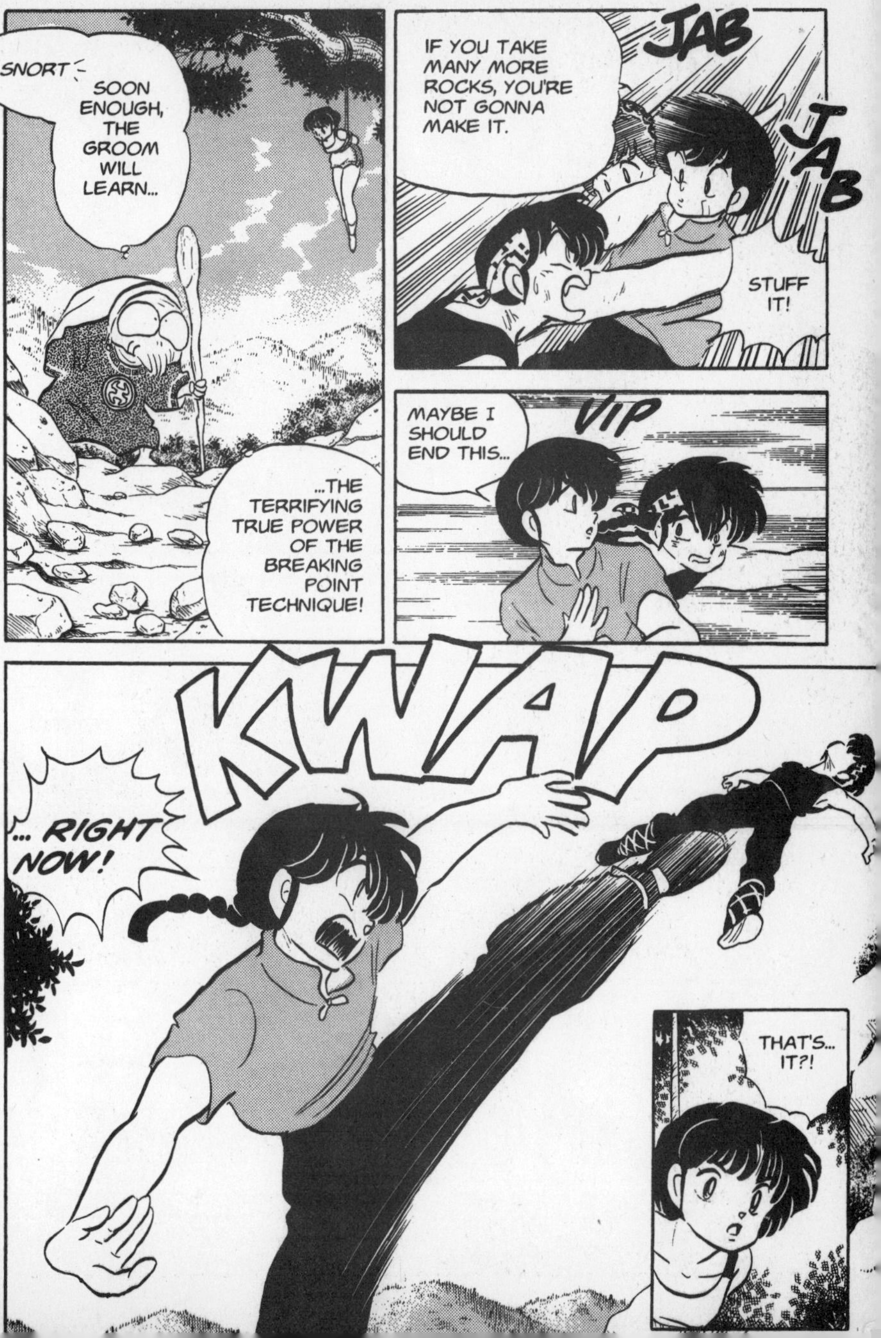
SNORT
SOON ENOUGH, THE GROOM WILL LEARN...
...THE TERRIFYING TRUE POWER OF THE BREAKING POINT TECHNIQUE!
IF YOU TAKE MANY MORE ROCKS, YOU'RE NOT GONNA MAKE IT.
JAB
JAB
STUFF IT!
MAYBE I SHOULD END THIS...
VIP
KWAP
... RIGHT NOW!
THAT'S... IT?!

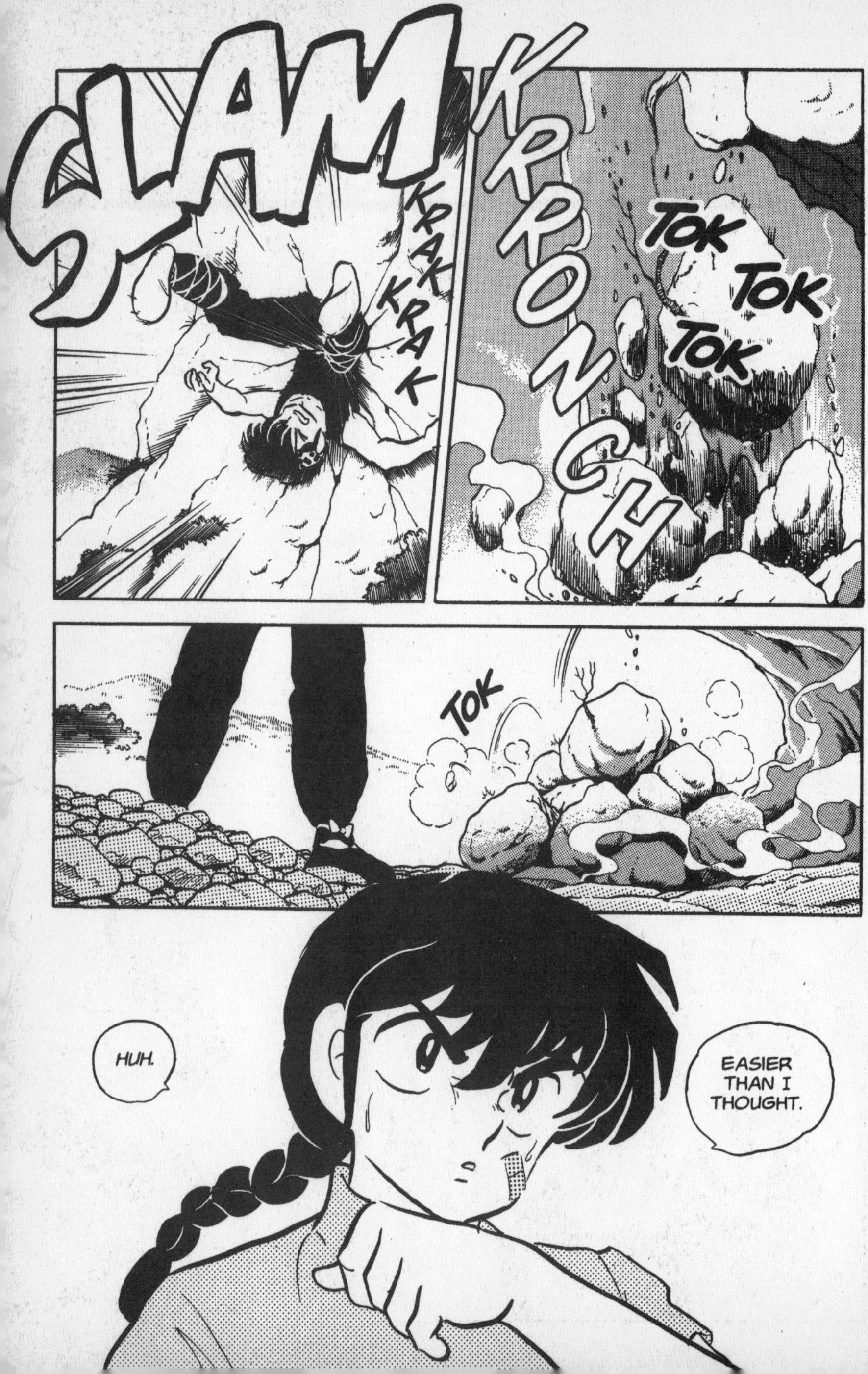
KRONCH
TOK
TOK
TOK
SLAM
KRAK KRAK
TOK
EASIER THAN I THOUGHT.
HUH.

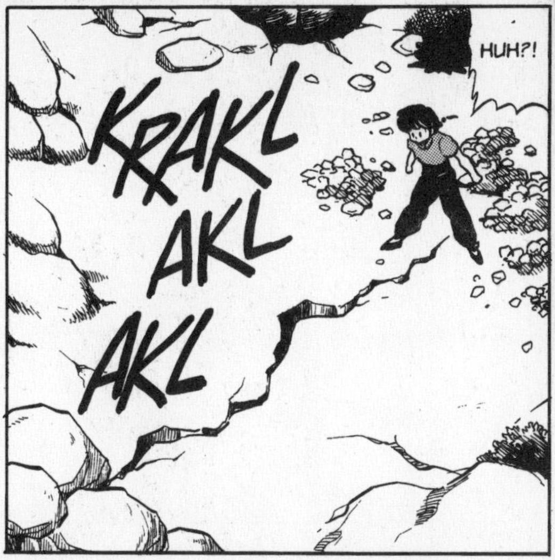
HUH?!
KRAKL
AKL
AKL

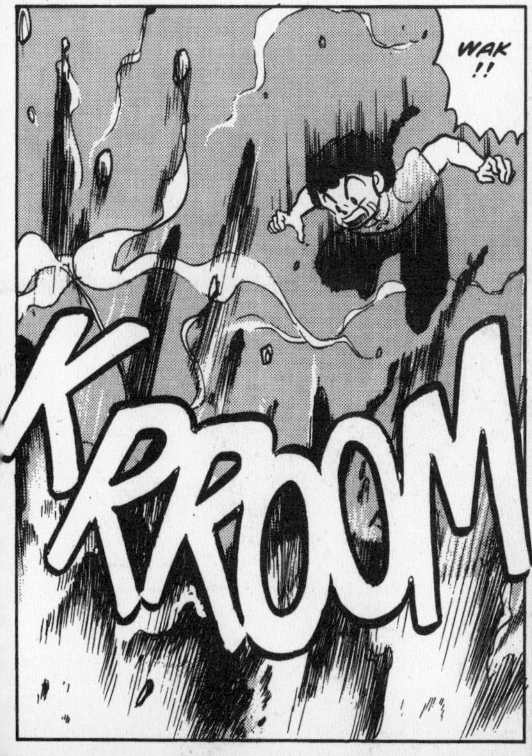
WAK !!
KRROOM

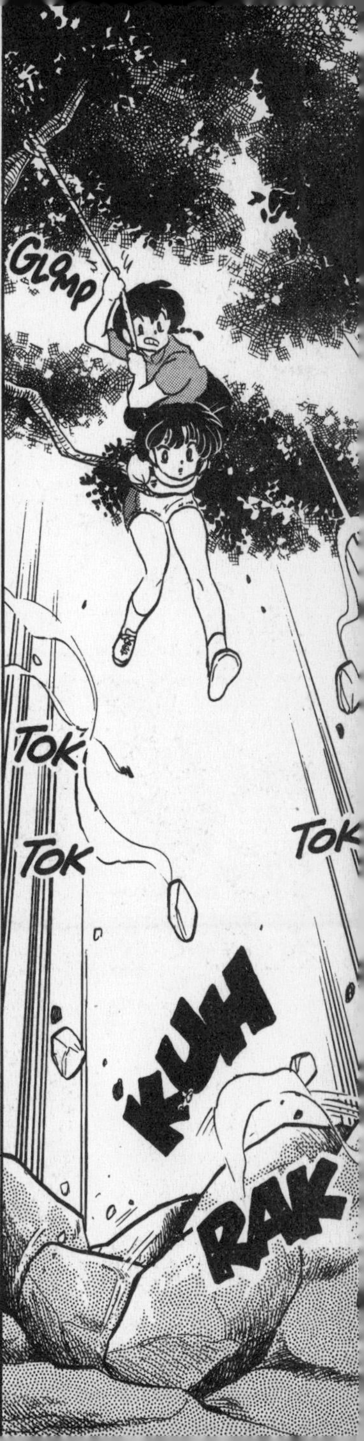
GLOMP
TOK
TOK
TOK
KUH
RAK

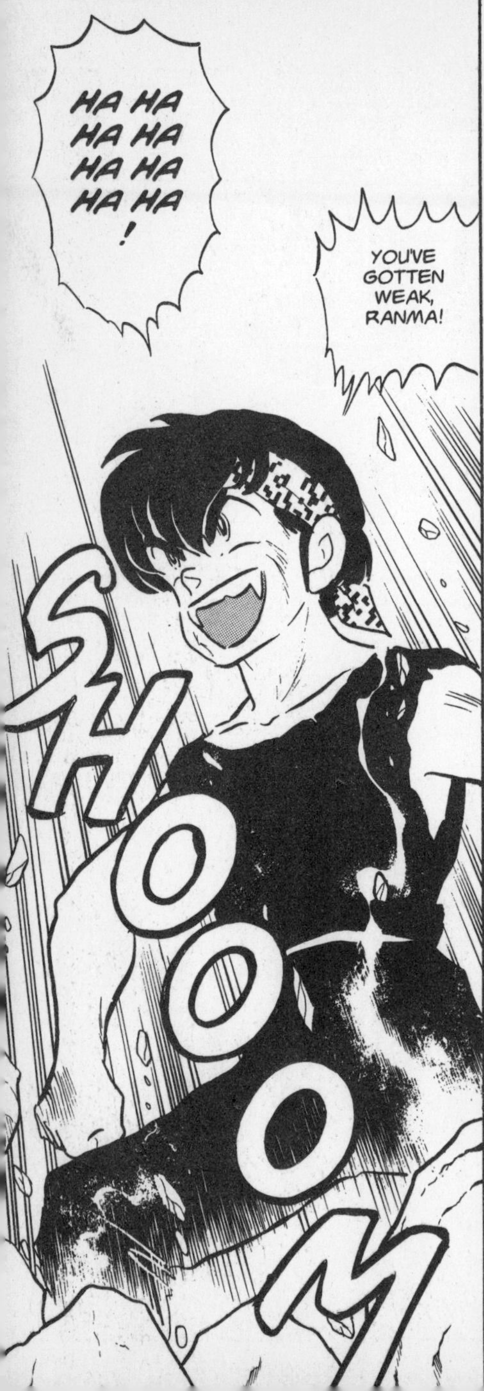
HA HA HA HA HA HA HA HA!
YOU'VE GOTTEN WEAK, RANMA!
SHOOOOM
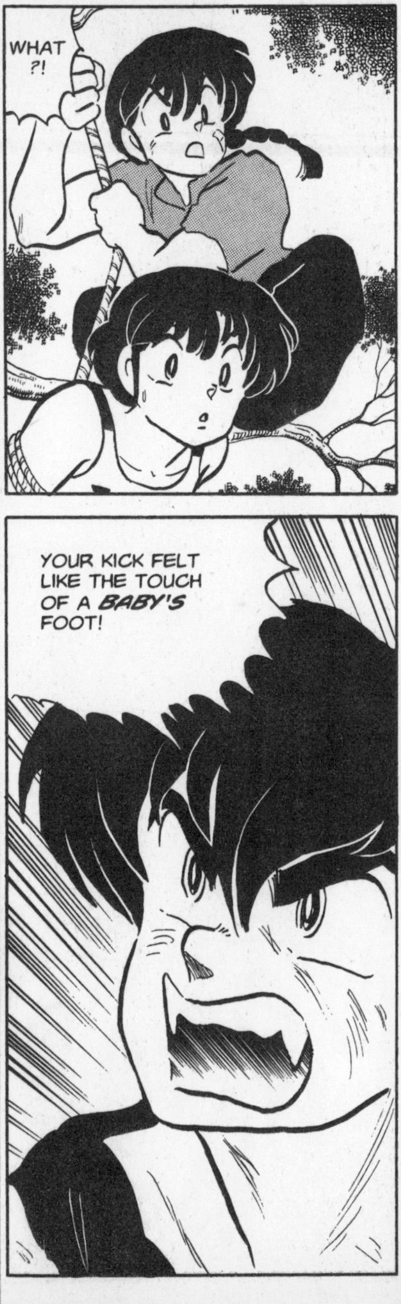
WHAT ?!
YOUR KICK FELT LIKE THE TOUCH OF A BABY'S FOOT!

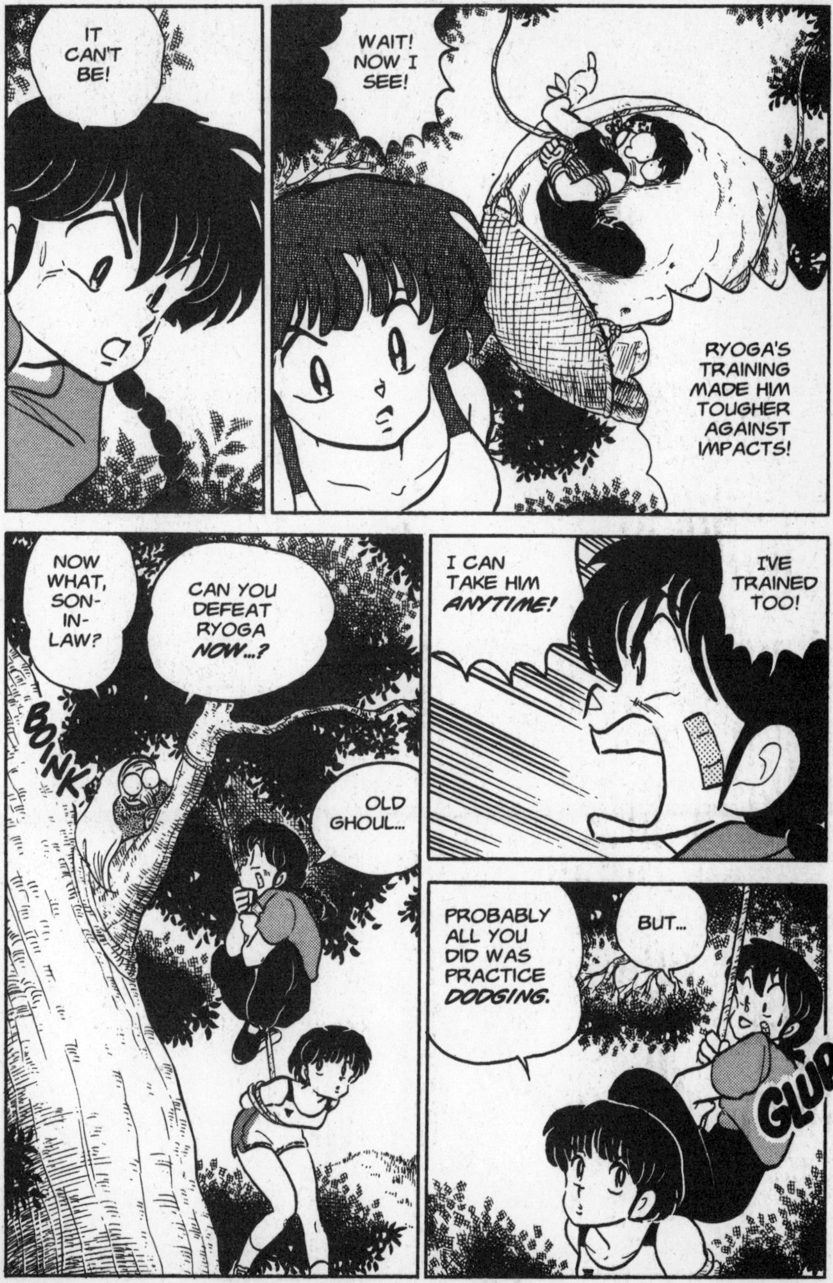
IT CAN'T BE!
WAIT! NOW I SEE!
RYOGA'S TRAINING MADE HIM TOUGHER AGAINST IMPACTS!
NOW WHAT, SON-IN-LAW?
CAN YOU DEFEAT RYOGA *NOW...?*
BOINK
OLD GHOUL...
I CAN TAKE HIM *ANYTIME!*
I'VE TRAINED TOO!
PROBABLY ALL YOU DID WAS PRACTICE *DODGING.*
BUT...
GLURK

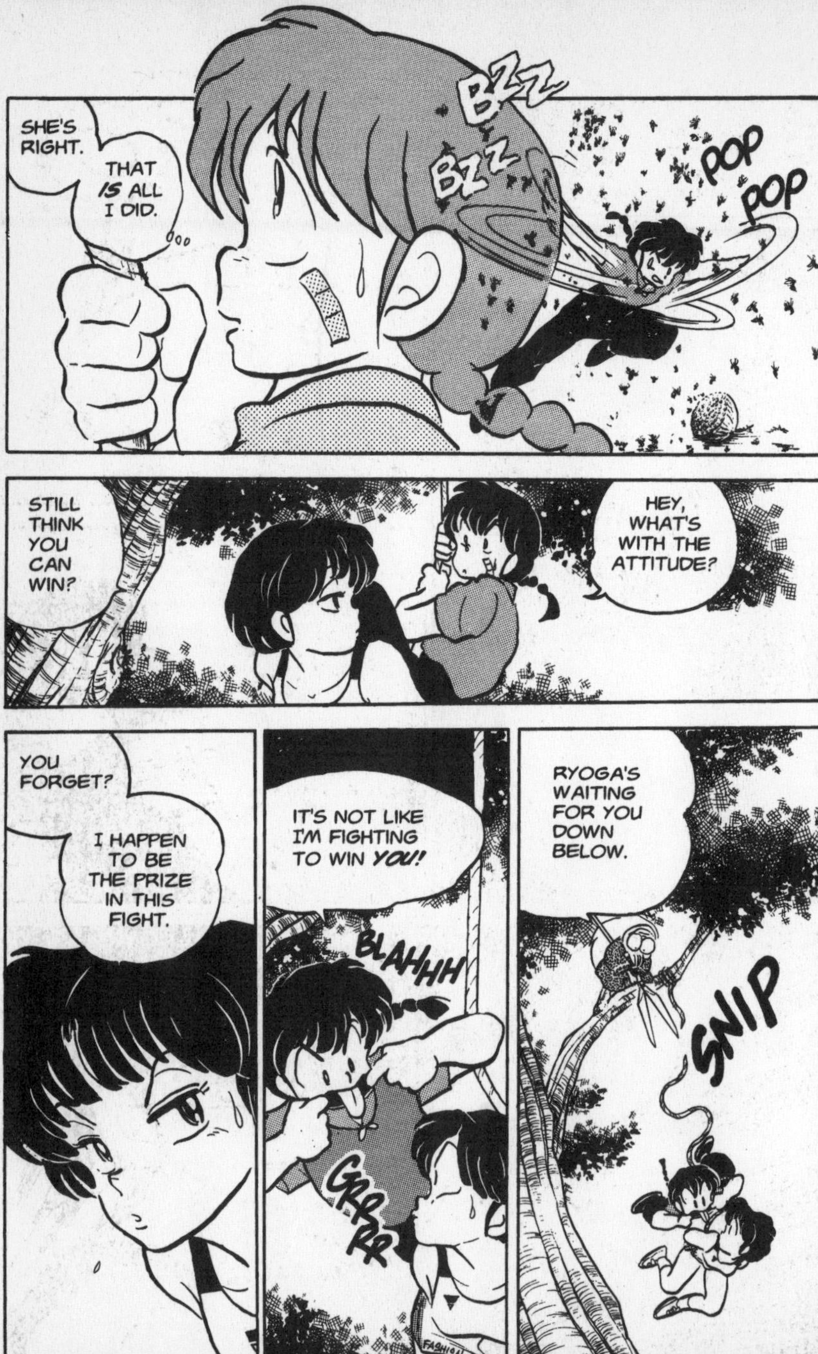
SHE'S RIGHT.
THAT *IS* ALL I DID.
BZZ
BZZ
POP
POP
STILL THINK YOU CAN WIN?
HEY, WHAT'S WITH THE ATTITUDE?
YOU FORGET?
I HAPPEN TO BE THE PRIZE IN THIS FIGHT.
IT'S NOT LIKE I'M FIGHTING TO WIN *YOU!*
BLAHHH
GRRRR
RYOGA'S WAITING FOR YOU DOWN BELOW.
SNIP

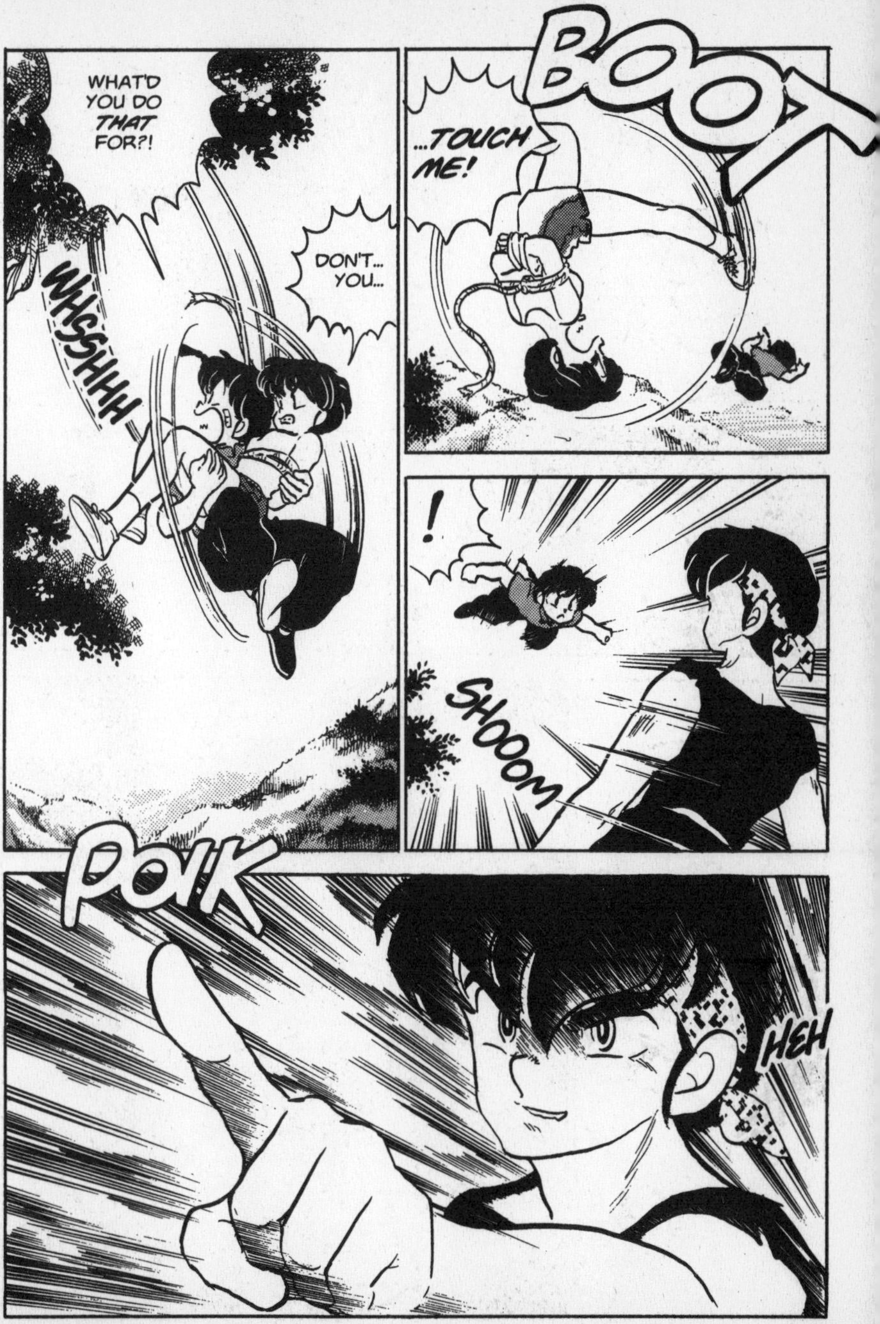
WHAT'D YOU DO *THAT* FOR?!
WHCSSHHH
DON'T... YOU...
BOOT
...TOUCH ME!
!
SHOOOM
POIK
HEH

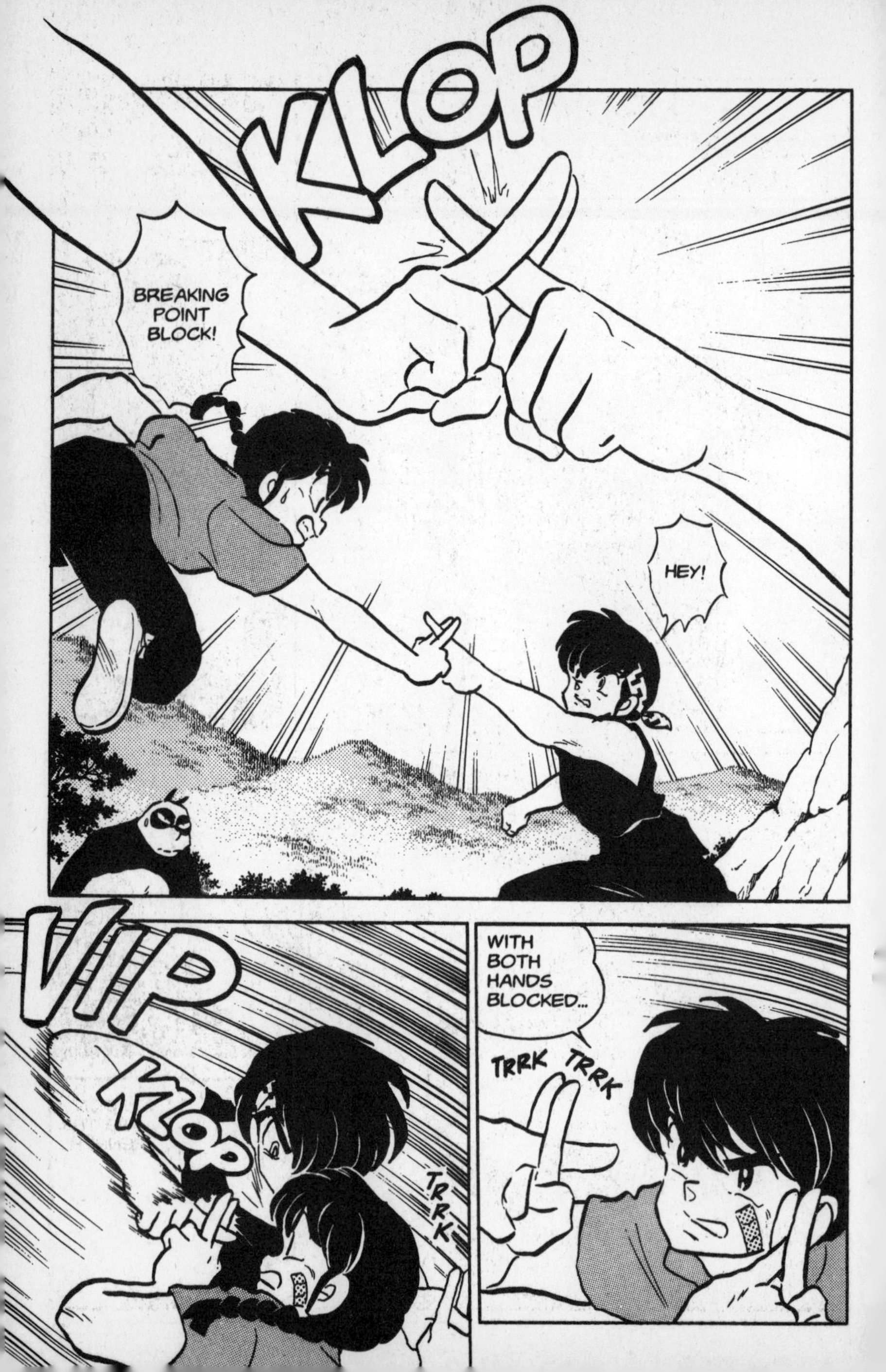
KLOP
BREAKING POINT BLOCK!
HEY!
VIP
KLOP
TRRK
WITH BOTH HANDS BLOCKED...
TRRK TRRK

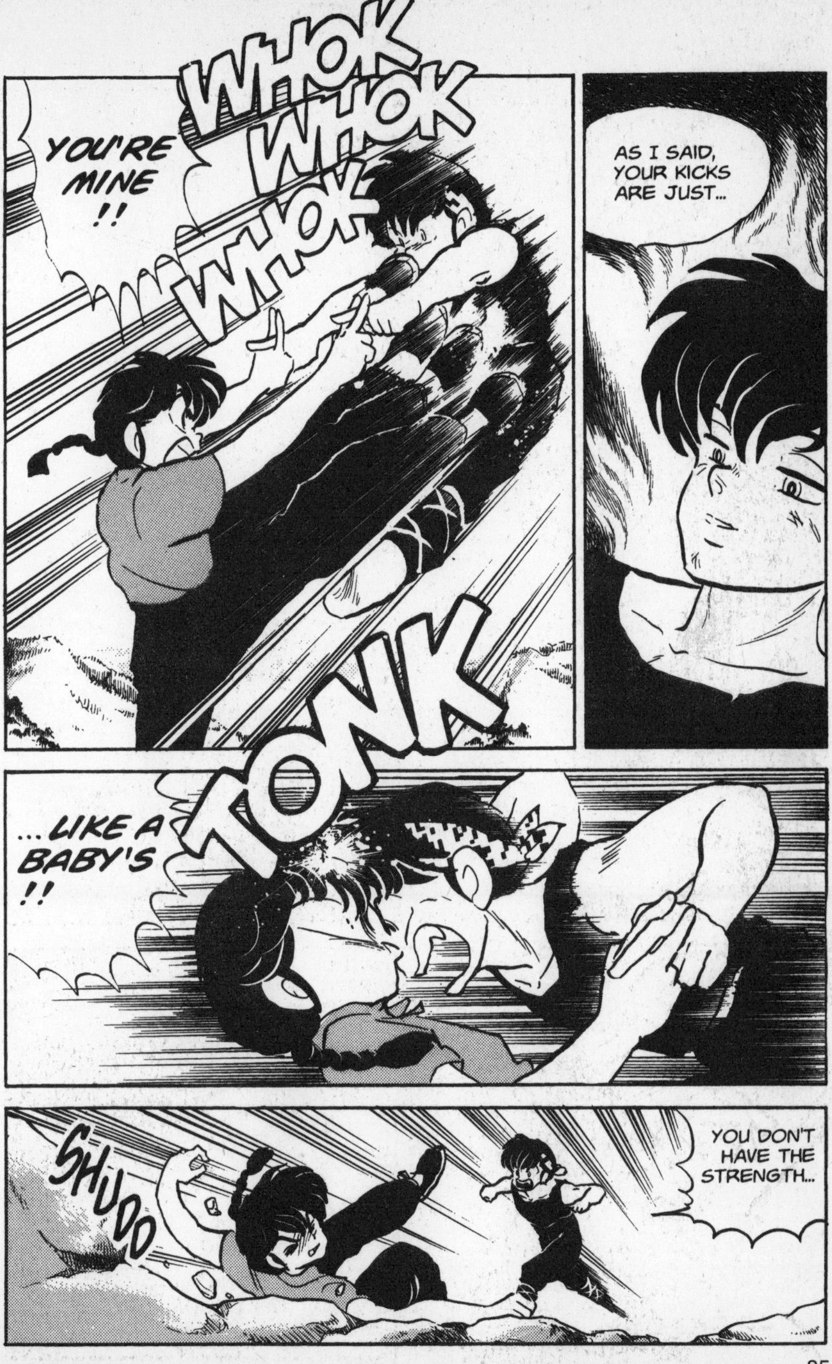
AS I SAID, YOUR KICKS ARE JUST...
WHOK WHOK WHOK
YOU'RE MINE !!
TONK
...LIKE A BABY'S !!
YOU DON'T HAVE THE STRENGTH...
SHUDO

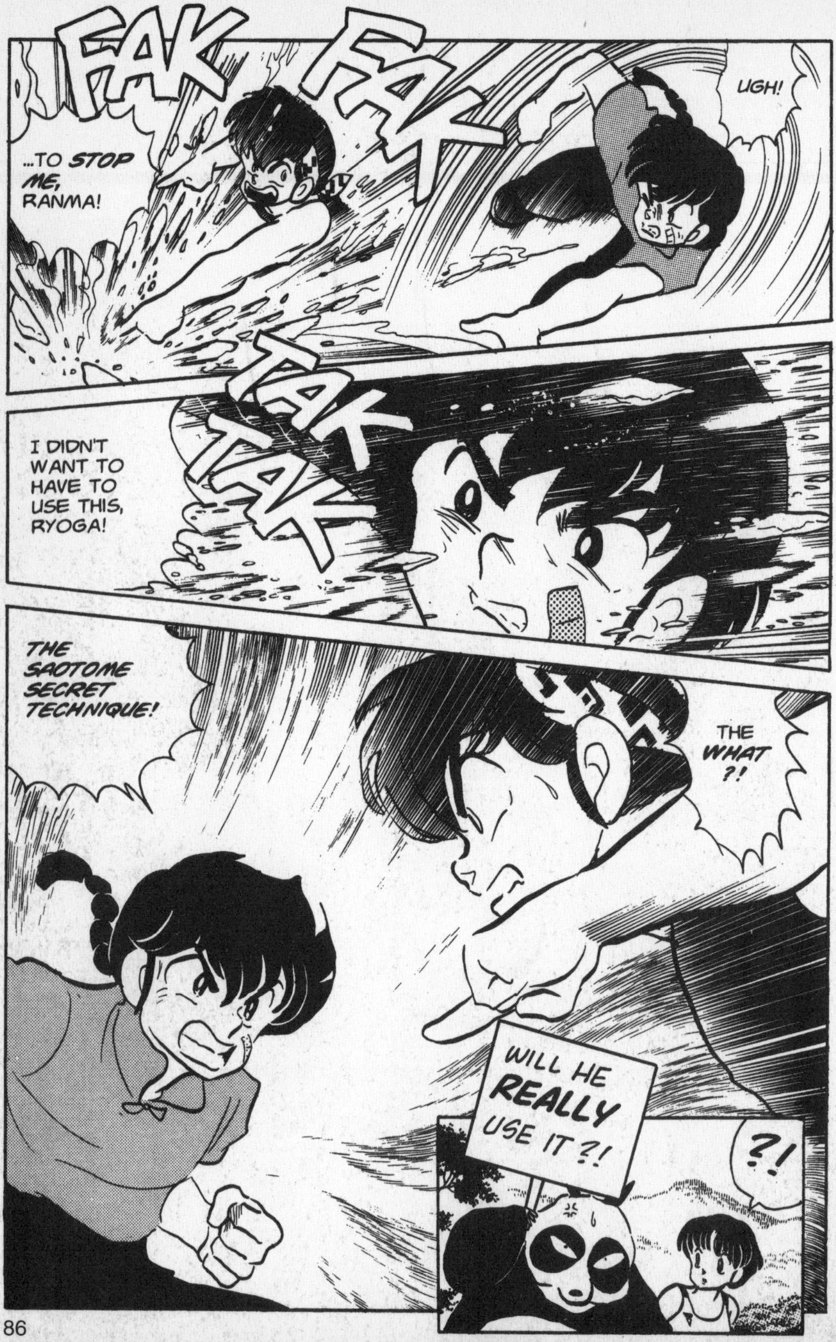
FAK
FAK
...TO STOP ME, RANMA!
UGH!
TAK
TAK
I DIDN'T WANT TO HAVE TO USE THIS, RYOGA!
THE SAOTOME SECRET TECHNIQUE!
THE WHAT?!
WILL HE REALLY USE IT?!
?!

Part 6

FAST BREAK

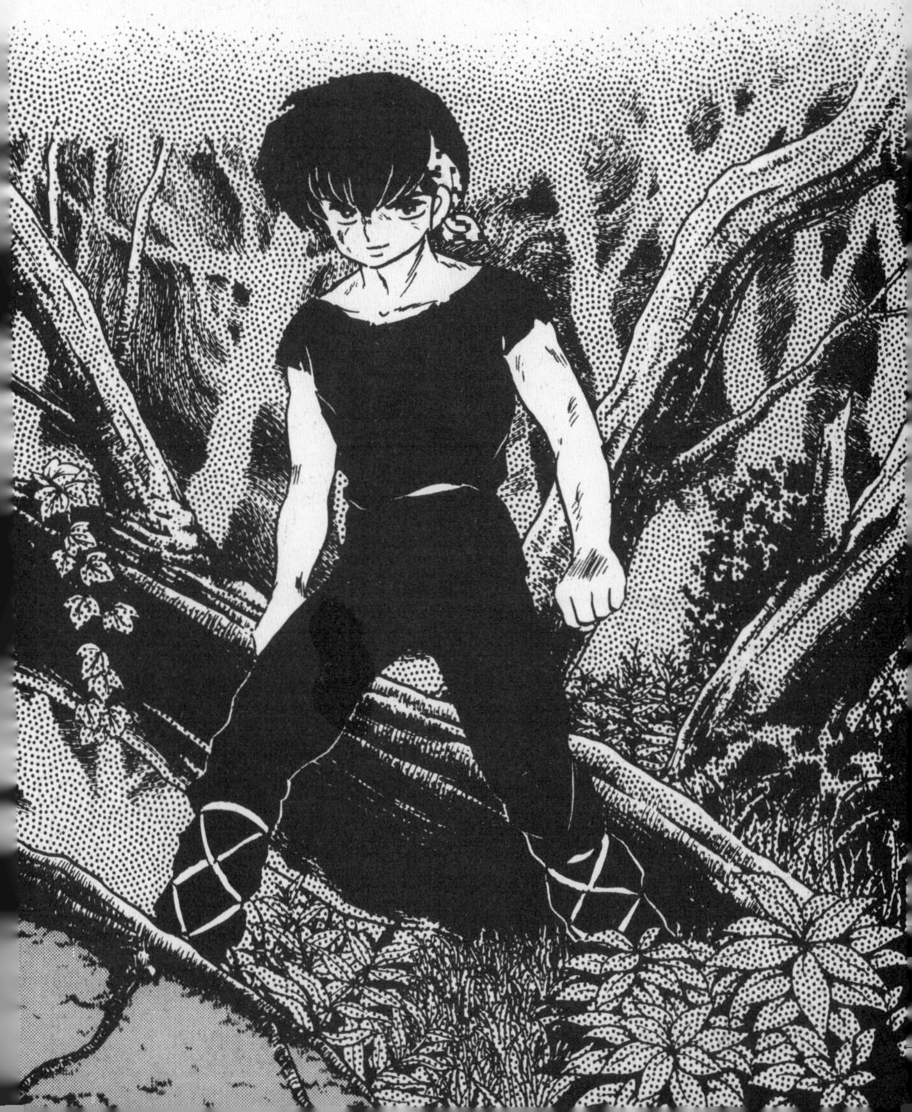

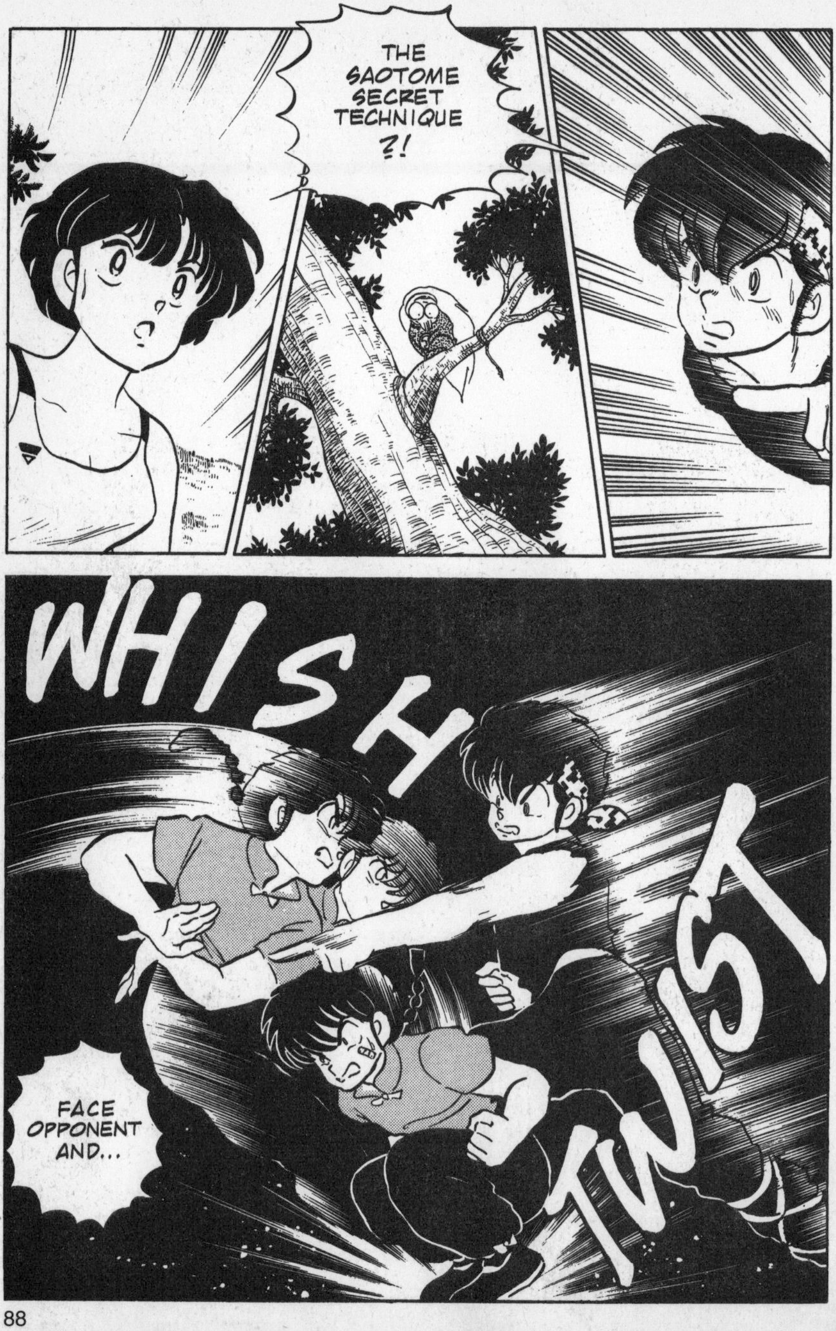
THE SAOTOME SECRET TECHNIQUE ?!
WHISH
TWIST
FACE OPPONENT AND...

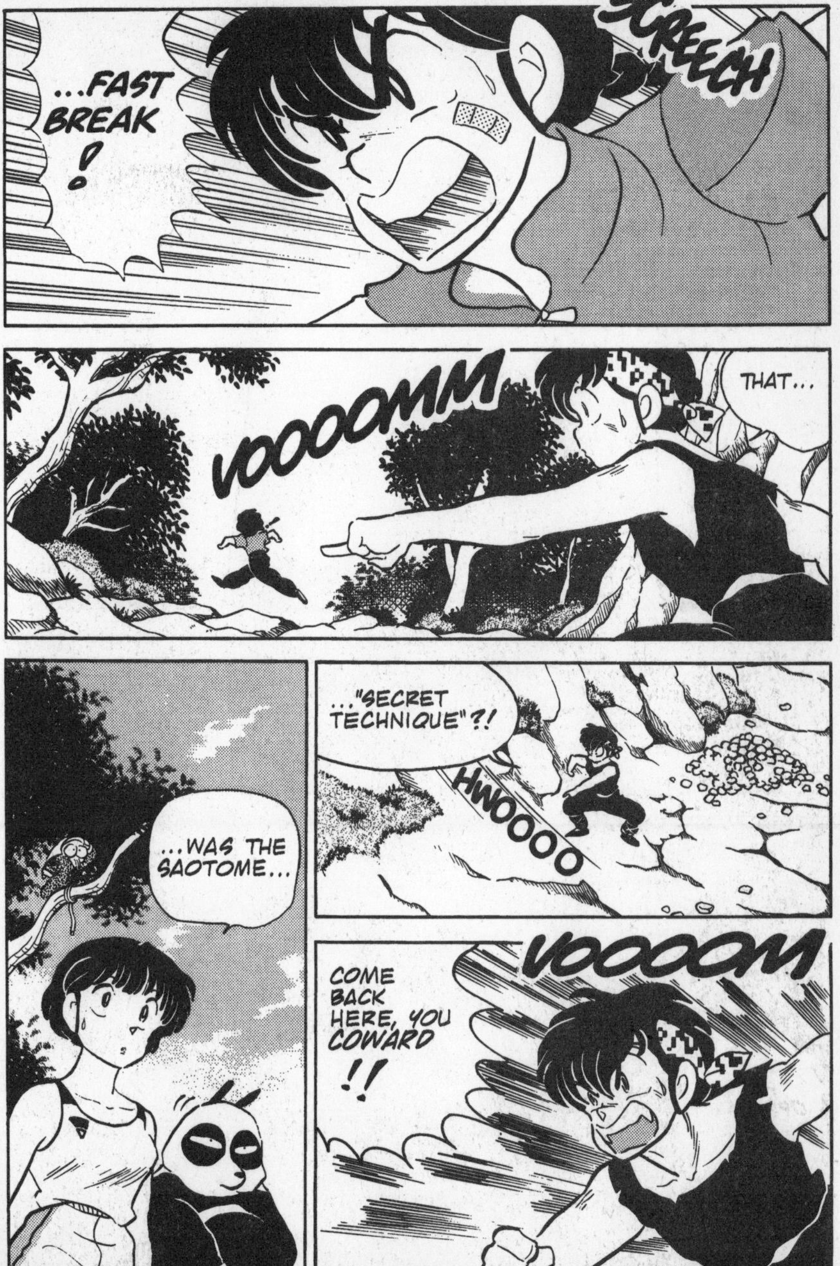
...FAST BREAK !
SCREECH
VOOOOMM
THAT...
...WAS THE SAOTOME...
..."SECRET TECHNIQUE"?!
HWOOOO
VOOOOM
COME BACK HERE, YOU COWARD !!

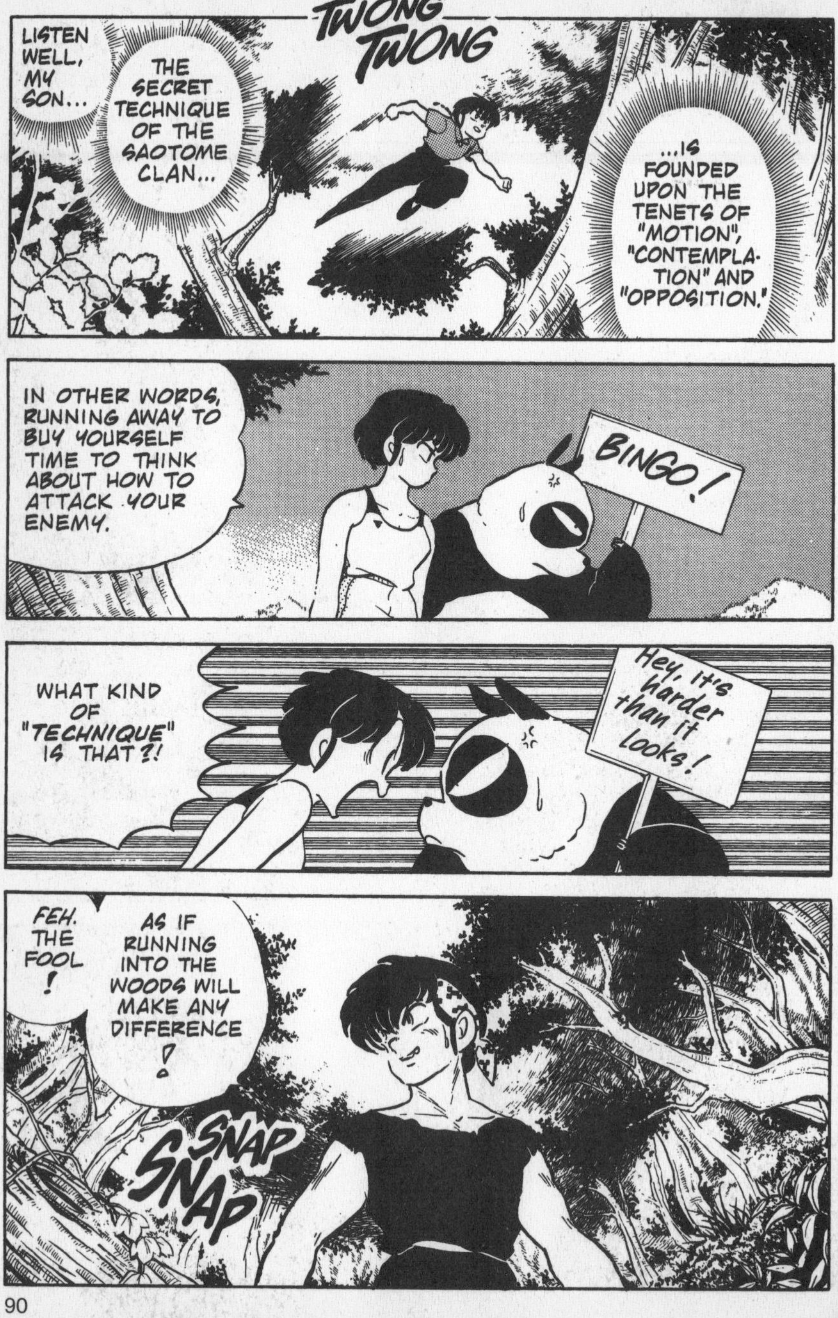
TWONG TWONG
LISTEN WELL, MY SON...
THE SECRET TECHNIQUE OF THE SAOTOME CLAN...
...IS FOUNDED UPON THE TENETS OF "MOTION", "CONTEMPLATION" AND "OPPOSITION."
IN OTHER WORDS, RUNNING AWAY TO BUY YOURSELF TIME TO THINK ABOUT HOW TO ATTACK YOUR ENEMY.
BINGO!
WHAT KIND OF "TECHNIQUE" IS THAT?!
Hey, it's harder than it looks!
FEH. THE FOOL!
AS IF RUNNING INTO THE WOODS WILL MAKE ANY DIFFERENCE!
SNAP SNAP

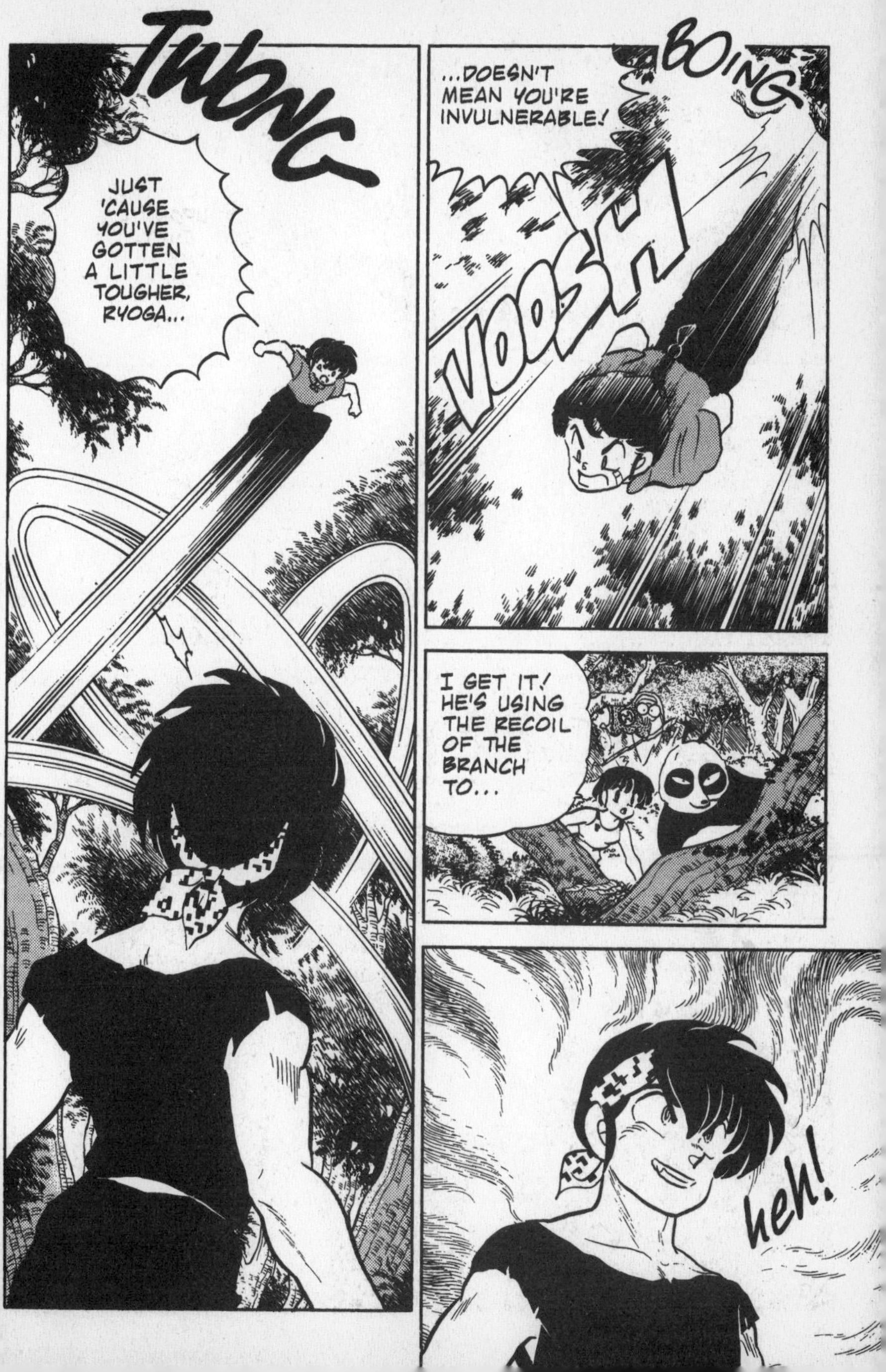
TWANG
JUST 'CAUSE YOU'VE GOTTEN A LITTLE TOUGHER, RYOGA...
...DOESN'T MEAN YOU'RE INVULNERABLE!
BOING
VOOSH
I GET IT! HE'S USING THE RECOIL OF THE BRANCH TO...
heh!

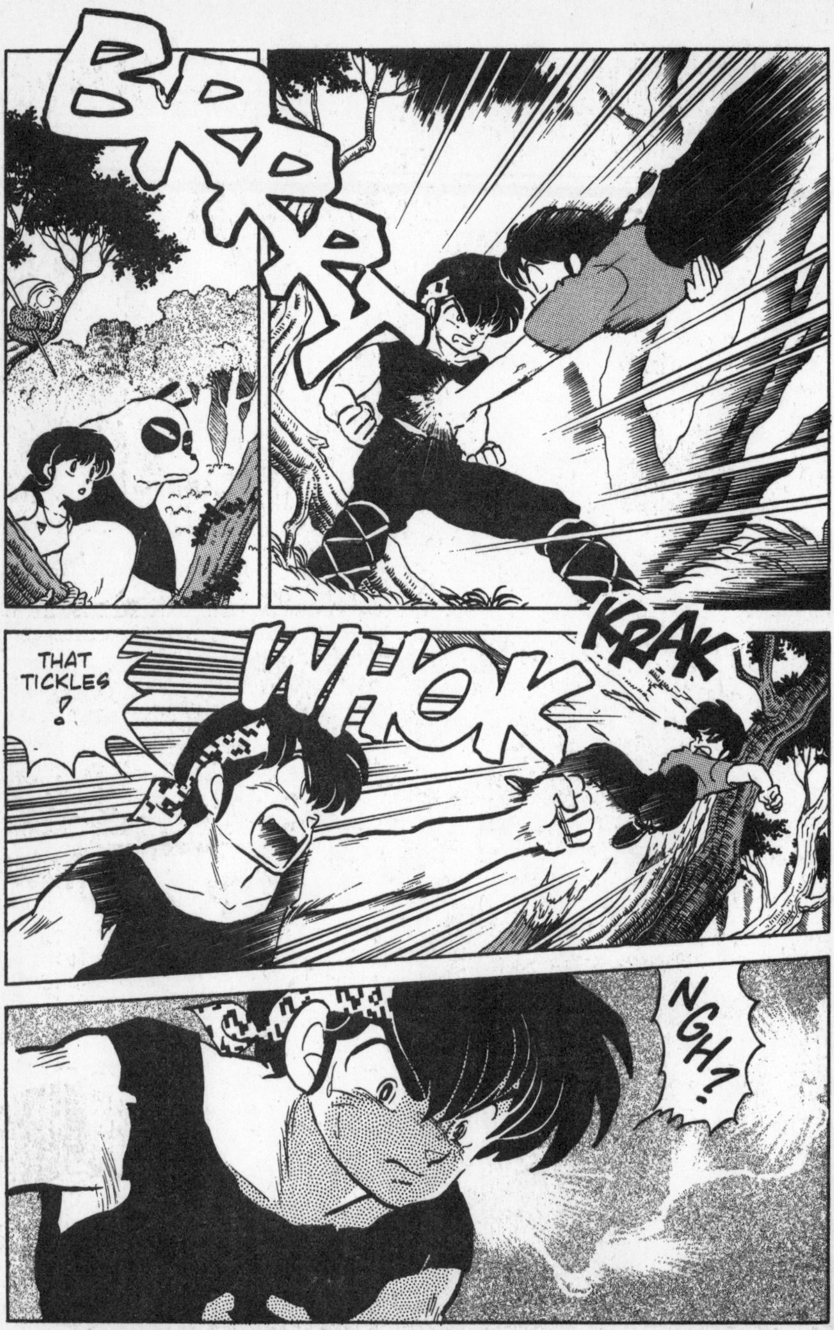
BRRRRY
THAT TICKLES!
WHOK
KRAK
NGH?!

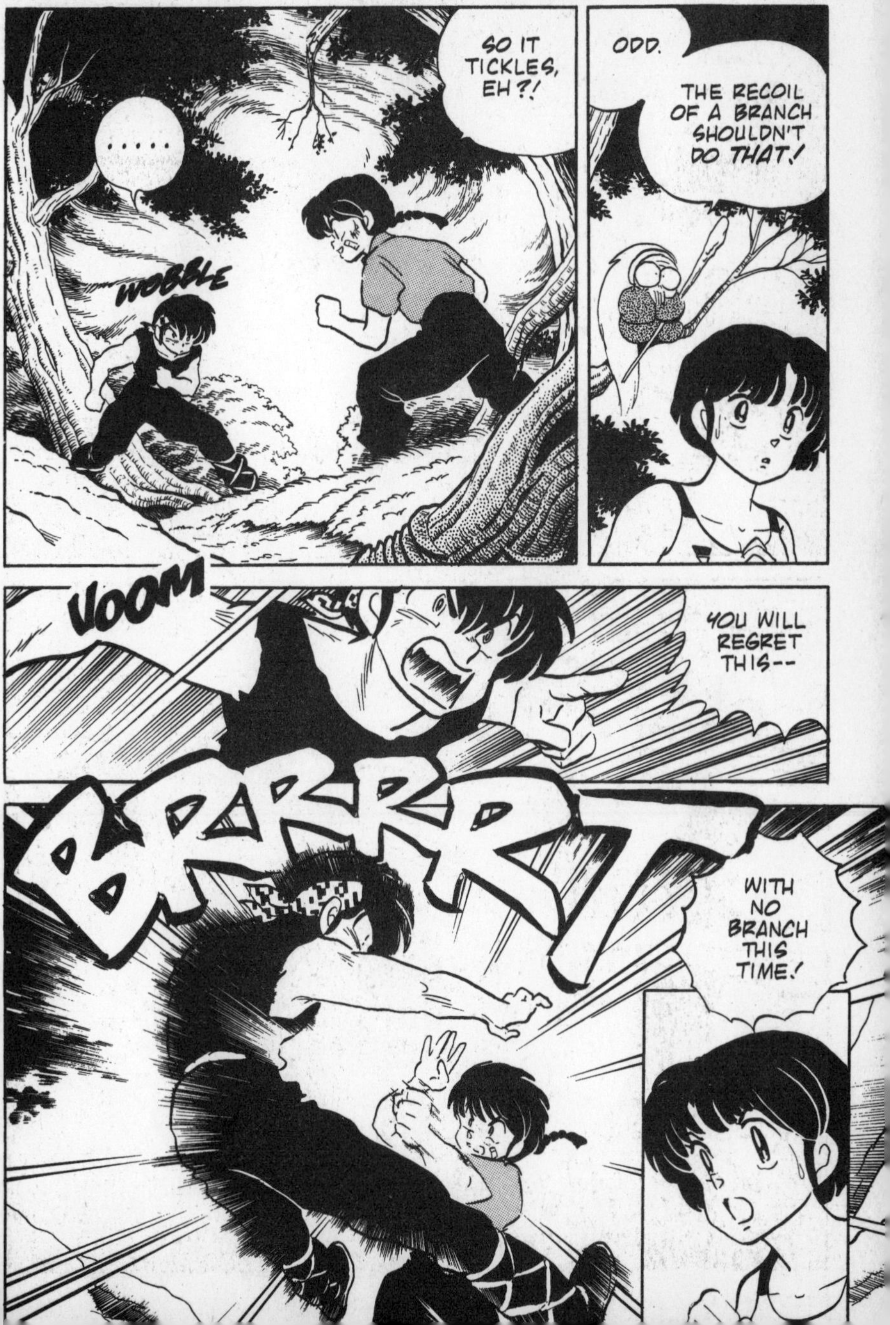
......
SO IT TICKLES, EH?!
WOBBLE
ODD.
THE RECOIL OF A BRANCH SHOULDN'T DO THAT!
VOOM
YOU WILL REGRET THIS--
BRRRT
WITH NO BRANCH THIS TIME!

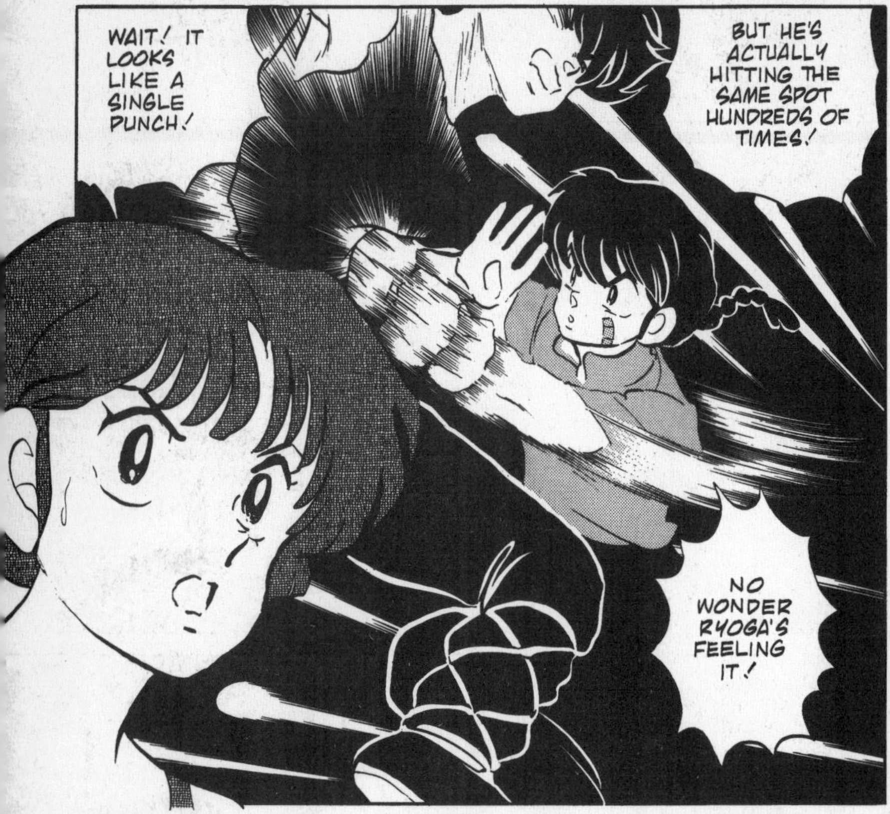
WAIT! IT LOOKS LIKE A SINGLE PUNCH!
BUT HE'S ACTUALLY HITTING THE SAME SPOT HUNDREDS OF TIMES!
NO WONDER RYOGA'S FEELING IT!

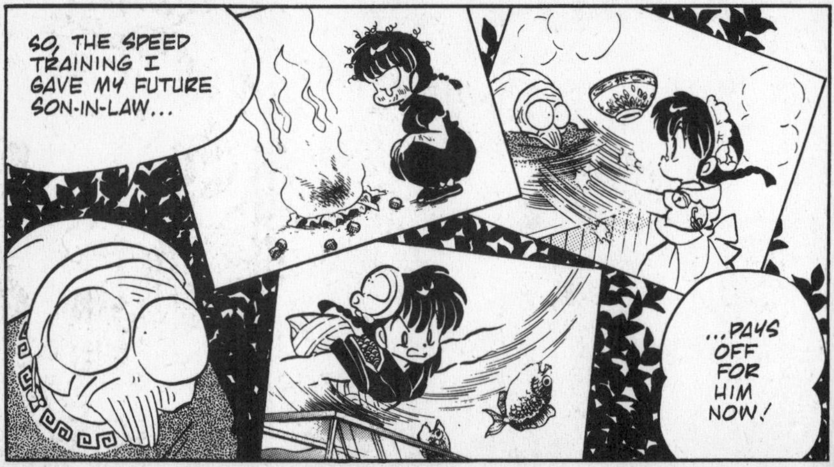
SO, THE SPEED TRAINING I GAVE MY FUTURE SON-IN-LAW...
...PAYS OFF FOR HIM NOW!

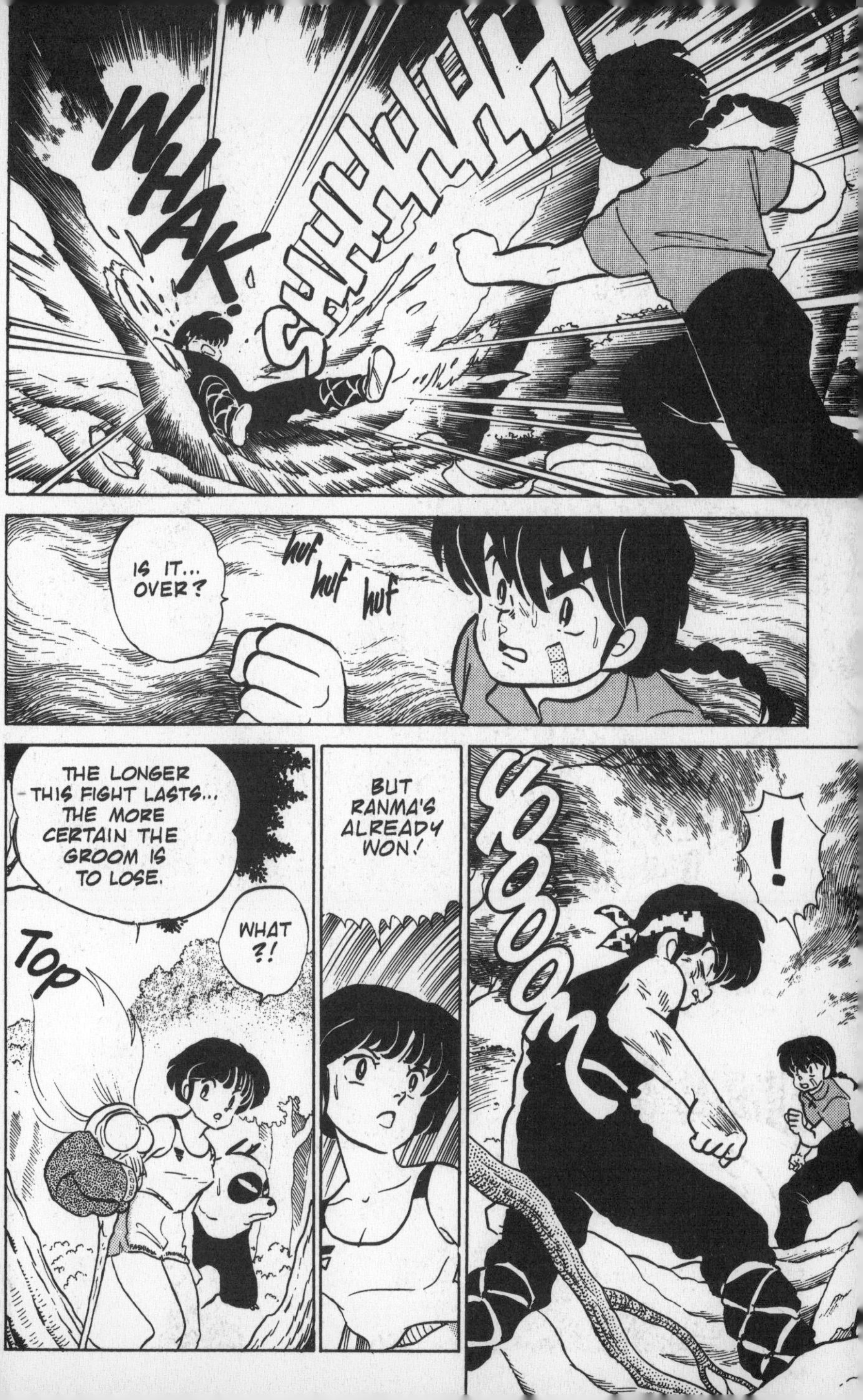
WHAK
SHHHHHHAAA
IS IT... OVER?
huf huf huf
THE LONGER THIS FIGHT LASTS... THE MORE CERTAIN THE GROOM IS TO LOSE.
WHAT ?!
TOP
BUT RANMA'S ALREADY WON!
VOOOOM
!

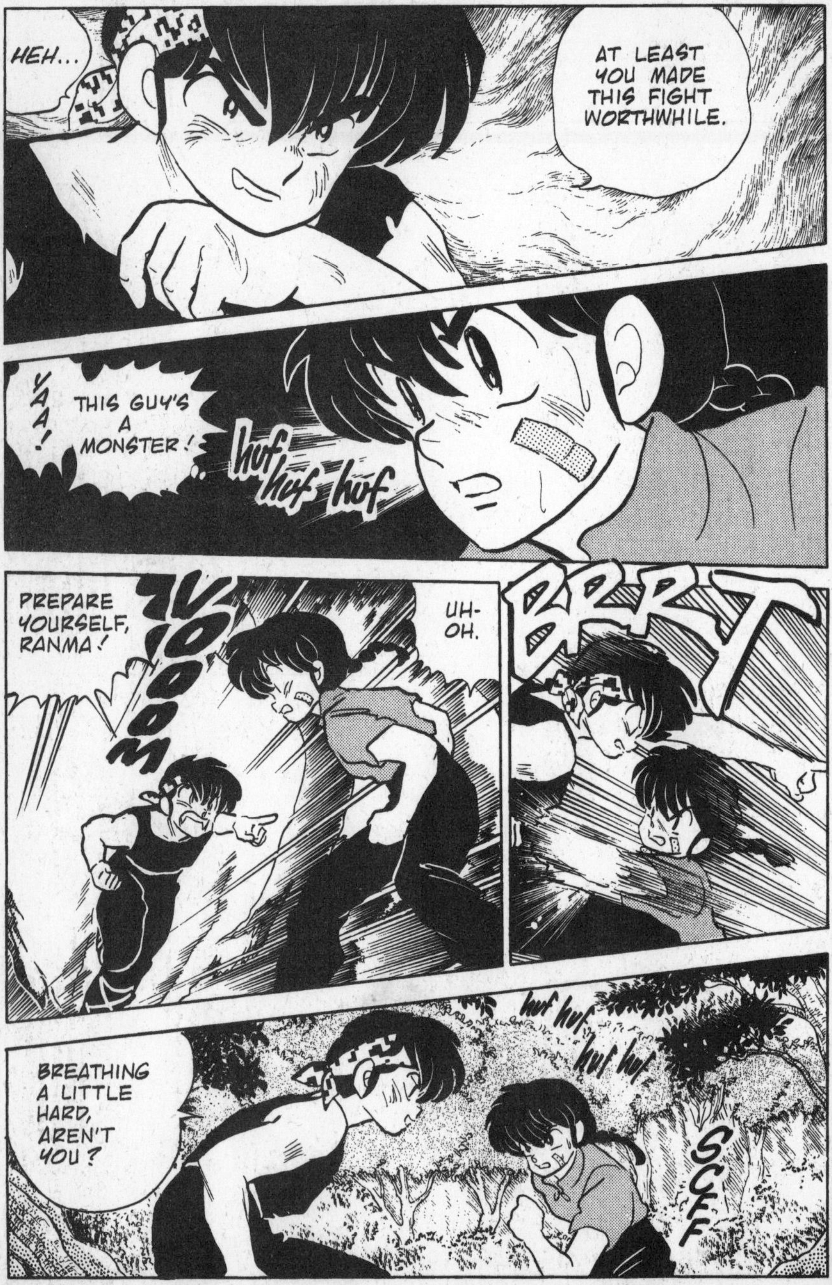
HEH...
AT LEAST YOU MADE THIS FIGHT WORTHWHILE.
YAA! THIS GUY'S A MONSTER!
huf huf huf
PREPARE YOURSELF, RANMA!
VOOOOOM
UH-OH.
BRRT
BREATHING A LITTLE HARD, AREN'T YOU?
huf huf
huf huf
SCFF

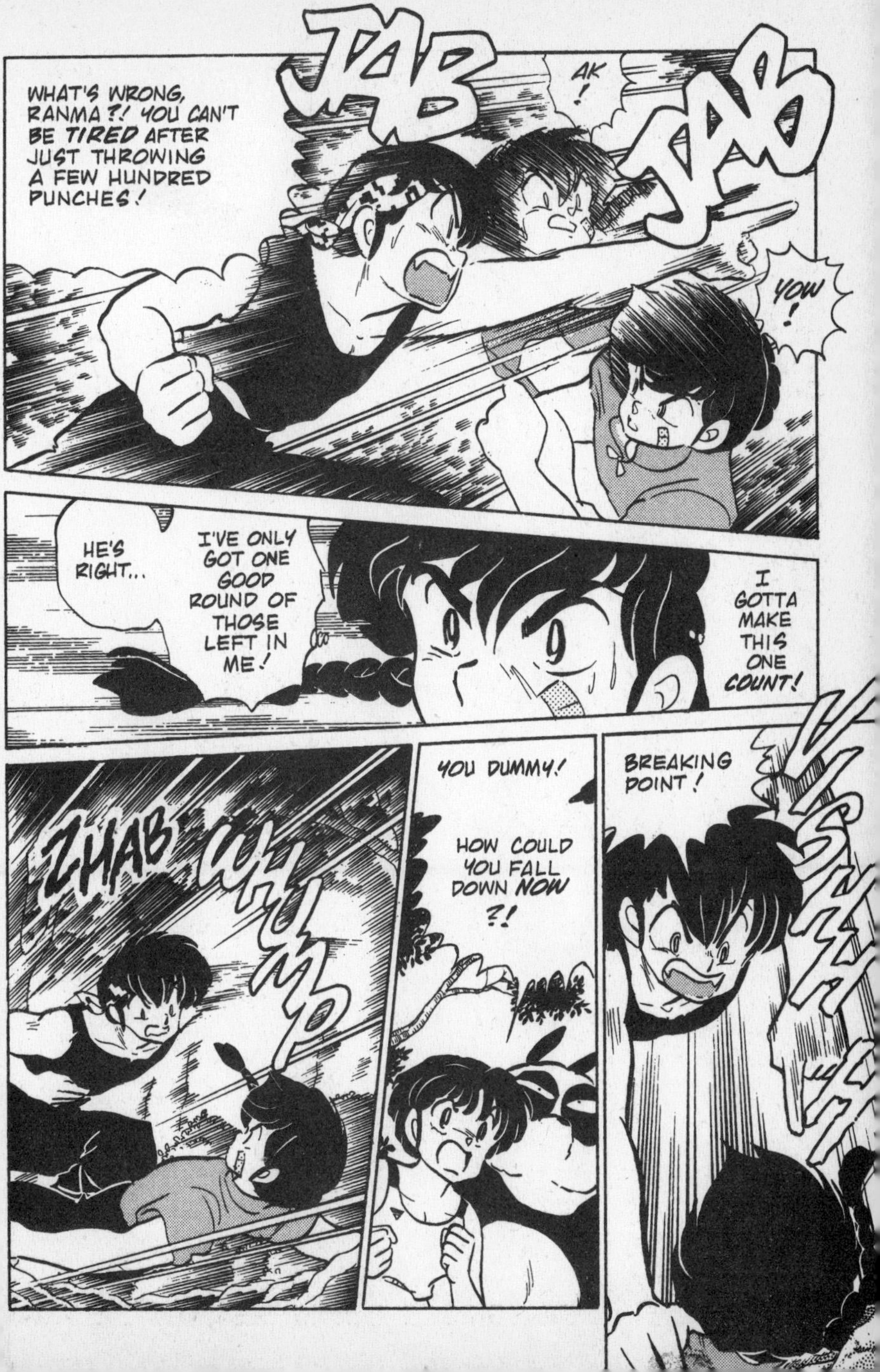
JAB
WHAT'S WRONG, RANMA ?! YOU CAN'T BE TIRED AFTER JUST THROWING A FEW HUNDRED PUNCHES!
AK!
JAB
YOW!
HE'S RIGHT...
I'VE ONLY GOT ONE GOOD ROUND OF THOSE LEFT IN ME!
I GOTTA MAKE THIS ONE COUNT!
ZHAB
WHUMP
YOU DUMMY!
HOW COULD YOU FALL DOWN NOW ?!
BREAKING POINT!

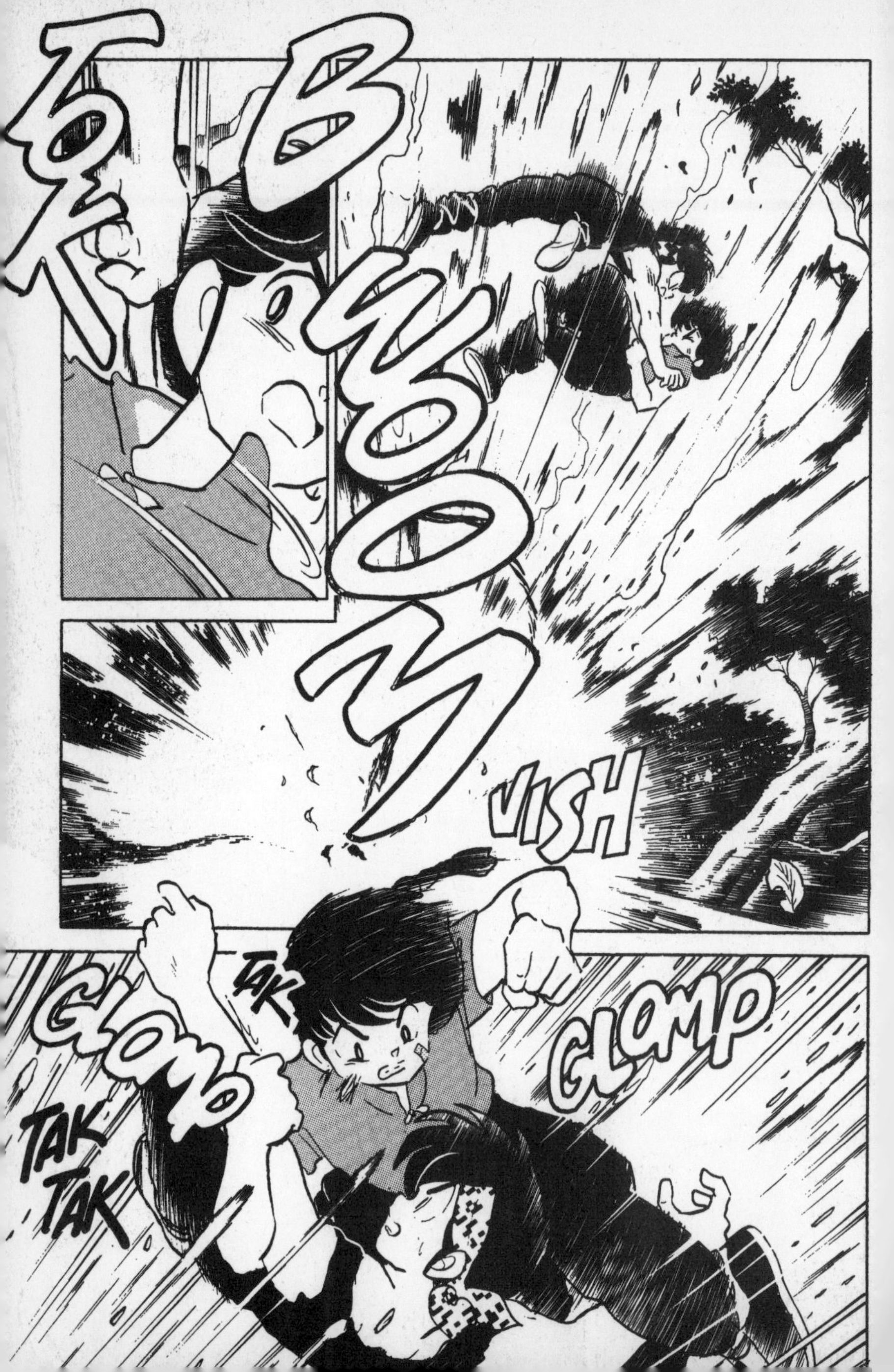
TOOF
BWOOOM
VISH
GLOMP
TAK
GLOMP
TAK TAK

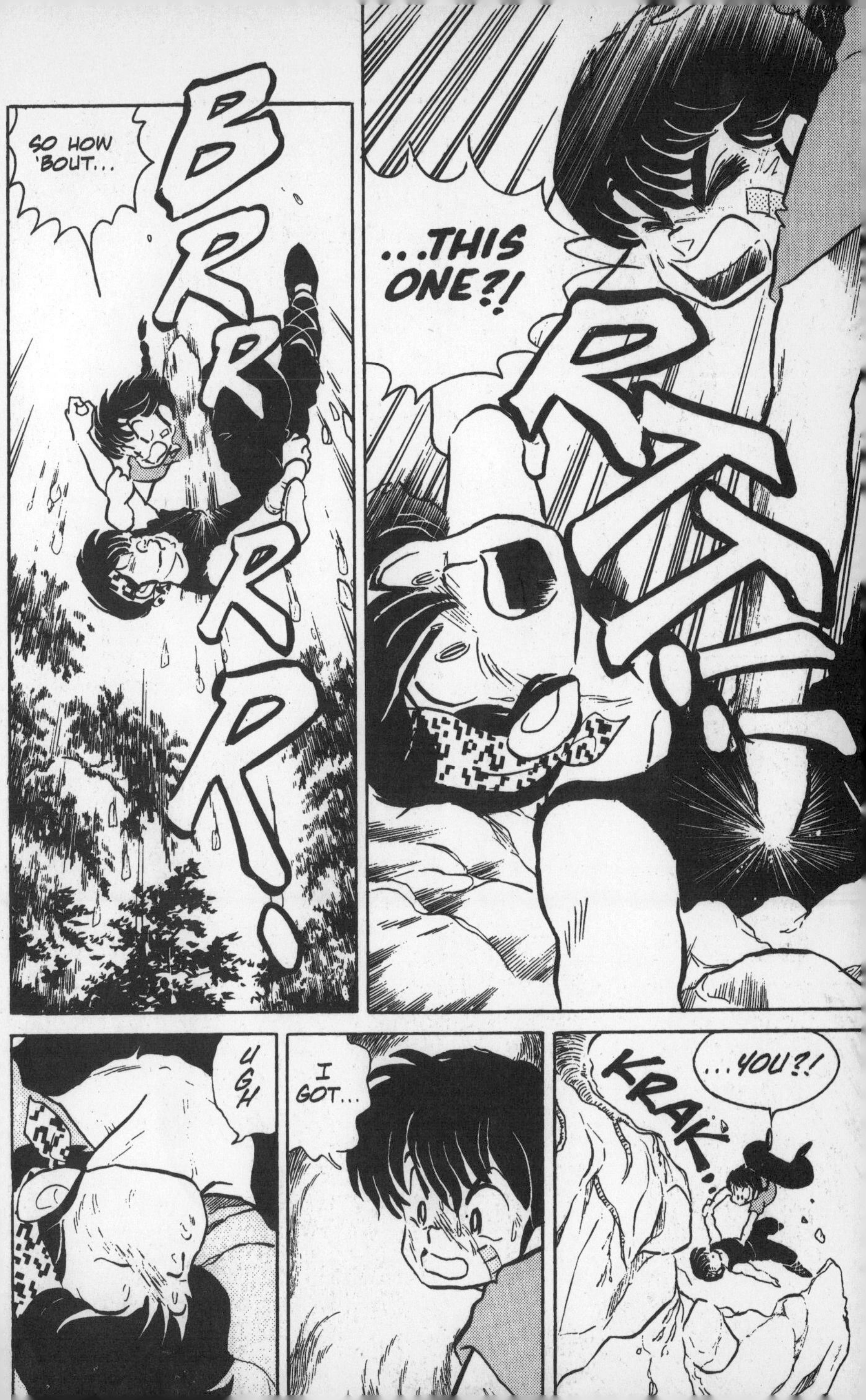
SO HOW 'BOUT...
BRRRR!
...THIS ONE?!
UGH
I GOT...
KRAK
...YOU?!

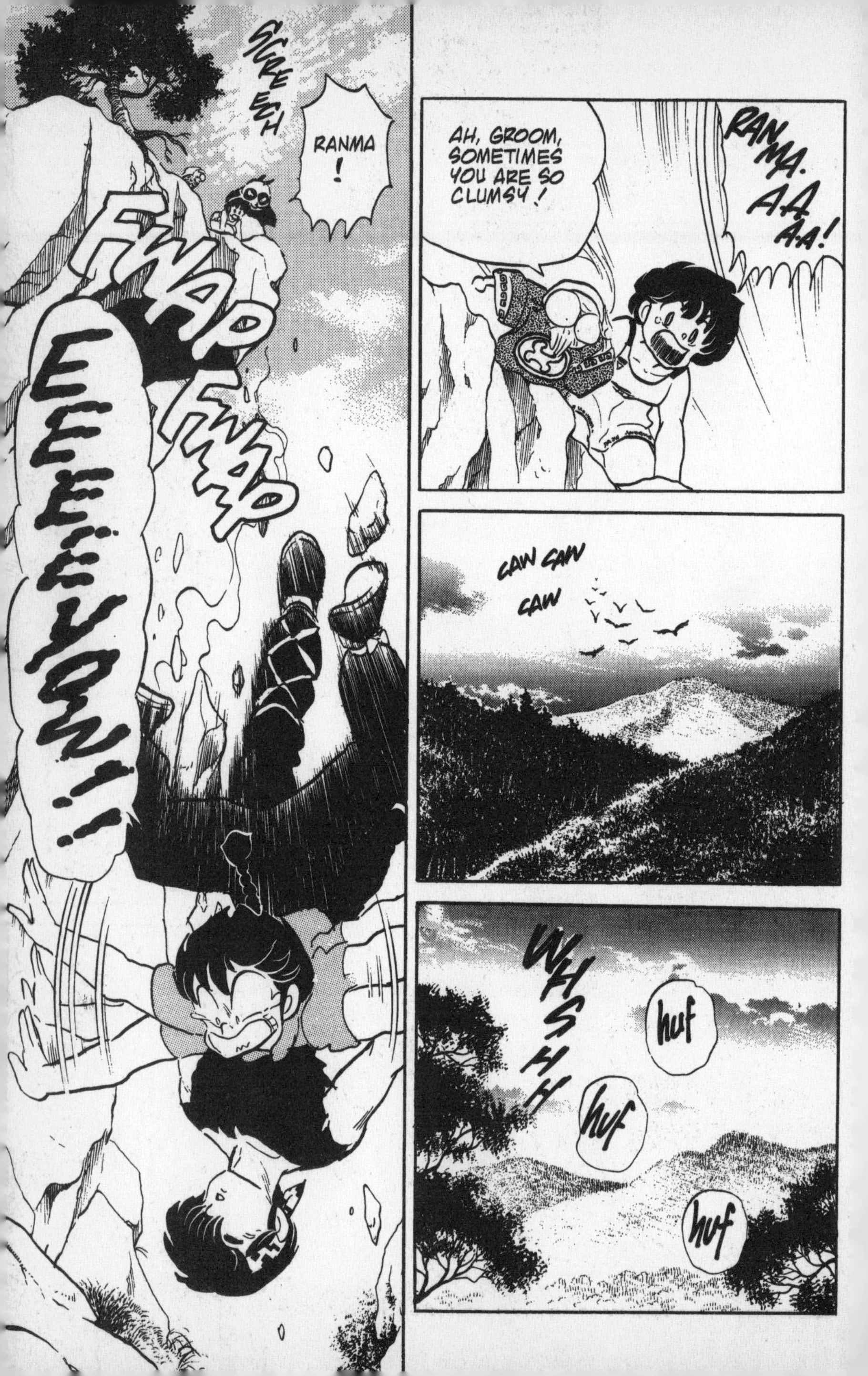
SCREEECH
RANMA!
FWAP FWAP
EEEEYOW!!!
RANMA-AAAAA!
AH, GROOM, SOMETIMES YOU ARE SO CLUMSY!
CAW CAW CAW
WHSHH
huf
huf
huf

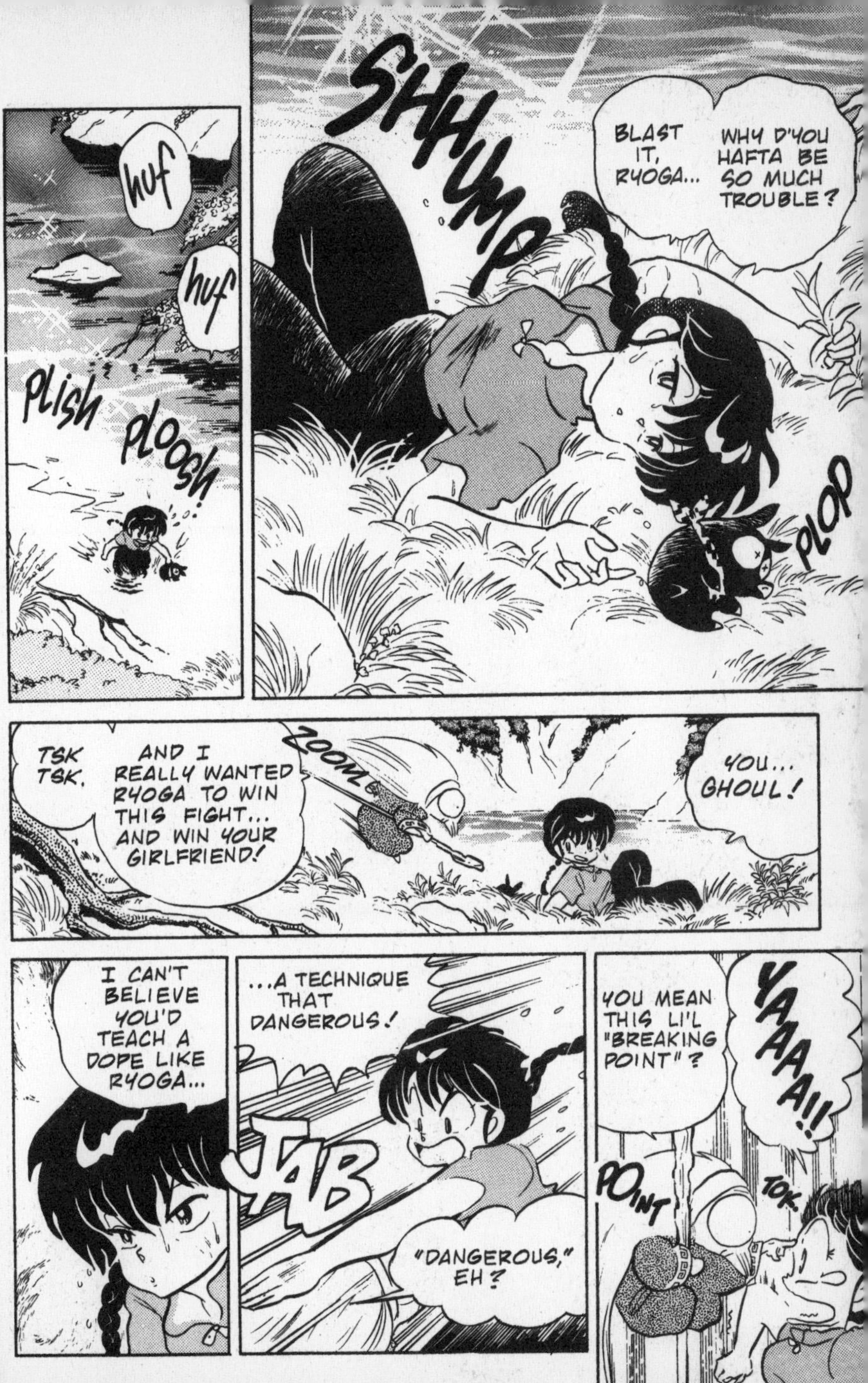
huf
huf
PLISH
PLOOSH
SHHUMP
BLAST IT, RYOGA...
WHY D'YOU HAFTA BE SO MUCH TROUBLE?
PLOP
TSK TSK.
AND I REALLY WANTED RYOGA TO WIN THIS FIGHT... AND WIN YOUR GIRLFRIEND!
ZOOM
YOU... GHOUL!
I CAN'T BELIEVE YOU'D TEACH A DOPE LIKE RYOGA...
...A TECHNIQUE THAT DANGEROUS!
JAB
"DANGEROUS," EH?
YOU MEAN THIS LI'L "BREAKING POINT"?
YAAAAA!!
POINT
TOK

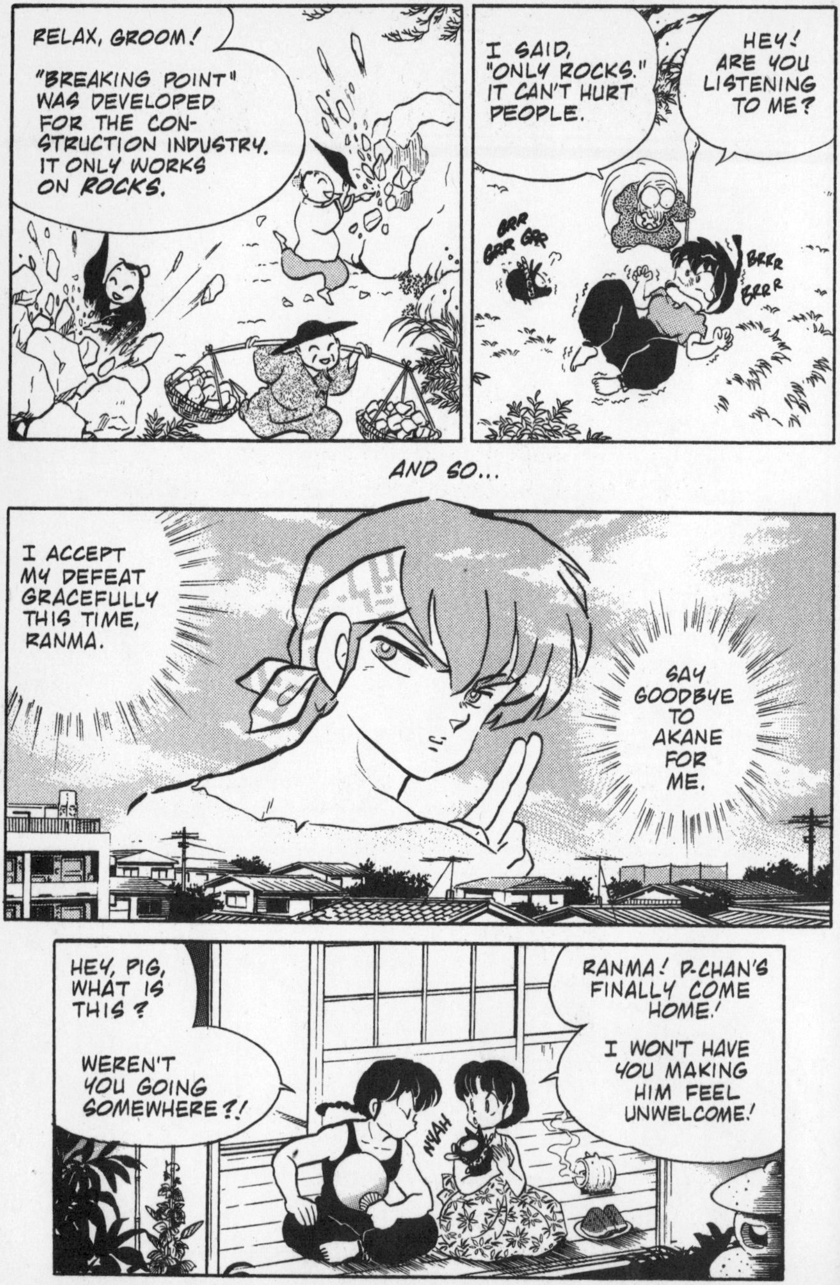
RELAX, GROOM!
"BREAKING POINT" WAS DEVELOPED FOR THE CON-STRUCTION INDUSTRY. IT ONLY WORKS ON *ROCKS*.
I SAID, "ONLY ROCKS." IT CAN'T HURT PEOPLE.
HEY! ARE YOU LISTENING TO ME?
GRR GRR GRR
BRRR BRRR
AND SO...
I ACCEPT MY DEFEAT GRACEFULLY THIS TIME, RANMA.
SAY GOODBYE TO AKANE FOR ME.
HEY, PIG, WHAT IS THIS?
WEREN'T YOU GOING SOMEWHERE?!
NYAH
RANMA! P-CHAN'S FINALLY COME HOME!
I WON'T HAVE YOU MAKING HIM FEEL UNWELCOME!

Part 7
THE WAY OF TEA

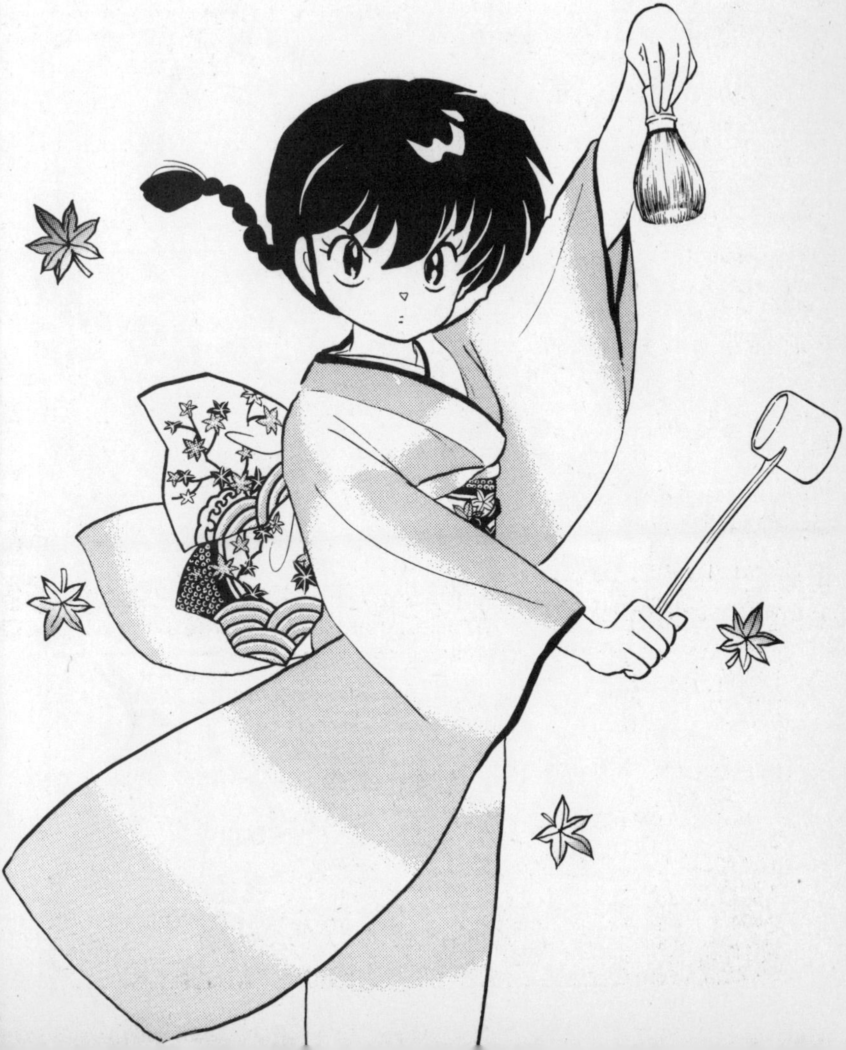

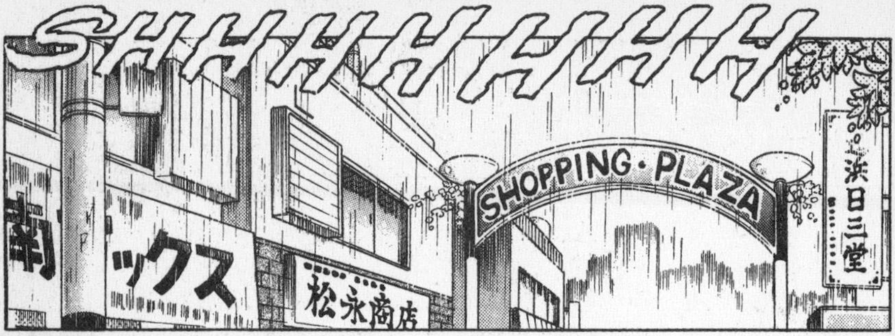
SHHHHHHHH
SHOPPING · PLAZA
ックス
松永商店
浜日三堂

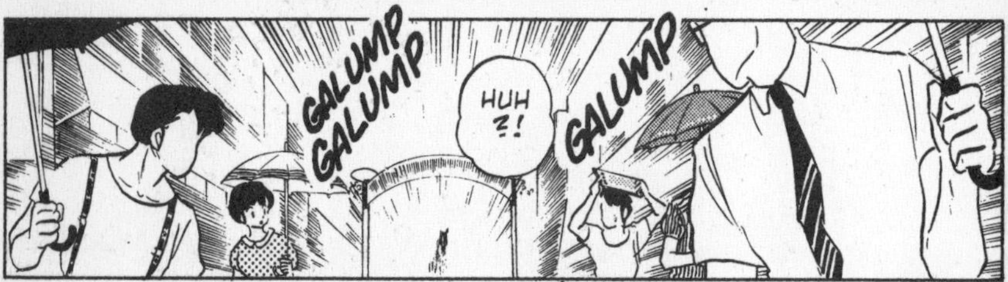
GALUMP GALUMP
HUH ?!
GALUMP

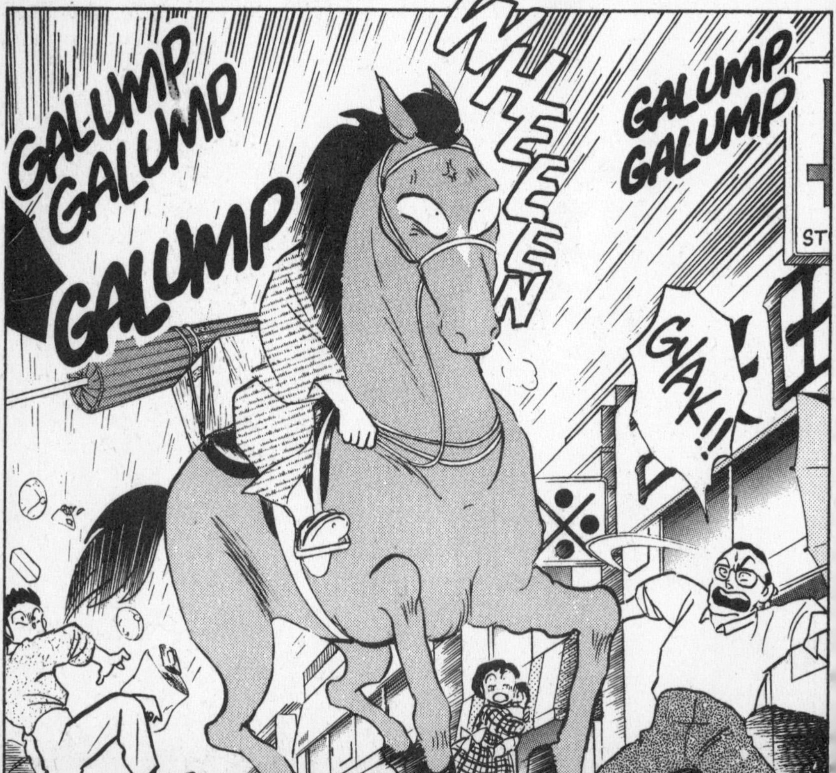
GAL-UMP GALUMP
GALUMP
WHEEEEN
GALUMP GALUMP
GYAK!!

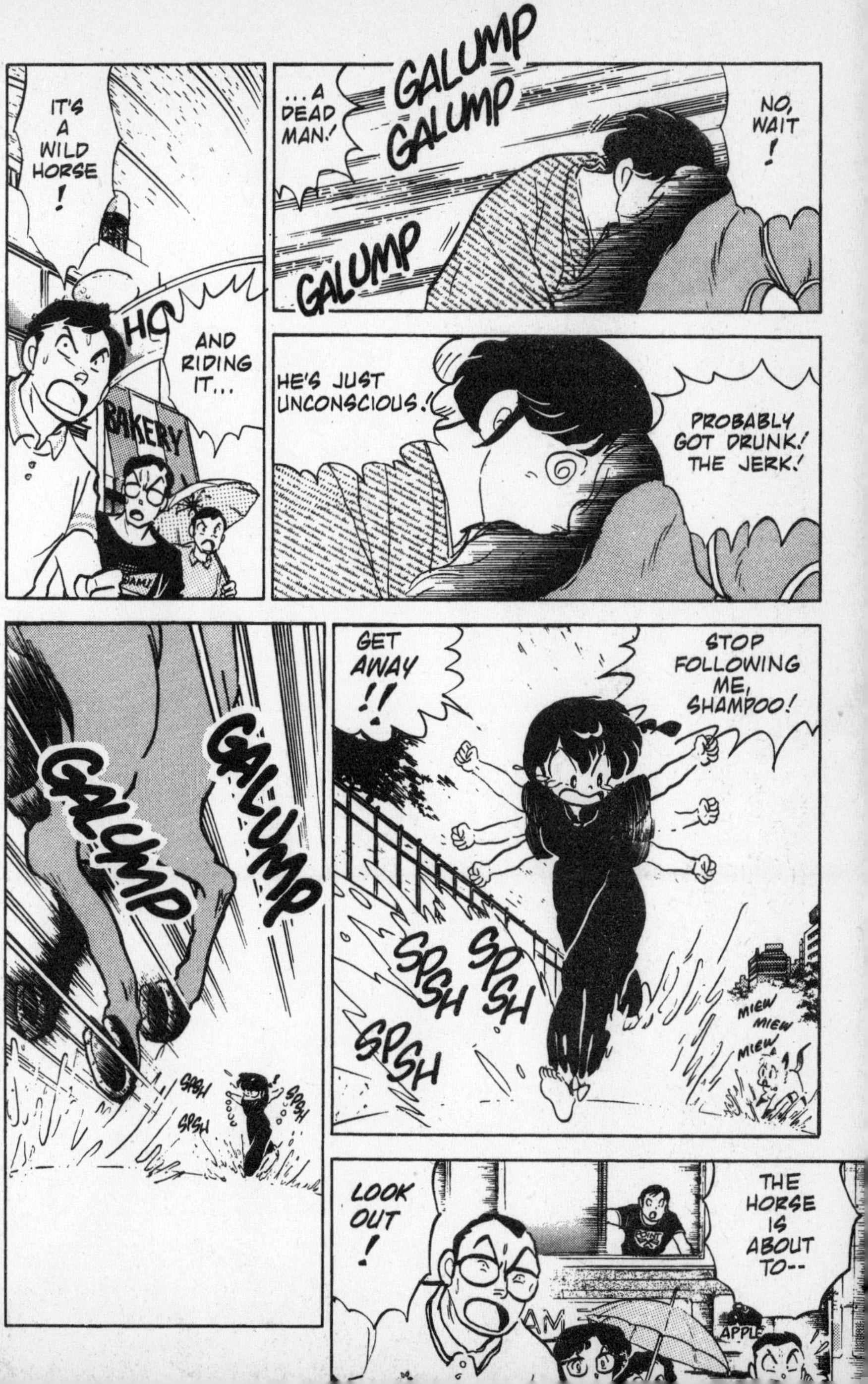
IT'S A WILD HORSE!
HO
AND RIDING IT...
BAKERY
...A DEAD MAN!
GALUMP GALUMP
NO, WAIT!
GALUMP
HE'S JUST UNCONSCIOUS!
PROBABLY GOT DRUNK! THE JERK!
GALUMP GALUMP
SPSH
SPSH
SPSH
GET AWAY!!
STOP FOLLOWING ME, SHAMPOO!
SPSH SPSH SPSH
MIEW MIEW MIEW
LOOK OUT!
THE HORSE IS ABOUT TO--
APPLE

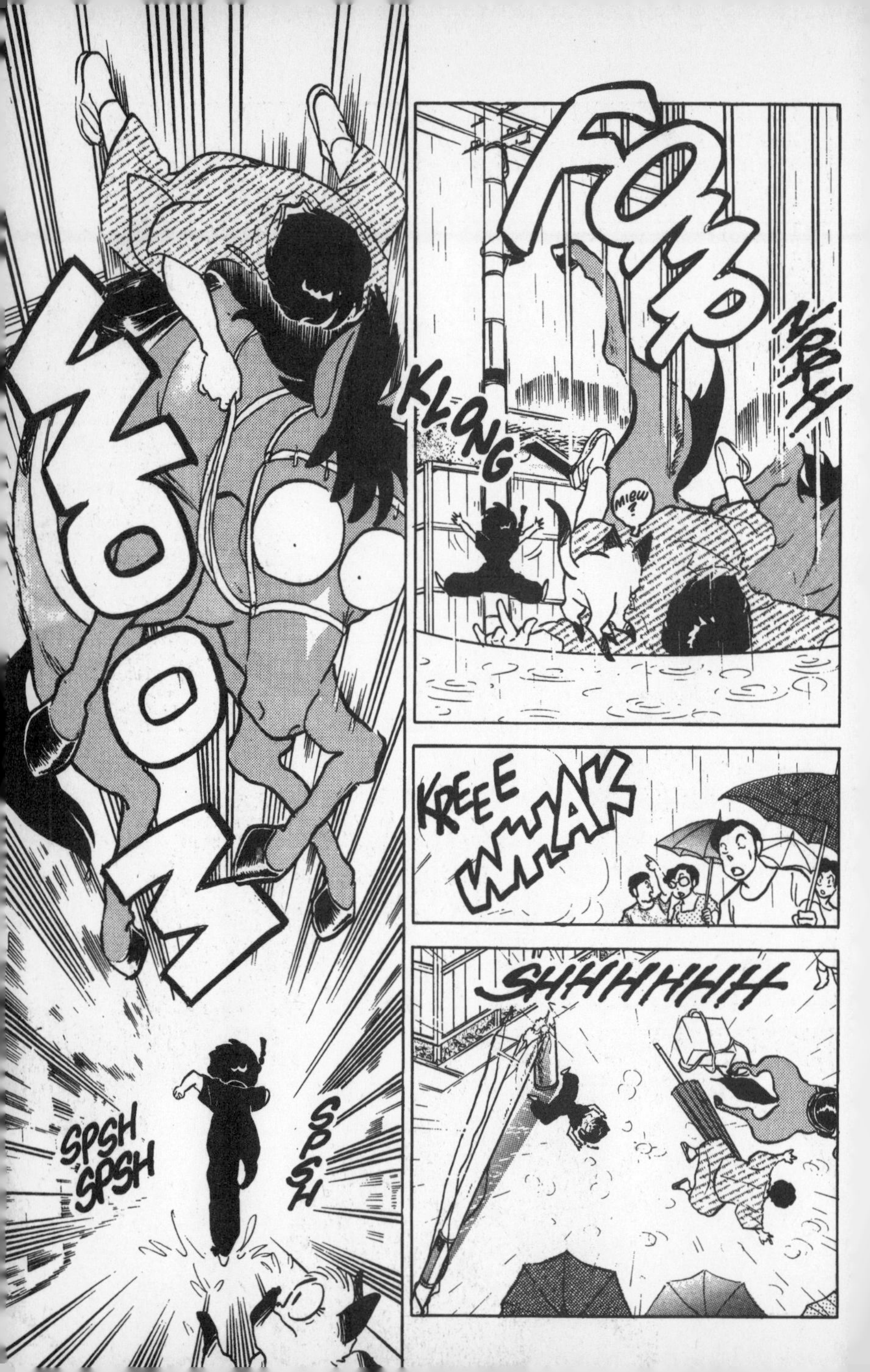

WOOM
SPSH SPSH
SPSH
FOMP
KLONG
MIEW?
KREEE WHAK
SHHHHHHH

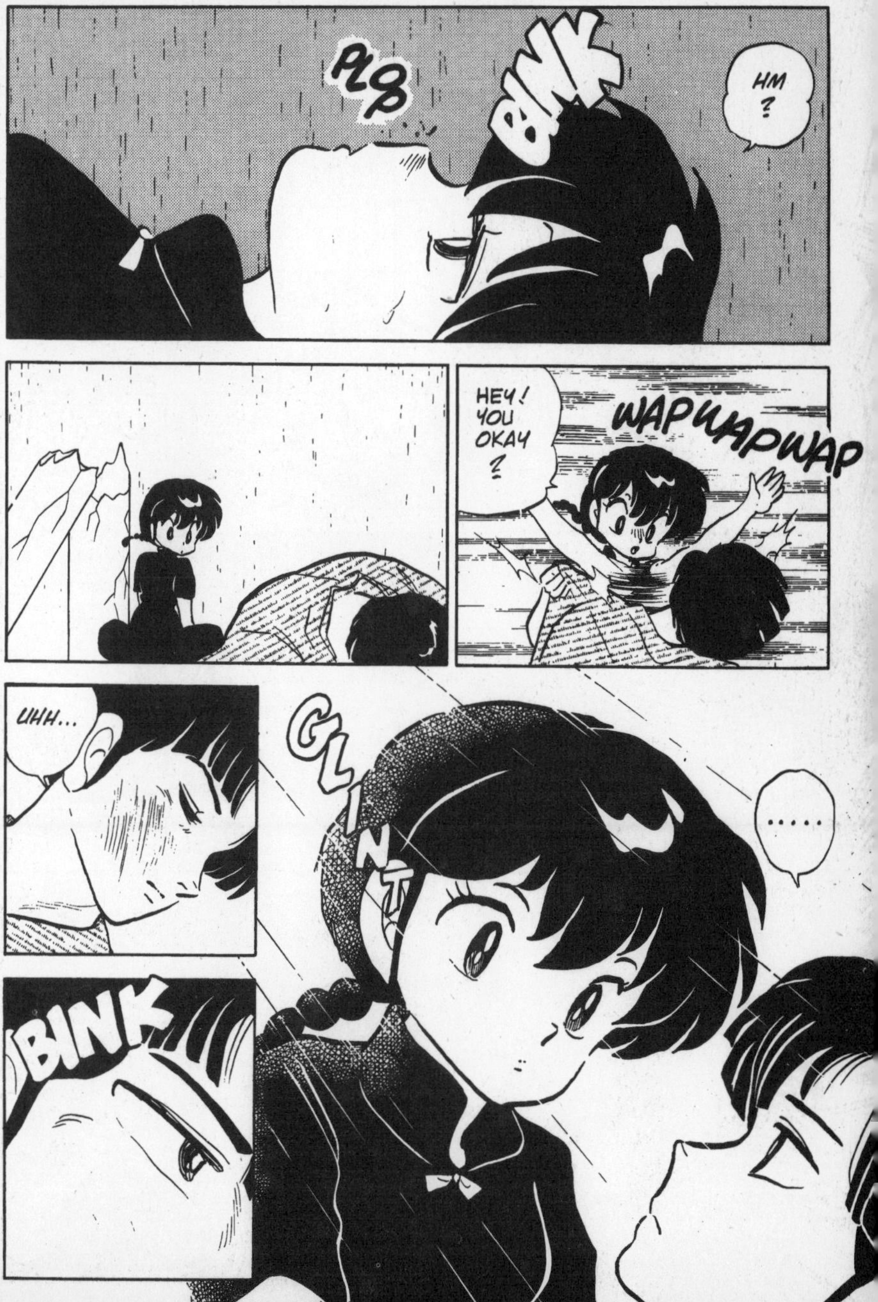
PLOP
BINK
HM ?
HEY! YOU OKAY ?
WAPWAPWAP
UHH...
GLINT
.....
BINK

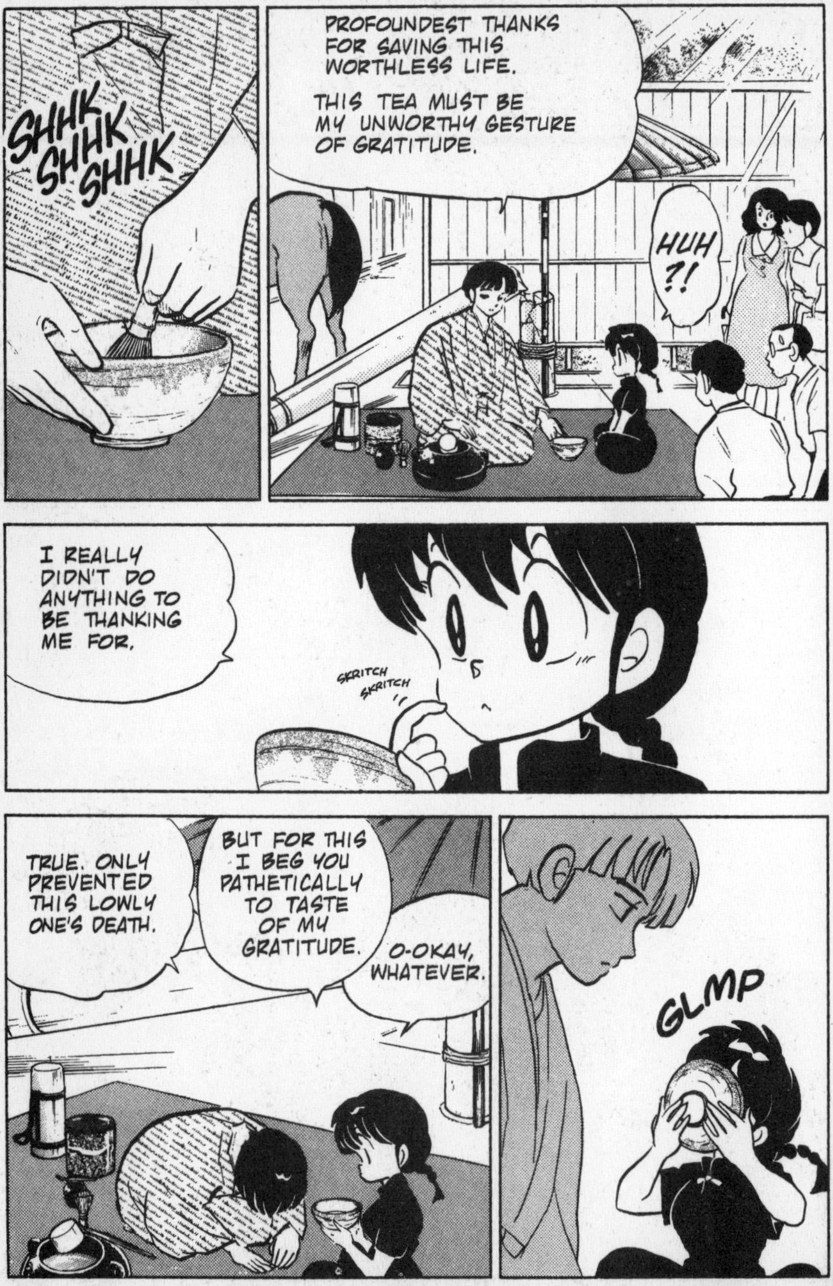
SHHK SHHK SHHK
PROFOUNDEST THANKS FOR SAVING THIS WORTHLESS LIFE.
THIS TEA MUST BE MY UNWORTHY GESTURE OF GRATITUDE.
HUH ?!
I REALLY DIDN'T DO ANYTHING TO BE THANKING ME FOR.
SKRITCH SKRITCH
TRUE. ONLY PREVENTED THIS LOWLY ONE'S DEATH.
BUT FOR THIS I BEG YOU PATHETICALLY TO TASTE OF MY GRATITUDE.
O-OKAY, WHATEVER.
GLMP

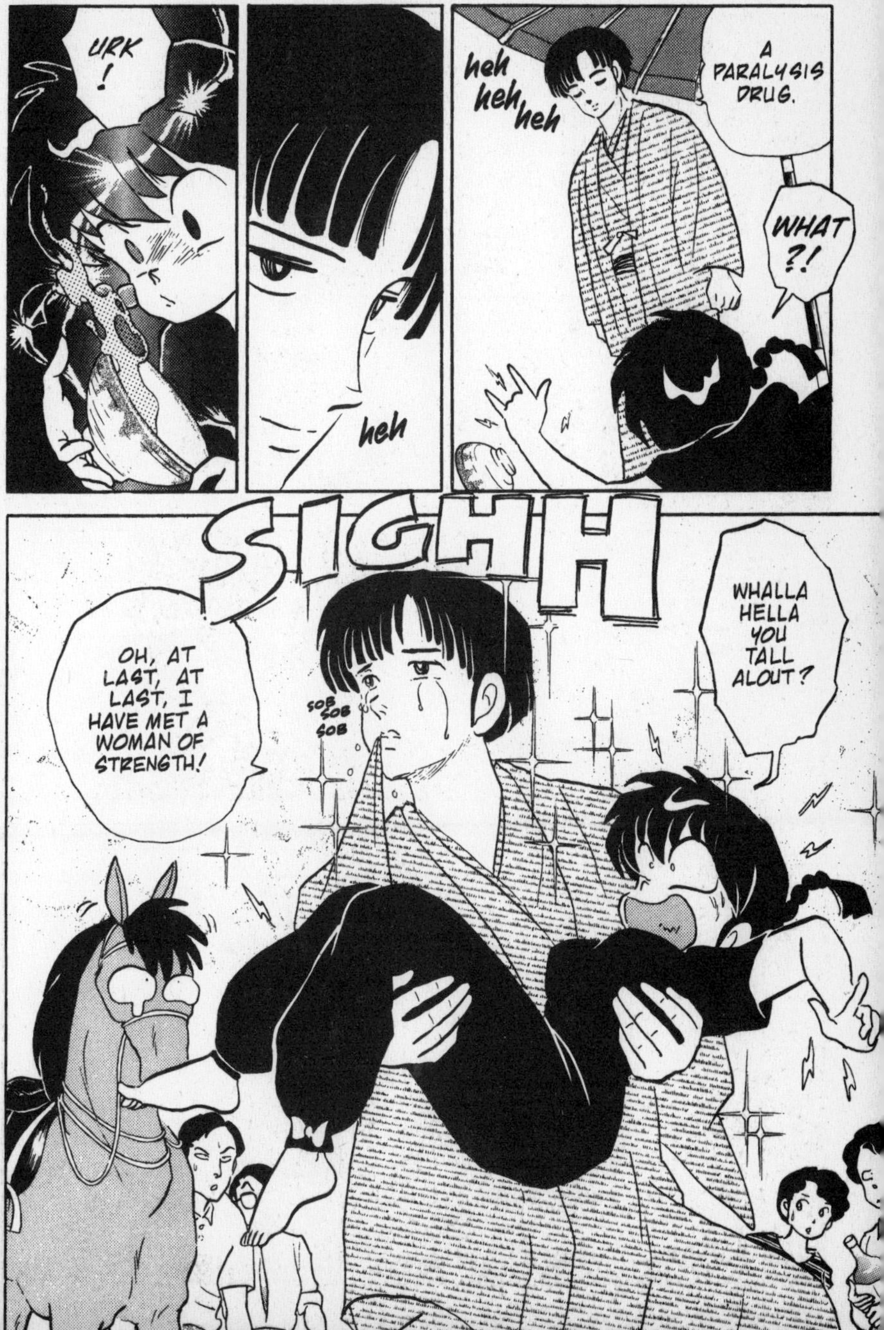
URK!
heh
heh heh heh
A PARALYSIS DRUG.
WHAT?!
SIGHH
OH, AT LAST, AT LAST, I HAVE MET A WOMAN OF STRENGTH!
SOB SOB SOB
WHALLA HELLA YOU TALL ALOUT?

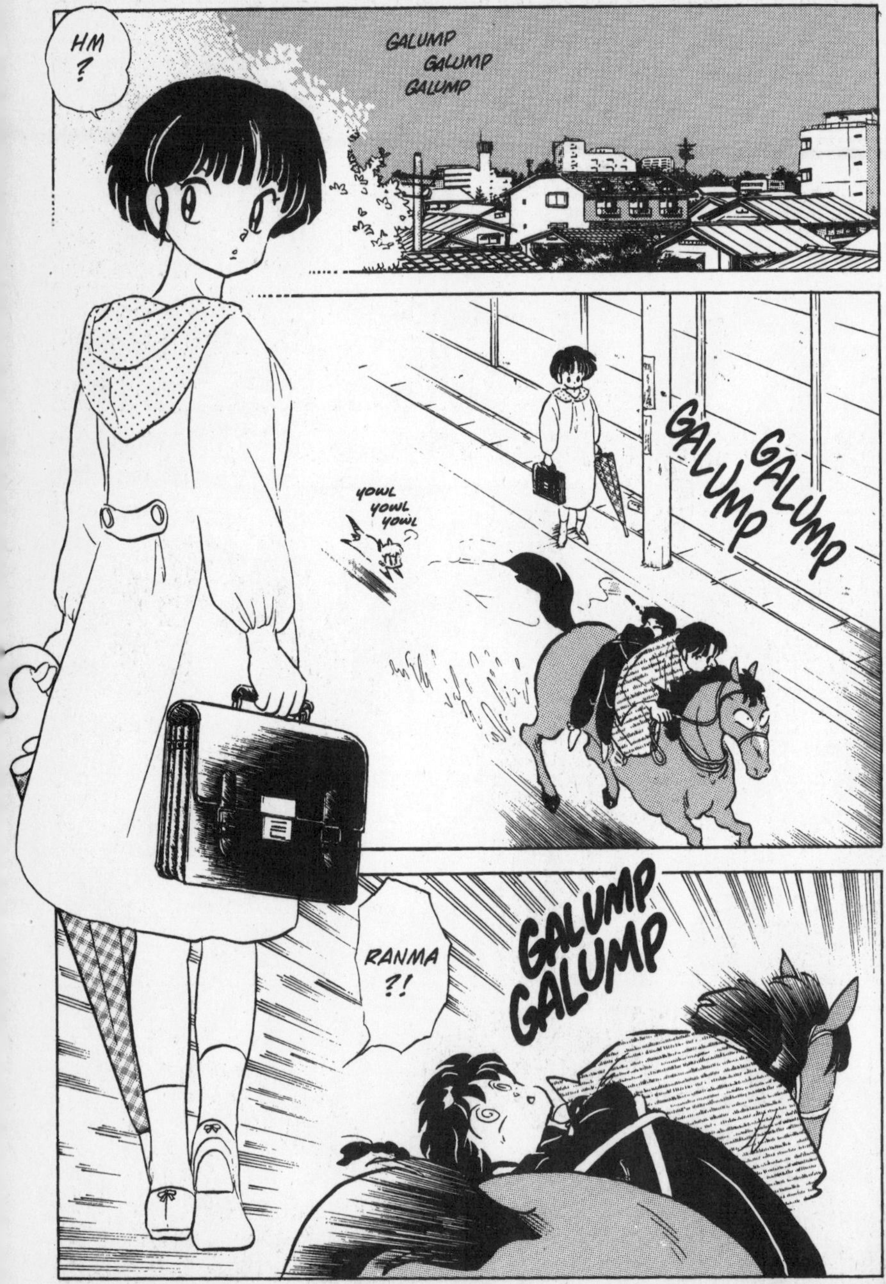
HM ?
GALUMP GALUMP GALUMP
YOWL YOWL YOWL
GALUMP GALUMP
RANMA ?!
GALUMP GALUMP

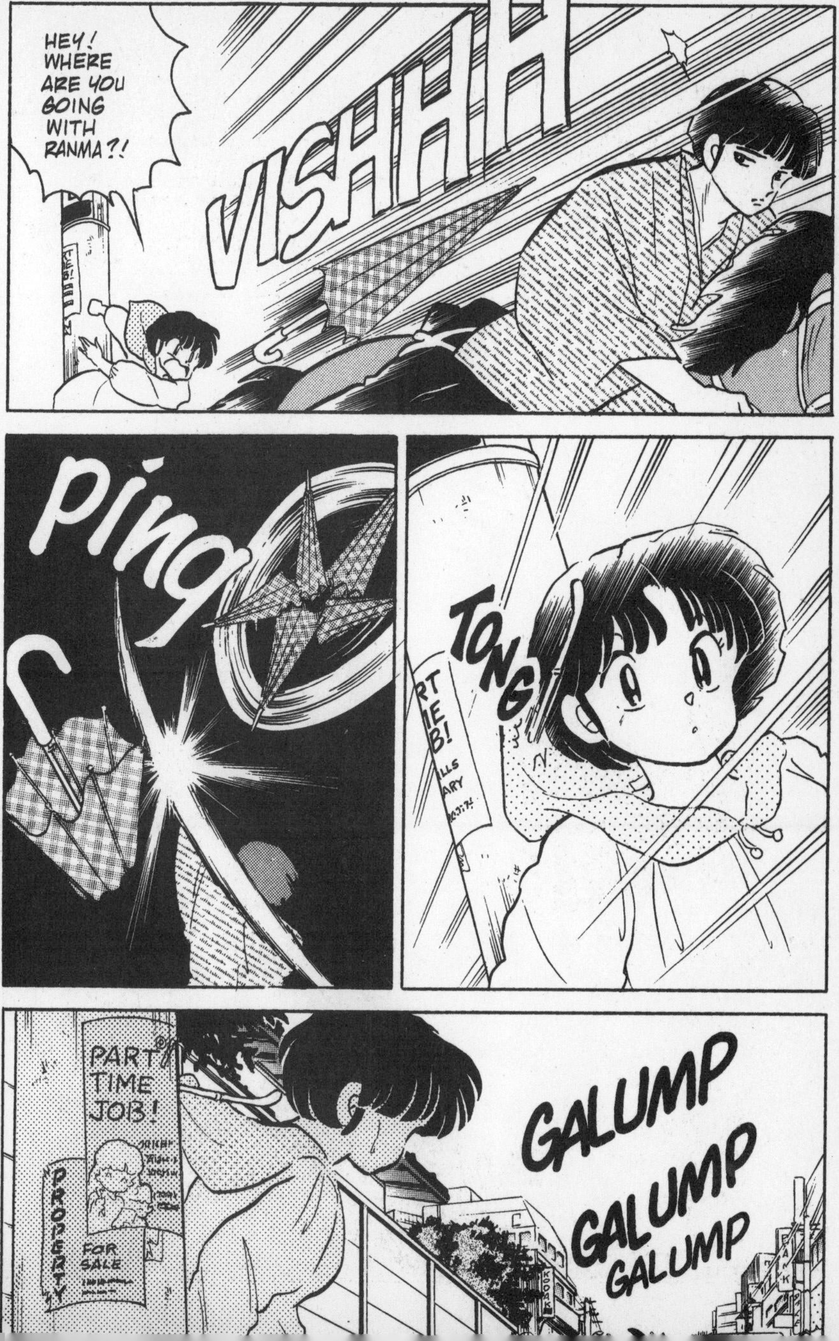
HEY! WHERE ARE YOU GOING WITH RANMA?!
VISHHH
ping
TONG
PART TIME JOB!
PROPERTY
FOR SALE
GALUMP
GALUMP
GALUMP

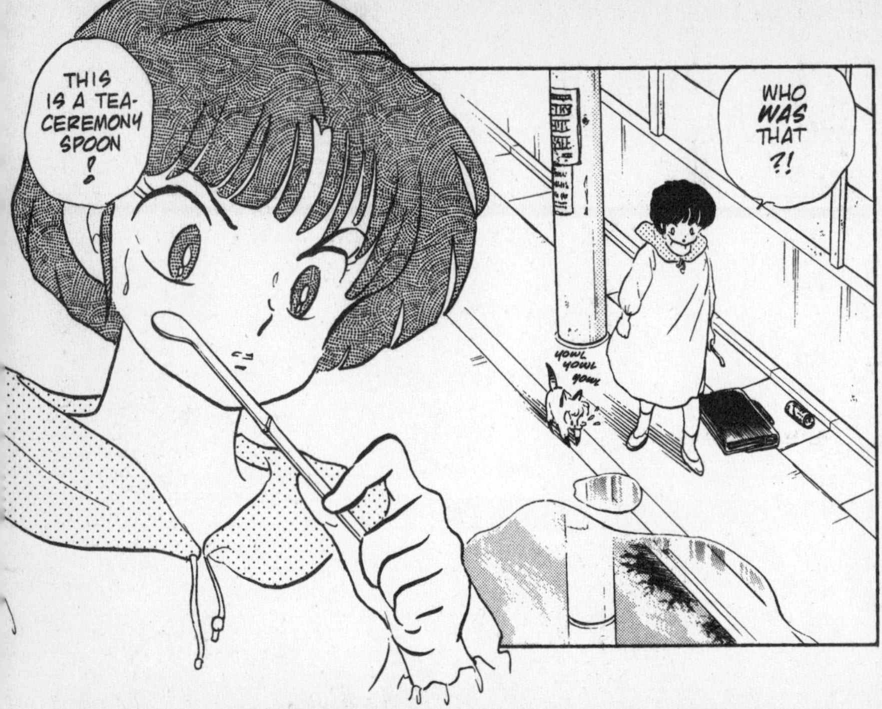
THIS IS A TEA-CEREMONY SPOON !
WHO WAS THAT ?!
YOWL YOWL YOWL

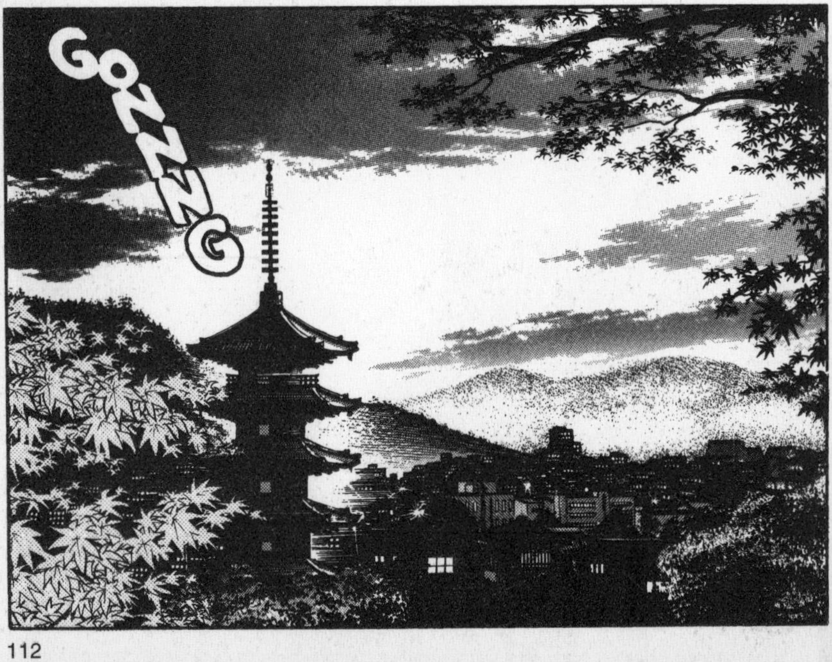
GOZZZG

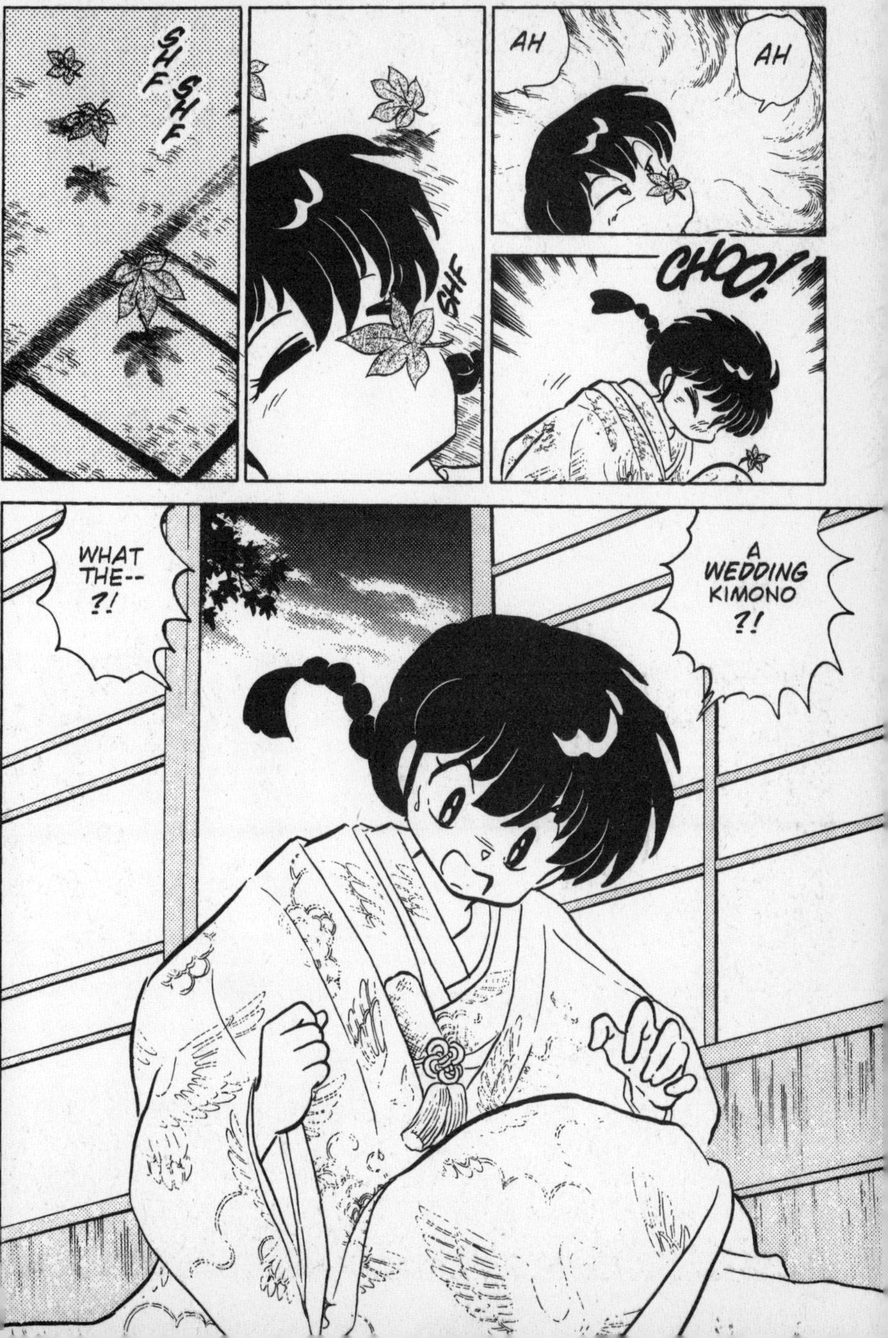
SHF SHF SHF
SHF
AH
AH
CHOO!
WHAT THE-- ?!
A WEDDING KIMONO ?!

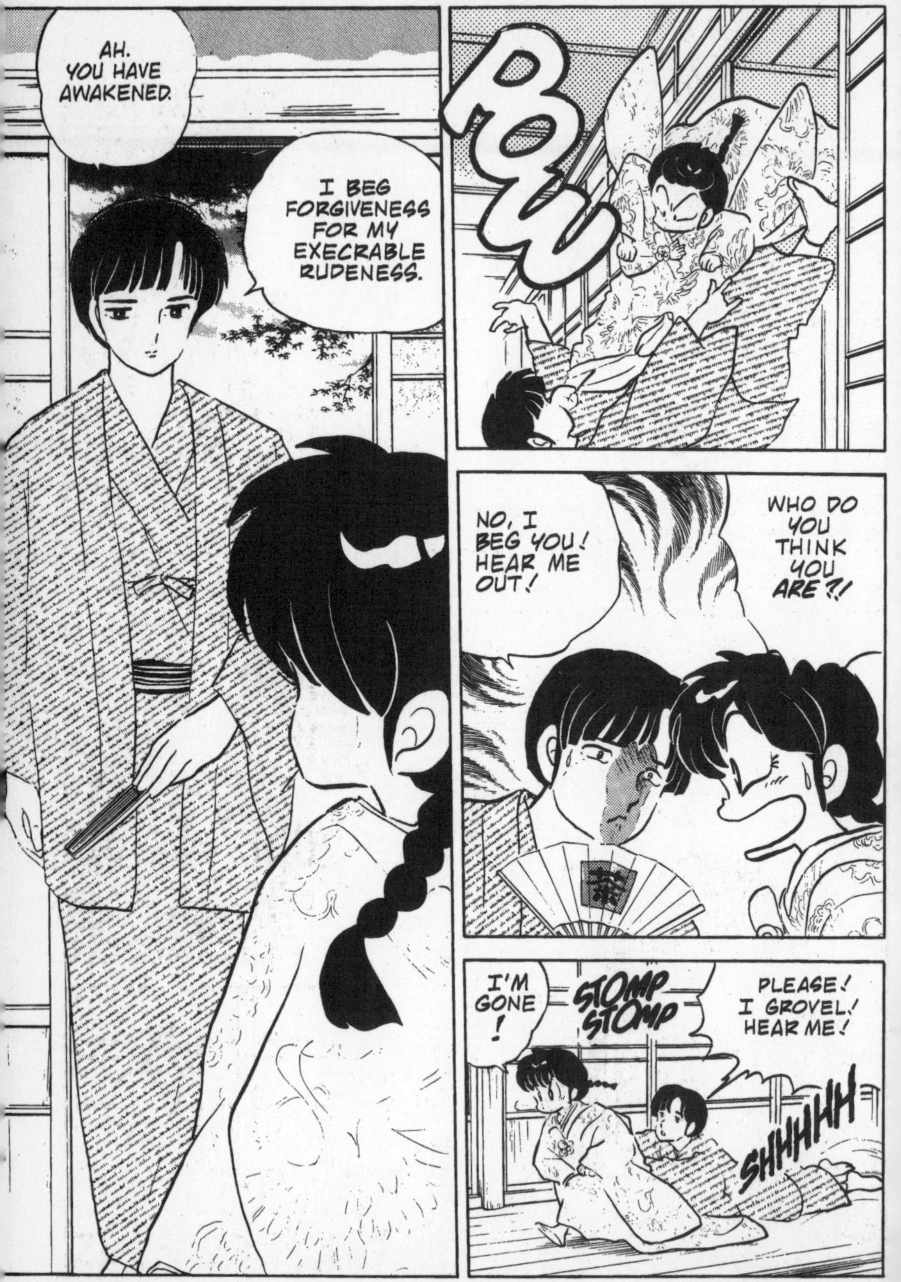

AH. YOU HAVE AWAKENED.
I BEG FORGIVENESS FOR MY EXECRABLE RUDENESS.
POW
NO, I BEG YOU! HEAR ME OUT!
WHO DO YOU THINK YOU ARE ?!
I'M GONE!
STOMP STOMP
PLEASE! I GROVEL! HEAR ME!
SHHHHH

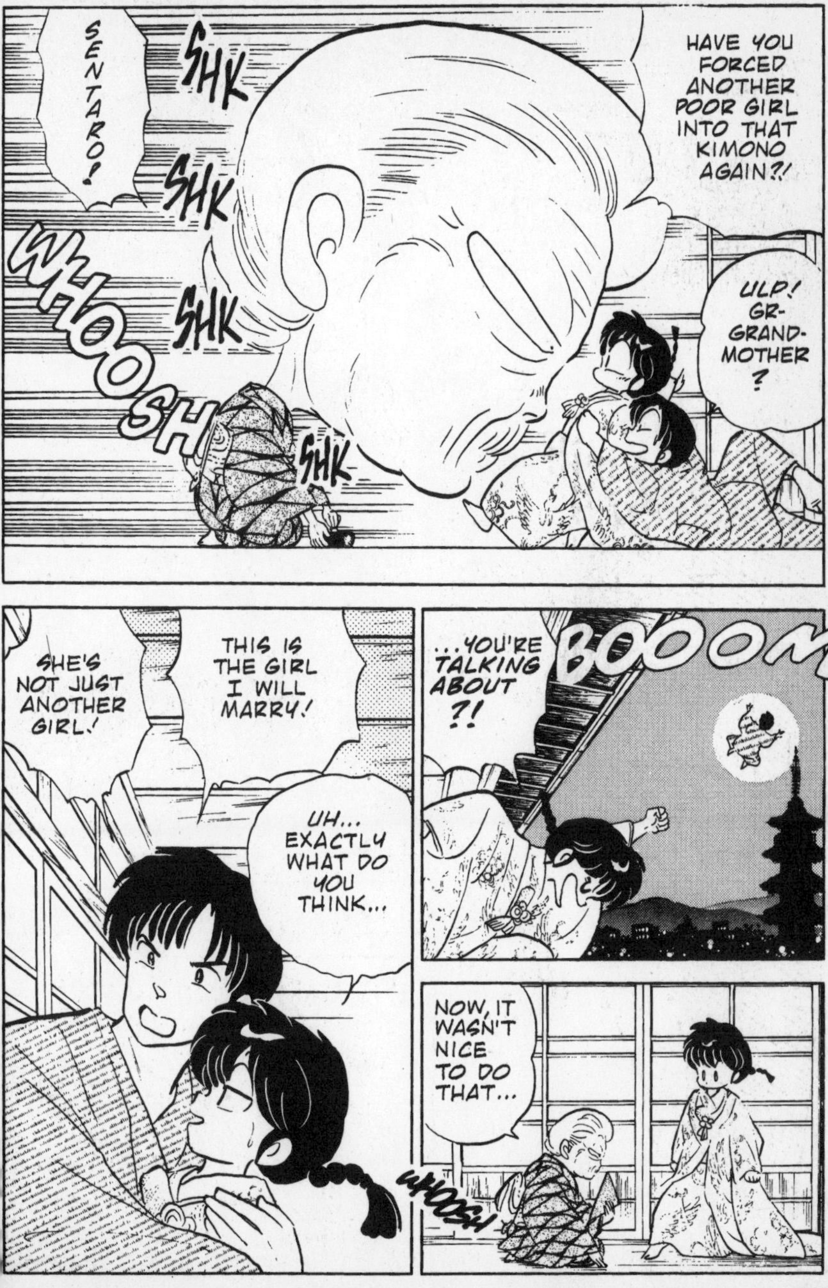
SENTARO!
SHK
SHK
WHOOSH
SHK
SHK
HAVE YOU FORCED ANOTHER POOR GIRL INTO THAT KIMONO AGAIN?!
ULP! GR-GRAND-MOTHER?
SHE'S NOT JUST ANOTHER GIRL!
THIS IS THE GIRL I WILL MARRY!
UH... EXACTLY WHAT DO YOU THINK...
...YOU'RE TALKING ABOUT?!
BOOOM
NOW, IT WASN'T NICE TO DO THAT...
WHOOSH

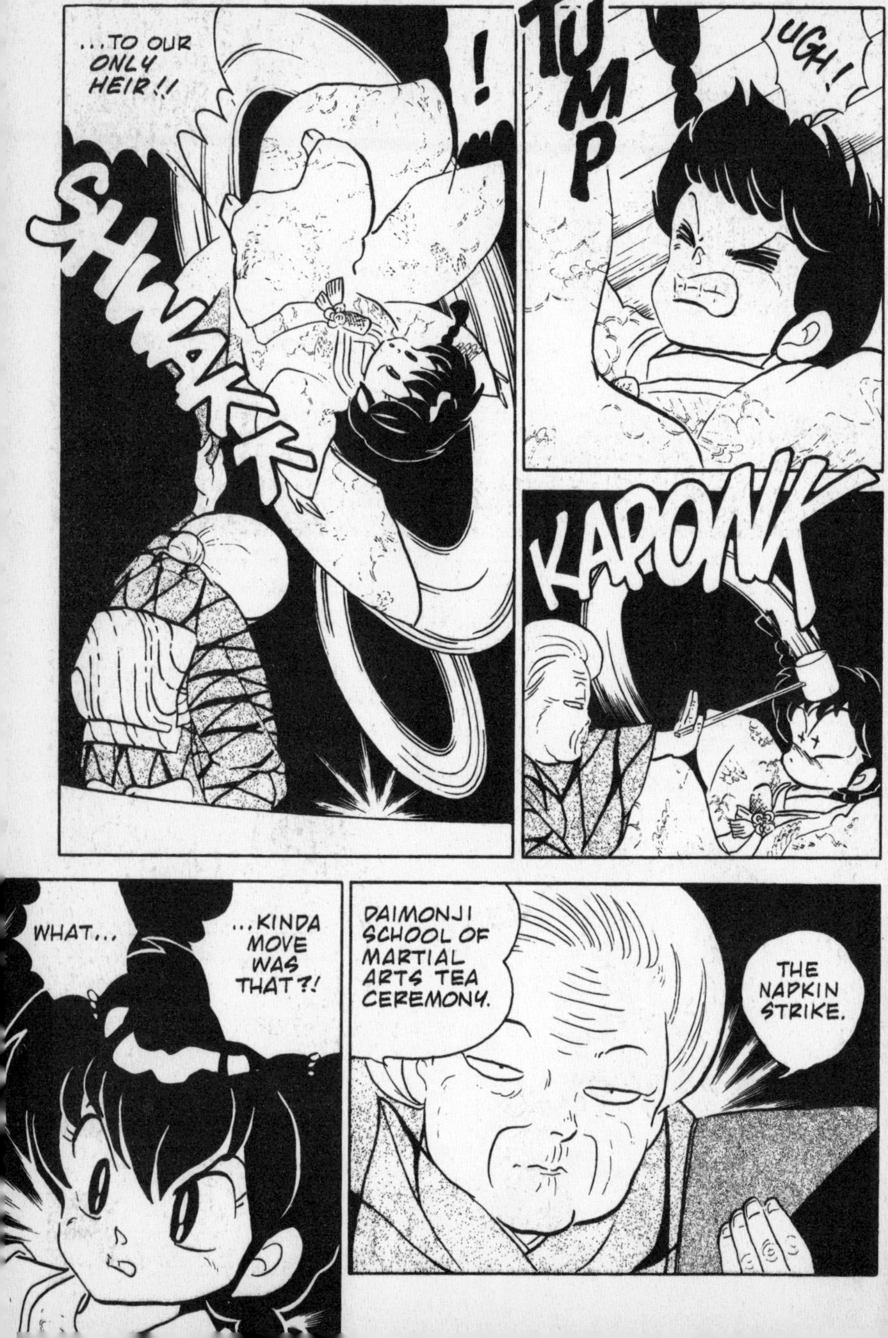
...TO OUR ONLY HEIR!!
!
SHWAKK
TUMP
UGH!
KAPONK
WHAT...
...KINDA MOVE WAS THAT?!
DAIMONJI SCHOOL OF MARTIAL ARTS TEA CEREMONY.
THE NAPKIN STRIKE.

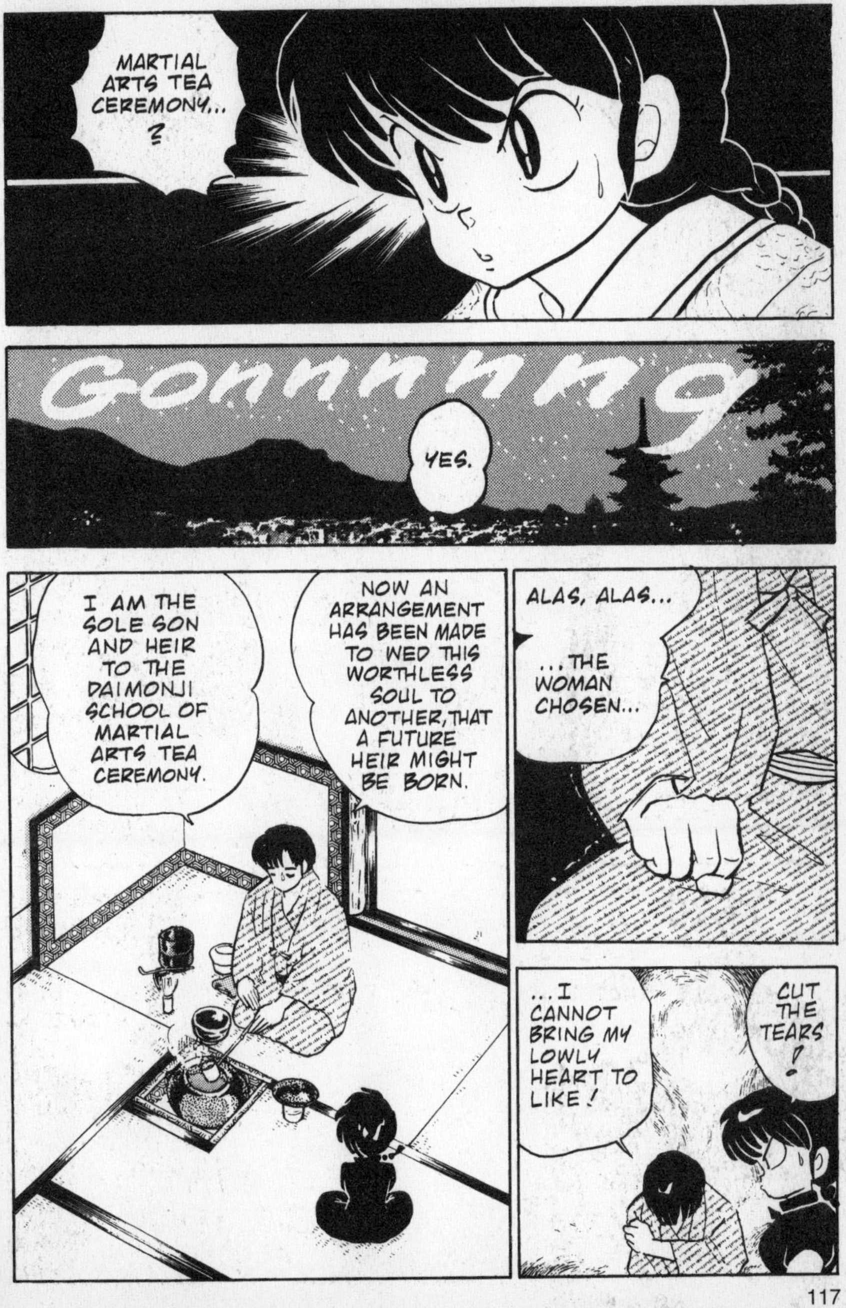
MARTIAL ARTS TEA CEREMONY...?
Gonnnng
YES.
I AM THE SOLE SON AND HEIR TO THE DAIMONJI SCHOOL OF MARTIAL ARTS TEA CEREMONY.
NOW AN ARRANGEMENT HAS BEEN MADE TO WED THIS WORTHLESS SOUL TO ANOTHER, THAT A FUTURE HEIR MIGHT BE BORN.
ALAS, ALAS...
...THE WOMAN CHOSEN...
...I CANNOT BRING MY LOWLY HEART TO LIKE!
CUT THE TEARS!

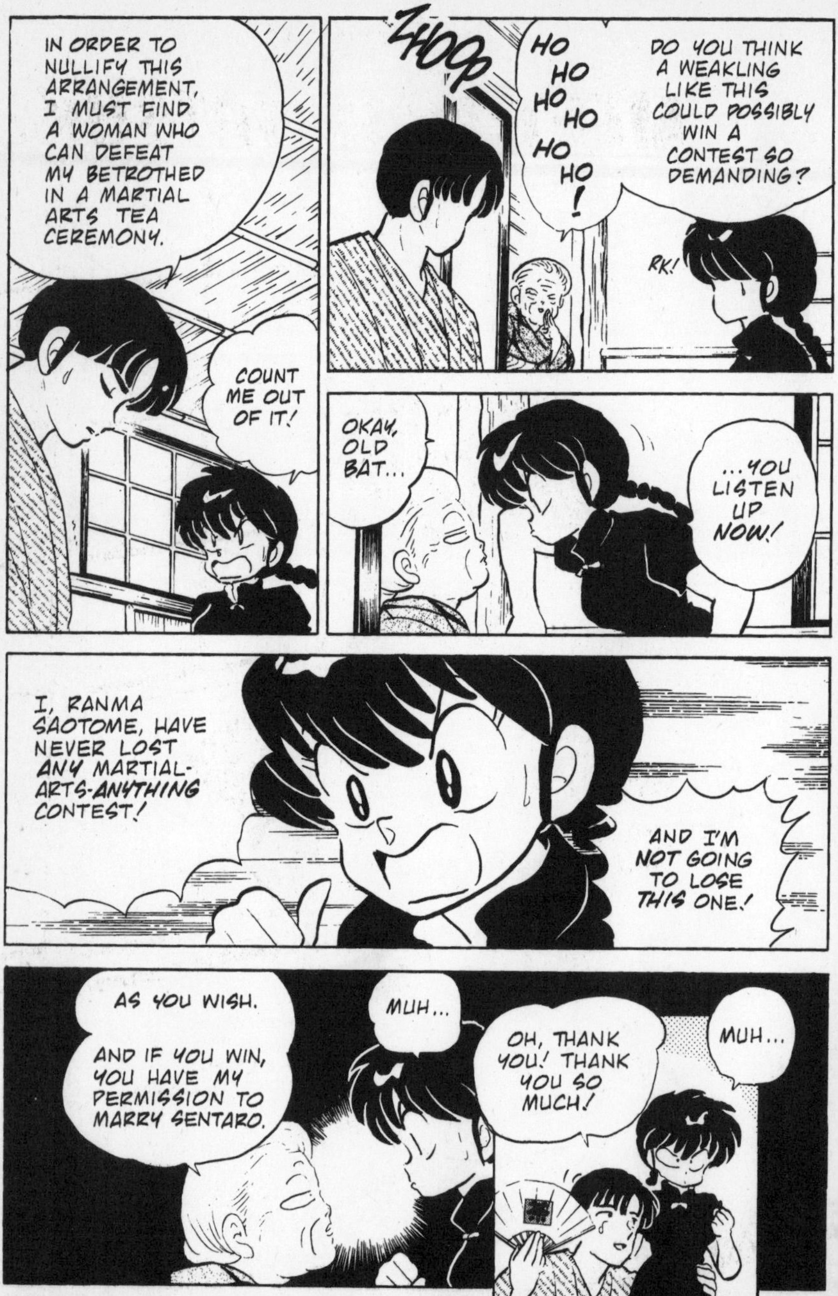

IN ORDER TO NULLIFY THIS ARRANGEMENT, I MUST FIND A WOMAN WHO CAN DEFEAT MY BETROTHED IN A MARTIAL ARTS TEA CEREMONY.
COUNT ME OUT OF IT!
ZHOOP
HO HO HO HO HO HO!
DO YOU THINK A WEAKLING LIKE THIS COULD POSSIBLY WIN A CONTEST SO DEMANDING?
RK!
OKAY, OLD BAT...
...YOU LISTEN UP NOW!
I, RANMA SAOTOME, HAVE NEVER LOST ANY MARTIAL-ARTS-ANYTHING CONTEST!
AND I'M NOT GOING TO LOSE THIS ONE!
AS YOU WISH.
AND IF YOU WIN, YOU HAVE MY PERMISSION TO MARRY SENTARO.
MUH...
OH, THANK YOU! THANK YOU SO MUCH!
MUH...

Part 8
MEET MISS SATSUKI

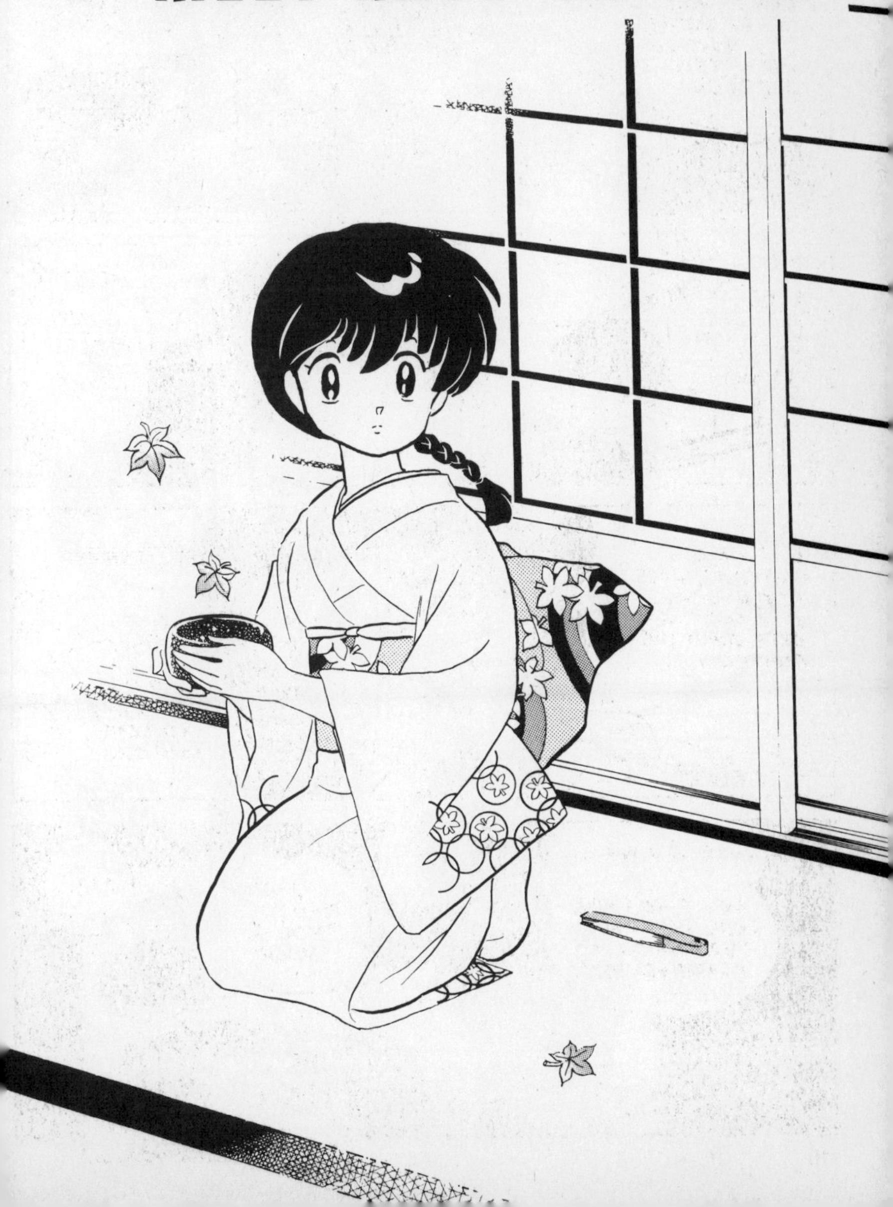

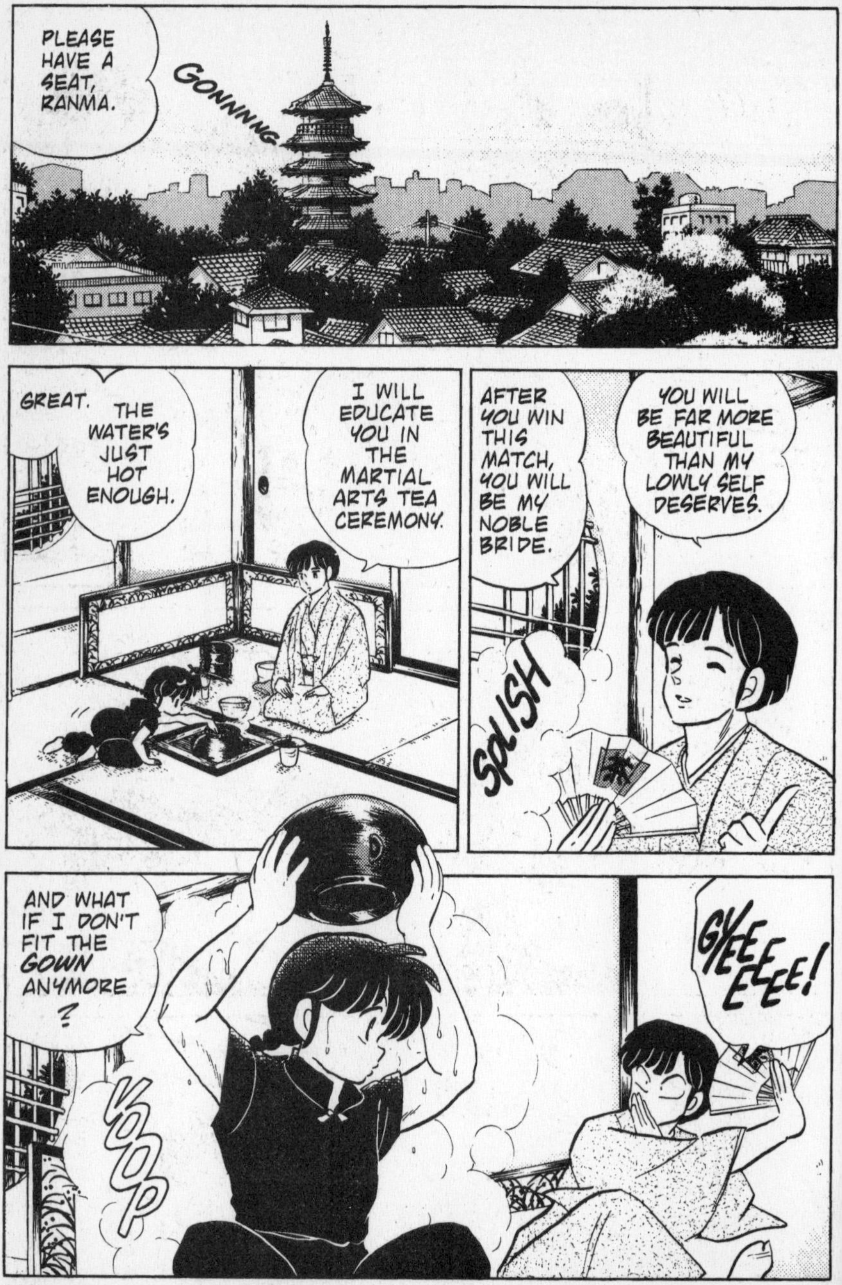
PLEASE HAVE A SEAT, RANMA.
GONNNNG
GREAT.
THE WATER'S JUST HOT ENOUGH.
I WILL EDUCATE YOU IN THE MARTIAL ARTS TEA CEREMONY.
AFTER YOU WIN THIS MATCH, YOU WILL BE MY NOBLE BRIDE.
YOU WILL BE FAR MORE BEAUTIFUL THAN MY LOWLY SELF DESERVES.
SPLISH
AND WHAT IF I DON'T FIT THE GOWN ANYMORE?
VOOP
GYEEEEEEE!

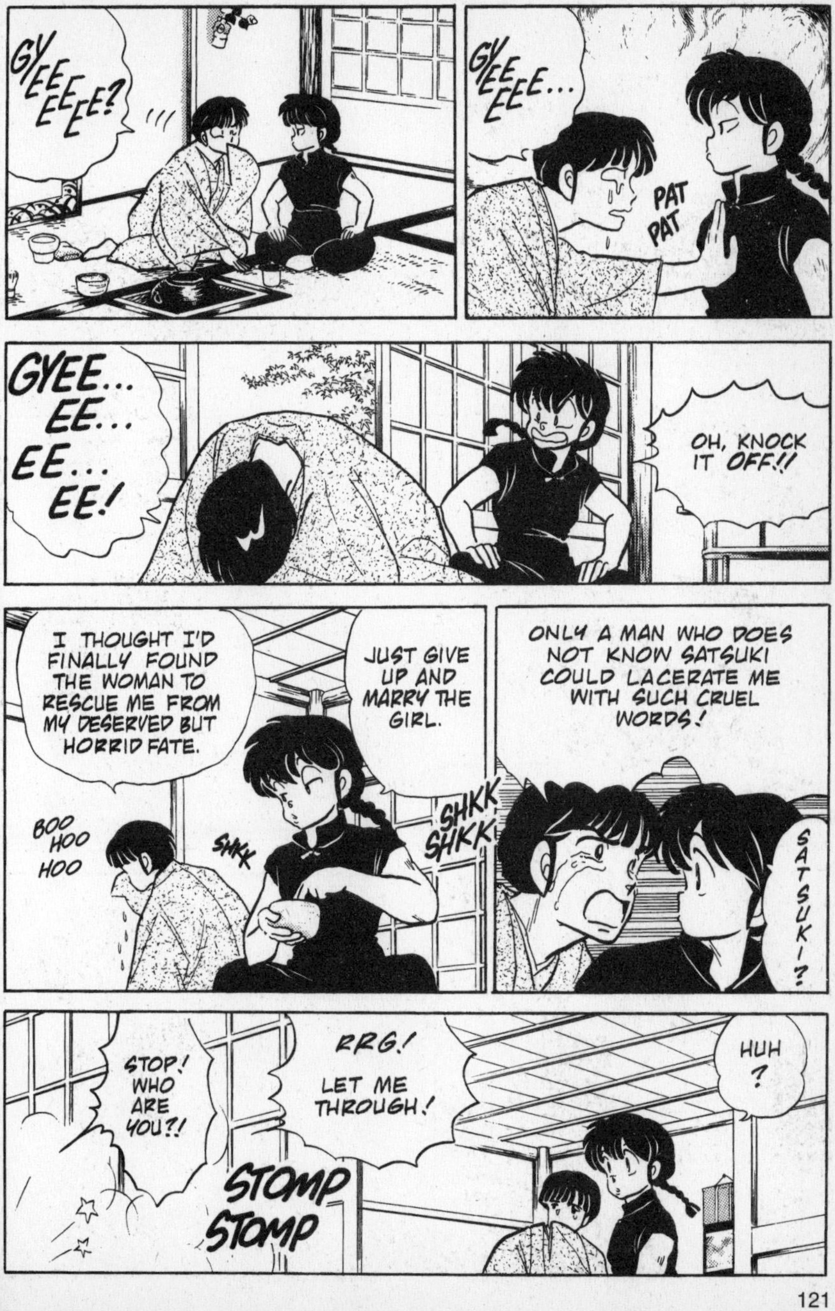
GYEEEEEE?
GYEEEE...
PAT PAT
GYEE... EE... EE... EE!
OH, KNOCK IT OFF!!
I THOUGHT I'D FINALLY FOUND THE WOMAN TO RESCUE ME FROM MY DESERVED BUT HORRID FATE.
JUST GIVE UP AND MARRY THE GIRL.
BOO HOO HOO
SHKK
ONLY A MAN WHO DOES NOT KNOW SATSUKI COULD LACERATE ME WITH SUCH CRUEL WORDS!
SHKK SHKK
SATSUKI?
STOP! WHO ARE YOU?!
RRG!
LET ME THROUGH!
HUH?
STOMP STOMP

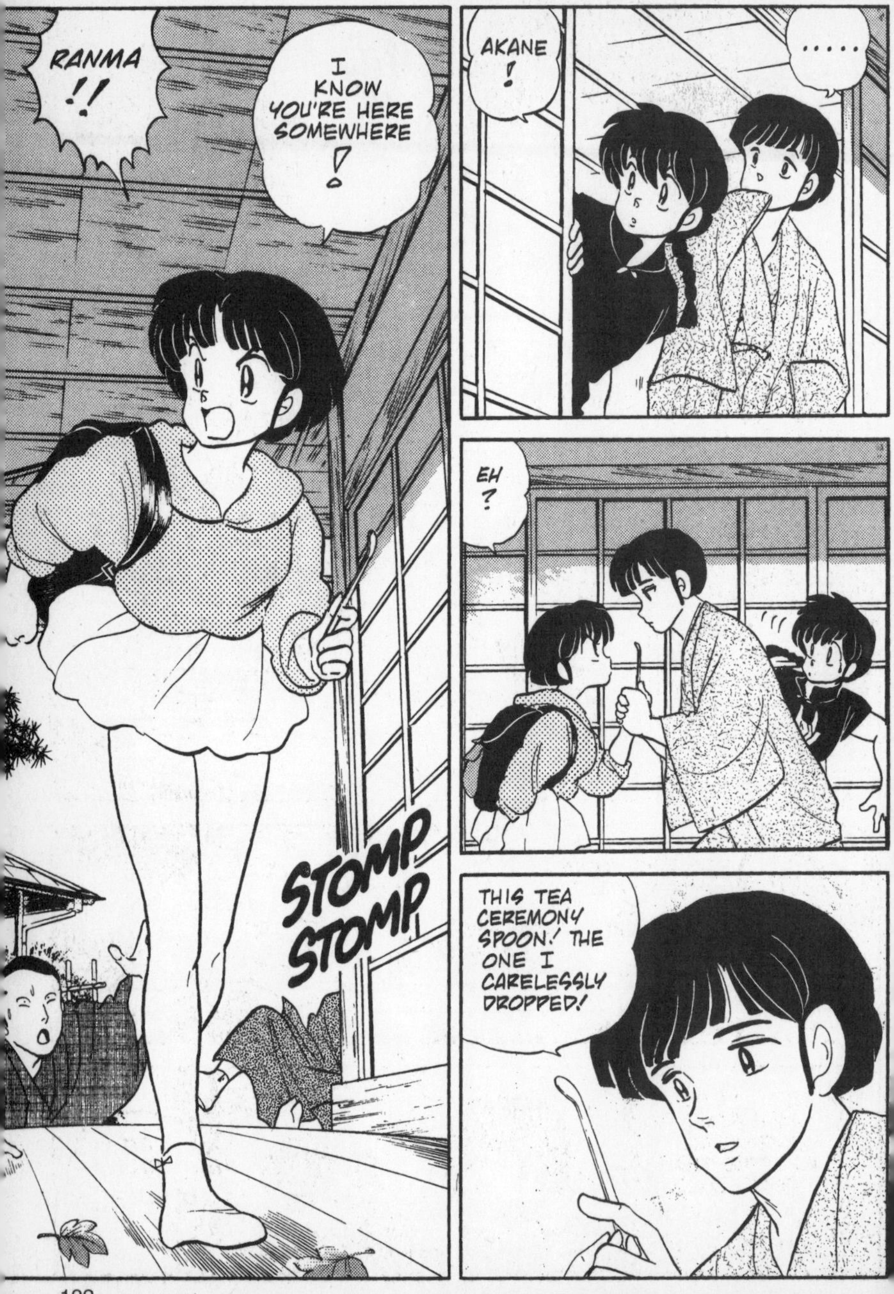
RANMA !!
I KNOW YOU'RE HERE SOMEWHERE !
STOMP STOMP
AKANE !
.....
EH ?
THIS TEA CEREMONY SPOON! THE ONE I CARELESSLY DROPPED!

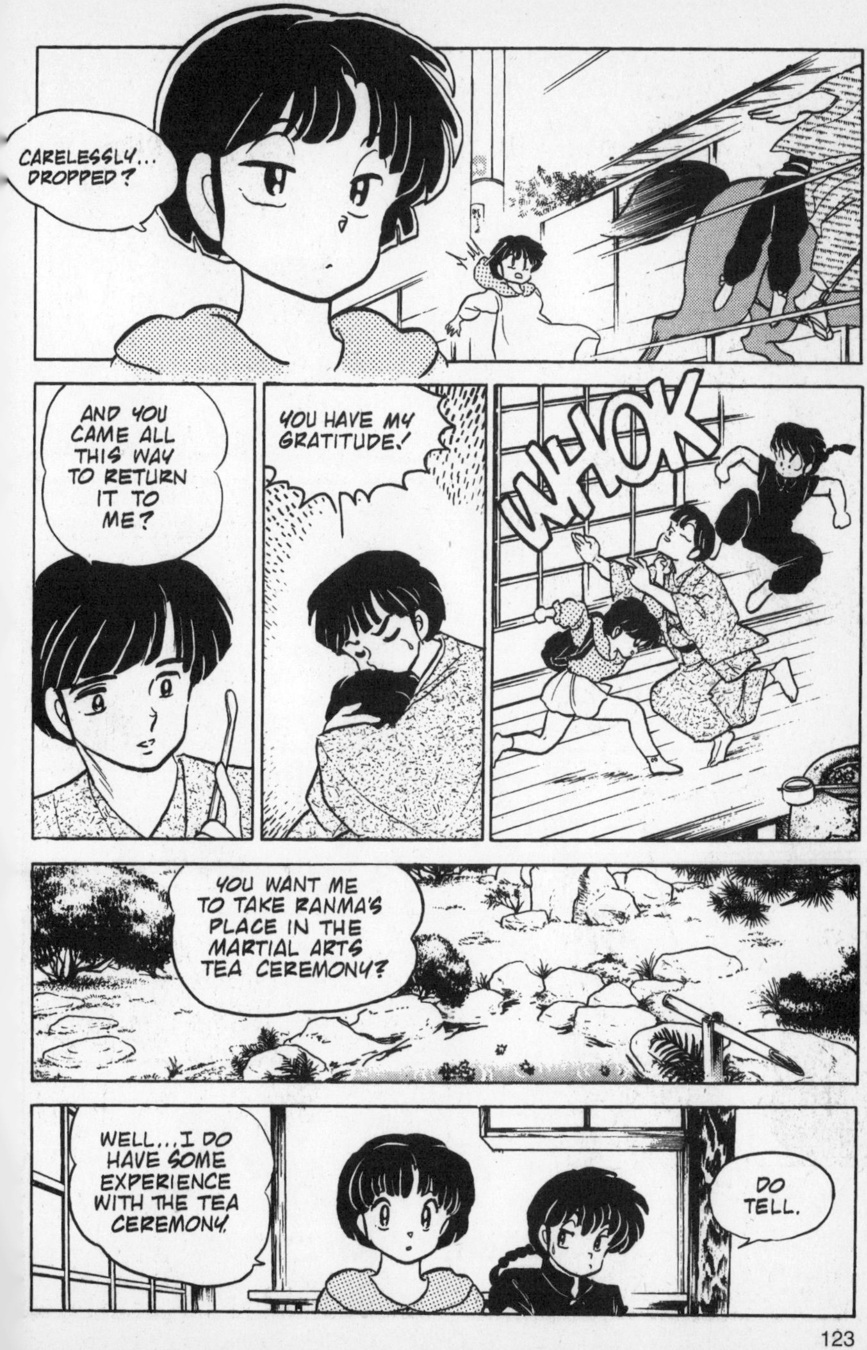
CARELESSLY... DROPPED?
AND YOU CAME ALL THIS WAY TO RETURN IT TO ME?
YOU HAVE MY GRATITUDE!
WHOK
YOU WANT ME TO TAKE RANMA'S PLACE IN THE MARTIAL ARTS TEA CEREMONY?
WELL...I DO HAVE SOME EXPERIENCE WITH THE TEA CEREMONY.
DO TELL.

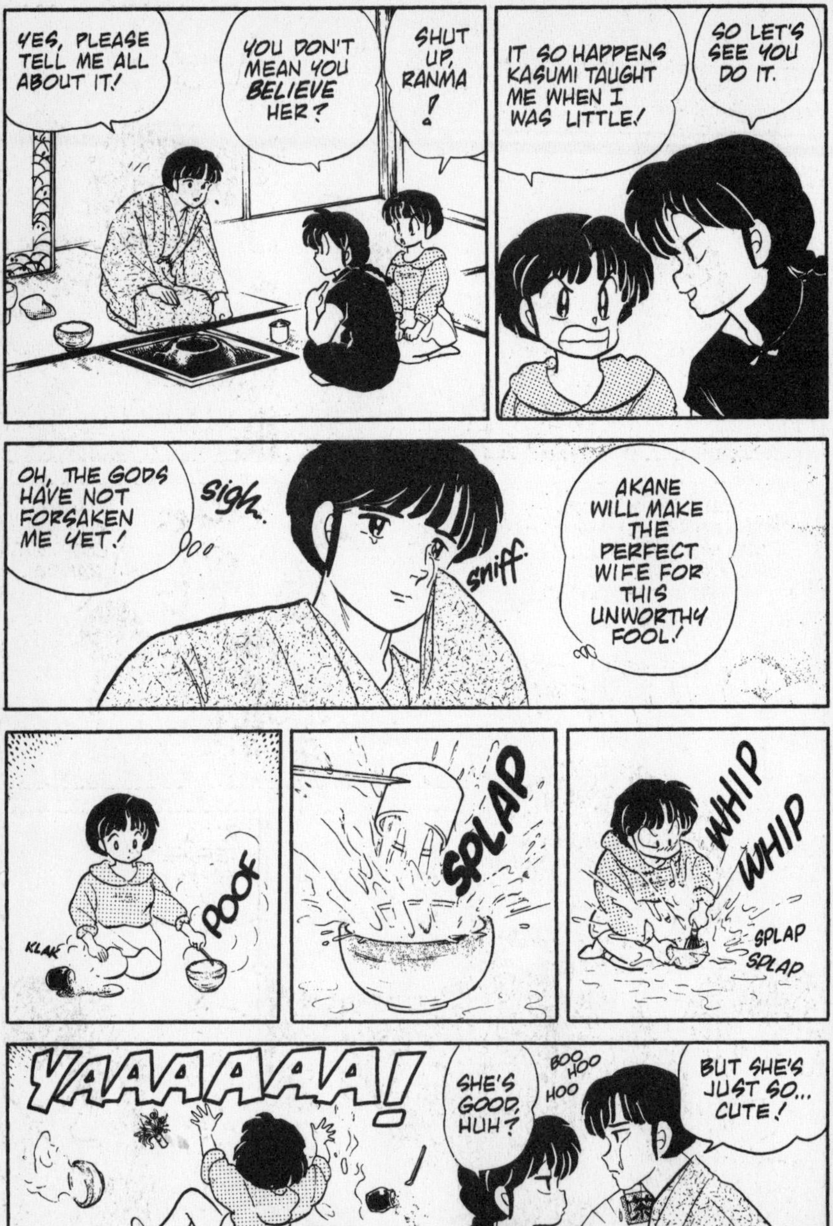
YES, PLEASE TELL ME ALL ABOUT IT!
YOU DON'T MEAN YOU BELIEVE HER?
SHUT UP, RANMA!
IT SO HAPPENS KASUMI TAUGHT ME WHEN I WAS LITTLE!
SO LET'S SEE YOU DO IT.
OH, THE GODS HAVE NOT FORSAKEN ME YET!
sigh...
sniff.
AKANE WILL MAKE THE PERFECT WIFE FOR THIS UNWORTHY FOOL!
KLAK
POOF
SPLAP
WHIP
WHIP
SPLAP
SPLAP
YAAAAAA!
SHE'S GOOD, HUH?
BOO HOO HOO
BUT SHE'S JUST SO... CUTE!

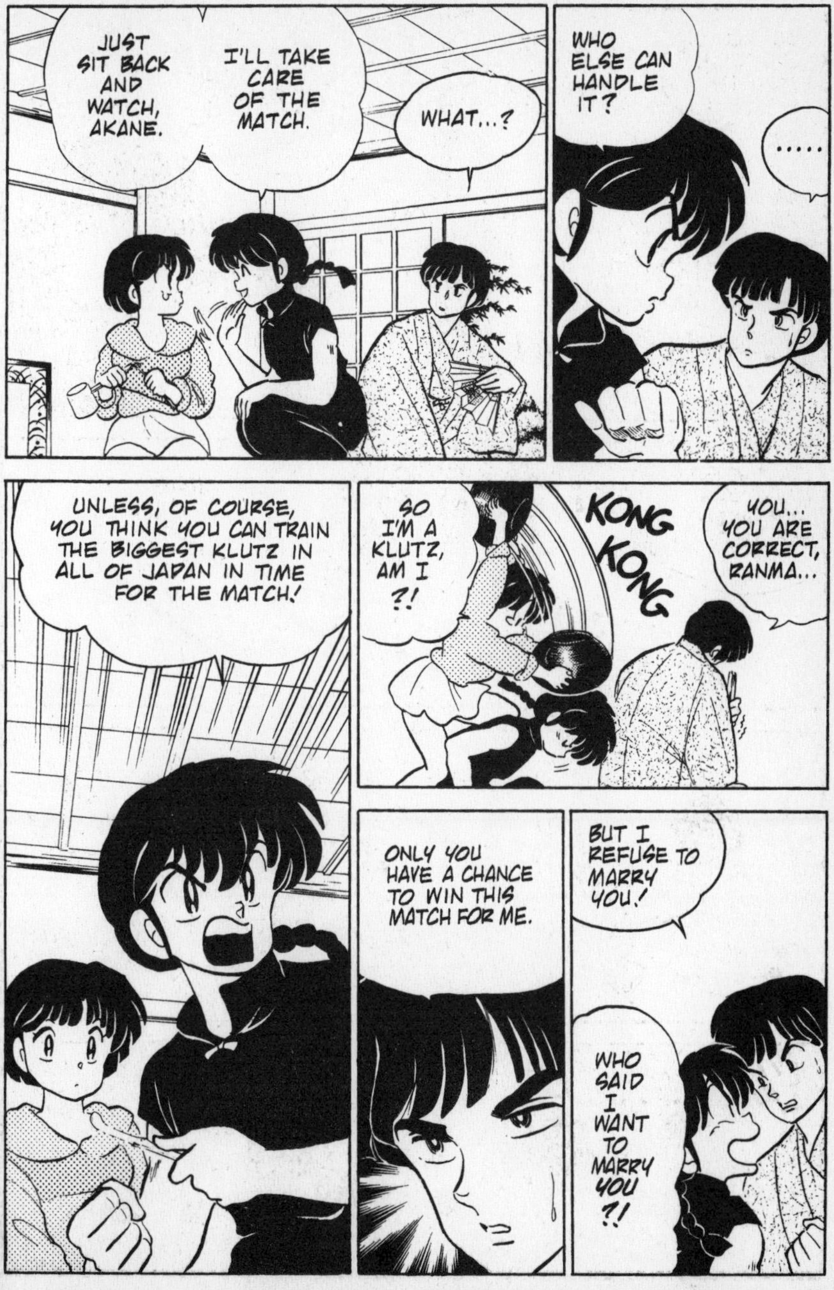
JUST SIT BACK AND WATCH, AKANE.
I'LL TAKE CARE OF THE MATCH.
WHAT...?
WHO ELSE CAN HANDLE IT?
.....
UNLESS, OF COURSE, YOU THINK YOU CAN TRAIN THE BIGGEST KLUTZ IN ALL OF JAPAN IN TIME FOR THE MATCH!
SO I'M A KLUTZ, AM I ?!
KONG KONG
YOU... YOU ARE CORRECT, RANMA...
ONLY YOU HAVE A CHANCE TO WIN THIS MATCH FOR ME.
BUT I REFUSE TO MARRY YOU!
WHO SAID I WANT TO MARRY YOU ?!

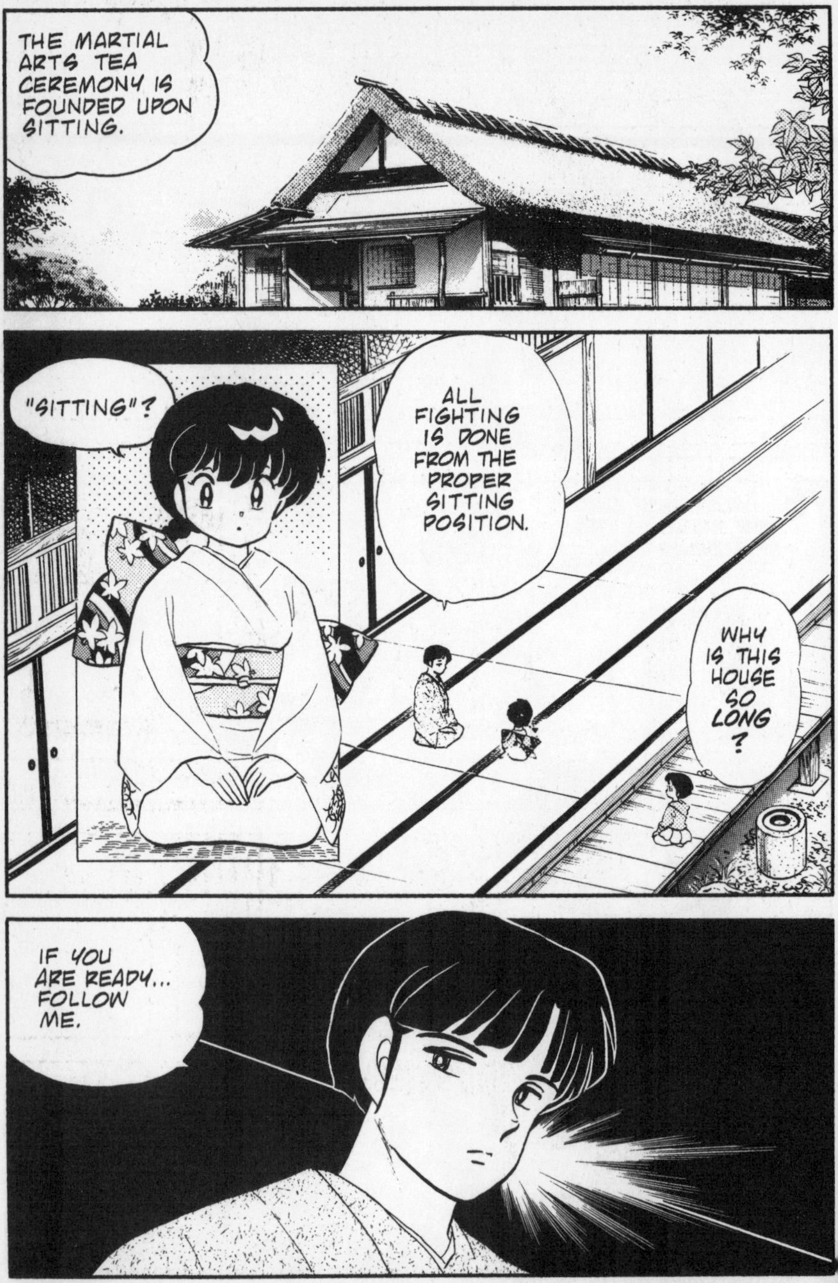
THE MARTIAL ARTS TEA CEREMONY IS FOUNDED UPON SITTING.
"SITTING"?
ALL FIGHTING IS DONE FROM THE PROPER SITTING POSITION.
WHY IS THIS HOUSE SO LONG?
IF YOU ARE READY... FOLLOW ME.

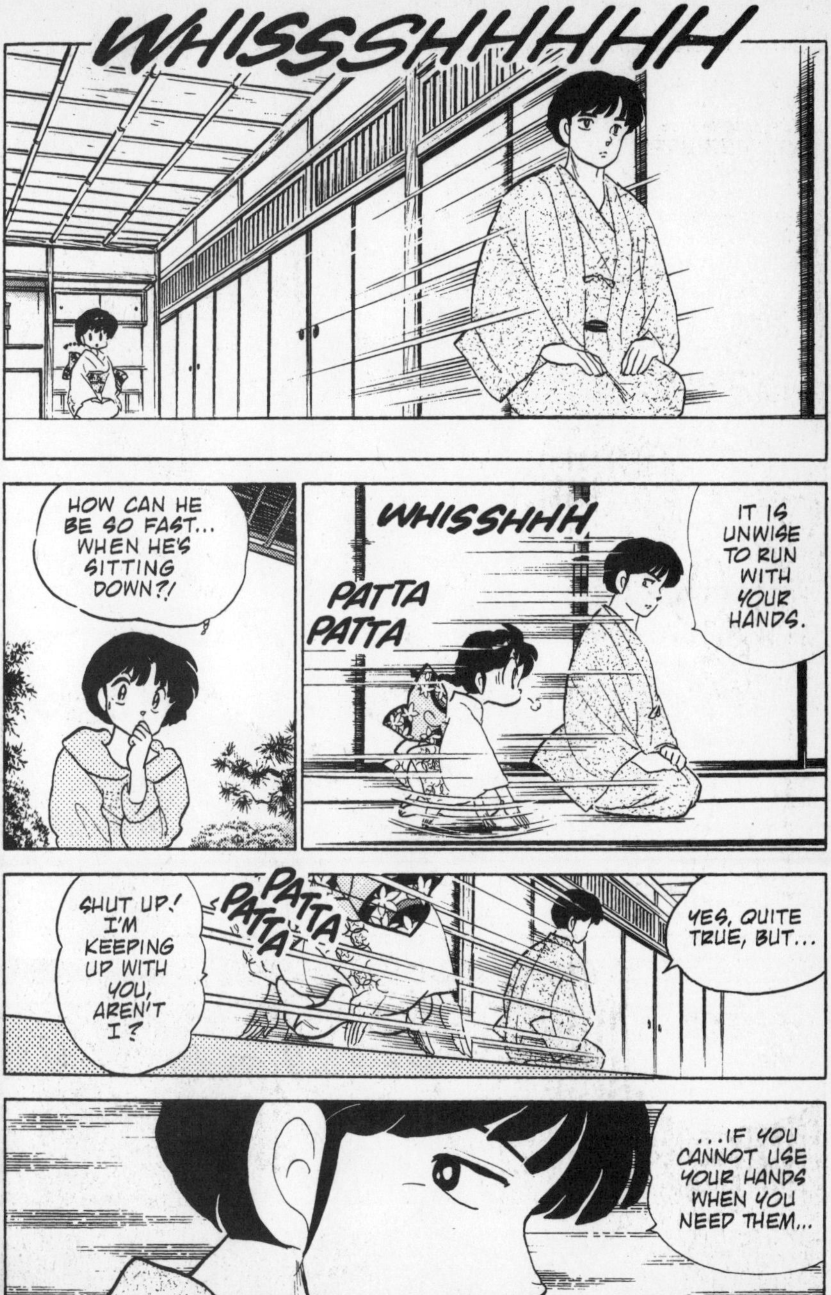
WHISSSHHHHH
HOW CAN HE BE SO FAST... WHEN HE'S SITTING DOWN?!
WHISSHHH
PATTA PATTA
IT IS UNWISE TO RUN WITH YOUR HANDS.
SHUT UP! I'M KEEPING UP WITH YOU, AREN'T I?
PATTA PATTA
YES, QUITE TRUE, BUT...
...IF YOU CANNOT USE YOUR HANDS WHEN YOU NEED THEM...

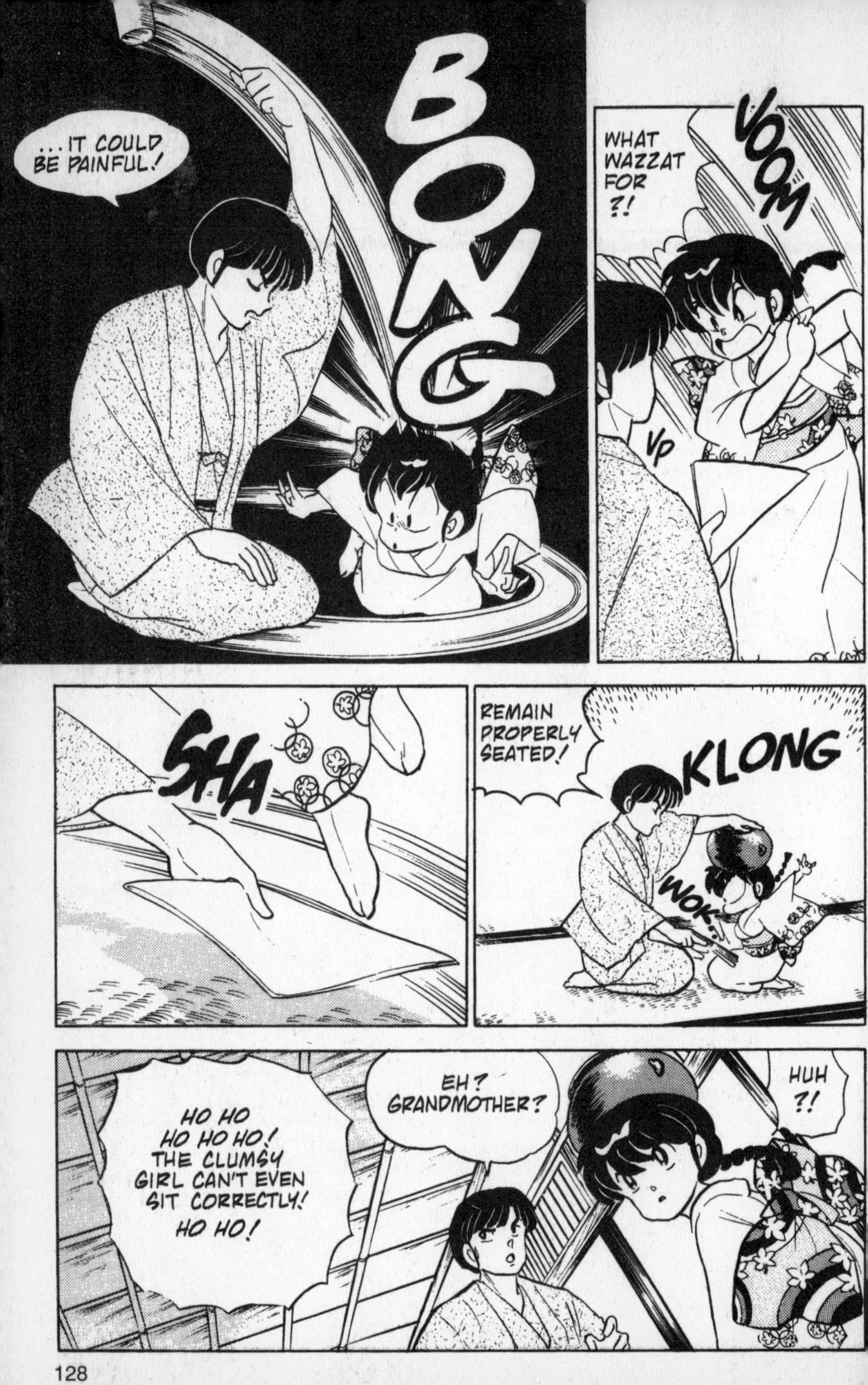
...IT COULD BE PAINFUL!
BONG
WHAT WAZZAT FOR ?!
VOOM
UP
SHA
REMAIN PROPERLY SEATED!
KLONG
WOK
HO HO HO HO HO! THE CLUMSY GIRL CAN'T EVEN SIT CORRECTLY! HO HO!
EH? GRANDMOTHER?
HUH ?!

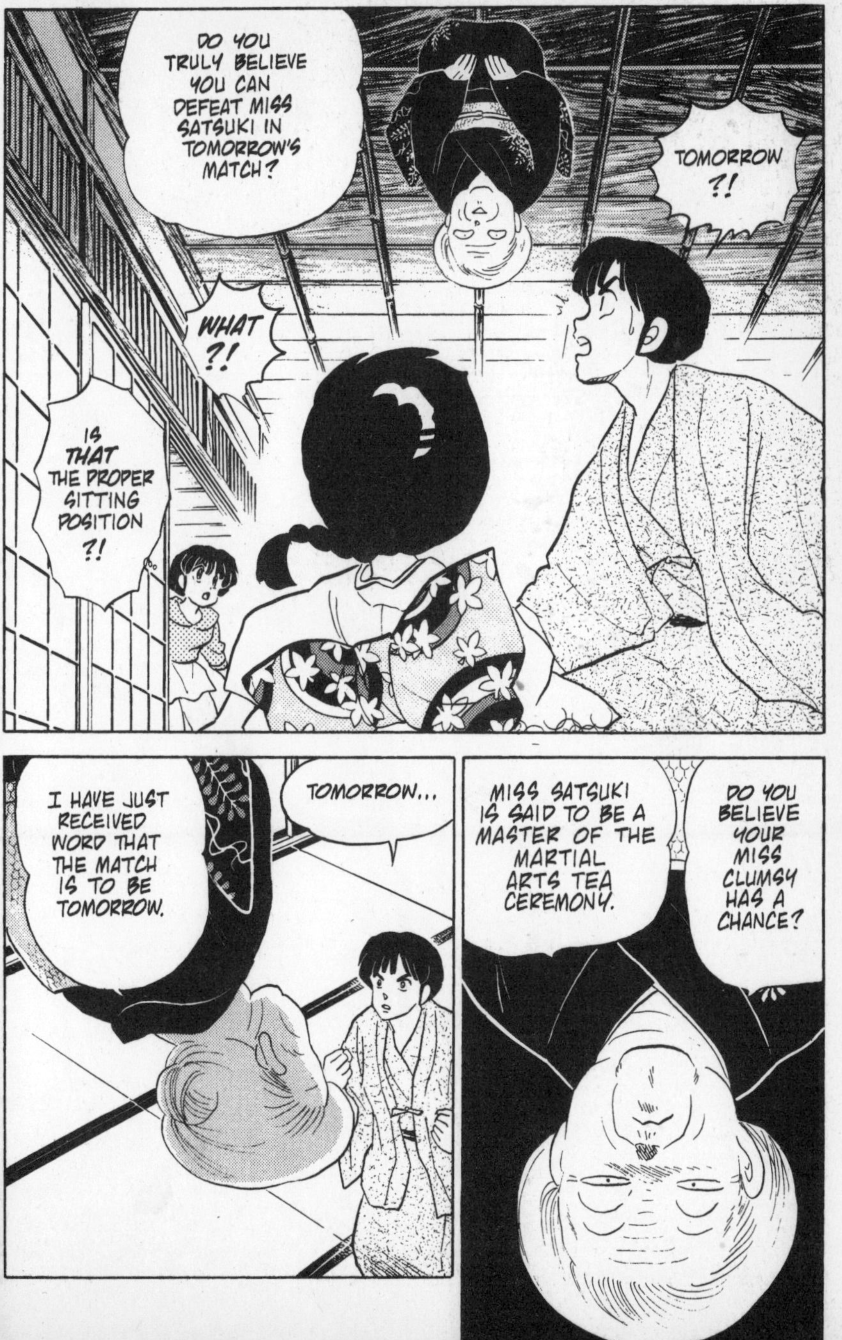
DO YOU TRULY BELIEVE YOU CAN DEFEAT MISS SATSUKI IN TOMORROW'S MATCH?
TOMORROW ?!
WHAT ?!
IS THAT THE PROPER SITTING POSITION ?!
I HAVE JUST RECEIVED WORD THAT THE MATCH IS TO BE TOMORROW.
TOMORROW...
MISS SATSUKI IS SAID TO BE A MASTER OF THE MARTIAL ARTS TEA CEREMONY.
DO YOU BELIEVE YOUR MISS CLUMSY HAS A CHANCE?

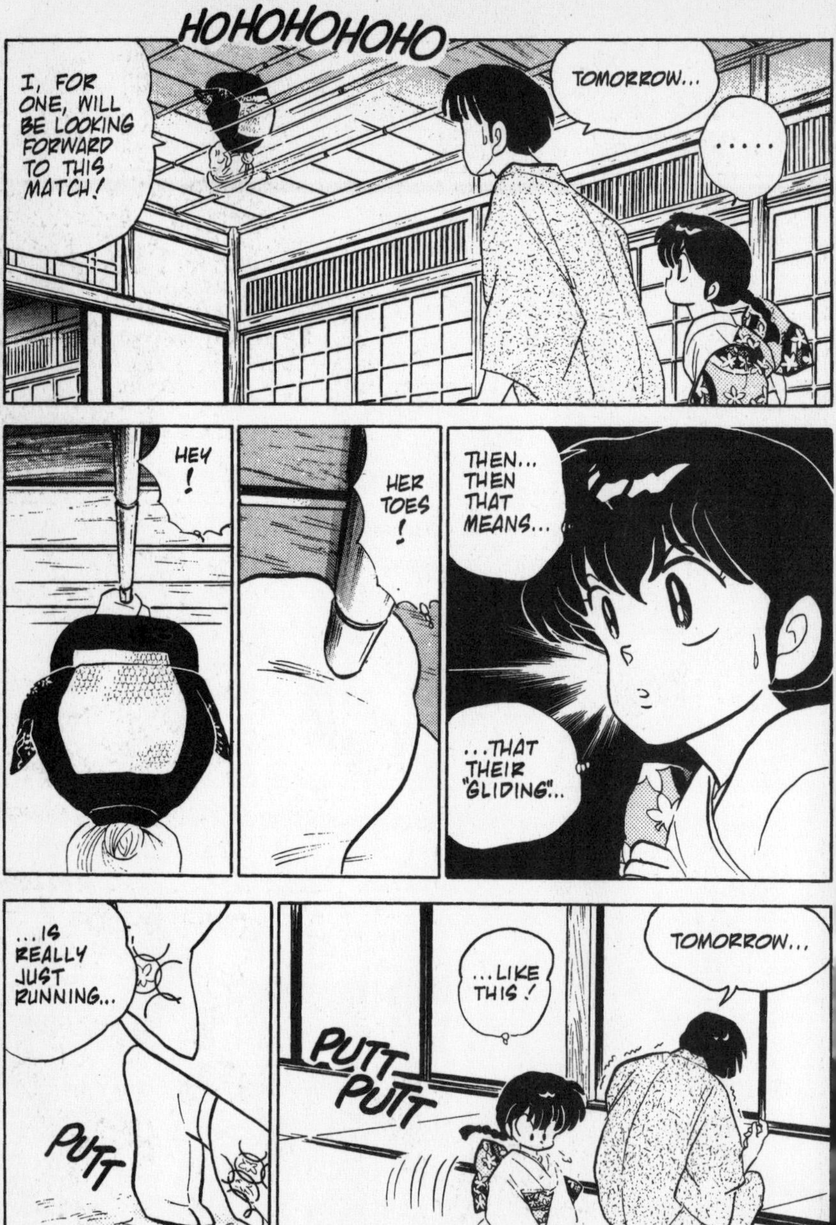
HOHOHOHOHOHO
I, FOR ONE, WILL BE LOOKING FORWARD TO THIS MATCH!
TOMORROW...
.....
HEY!
HER TOES!
THEN... THEN THAT MEANS...
...THAT THEIR "GLIDING"...
...IS REALLY JUST RUNNING...
PUTT
...LIKE THIS!
PUTT-PUTT
TOMORROW...

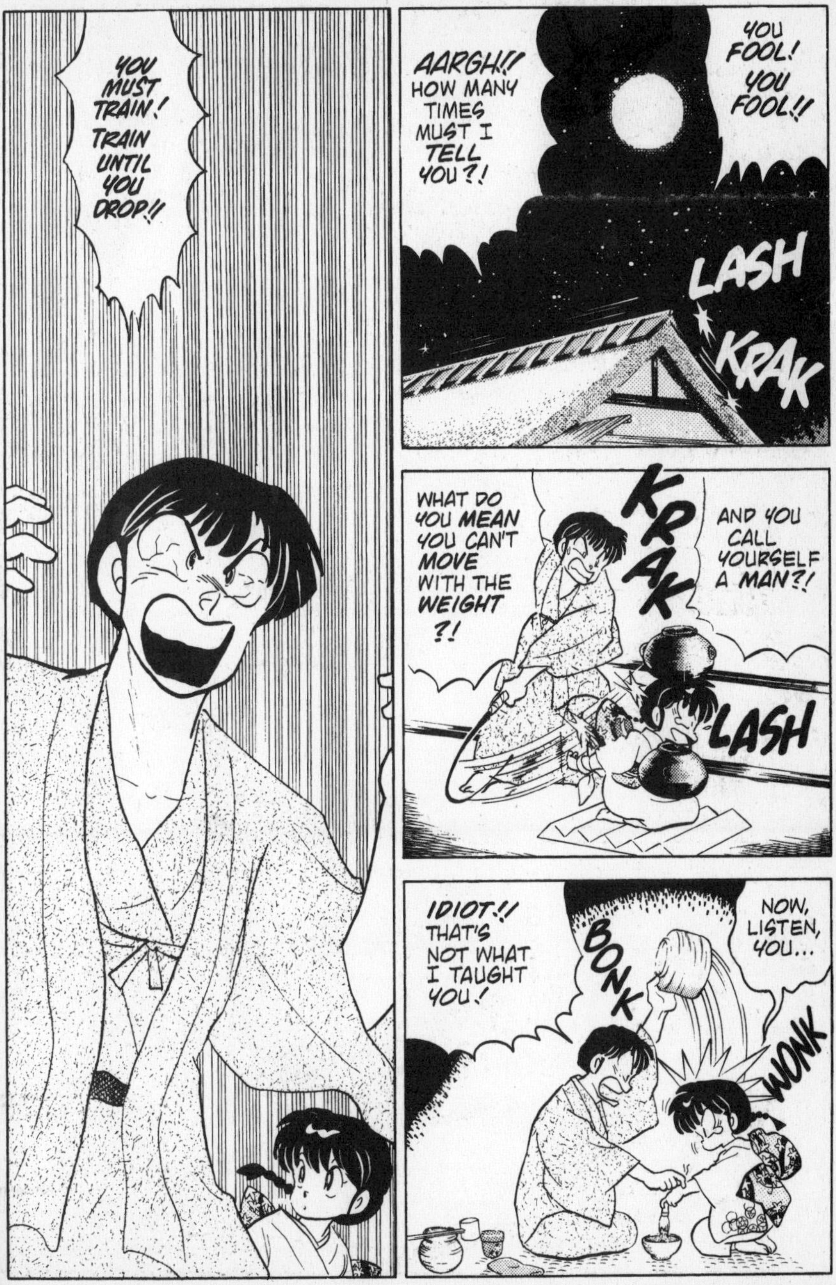
YOU MUST TRAIN! TRAIN UNTIL YOU DROP!!
AARGH!! HOW MANY TIMES MUST I TELL YOU?!
YOU FOOL! YOU FOOL!!
LASH
KRAK
WHAT DO YOU MEAN YOU CAN'T MOVE WITH THE WEIGHT?!
KRAK
AND YOU CALL YOURSELF A MAN?!
LASH
IDIOT!! THAT'S NOT WHAT I TAUGHT YOU!
BONK
NOW, LISTEN, YOU...
WONK

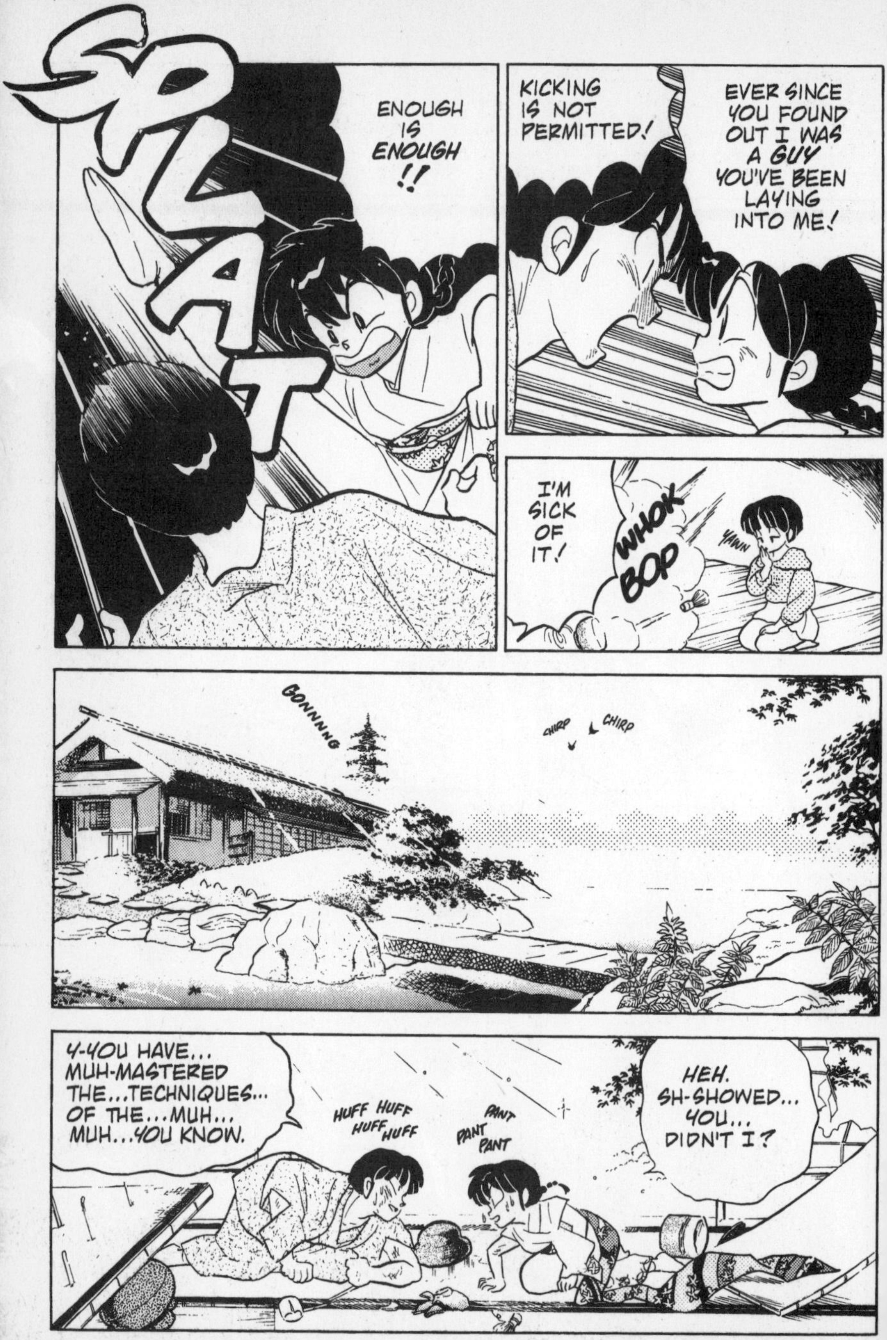

SPLAT
ENOUGH IS ENOUGH!!
KICKING IS NOT PERMITTED!
EVER SINCE YOU FOUND OUT I WAS A GUY YOU'VE BEEN LAYING INTO ME!
I'M SICK OF IT!
WHOK
BOP
YAWN
GONNNNG
CHIRP
CHIRP
Y-YOU HAVE... MUH-MASTERED THE...TECHNIQUES... OF THE...MUH... MUH...YOU KNOW.
HUFF HUFF HUFF HUFF
PANT PANT PANT
HEH. SH-SHOWED... YOU... DIDN'T I?

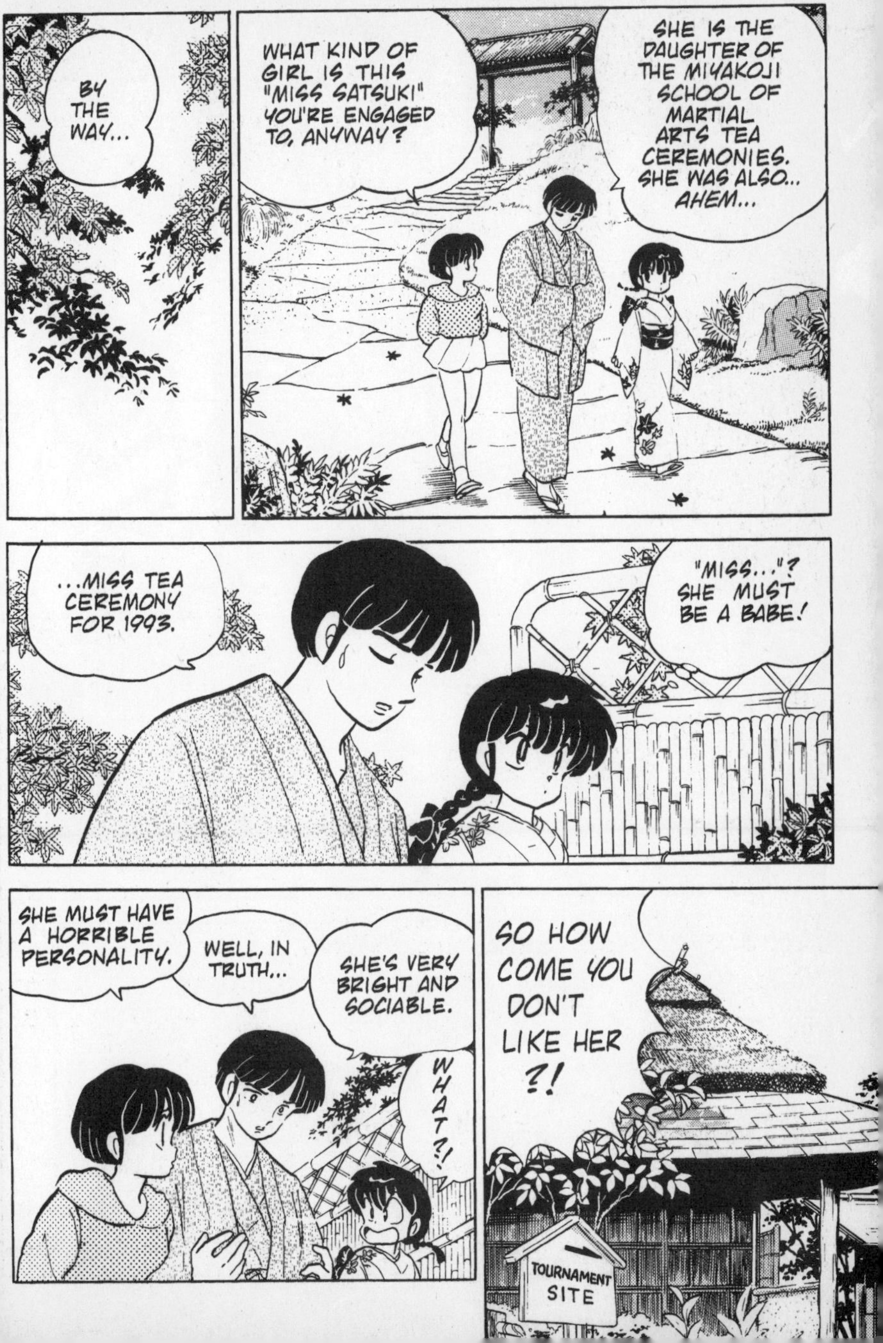
BY THE WAY...
WHAT KIND OF GIRL IS THIS "MISS SATSUKI" YOU'RE ENGAGED TO, ANYWAY?
SHE IS THE DAUGHTER OF THE MIYAKOJI SCHOOL OF MARTIAL ARTS TEA CEREMONIES. SHE WAS ALSO... AHEM...
...MISS TEA CEREMONY FOR 1993.
"MISS..."? SHE MUST BE A BABE!
SHE MUST HAVE A HORRIBLE PERSONALITY.
WELL, IN TRUTH...
SHE'S VERY BRIGHT AND SOCIABLE.
WHAT?!
SO HOW COME YOU DON'T LIKE HER ?!
TOURNAMENT SITE

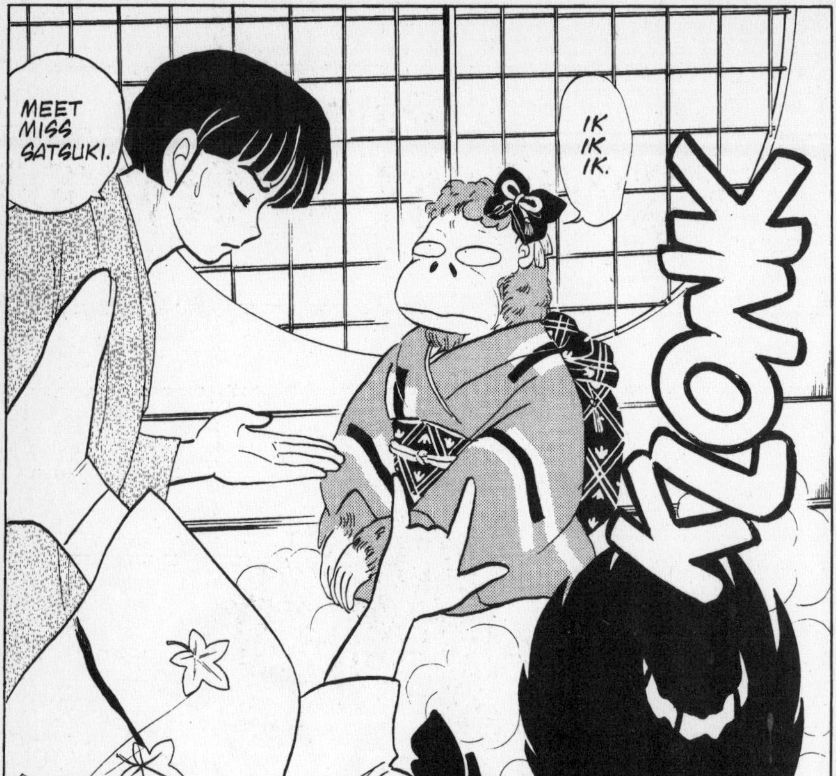
MEET MISS SATSUKI.
IK IK IK.
KLONK

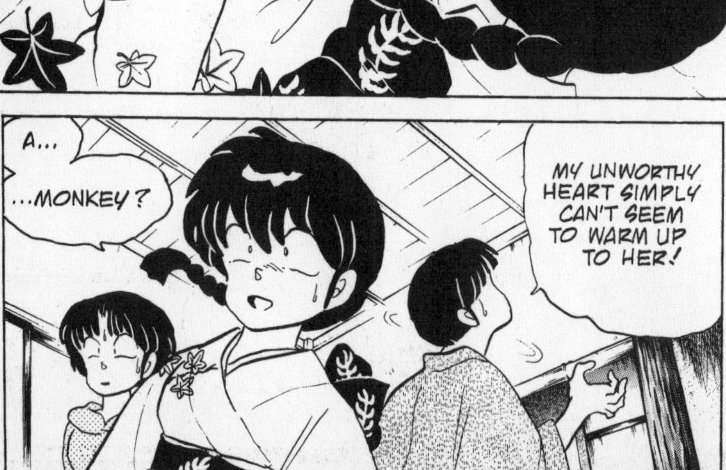
A...
...MONKEY?
MY UNWORTHY HEART SIMPLY CAN'T SEEM TO WARM UP TO HER!

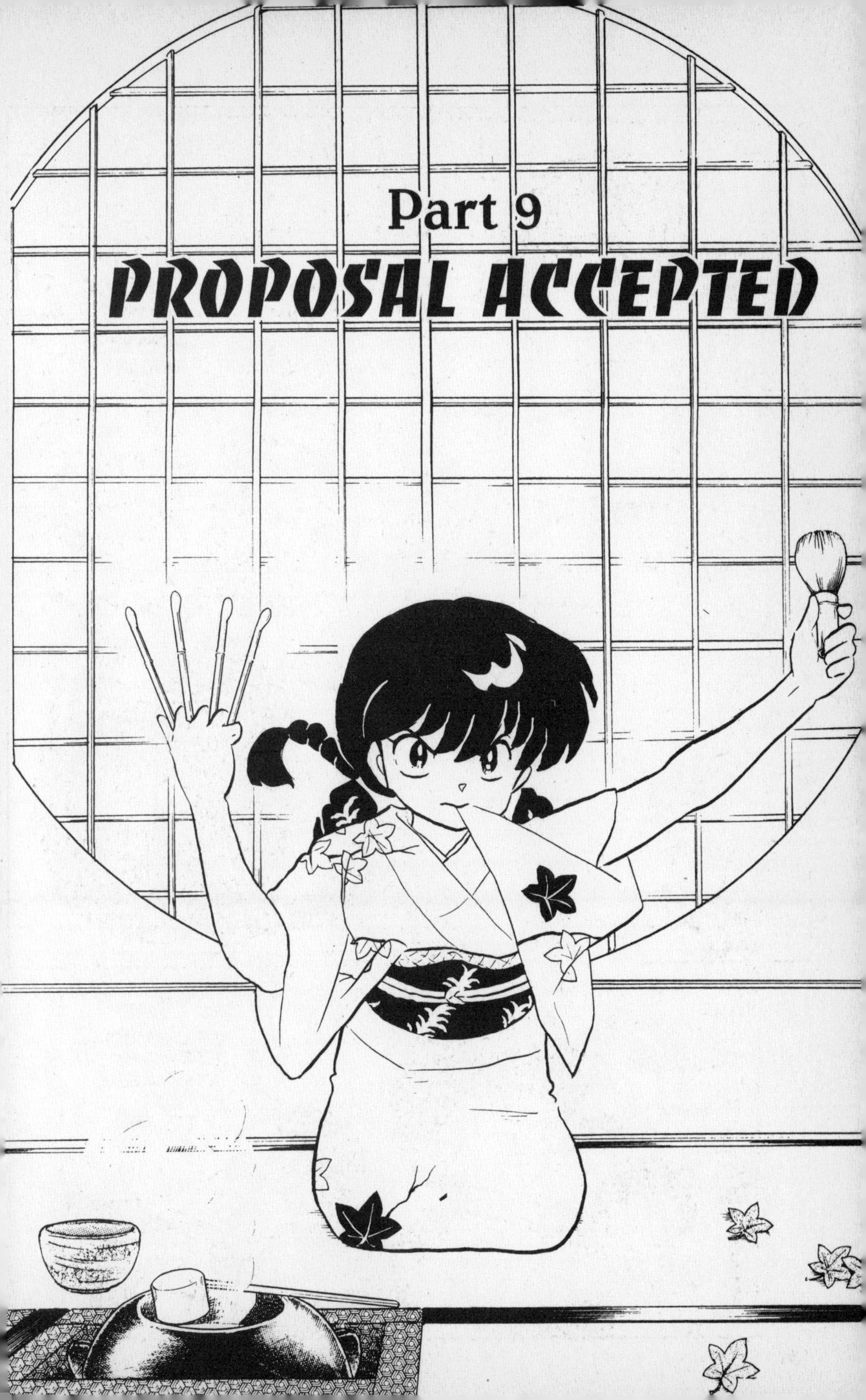
Part 9
PROPOSAL ACCEPTED

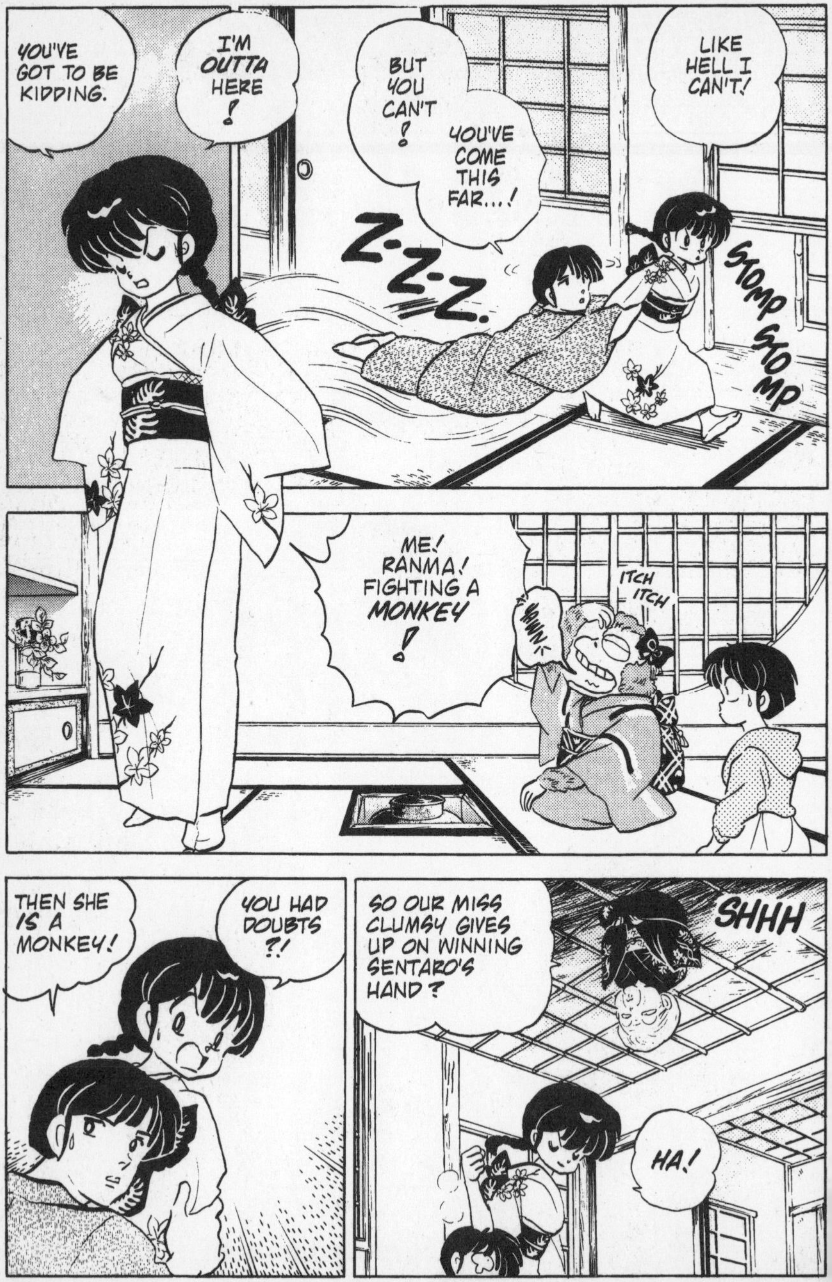

YOU'VE GOT TO BE KIDDING.
I'M OUTTA HERE!
BUT YOU CAN'T!
YOU'VE COME THIS FAR...!
Z-Z-Z.
LIKE HELL I CAN'T!
STOMP STOMP
ME! RANMA! FIGHTING A MONKEY!
ITCH ITCH
THEN SHE IS A MONKEY!
YOU HAD DOUBTS?!
SO OUR MISS CLUMSY GIVES UP ON WINNING SENTARO'S HAND?
SHHH
HA!

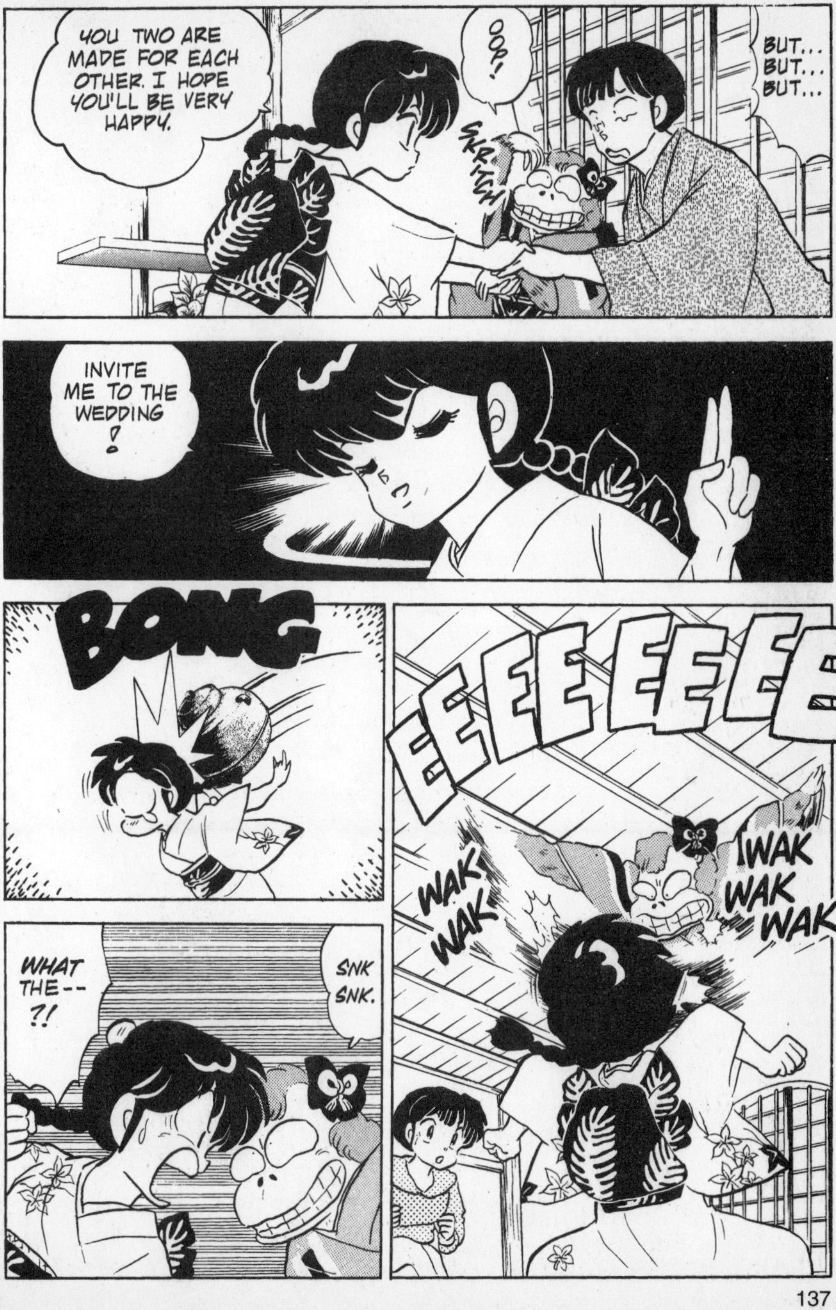
YOU TWO ARE MADE FOR EACH OTHER. I HOPE YOU'LL BE VERY HAPPY.
OOP!
SKRITCH
BUT... BUT... BUT...
INVITE ME TO THE WEDDING!
BONG
WHAT THE--?!
SNK SNK.
EEEEEEEE
WAK WAK
WAK WAK WAK

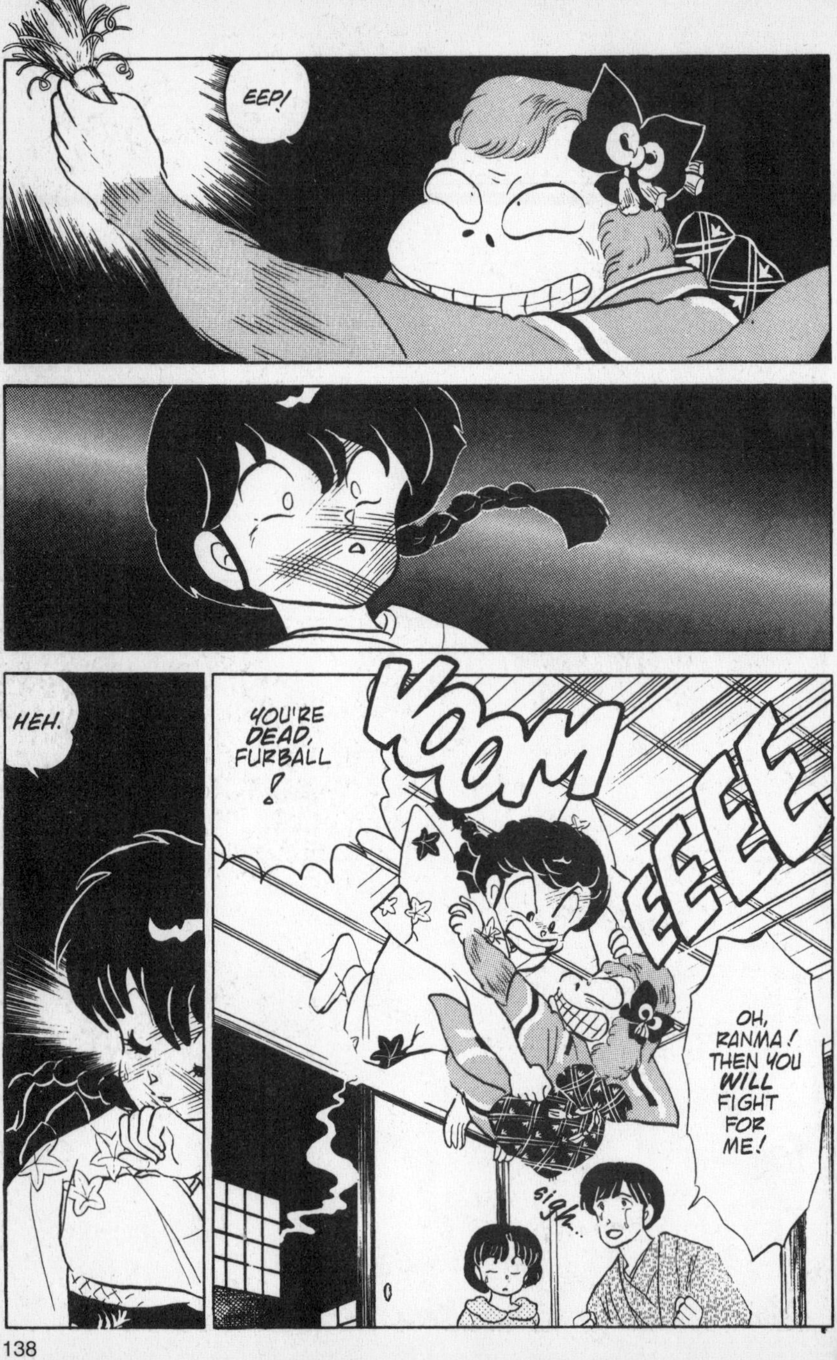
EEP!
HEH.
YOU'RE DEAD, FURBALL!
VOOM
EEEE
OH, RANMA! THEN YOU WILL FIGHT FOR ME!
sigh...

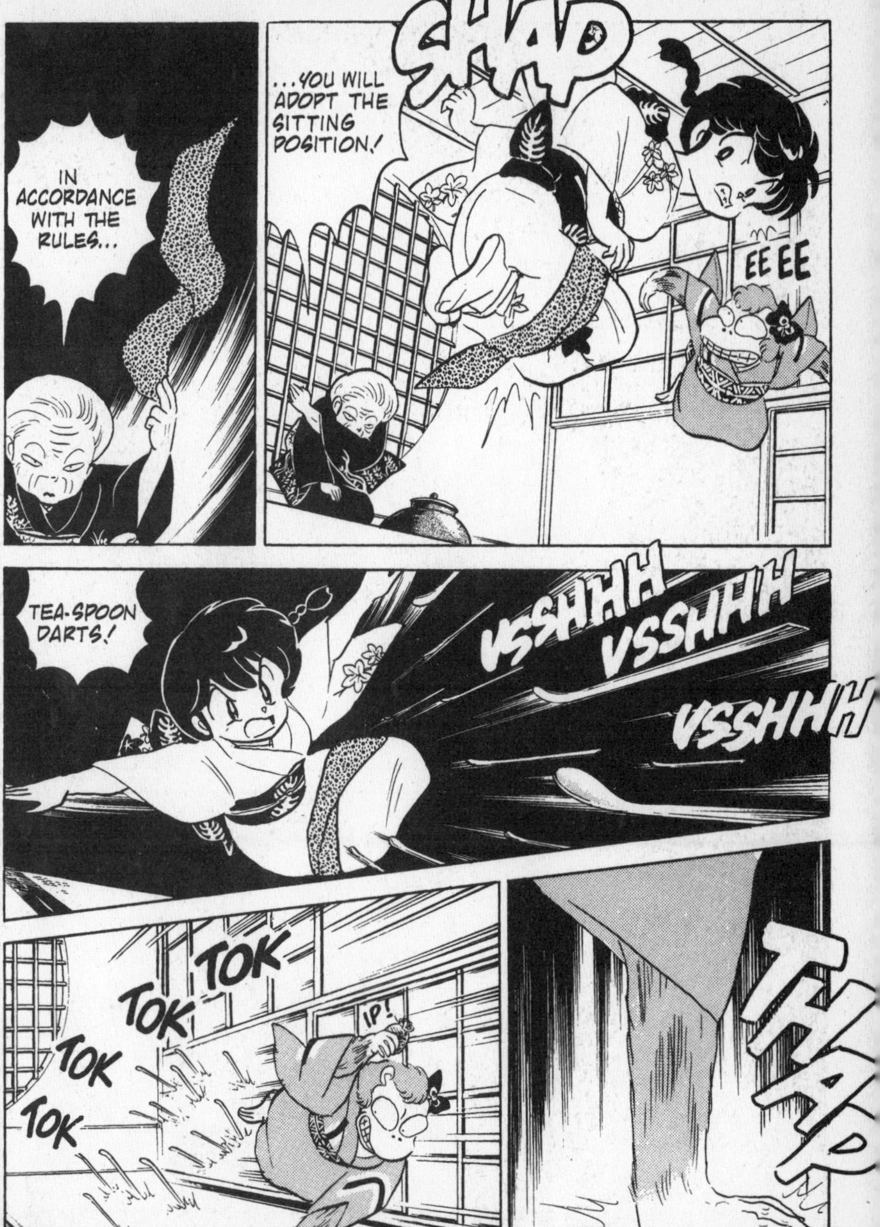
IN ACCORDANCE WITH THE RULES...
SHAD
...YOU WILL ADOPT THE SITTING POSITION!
EE EE
TEA-SPOON DARTS!
VSSHHH
VSSHHH
VSSHHH
TOK
TOK
TOK
TOK
IP!
THAP

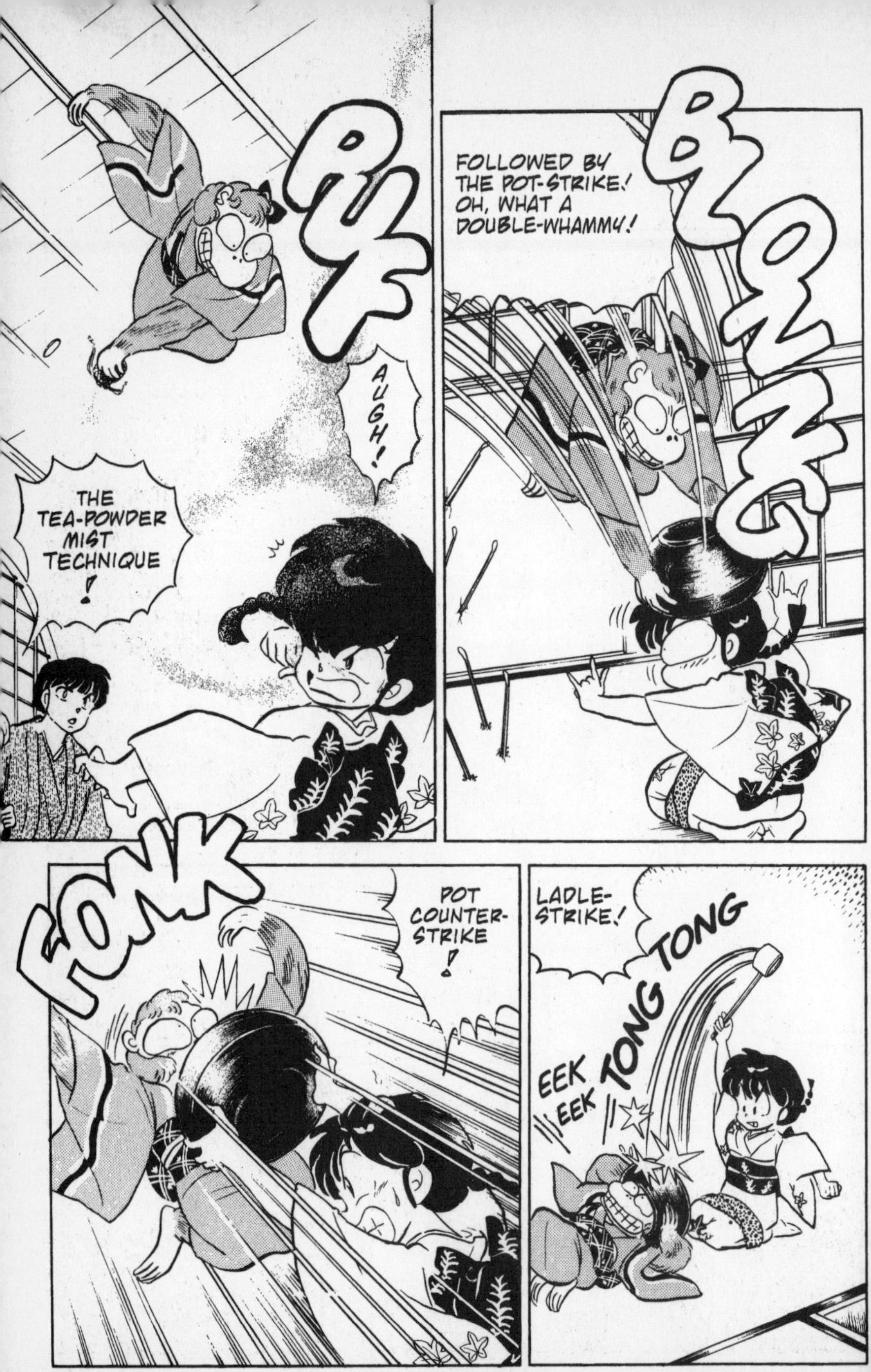
PUF
AUGH!
THE TEA-POWDER MIST TECHNIQUE!
BLONNG
FOLLOWED BY THE POT-STRIKE! OH, WHAT A DOUBLE-WHAMMY!
FONK
POT COUNTER-STRIKE!
LADLE-STRIKE!
TONG TONG
EEK EEK TONG

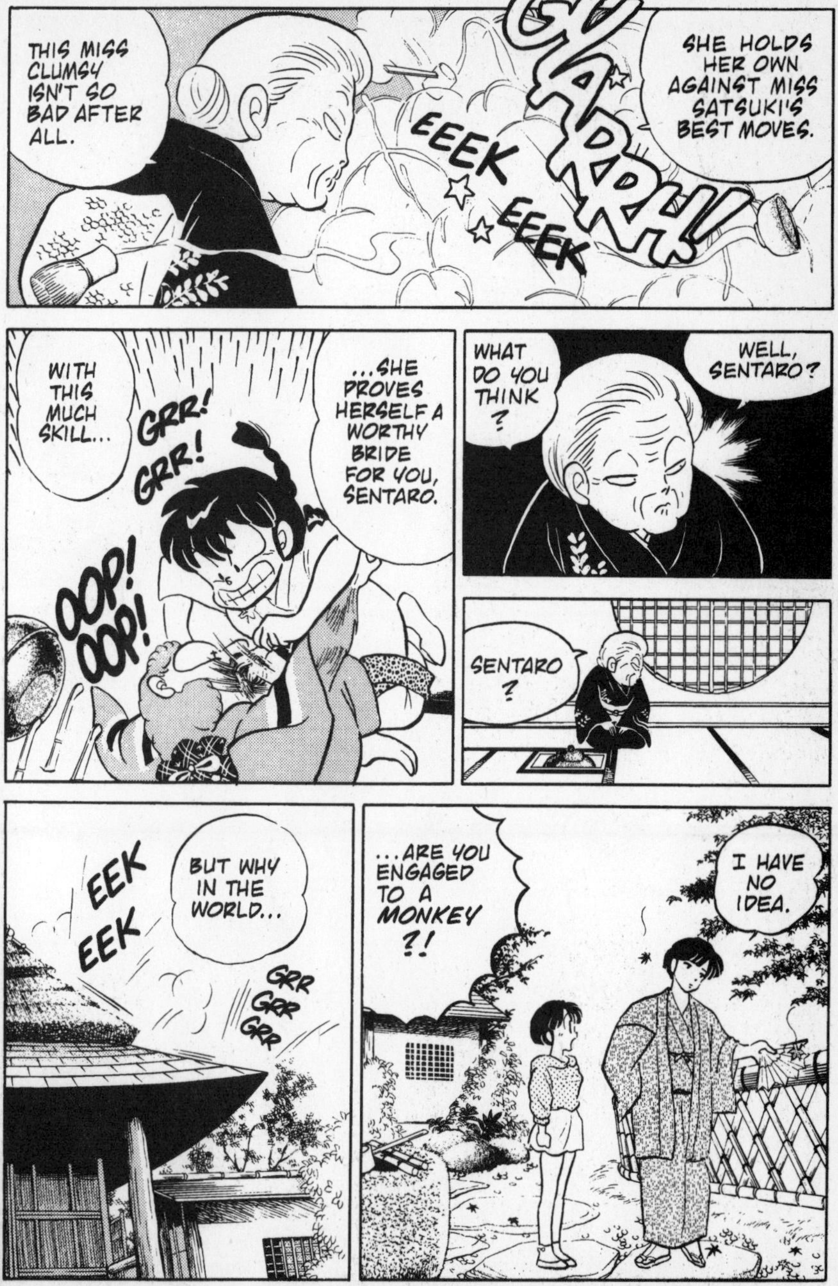
THIS MISS CLUMSY ISN'T SO BAD AFTER ALL.
GYAARH!!
EEEK
EEEK
SHE HOLDS HER OWN AGAINST MISS SATSUKI'S BEST MOVES.
WITH THIS MUCH SKILL...
GRR! GRR!
...SHE PROVES HERSELF A WORTHY BRIDE FOR YOU, SENTARO.
OOP! OOP!
WHAT DO YOU THINK ?
WELL, SENTARO?
SENTARO ?
EEK EEK
BUT WHY IN THE WORLD...
GRR GRR GRR
...ARE YOU ENGAGED TO A *MONKEY* ?!
I HAVE NO IDEA.

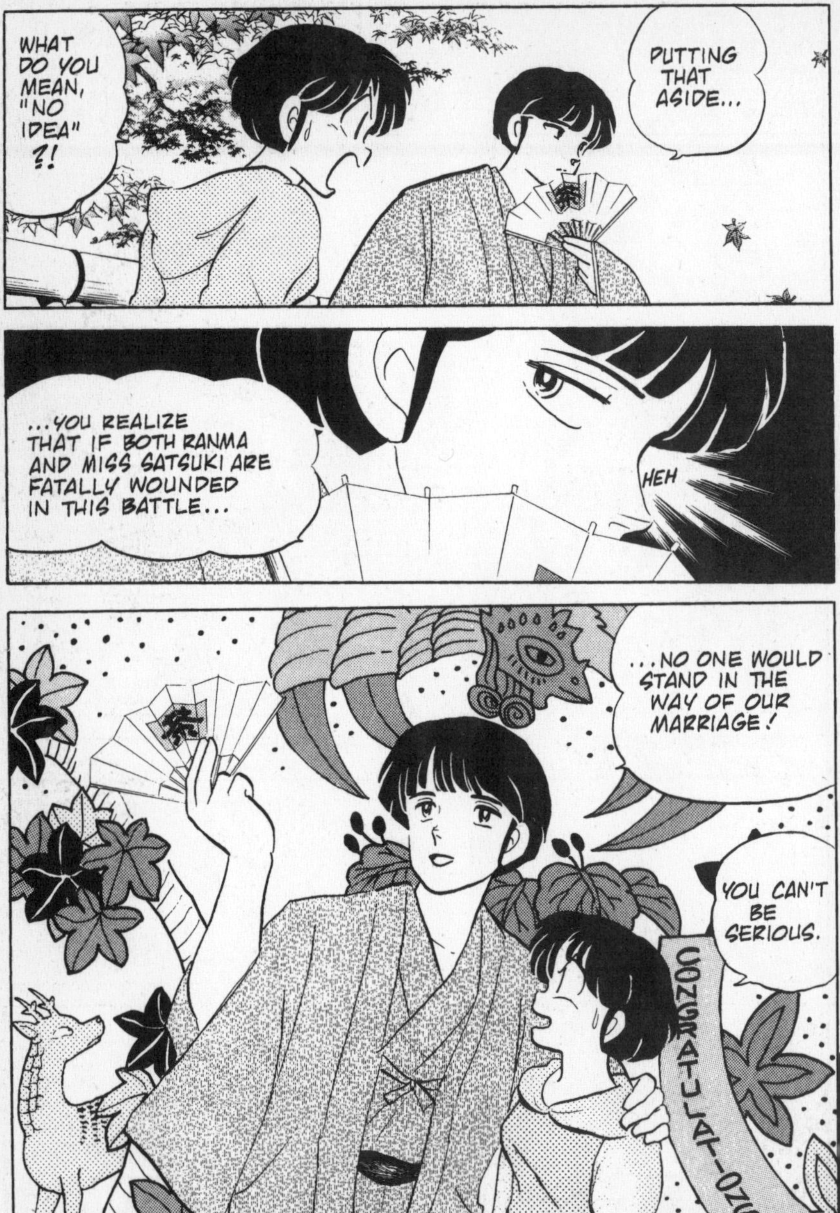
WHAT DO YOU MEAN, "NO IDEA" ?!
PUTTING THAT ASIDE...
...YOU REALIZE THAT IF BOTH RANMA AND MISS SATSUKI ARE FATALLY WOUNDED IN THIS BATTLE...
HEH
...NO ONE WOULD STAND IN THE WAY OF OUR MARRIAGE!
CONGRATULATIONS
YOU CAN'T BE SERIOUS.

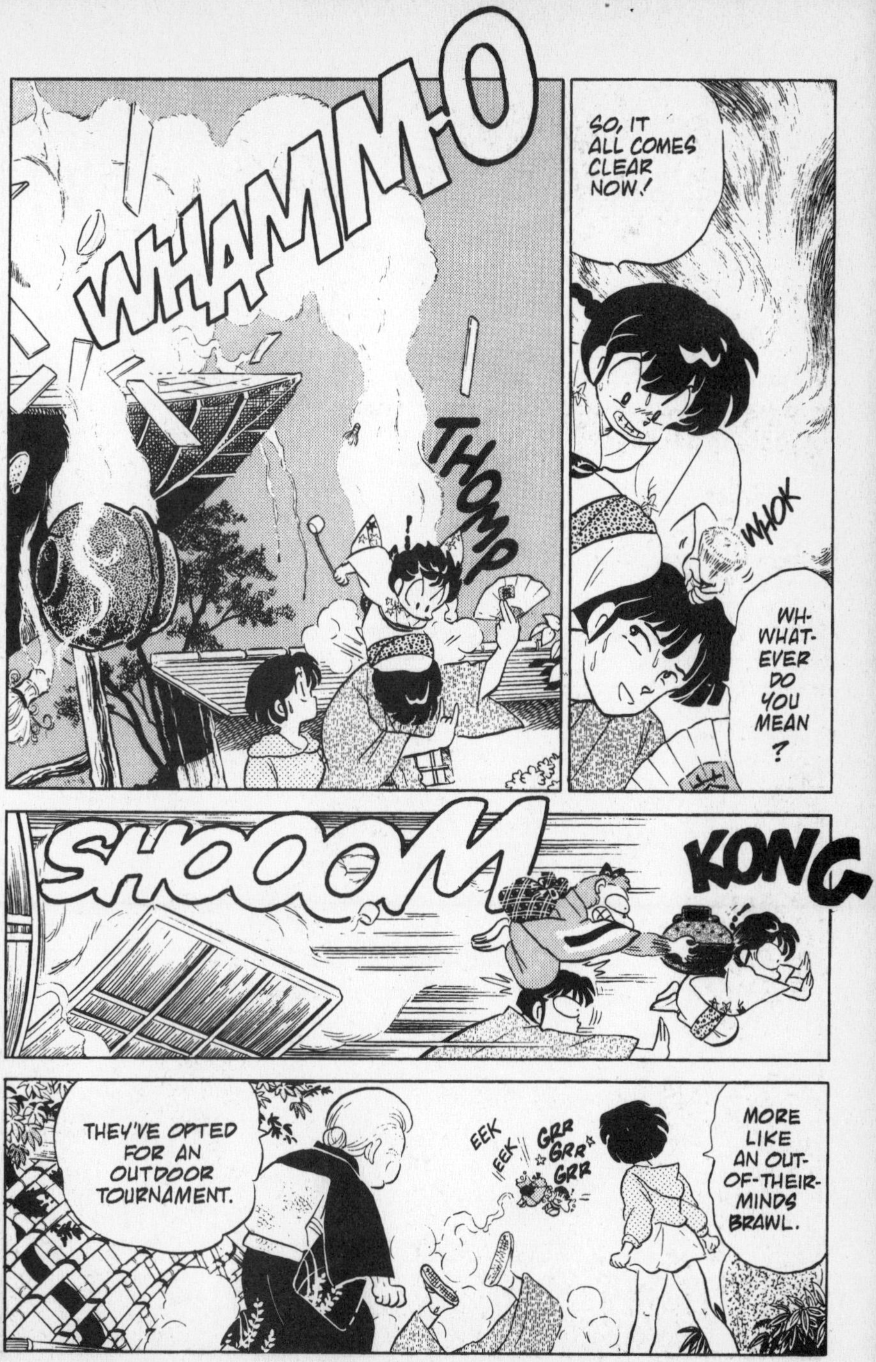
WHAMMO
THOMP
SO, IT ALL COMES CLEAR NOW!
WHOK
WH-WHAT-EVER DO YOU MEAN?
SHOOOM
KONG
THEY'VE OPTED FOR AN OUTDOOR TOURNAMENT.
EEK
EEK
GRR GRR GRR
MORE LIKE AN OUT-OF-THEIR-MINDS BRAWL.

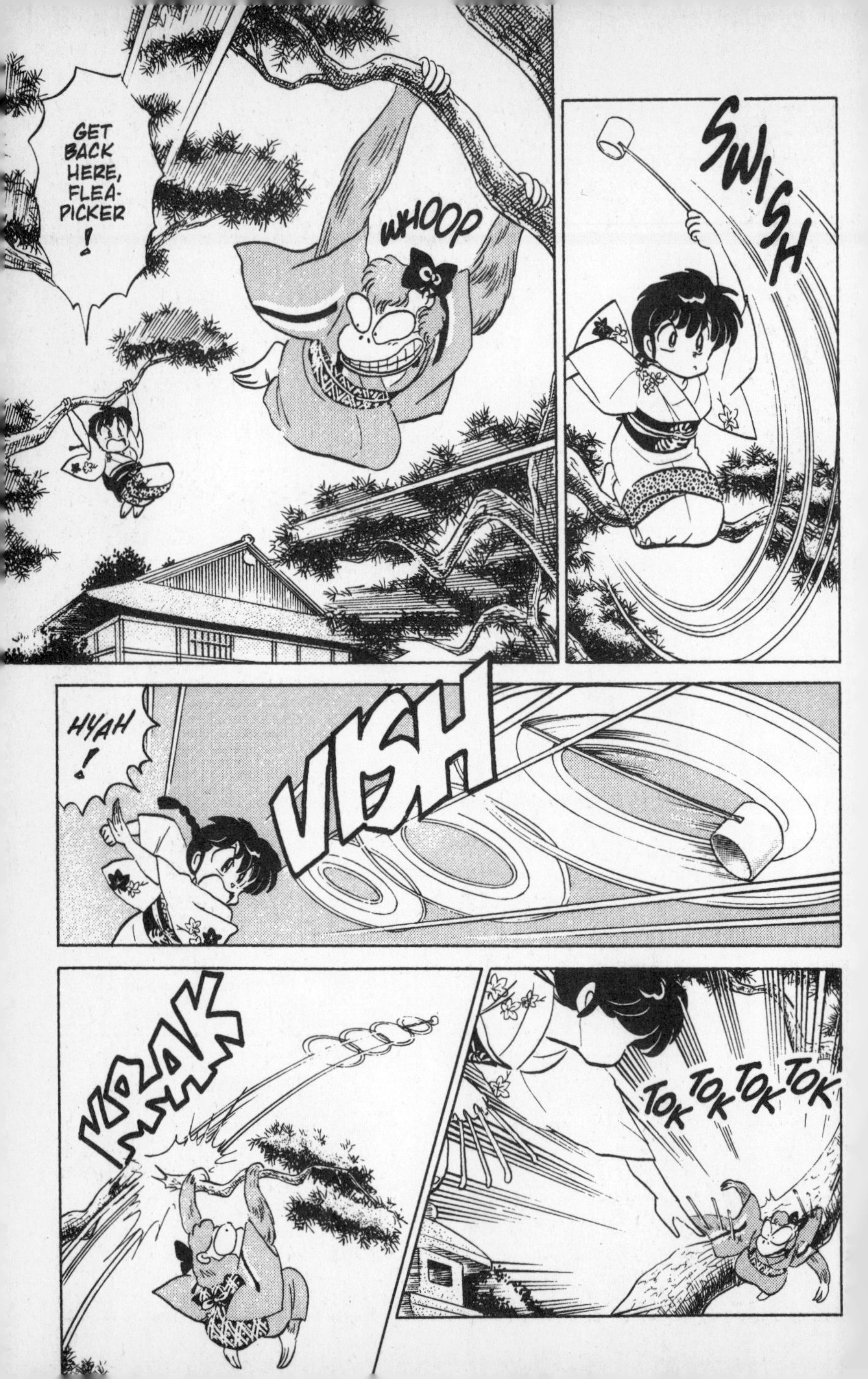
GET BACK HERE, FLEA-PICKER!
WHOOP
SWISH
HYAH!
VISH
KRAK
TOK TOK TOK TOK

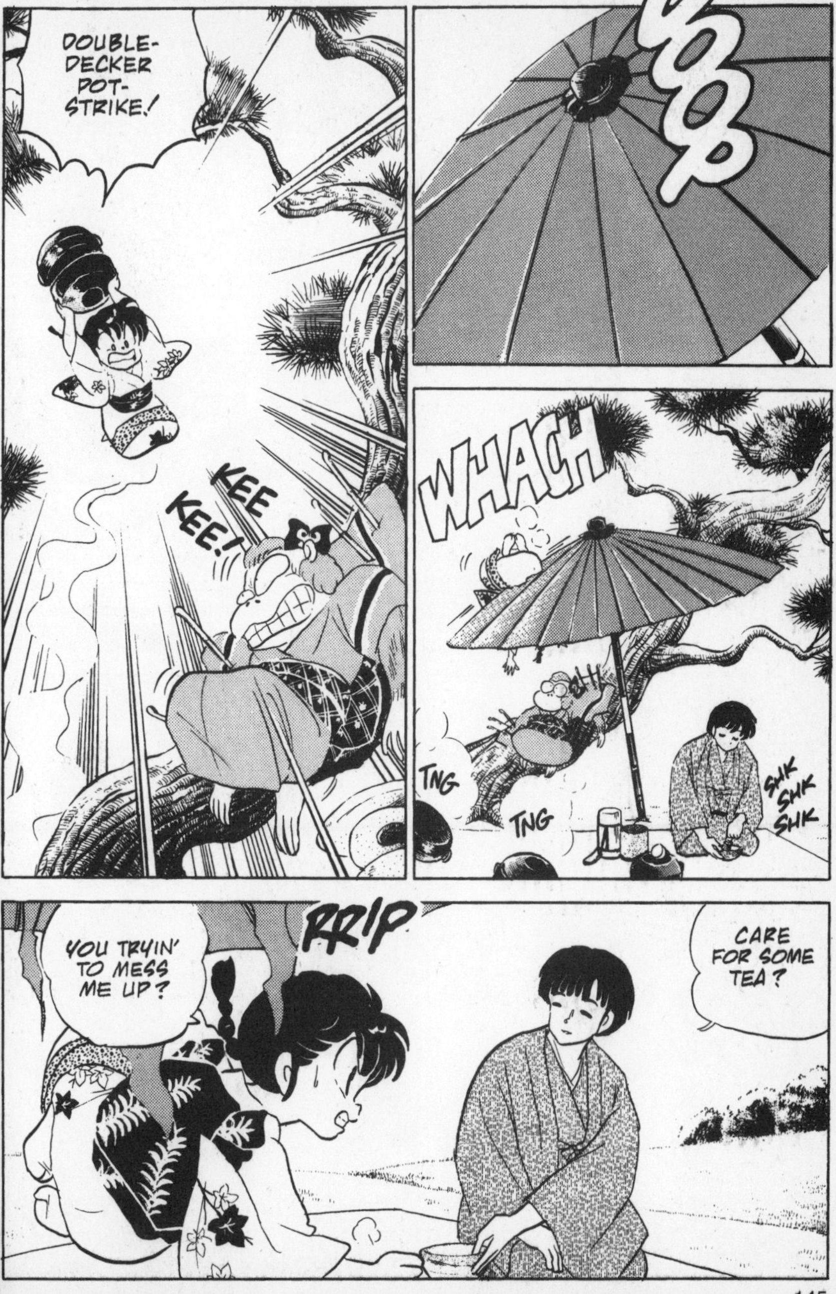
DOUBLE-DECKER POT-STRIKE!
KEE KEE!
YOOP
WHACH
TNG
TNG
SHK SHK SHK
YOU TRYIN' TO MESS ME UP?
RRIP
CARE FOR SOME TEA?

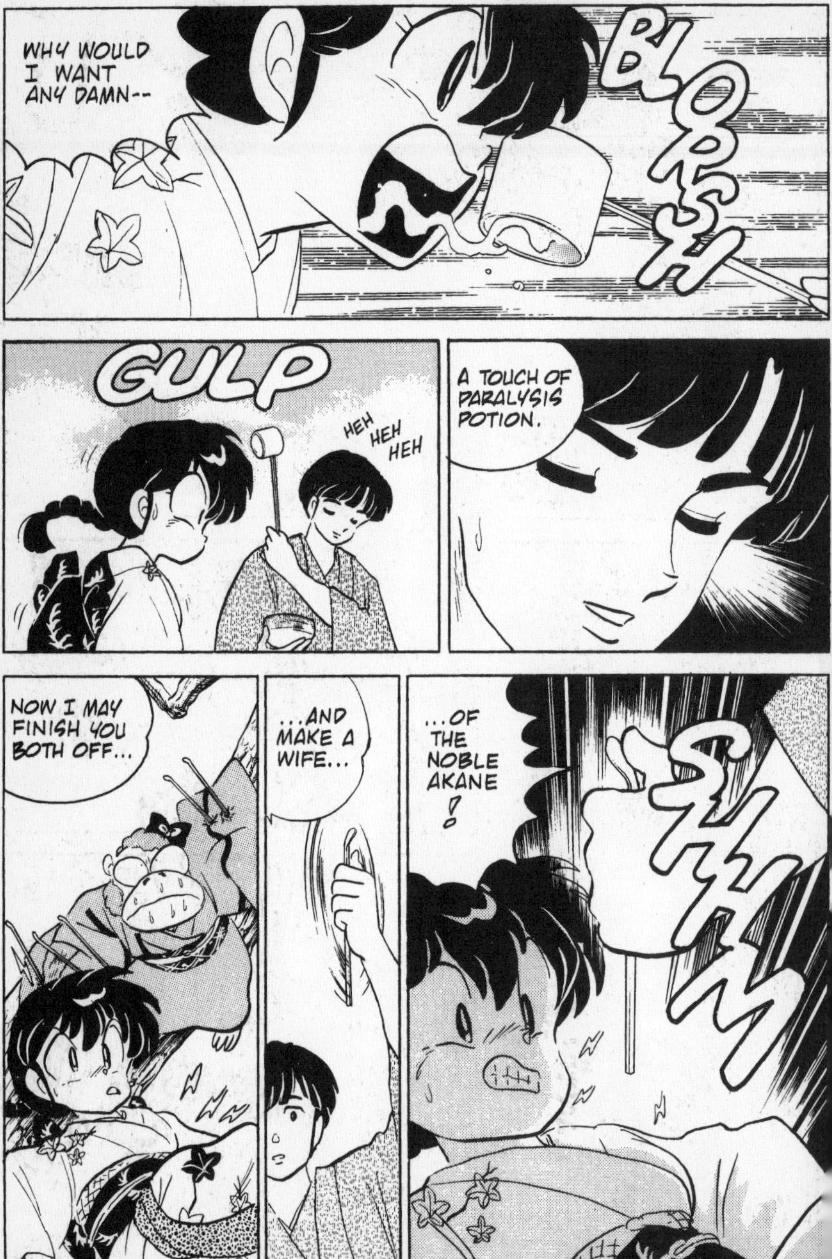
WHY WOULD I WANT ANY DAMN--
BLORSH
GULP
HEH HEH HEH
A TOUCH OF PARALYSIS POTION.
NOW I MAY FINISH YOU BOTH OFF...
...AND MAKE A WIFE...
...OF THE NOBLE AKANE!
SHHM

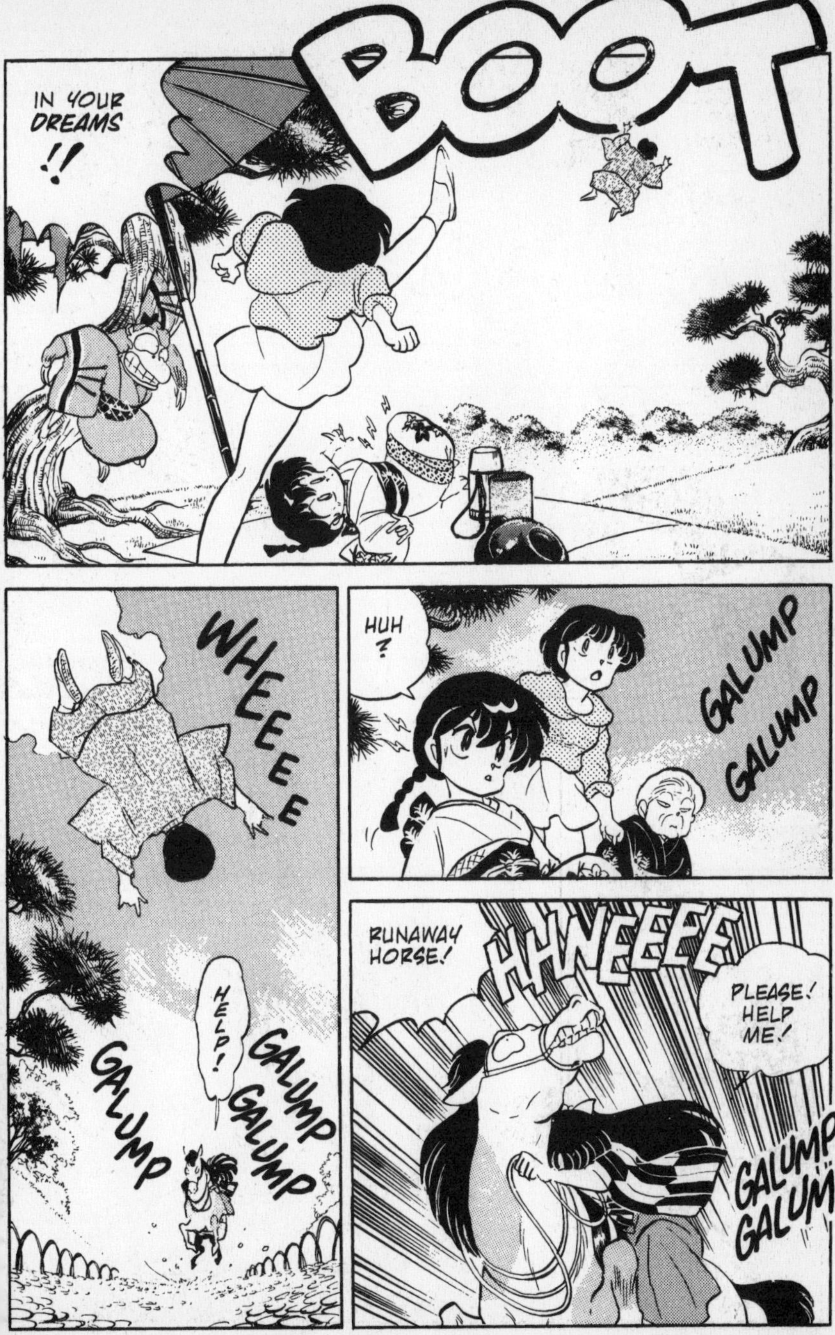
IN YOUR DREAMS!!
BOOT
WHEEEEE
HELP!
GALUMP GALUMP
GALUMP GALUMP
HUH?
GALUMP GALUMP
RUNAWAY HORSE!
HHWEEEE
PLEASE! HELP ME!
GALUMP GALUMP

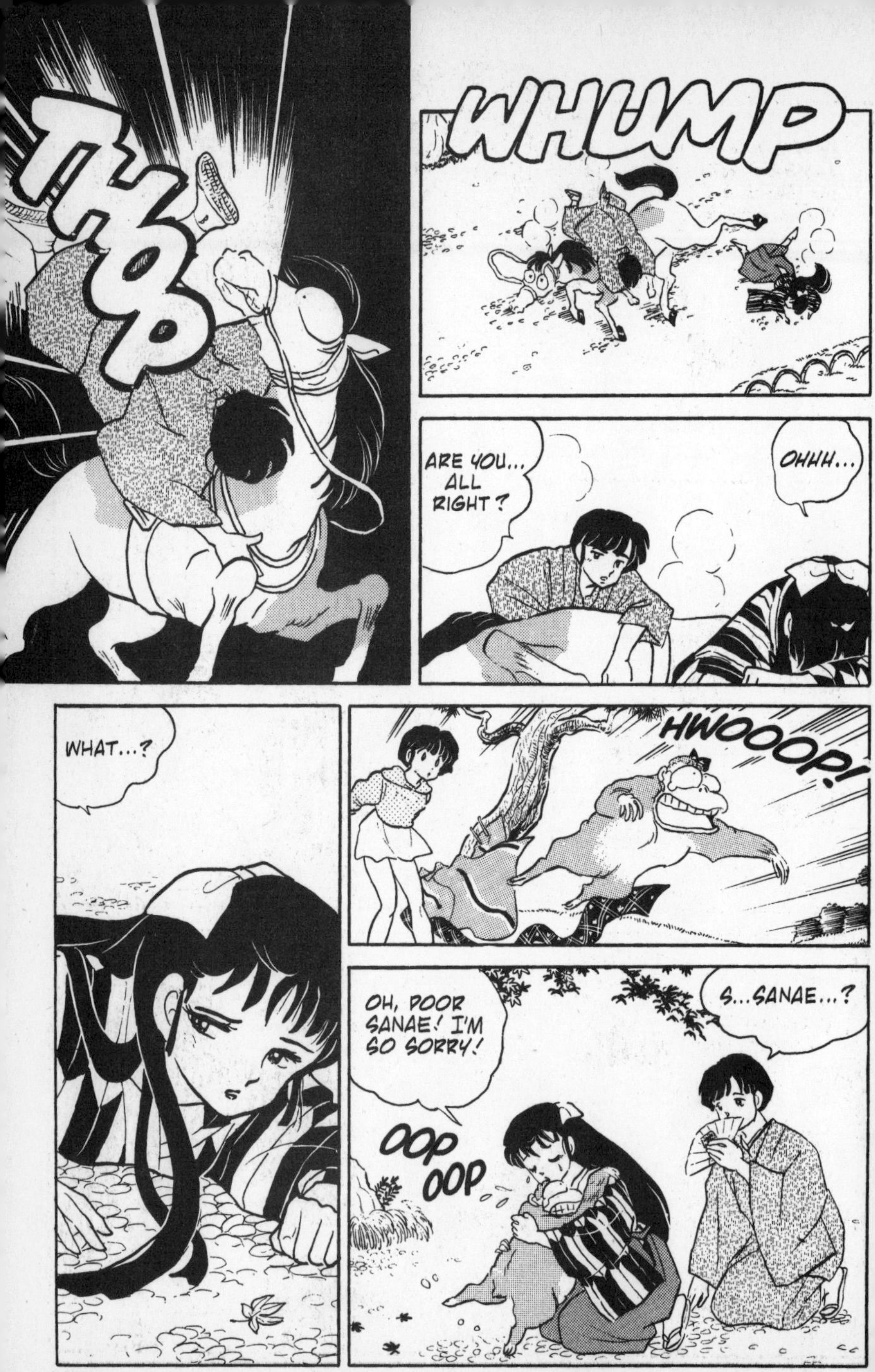
THOP
WHUMP
ARE YOU... ALL RIGHT?
OHHH...
WHAT...?
HWOOOOP!
OH, POOR SANAE! I'M SO SORRY!
OOP OOP
S...SANAE...?

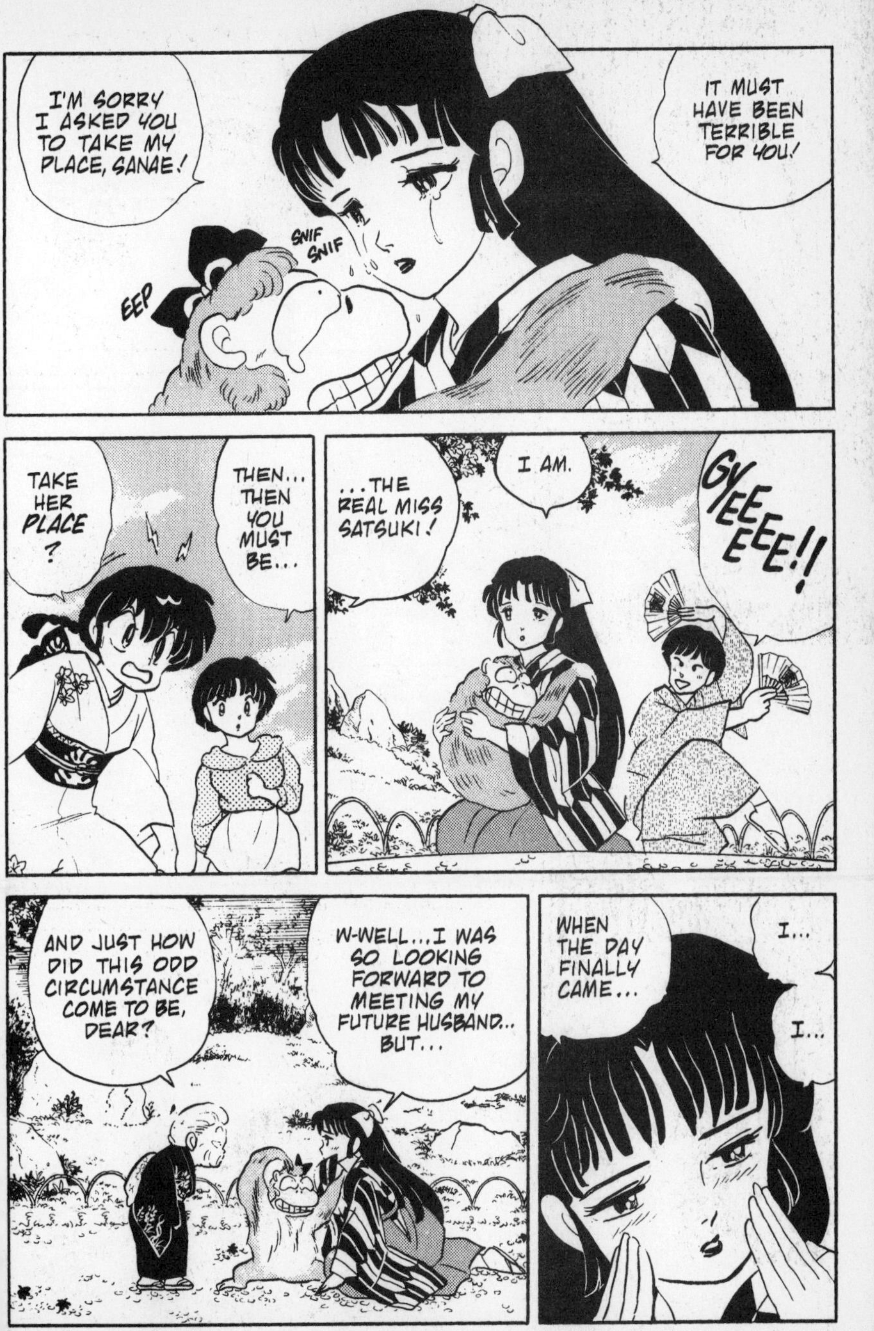
I'M SORRY I ASKED YOU TO TAKE MY PLACE, SANAE!
SNIF SNIF
EEP
IT MUST HAVE BEEN TERRIBLE FOR YOU!
TAKE HER PLACE?
THEN... THEN YOU MUST BE...
...THE REAL MISS SATSUKI!
I AM.
GYEEEEEE!!
AND JUST HOW DID THIS ODD CIRCUMSTANCE COME TO BE, DEAR?
W-WELL...I WAS SO LOOKING FORWARD TO MEETING MY FUTURE HUSBAND... BUT...
WHEN THE DAY FINALLY CAME...
I...
I...

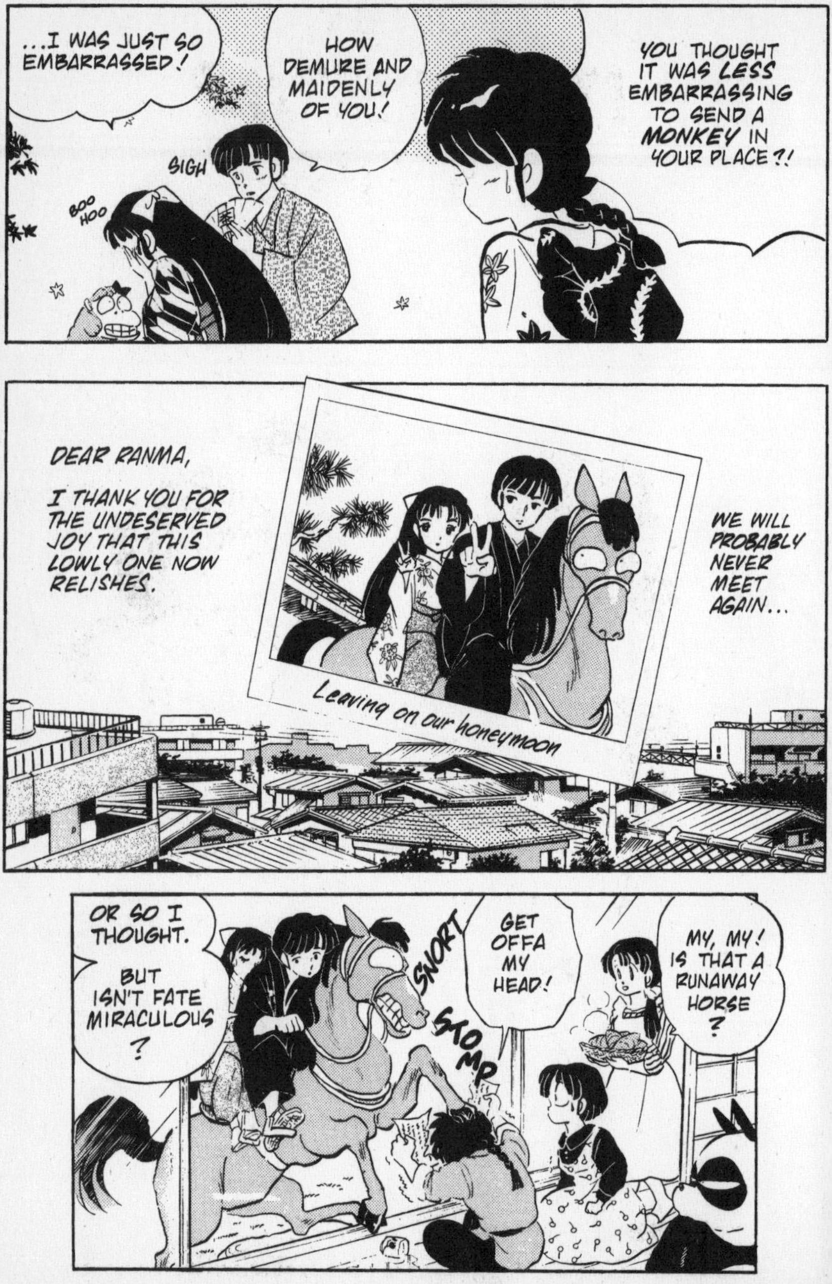
...I WAS JUST SO EMBARRASSED!
BOO HOO
SIGH
HOW DEMURE AND MAIDENLY OF YOU!
YOU THOUGHT IT WAS LESS EMBARRASSING TO SEND A MONKEY IN YOUR PLACE?!
DEAR RANMA,
I THANK YOU FOR THE UNDESERVED JOY THAT THIS LOWLY ONE NOW RELISHES.
Leaving on our honeymoon
WE WILL PROBABLY NEVER MEET AGAIN...
OR SO I THOUGHT.
BUT ISN'T FATE MIRACULOUS?
SNORT
STOMP
GET OFFA MY HEAD!
MY, MY! IS THAT A RUNAWAY HORSE?

Part 10
IT'S FAST OR IT'S FREE

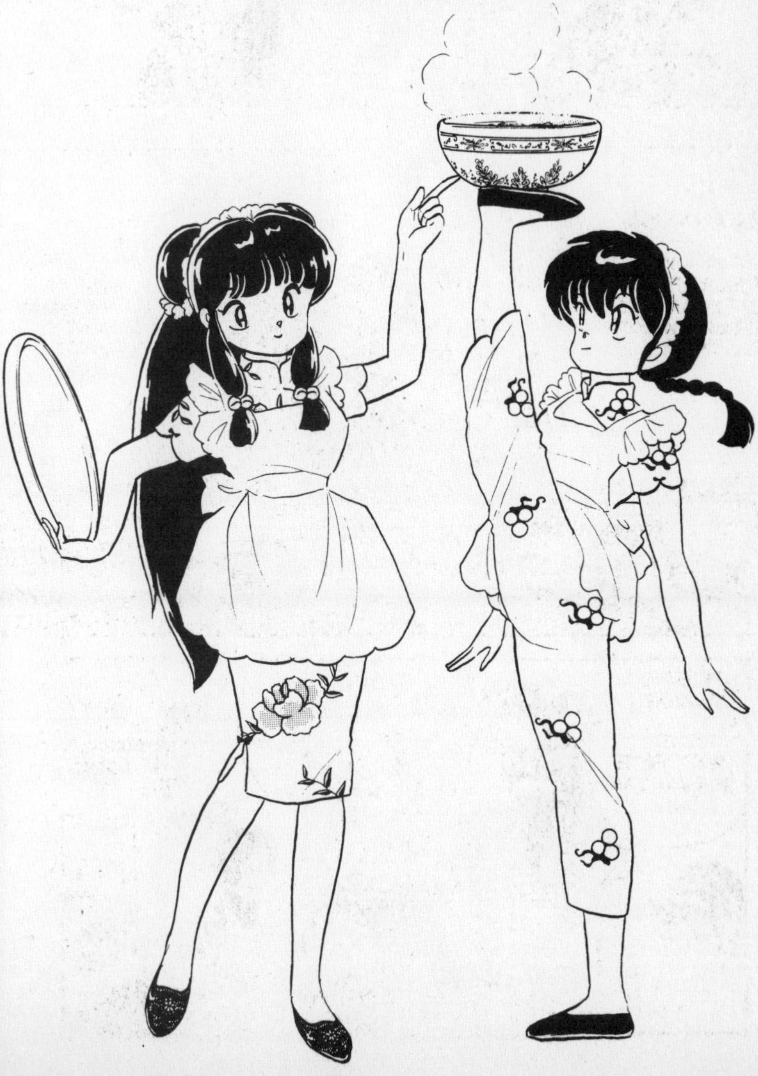

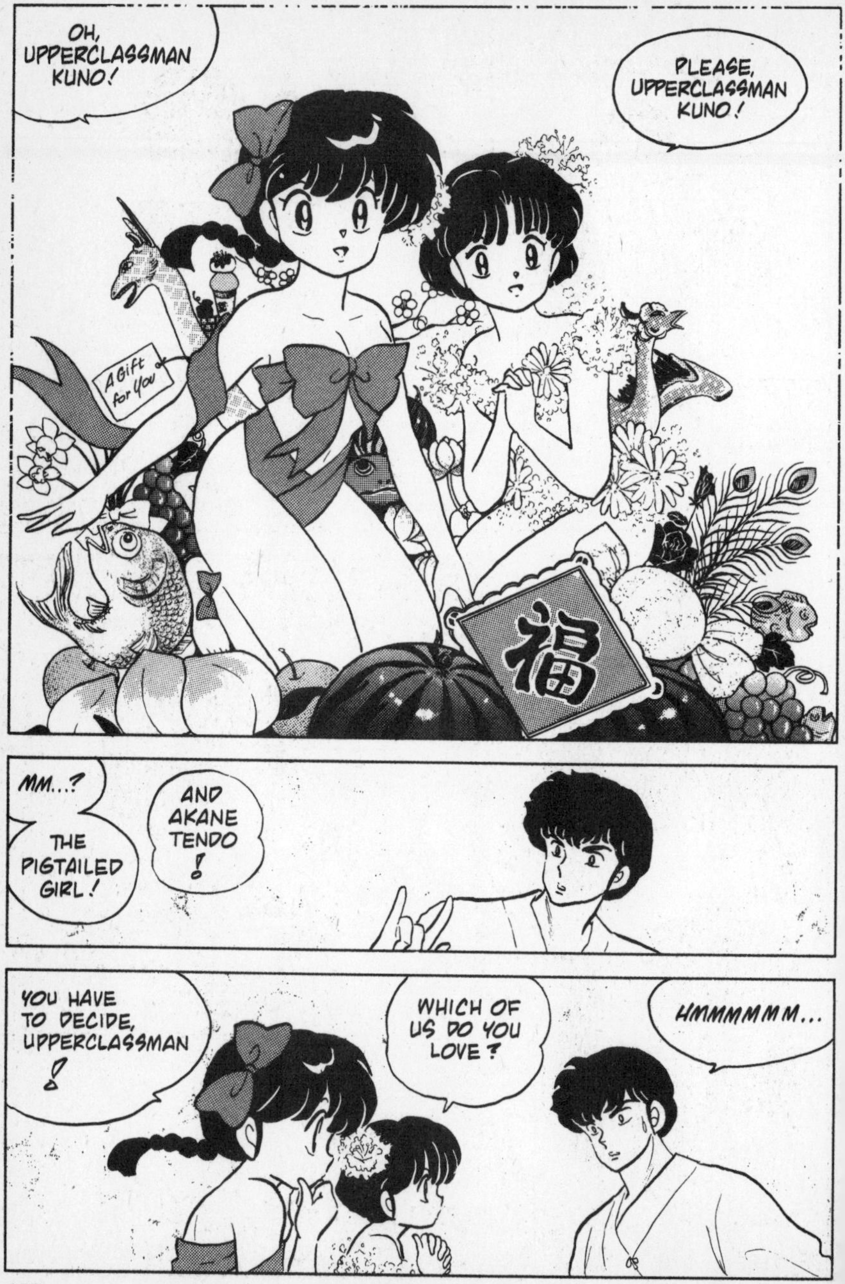
OH, UPPERCLASSMAN KUNO!
PLEASE, UPPERCLASSMAN KUNO!
A Gift for You
福
MM...?
THE PIGTAILED GIRL!
AND AKANE TENDO!
YOU HAVE TO DECIDE, UPPERCLASSMAN!
WHICH OF US DO YOU LOVE?
HMMMMMM...

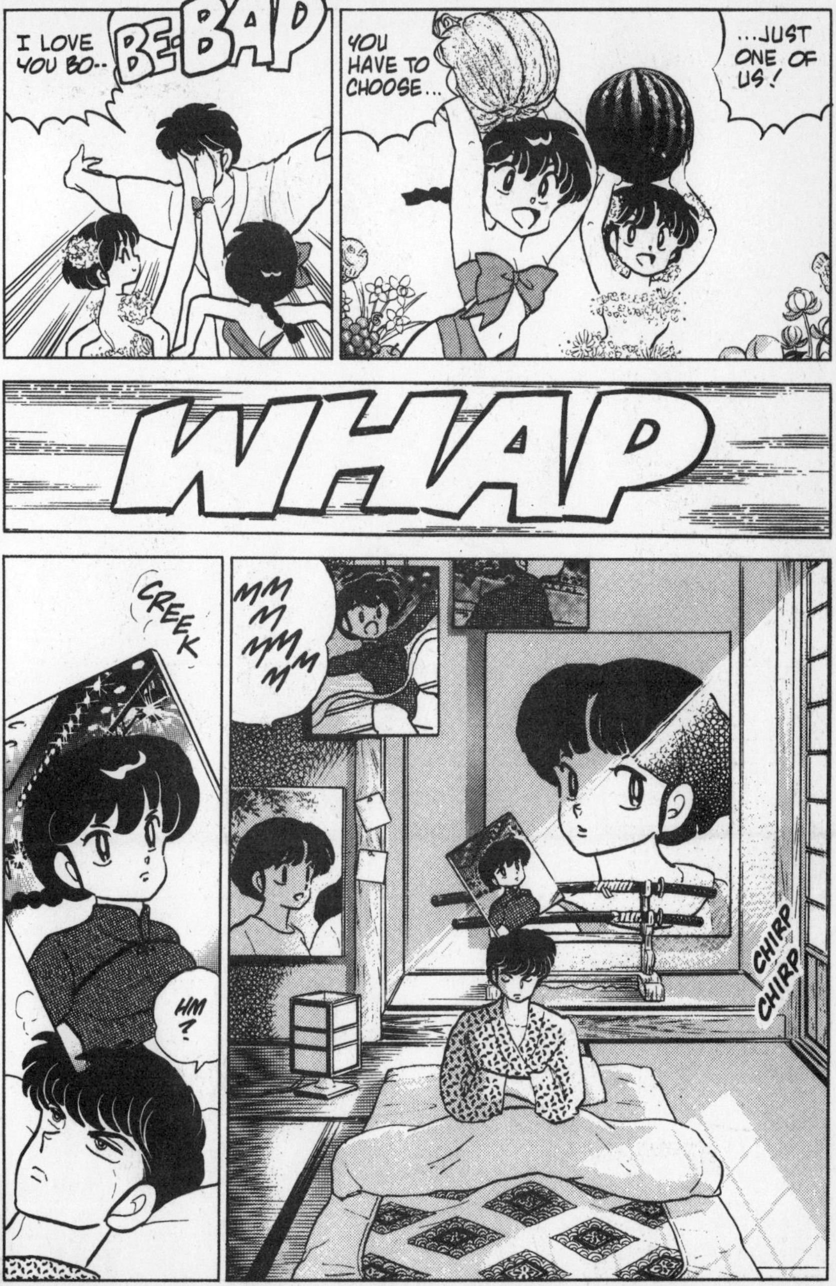
I LOVE YOU BO--
BE-BAP
YOU HAVE TO CHOOSE...
...JUST ONE OF US!
WHAP
CREEK
HM?
MMMMMMM
CHIRP CHIRP

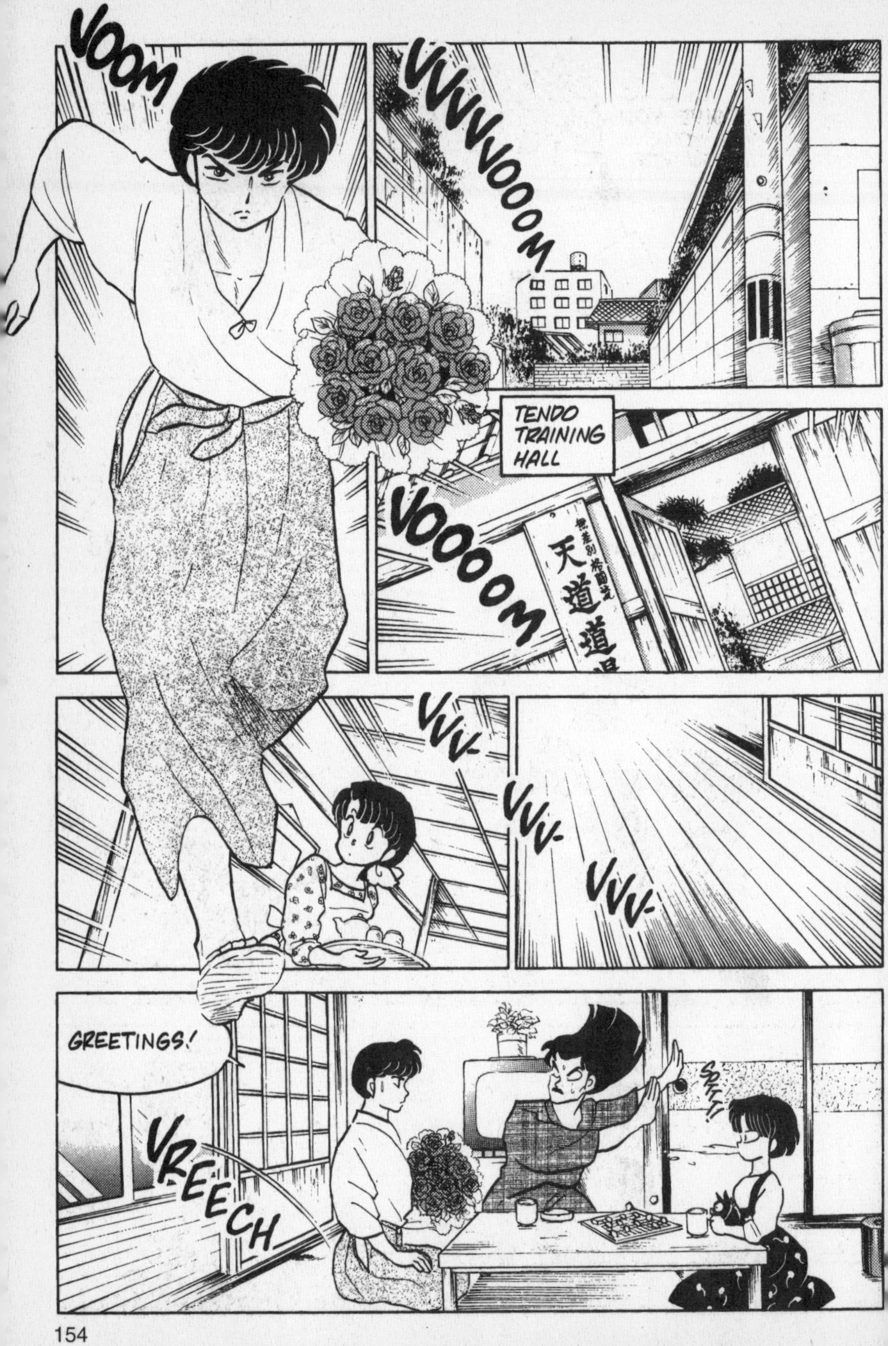
VOOM
VVVVVVOOOM
TENDO TRAINING HALL
VOOOOOM
天道道
VVV-
VVV-
VVV-
GREETINGS!
VREECH
SPKT!!

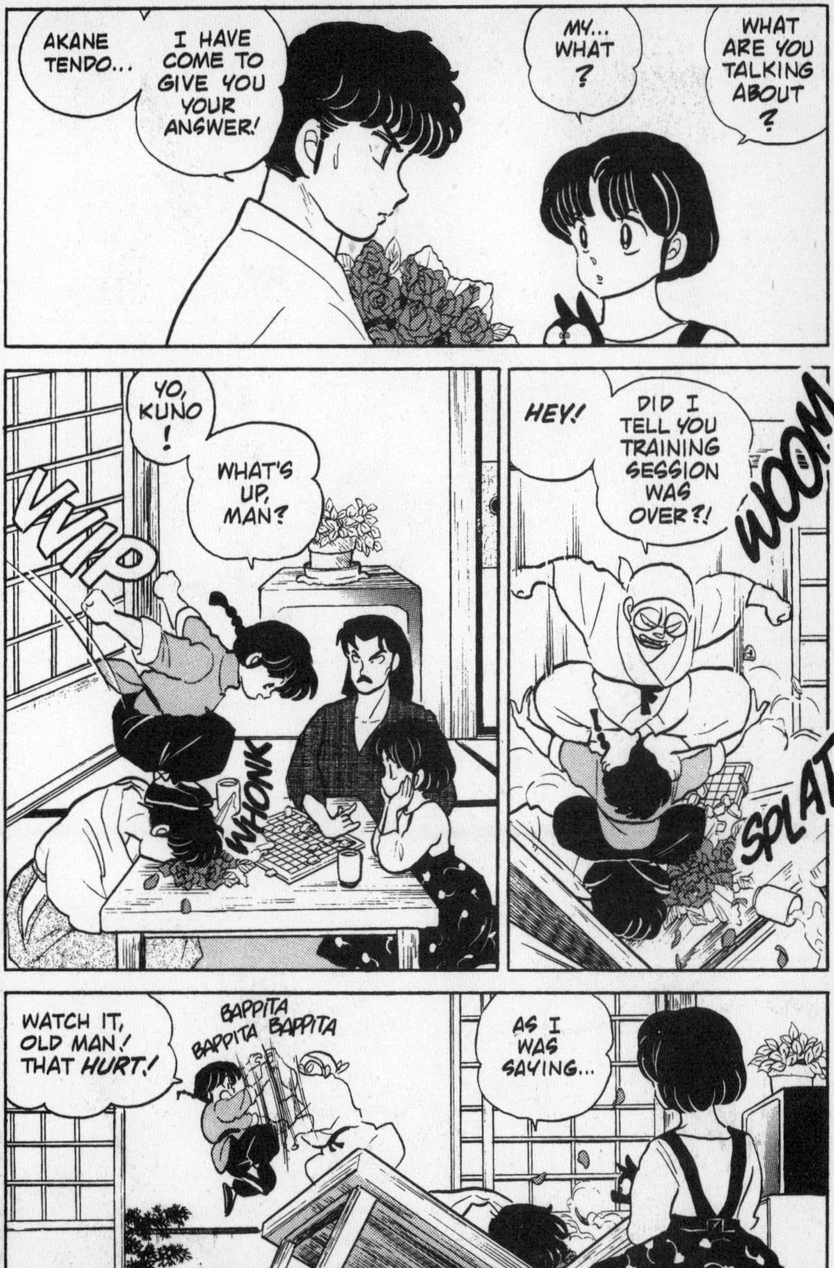
AKANE TENDO...
I HAVE COME TO GIVE YOU YOUR ANSWER!
MY... WHAT?
WHAT ARE YOU TALKING ABOUT?
YO, KUNO!
WHAT'S UP, MAN?
VWIP
WHONK
HEY!
DID I TELL YOU TRAINING SESSION WAS OVER?!
WOOM
SPLAT
WATCH IT, OLD MAN! THAT HURT!
BAPPITA BAPPITA BAPPITA
AS I WAS SAYING...

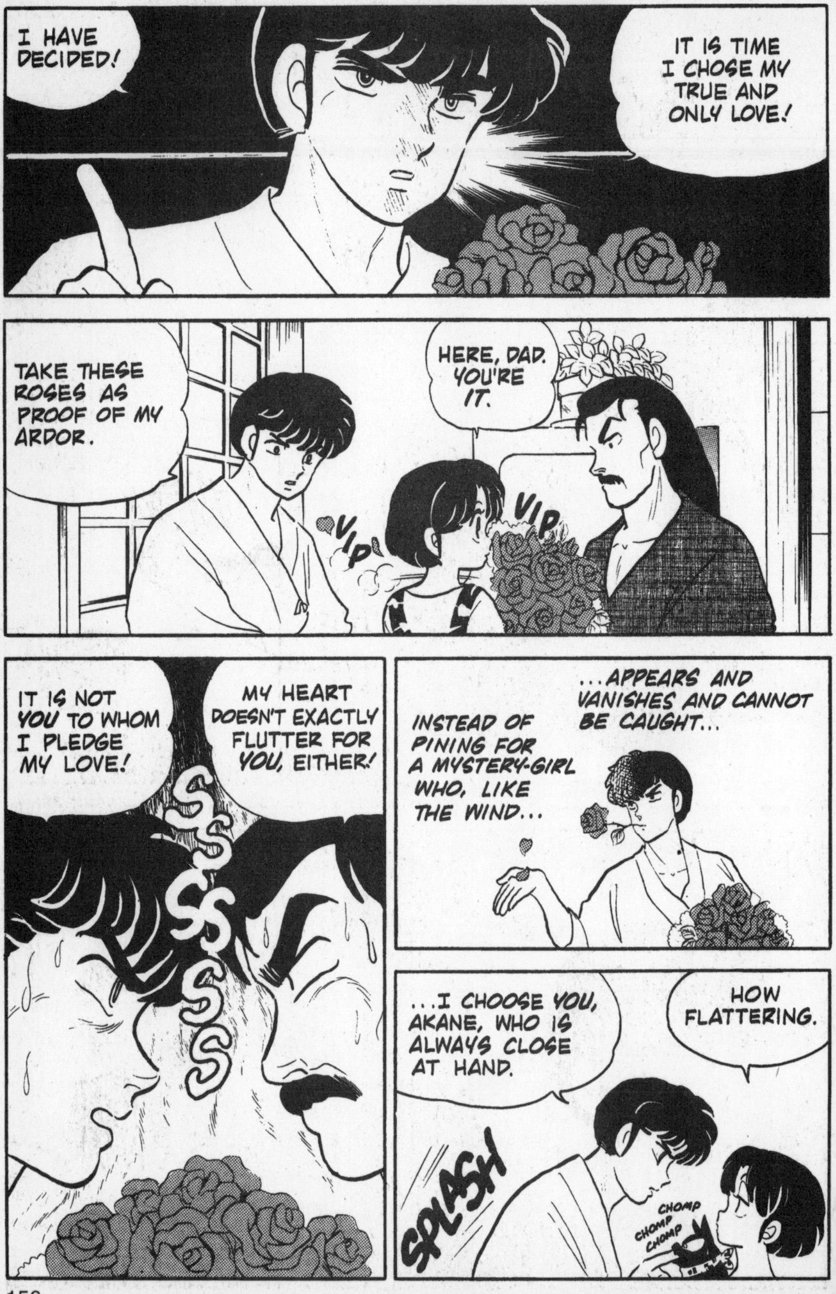
I HAVE DECIDED!
IT IS TIME I CHOSE MY TRUE AND ONLY LOVE!
TAKE THESE ROSES AS PROOF OF MY ARDOR.
HERE, DAD. YOU'RE IT.
VIP
VIP
IT IS NOT YOU TO WHOM I PLEDGE MY LOVE!
MY HEART DOESN'T EXACTLY FLUTTER FOR YOU, EITHER!
SSSSSS
INSTEAD OF PINING FOR A MYSTERY-GIRL WHO, LIKE THE WIND...
...APPEARS AND VANISHES AND CANNOT BE CAUGHT...
...I CHOOSE YOU, AKANE, WHO IS ALWAYS CLOSE AT HAND.
HOW FLATTERING.
SPLASH
CHOMP CHOMP CHOMP

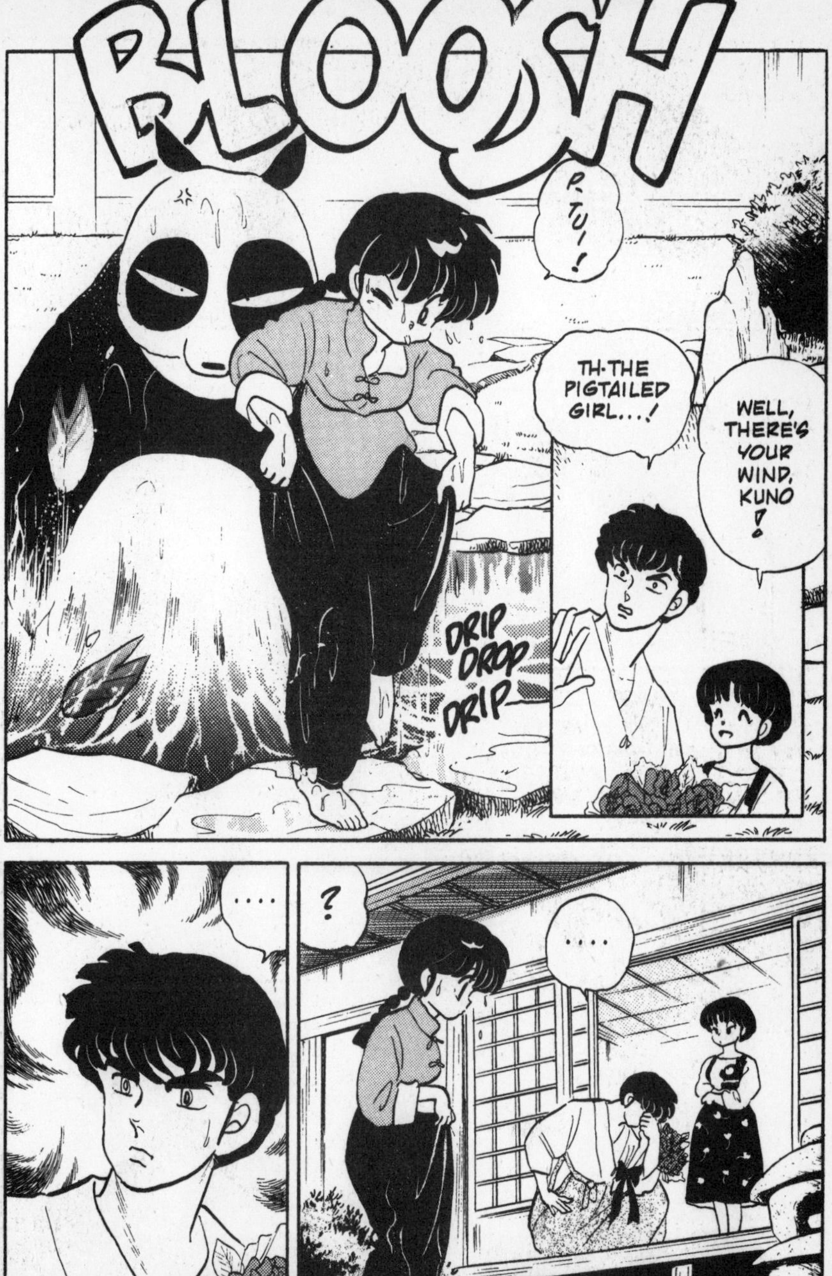
BLOOSH
P-TUI!
DRIP DROP DRIP
TH-THE PIGTAILED GIRL...!
WELL, THERE'S YOUR WIND, KUNO!
....
?
....

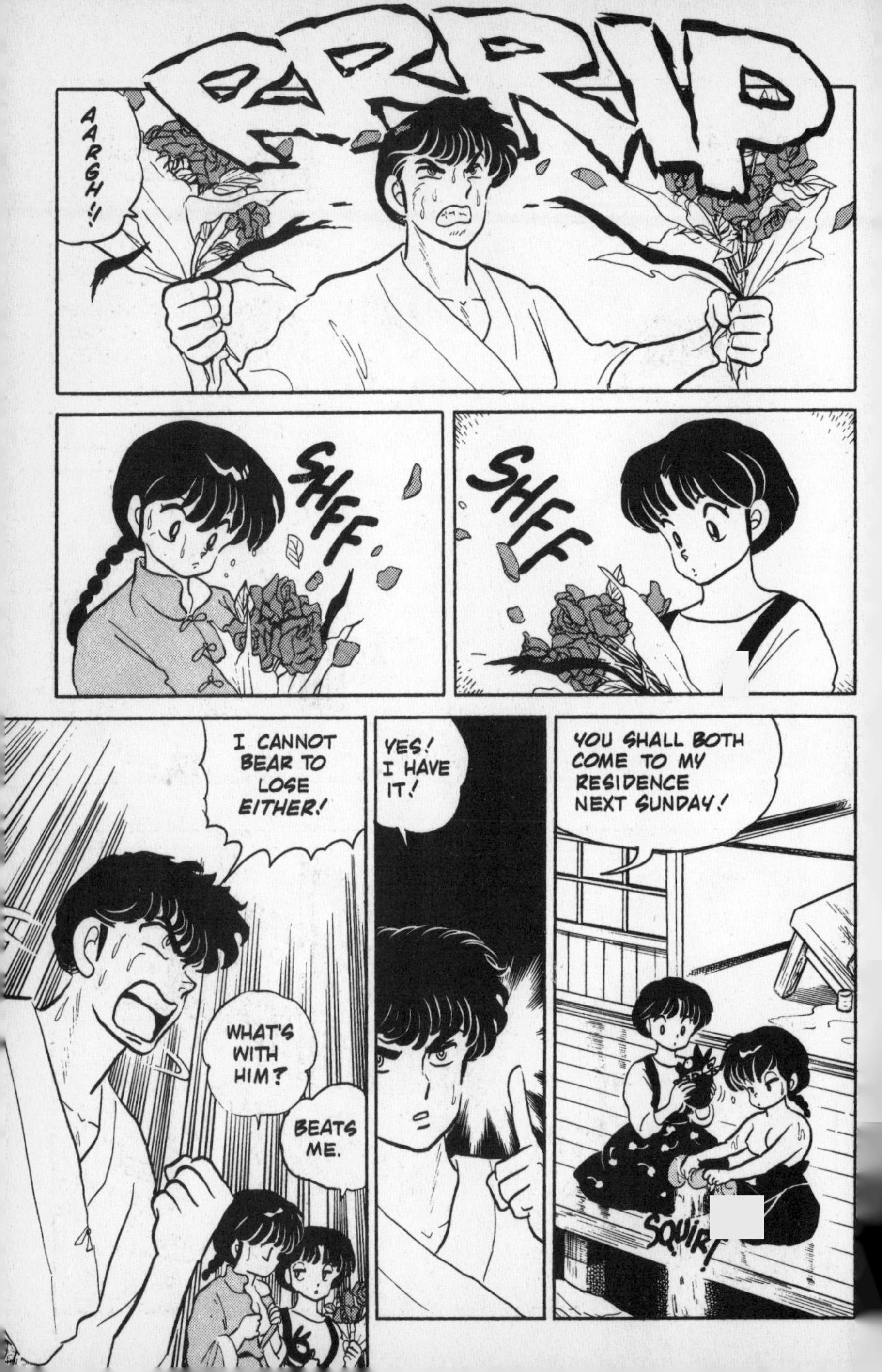

BRRRIP
AARGH!!
SHFF
SHFF
I CANNOT BEAR TO LOSE EITHER!
WHAT'S WITH HIM?
BEATS ME.
YES! I HAVE IT!
YOU SHALL BOTH COME TO MY RESIDENCE NEXT SUNDAY!
SQUIR!

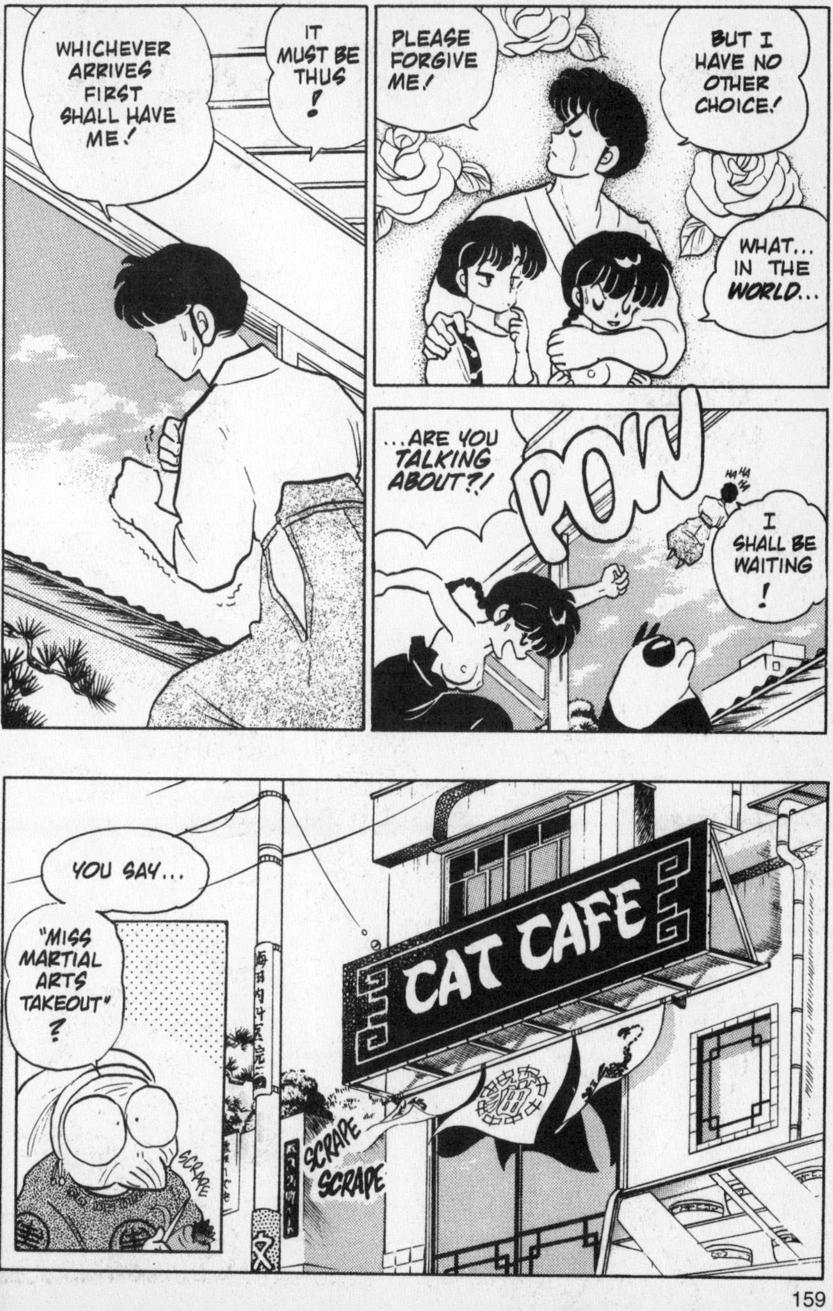
WHICHEVER ARRIVES FIRST SHALL HAVE ME!
IT MUST BE THUS!
PLEASE FORGIVE ME!
BUT I HAVE NO OTHER CHOICE!
WHAT... IN THE WORLD...
...ARE YOU TALKING ABOUT?!
POW
HA HA HA
I SHALL BE WAITING!
YOU SAY...
"MISS MARTIAL ARTS TAKEOUT"?
CAT CAFE
SCRAPE
SCRAPE
SCRAPE

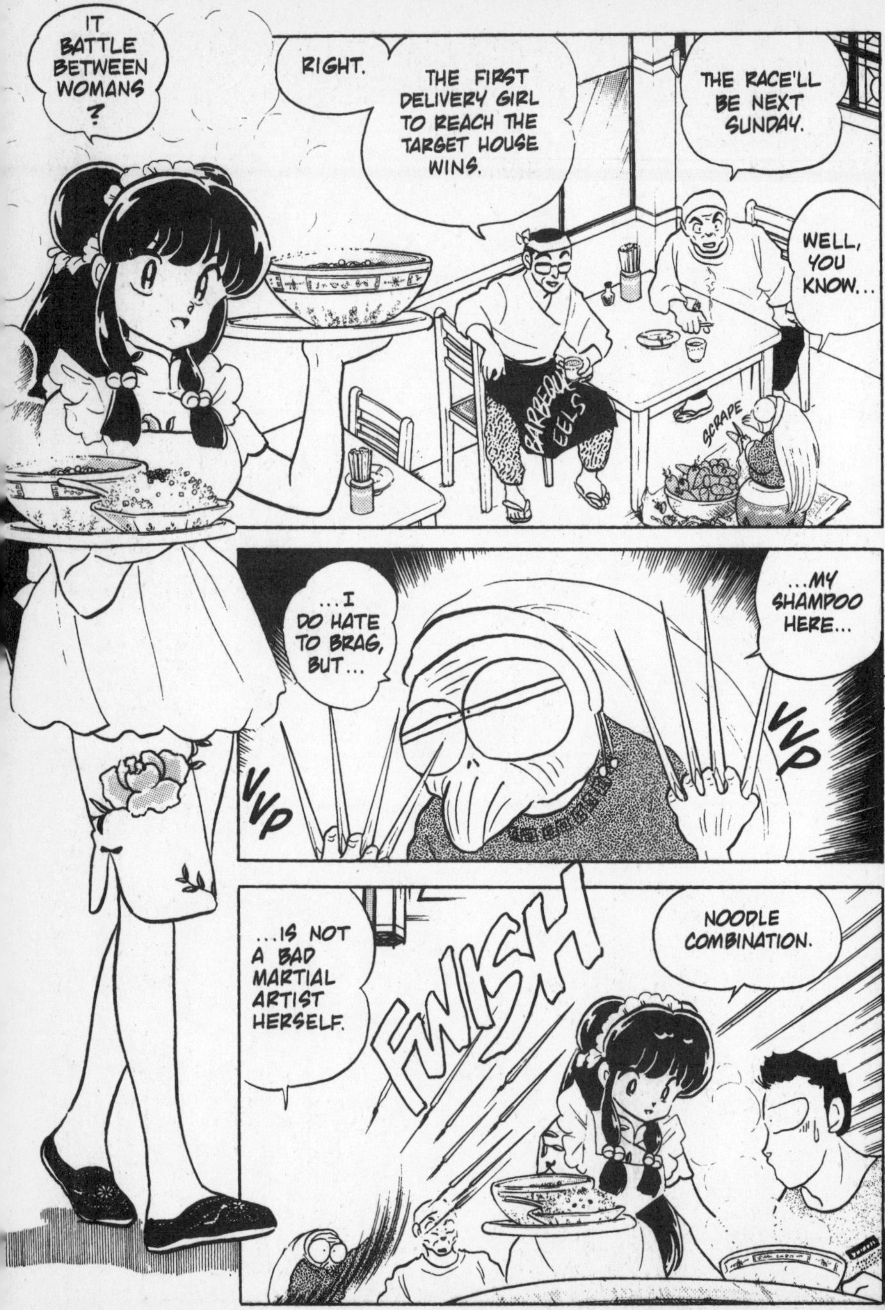
IT BATTLE BETWEEN WOMANS ?
RIGHT.
THE FIRST DELIVERY GIRL TO REACH THE TARGET HOUSE WINS.
THE RACE'LL BE NEXT SUNDAY.
WELL, YOU KNOW...
BARBEQUE EELS
SCRAPE
...I DO HATE TO BRAG, BUT...
...MY SHAMPOO HERE...
VVP
VVP
...IS NOT A BAD MARTIAL ARTIST HERSELF.
FWISH
NOODLE COMBINATION.

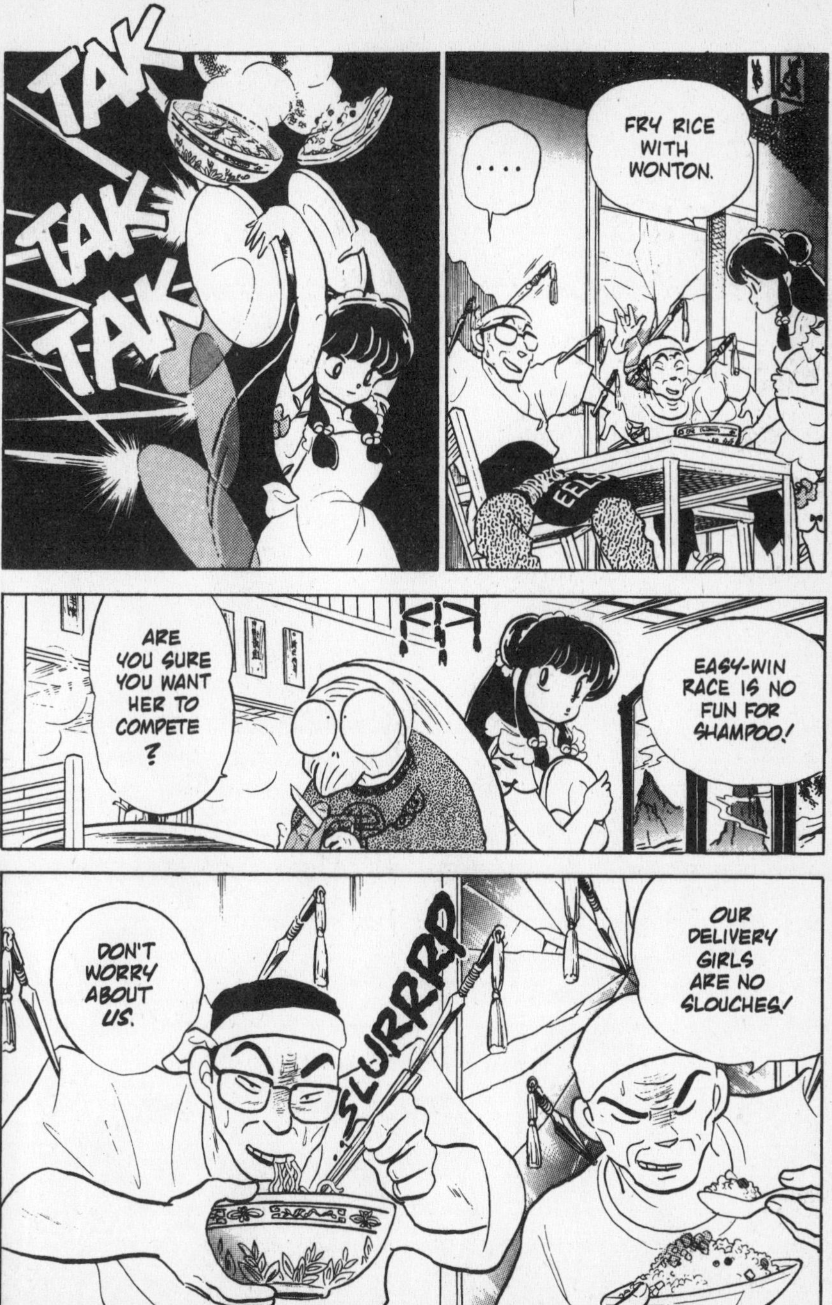
TAK TAK TAK
....
FRY RICE WITH WONTON.
ARE YOU SURE YOU WANT HER TO COMPETE?
EASY-WIN RACE IS NO FUN FOR SHAMPOO!
DON'T WORRY ABOUT US.
SLURRRP
OUR DELIVERY GIRLS ARE NO SLOUCHES!

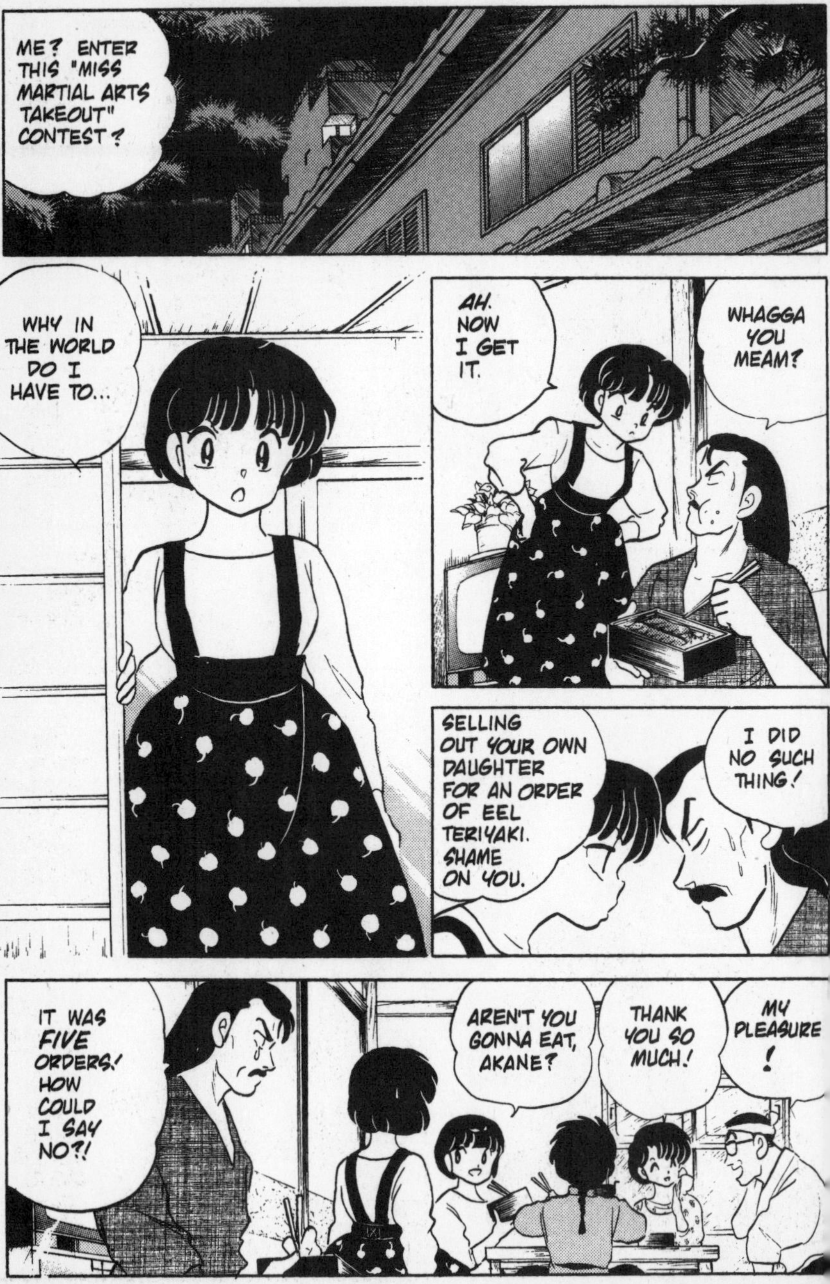
ME? ENTER THIS "MISS MARTIAL ARTS TAKEOUT" CONTEST?
WHY IN THE WORLD DO I HAVE TO...
AH. NOW I GET IT.
WHAGGA YOU MEAM?
SELLING OUT YOUR OWN DAUGHTER FOR AN ORDER OF EEL TERIYAKI. SHAME ON YOU.
I DID NO SUCH THING!
IT WAS FIVE ORDERS! HOW COULD I SAY NO?!
AREN'T YOU GONNA EAT, AKANE?
THANK YOU SO MUCH!
MY PLEASURE!

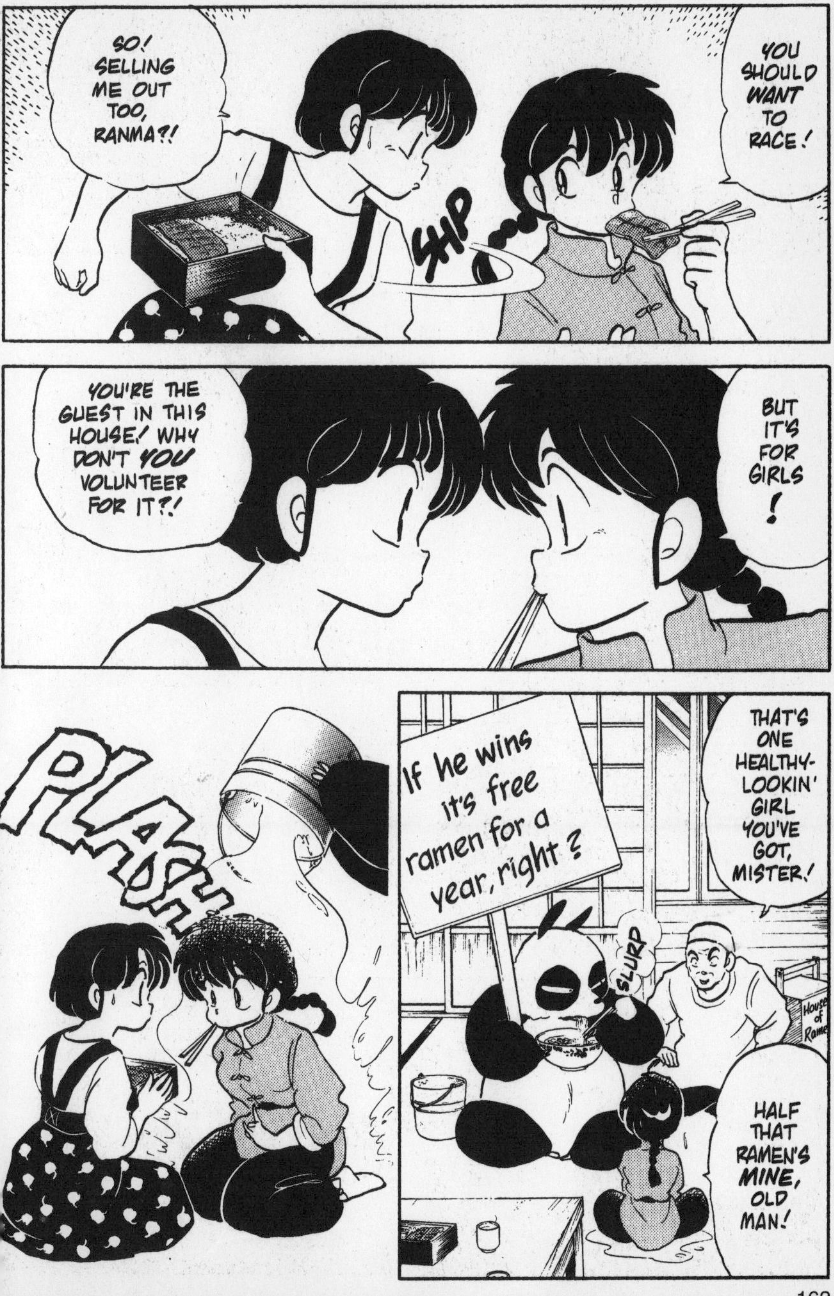
SO! SELLING ME OUT TOO, RANMA?!
SHP
YOU SHOULD WANT TO RACE!
YOU'RE THE GUEST IN THIS HOUSE! WHY DON'T YOU VOLUNTEER FOR IT?!
BUT IT'S FOR GIRLS!
PLASH
If he wins it's free ramen for a year, right?
SLURP
THAT'S ONE HEALTHY-LOOKIN' GIRL YOU'VE GOT, MISTER!
HALF THAT RAMEN'S MINE, OLD MAN!
House of Rame

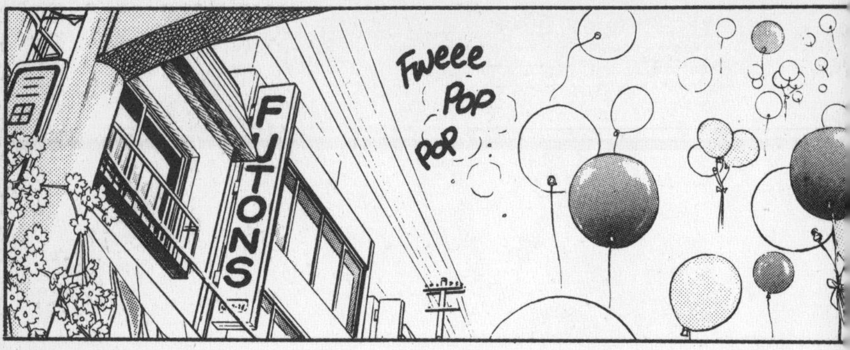
FUTONS
FWEEE
POP
POP

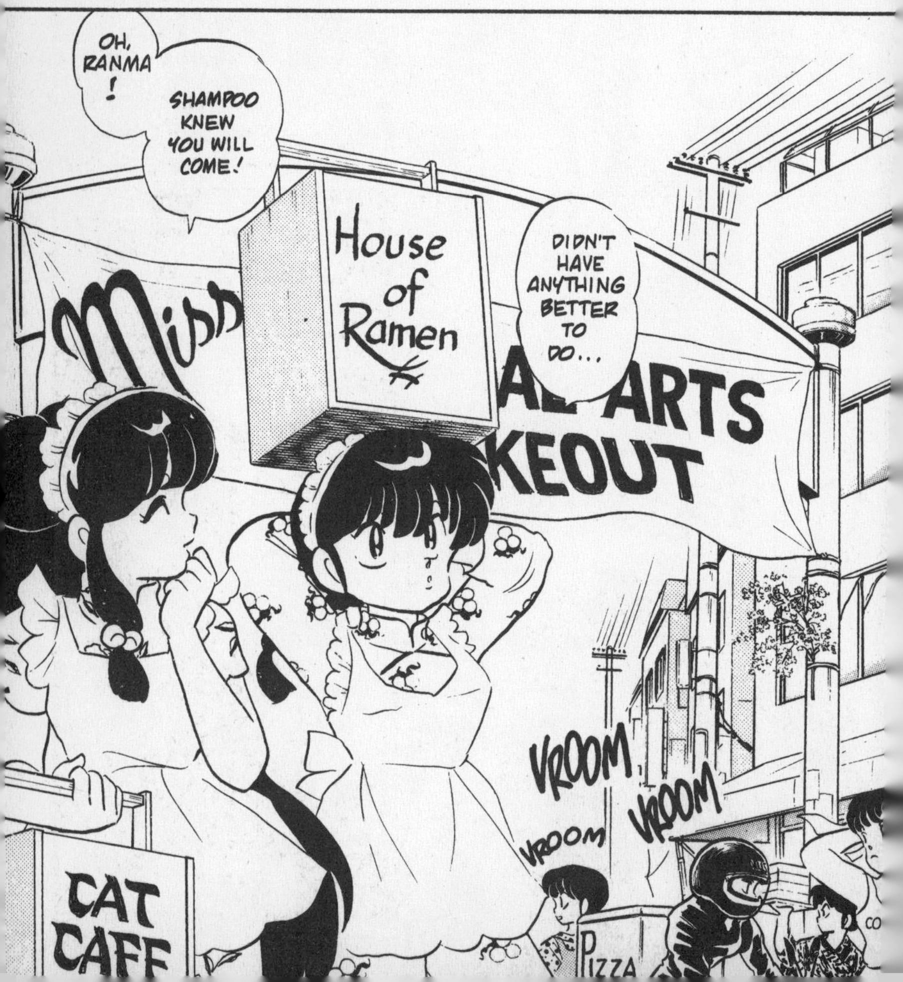
OH, RANMA!
SHAMPOO KNEW YOU WILL COME!
House of Ramen
DIDN'T HAVE ANYTHING BETTER TO DO...
VROOM
VROOM
VROOM
CAT
PIZZA

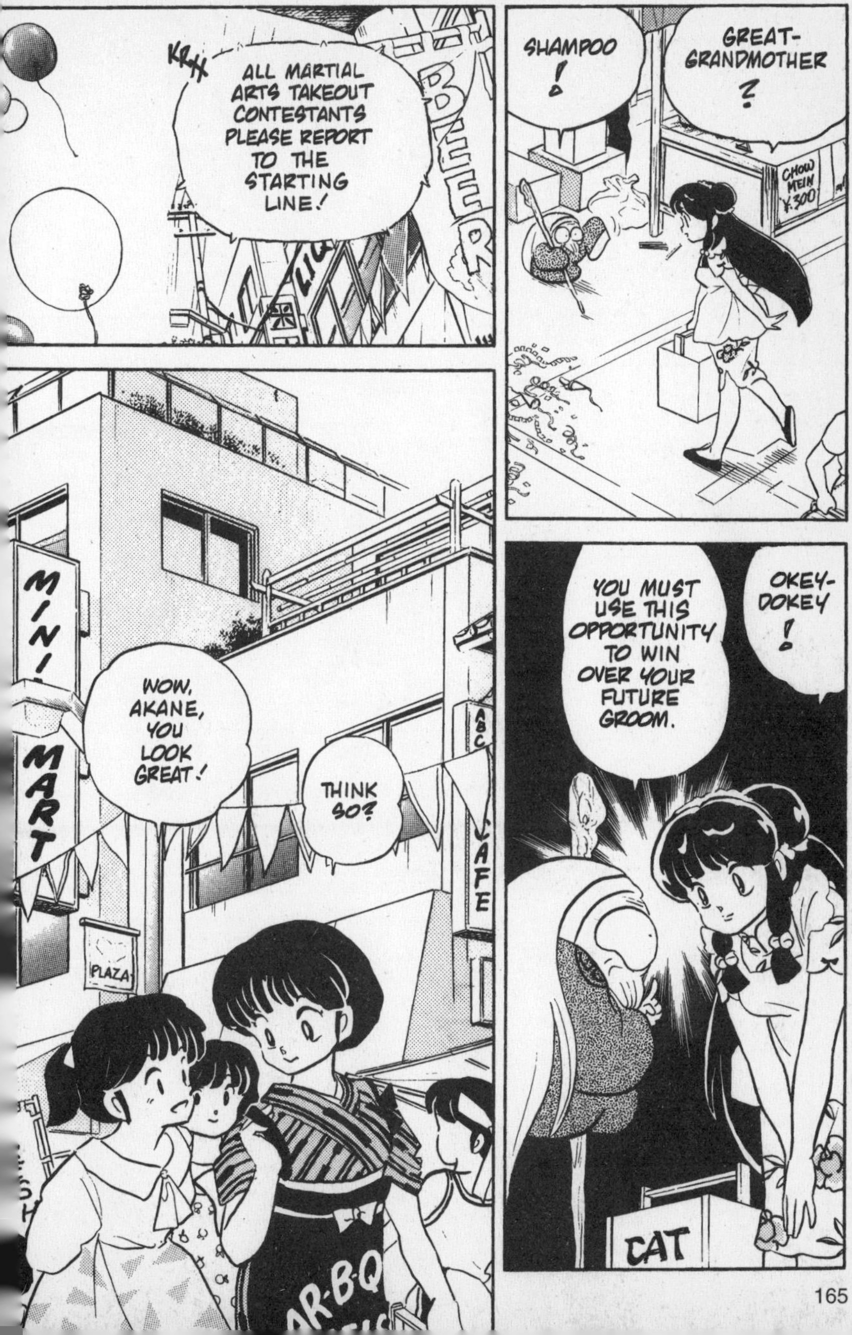
KRIIX
ALL MARTIAL ARTS TAKEOUT CONTESTANTS PLEASE REPORT TO THE STARTING LINE!
BEER
SHAMPOO!
GREAT-GRANDMOTHER?
CHOW MEIN ¥300
MINI MART
WOW, AKANE, YOU LOOK GREAT!
THINK SO?
ABC
CAFE
PLAZA
AR-B-Q
YOU MUST USE THIS OPPORTUNITY TO WIN OVER YOUR FUTURE GROOM.
OKEY-DOKEY!
CAT

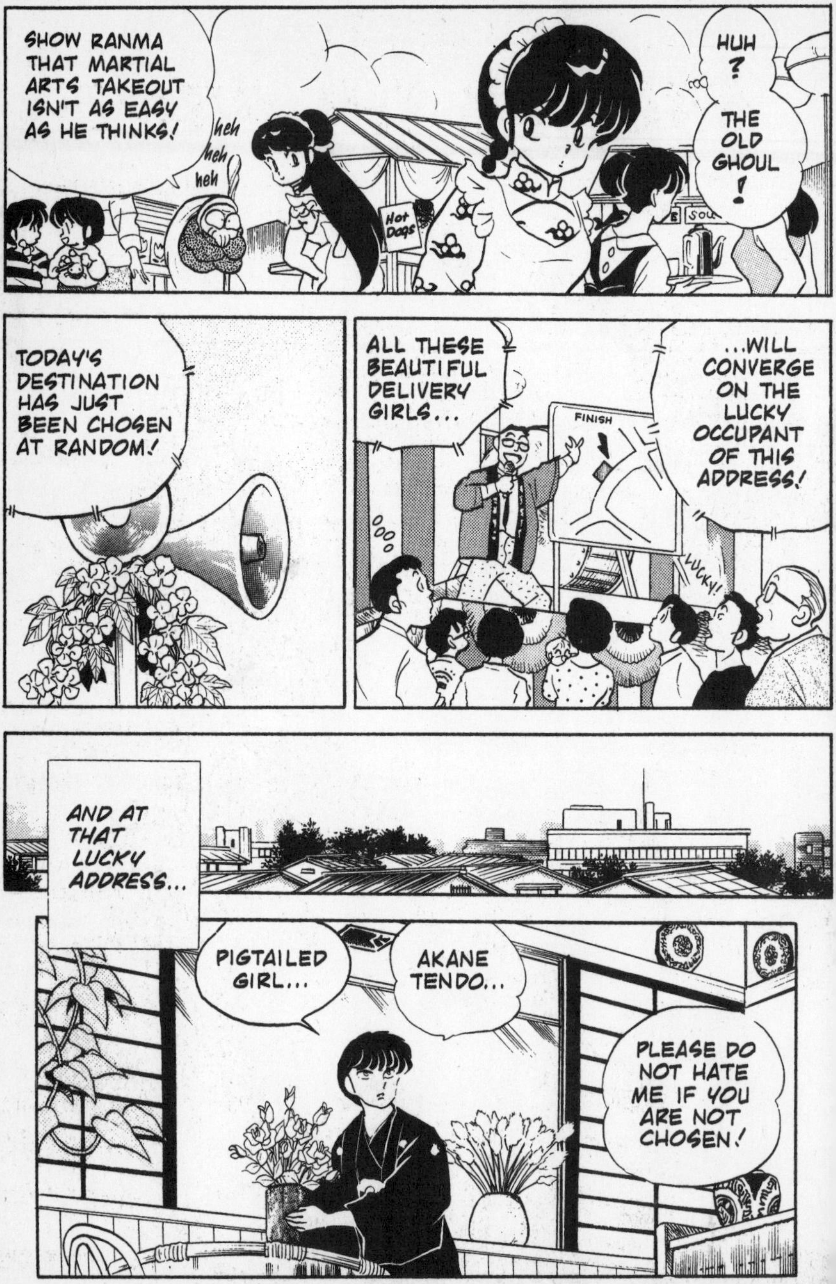
SHOW RANMA THAT MARTIAL ARTS TAKEOUT ISN'T AS EASY AS HE THINKS!
heh heh heh
Hot Dogs
HUH? THE OLD GHOUL!
TODAY'S DESTINATION HAS JUST BEEN CHOSEN AT RANDOM!
ALL THESE BEAUTIFUL DELIVERY GIRLS...
FINISH
...WILL CONVERGE ON THE LUCKY OCCUPANT OF THIS ADDRESS!
LUCKY!
AND AT THAT LUCKY ADDRESS...
PIGTAILED GIRL...
AKANE TENDO...
PLEASE DO NOT HATE ME IF YOU ARE NOT CHOSEN!

Part 11
EYES ON THE PRIZE

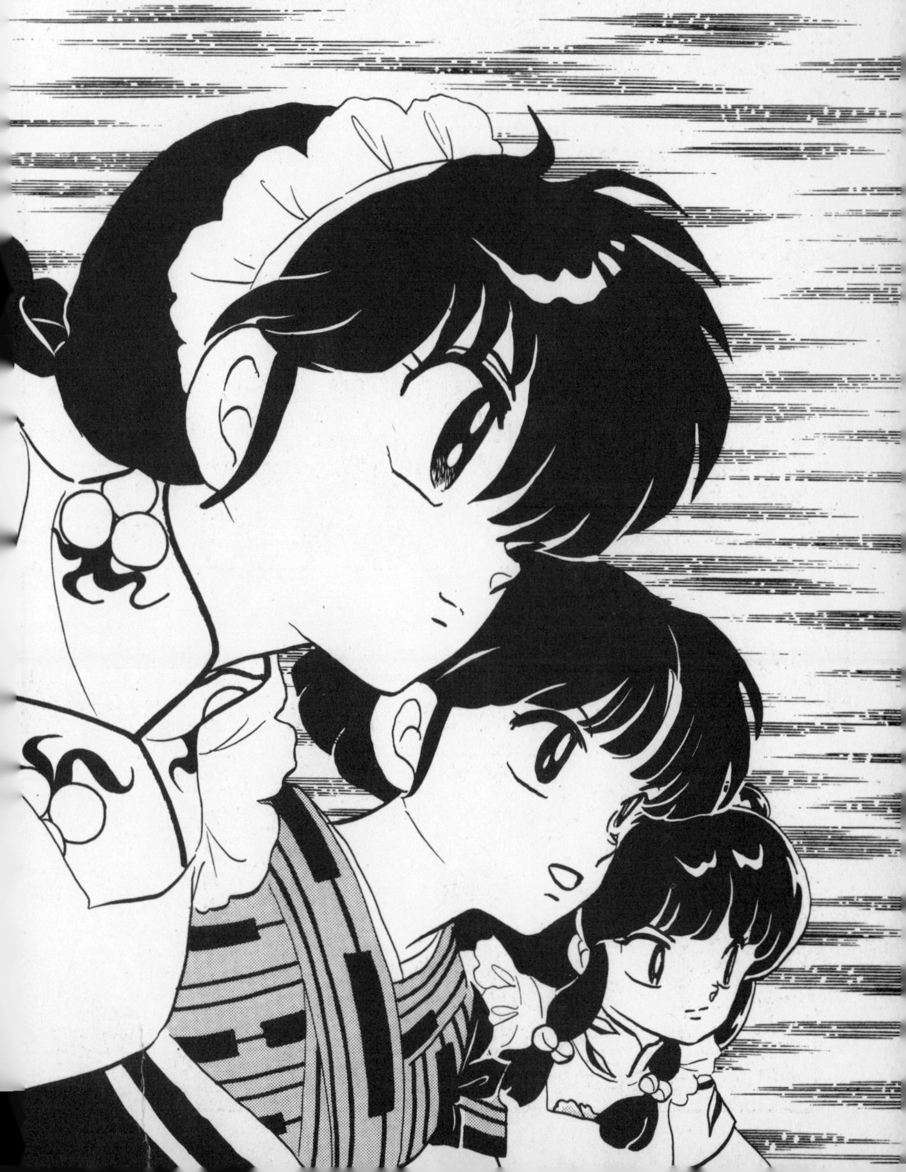

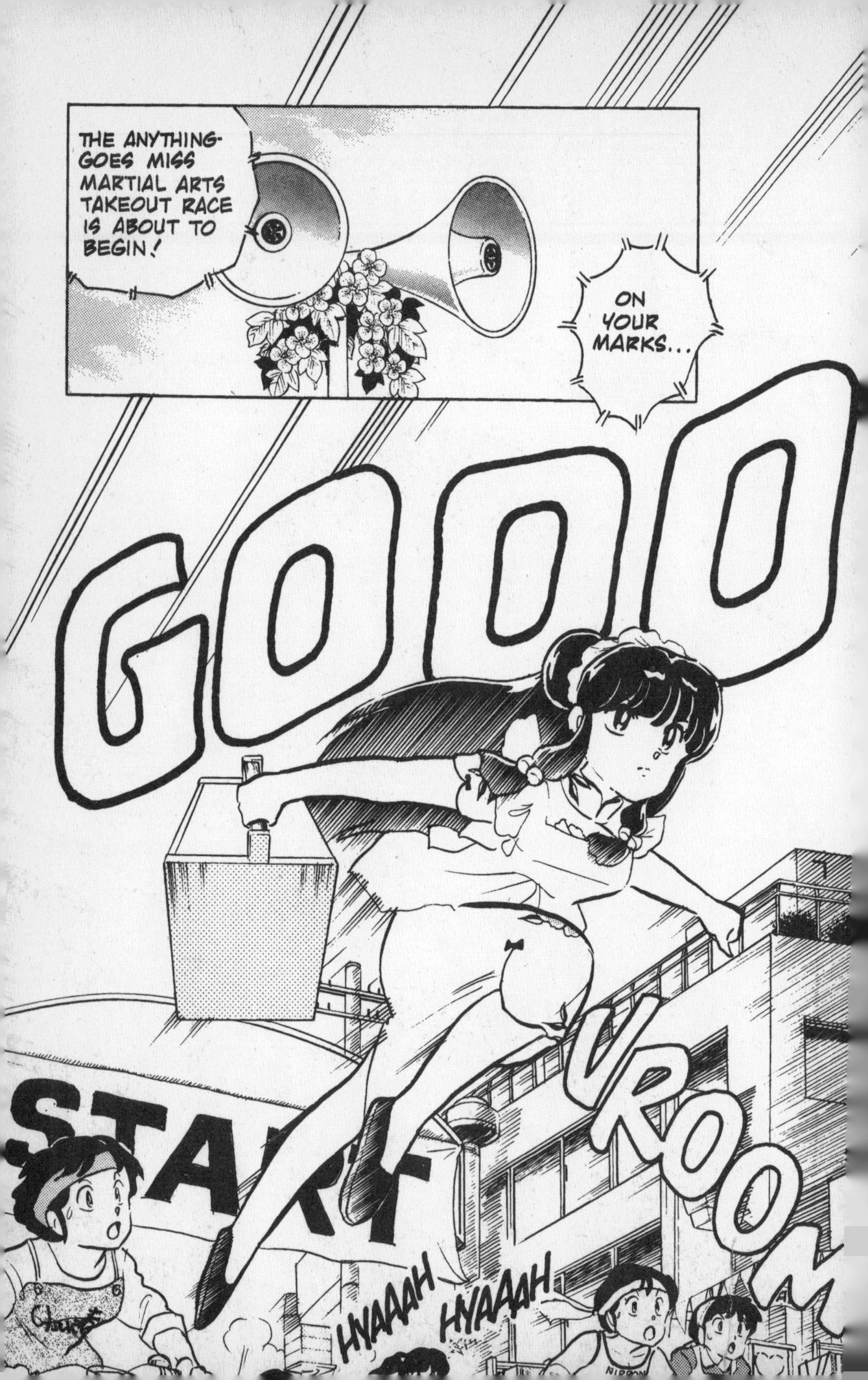
THE ANYTHING-GOES MISS MARTIAL ARTS TAKEOUT RACE IS ABOUT TO BEGIN!
ON YOUR MARKS...
GOOO
START
VROOOM
HYAAAH HYAAAH

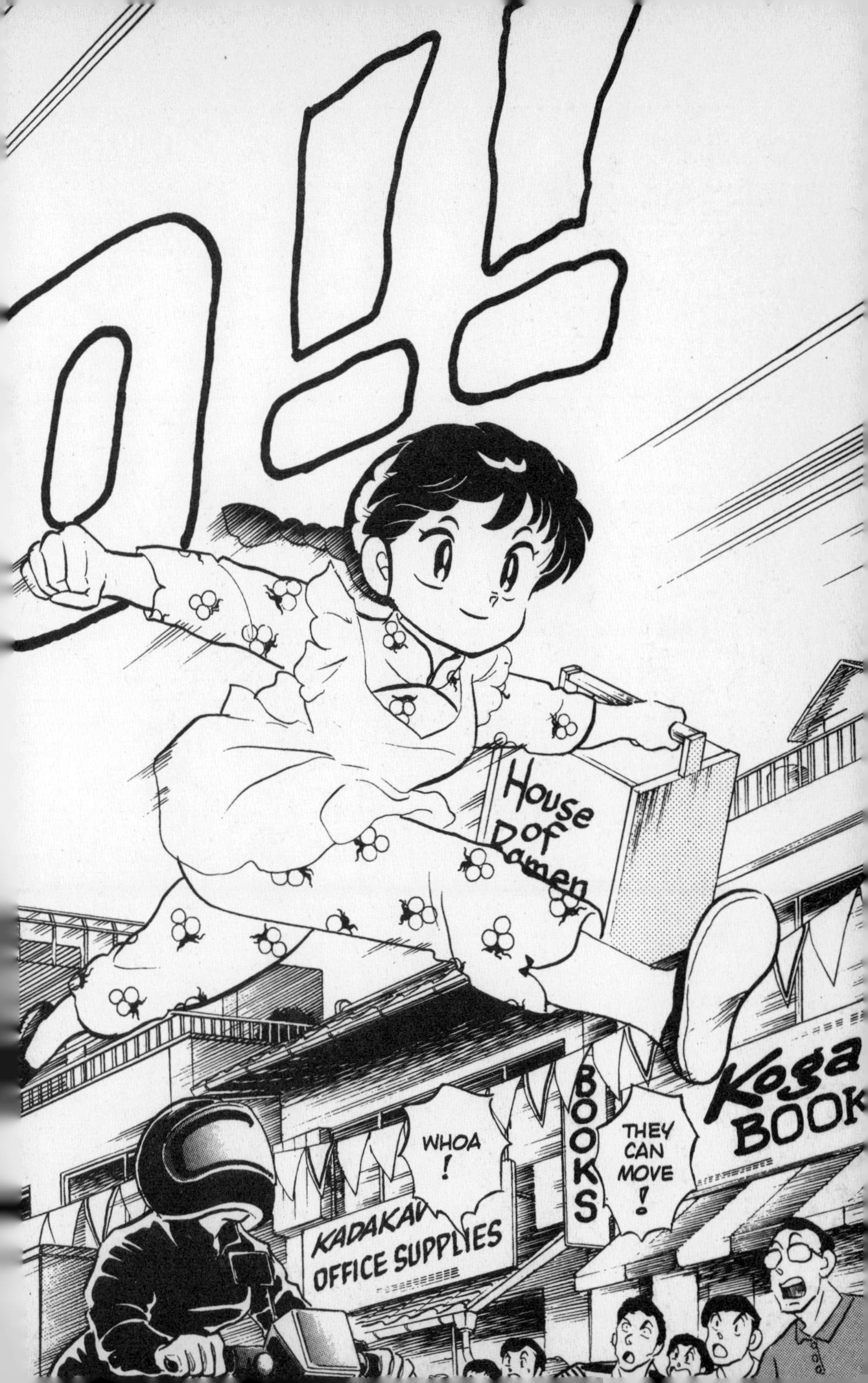
House of Ramen
Koga
BOOK
WHOA!
BOOKS
THEY CAN MOVE!
KADAKAV
OFFICE SUPPLIES

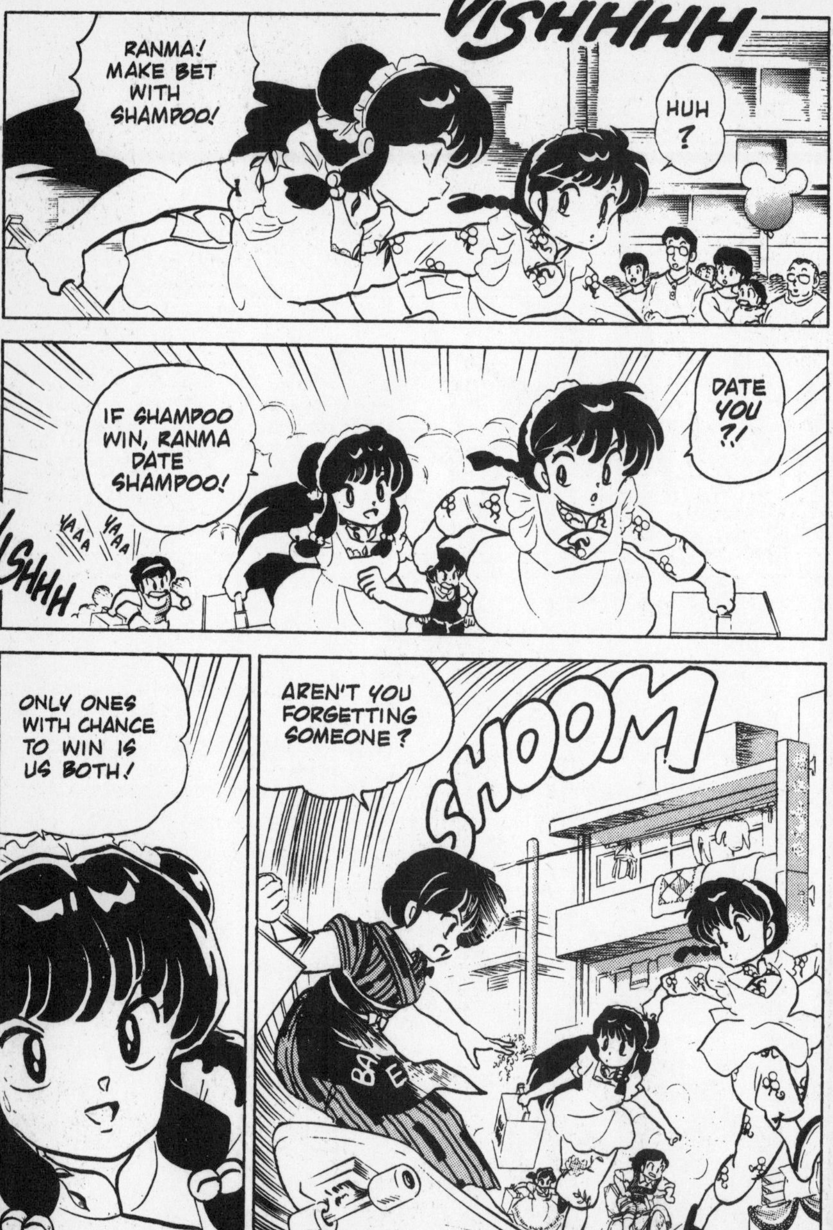
RANMA! MAKE BET WITH SHAMPOO!
VISHHHH
HUH ?
IF SHAMPOO WIN, RANMA DATE SHAMPOO!
DATE YOU ?!
VISHHH
YAAA
YAAA
ONLY ONES WITH CHANCE TO WIN IS US BOTH!
AREN'T YOU FORGETTING SOMEONE?
SHOOM

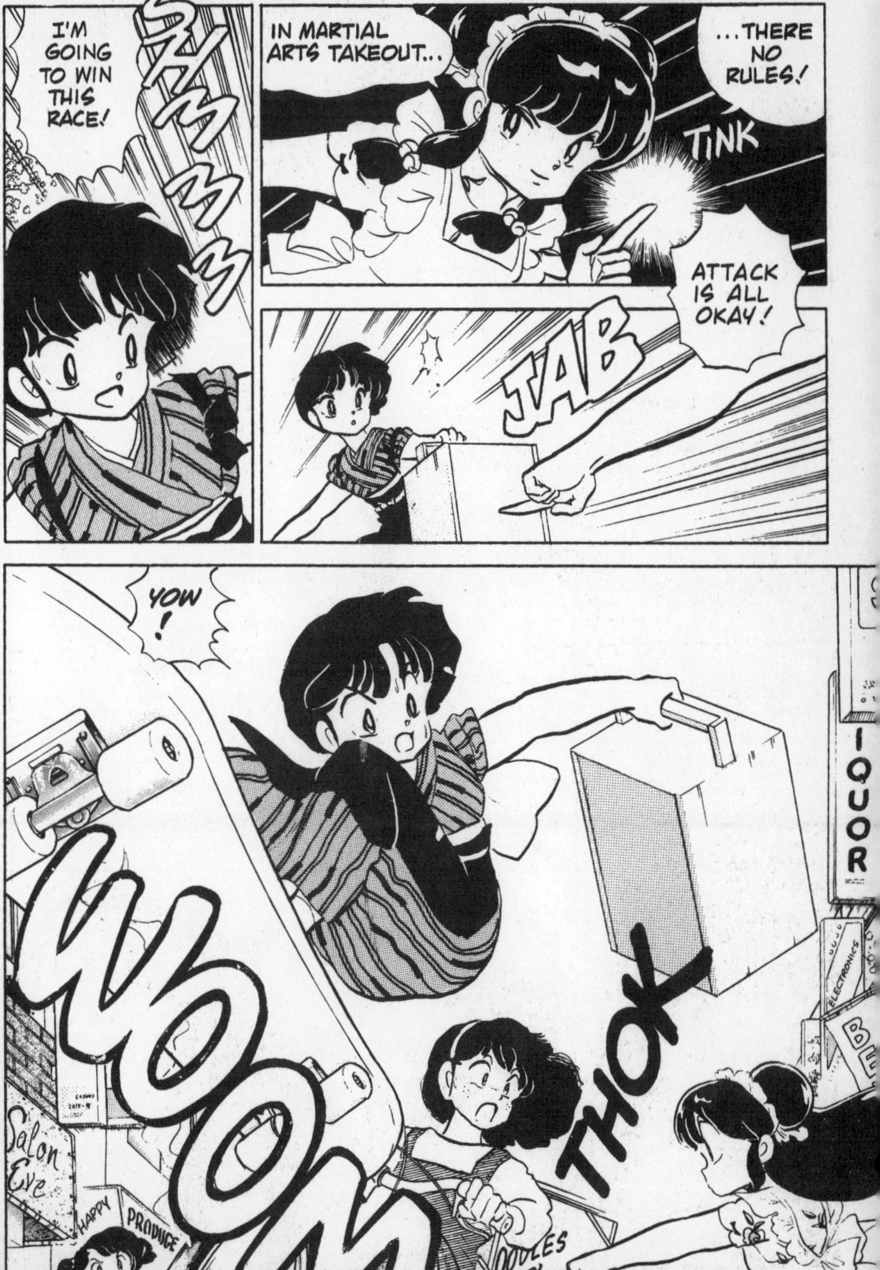
I'M GOING TO WIN THIS RACE!
SHMMMM
IN MARTIAL ARTS TAKEOUT...
...THERE NO RULES!
TINK
ATTACK IS ALL OKAY!
JAB
YOW!
IQUOR
ELECTRONICS
WOOOM
THOK
Salon Eve
HAPPY
PRODUCE
NOODLES O' NOODLES

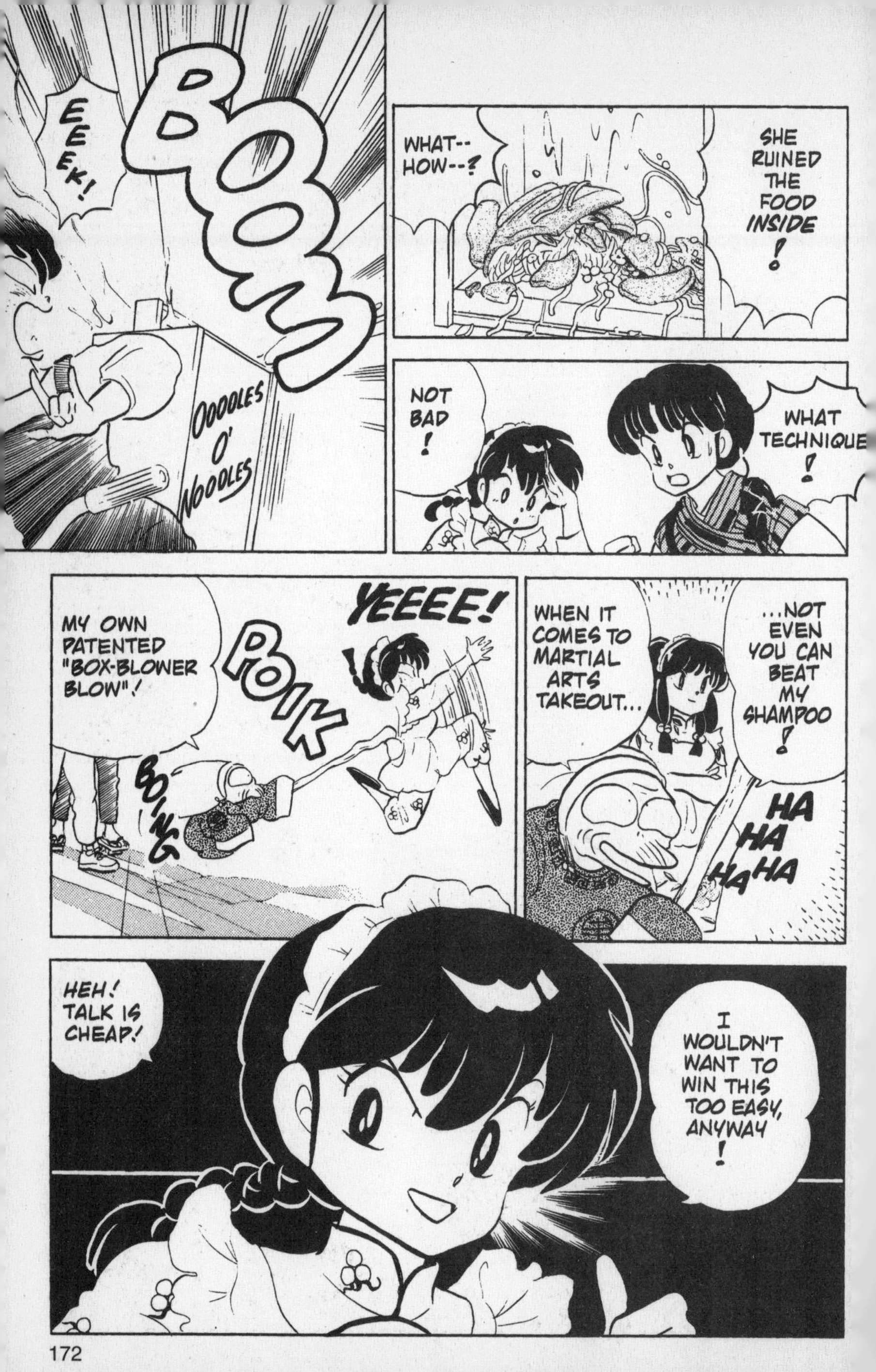
EEEEK!
BOOM
OOOODLES O' NOODLES
WHAT-- HOW--?
SHE RUINED THE FOOD INSIDE!
NOT BAD!
WHAT TECHNIQUE!
MY OWN PATENTED "BOX-BLOWER BLOW"!
YEEEE!
POIK
BOING
WHEN IT COMES TO MARTIAL ARTS TAKEOUT...
...NOT EVEN YOU CAN BEAT MY SHAMPOO!
HA HA HA HA HA
HEH! TALK IS CHEAP!
I WOULDN'T WANT TO WIN THIS TOO EASY, ANYWAY!

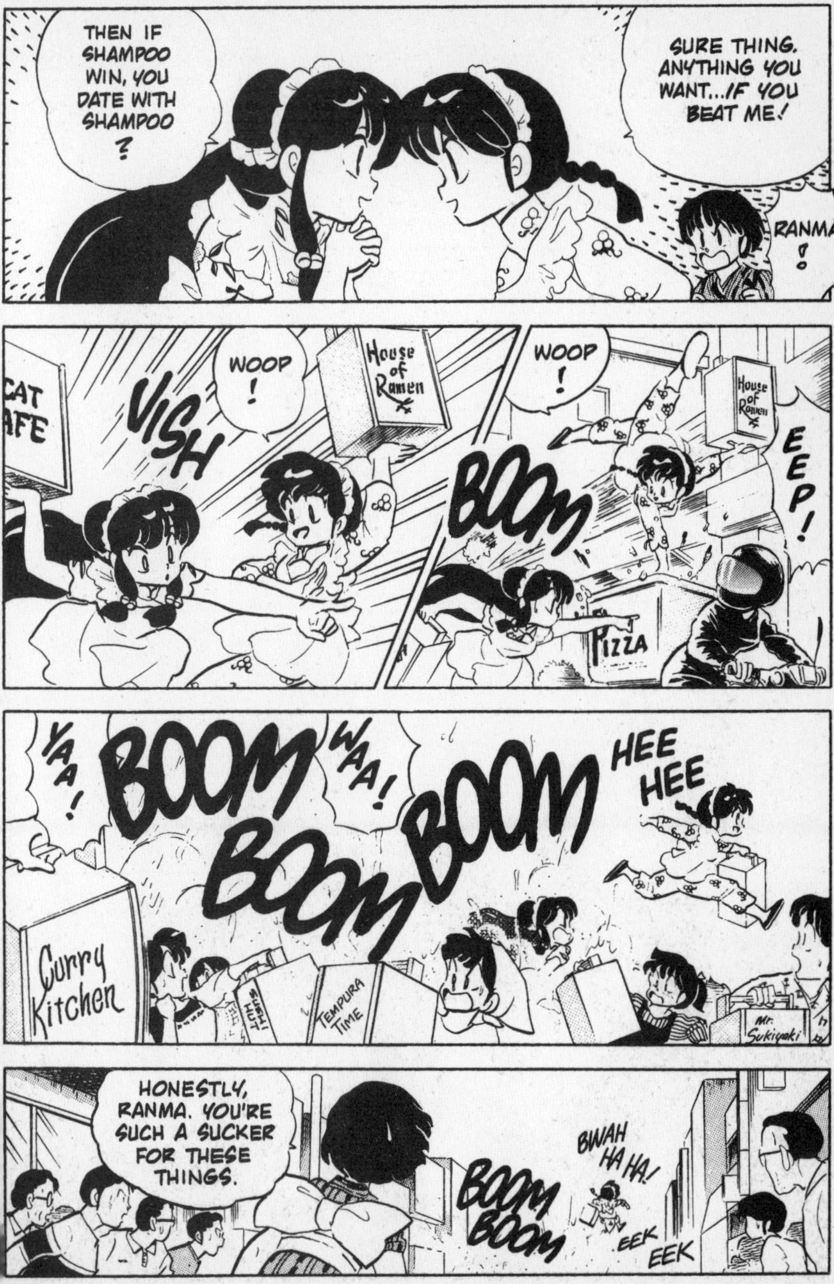
THEN IF SHAMPOO WIN, YOU DATE WITH SHAMPOO ?
SURE THING. ANYTHING YOU WANT...IF YOU BEAT ME!
RANMA !
CAT CAFE
WOOP !
House of Ramen
VISH
WOOP !
House of Ramen
BOOM
EEP!
PIZZA
YAA!
BOOM
BOOM
WAA!
BOOM
HEE HEE
Curry Kitchen
SUSHI HUT
TEMPURA TIME
Mr. Sukiyaki
HONESTLY, RANMA. YOU'RE SUCH A SUCKER FOR THESE THINGS.
BWAH HA HA!
BOOM BOOM
EEK EEK

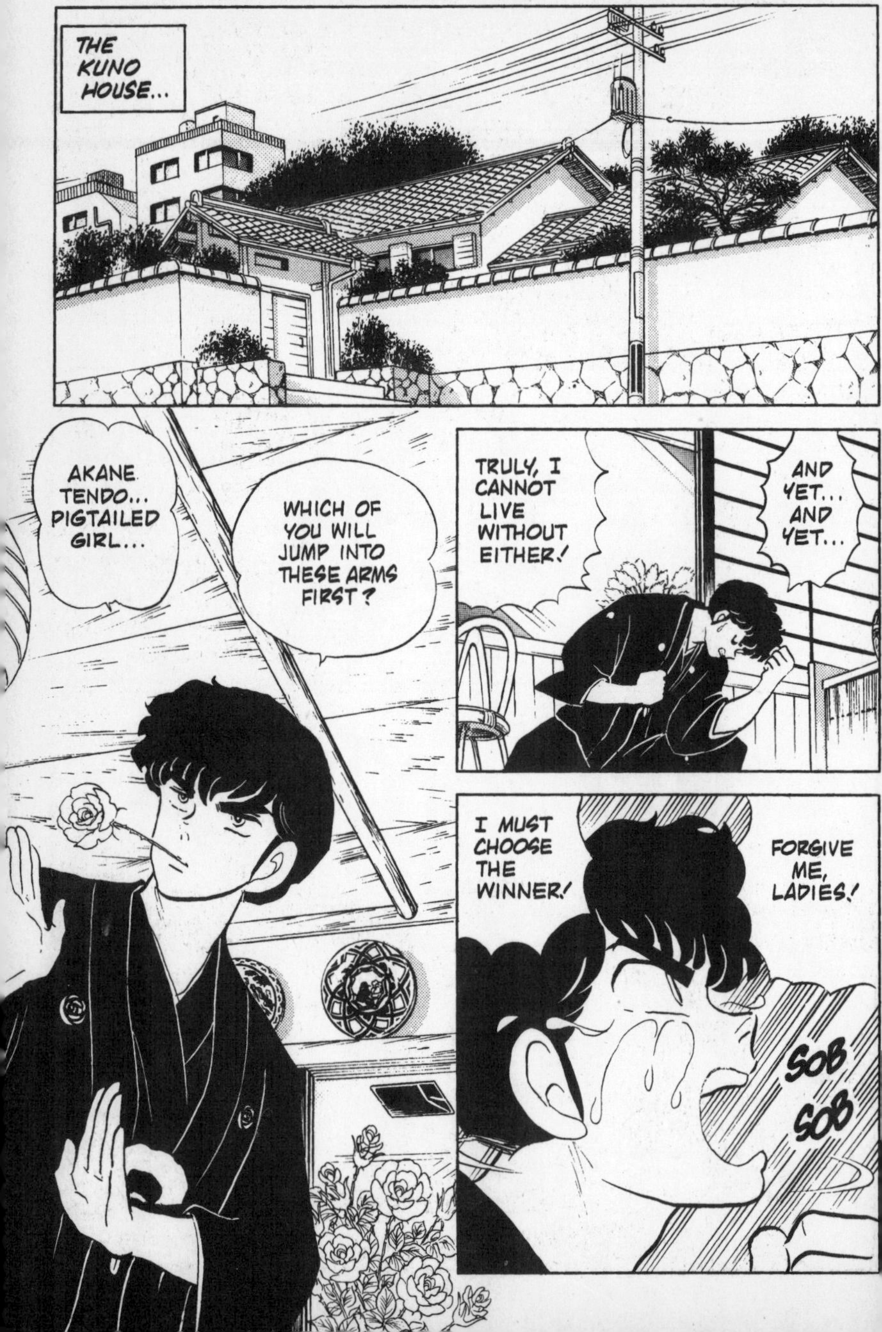
THE KUNO HOUSE...
AKANE TENDO... PIGTAILED GIRL...
WHICH OF YOU WILL JUMP INTO THESE ARMS FIRST?
TRULY, I CANNOT LIVE WITHOUT EITHER!
AND YET... AND YET...
I MUST CHOOSE THE WINNER!
FORGIVE ME, LADIES!
SOB SOB

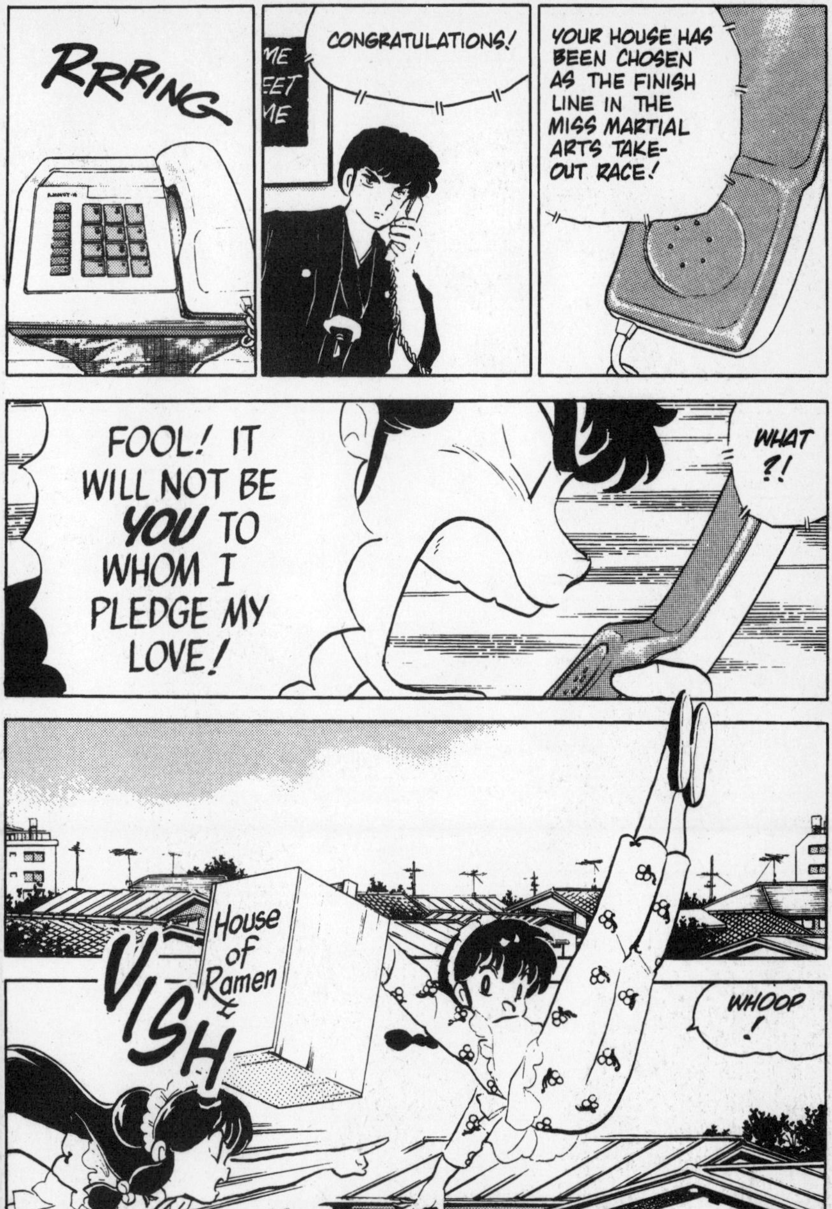
RRRING
CONGRATULATIONS!
YOUR HOUSE HAS BEEN CHOSEN AS THE FINISH LINE IN THE MISS MARTIAL ARTS TAKE-OUT RACE!
FOOL! IT WILL NOT BE YOU TO WHOM I PLEDGE MY LOVE!
WHAT?!
House of Ramen
VISH
WHOOP!

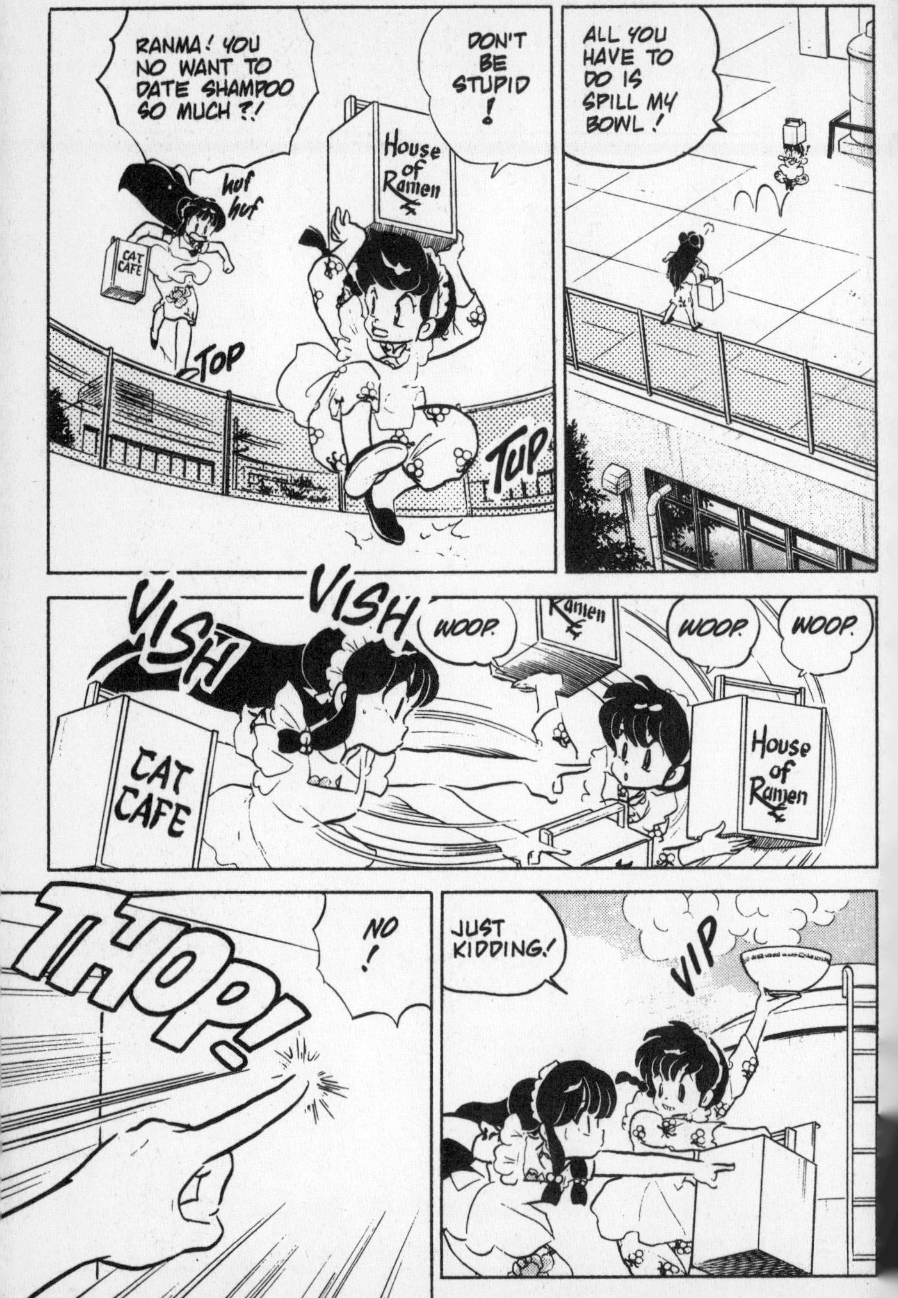
RANMA! YOU NO WANT TO DATE SHAMPOO SO MUCH ?!
huf huf
TOP
House of Ramen
DON'T BE STUPID !
TUP
ALL YOU HAVE TO DO IS SPILL MY BOWL !
VISH
VISH
Ramen
WOOP.
WOOP.
WOOP.
CAT CAFE
House of Ramen
THOP!
NO !
JUST KIDDING!
VIP

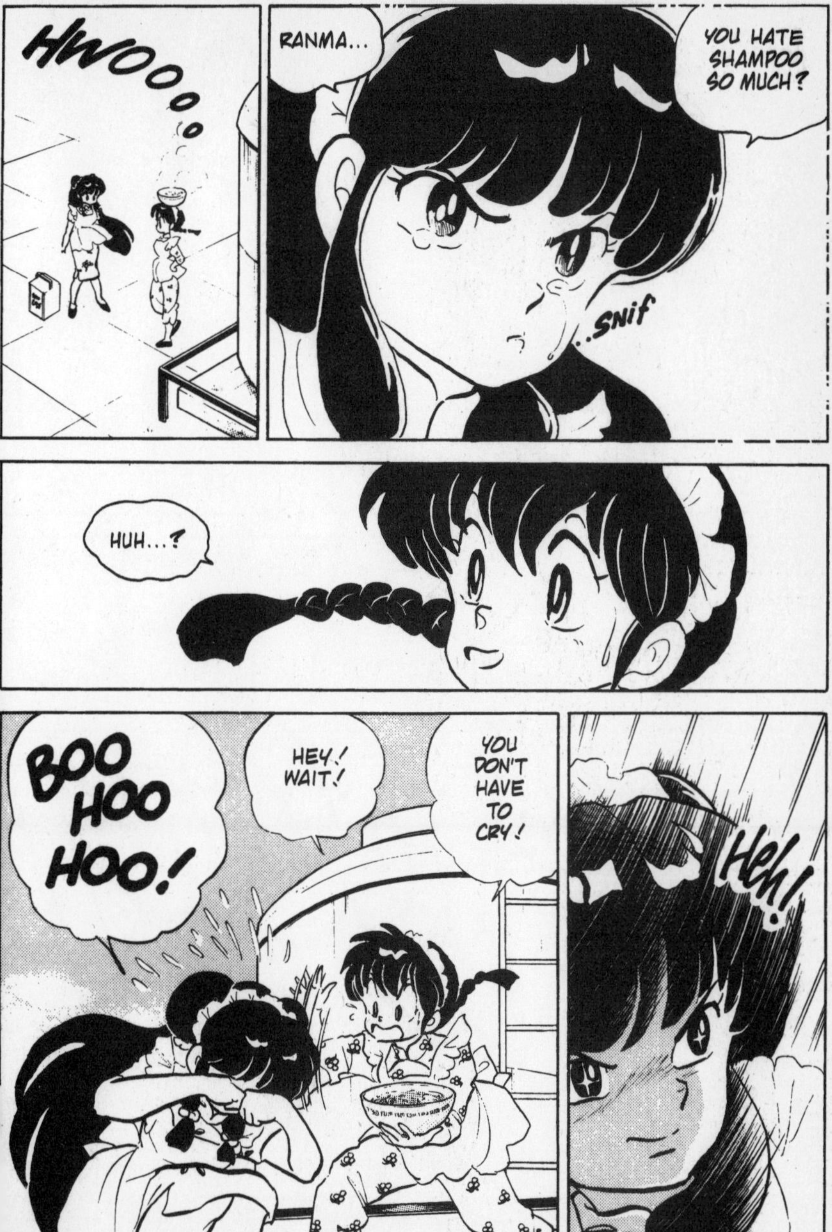
HWOOOOO
RANMA...
YOU HATE SHAMPOO SO MUCH?
...SNIF
HUH...?
BOO HOO HOO!
HEY! WAIT!
YOU DON'T HAVE TO CRY!
HEH!

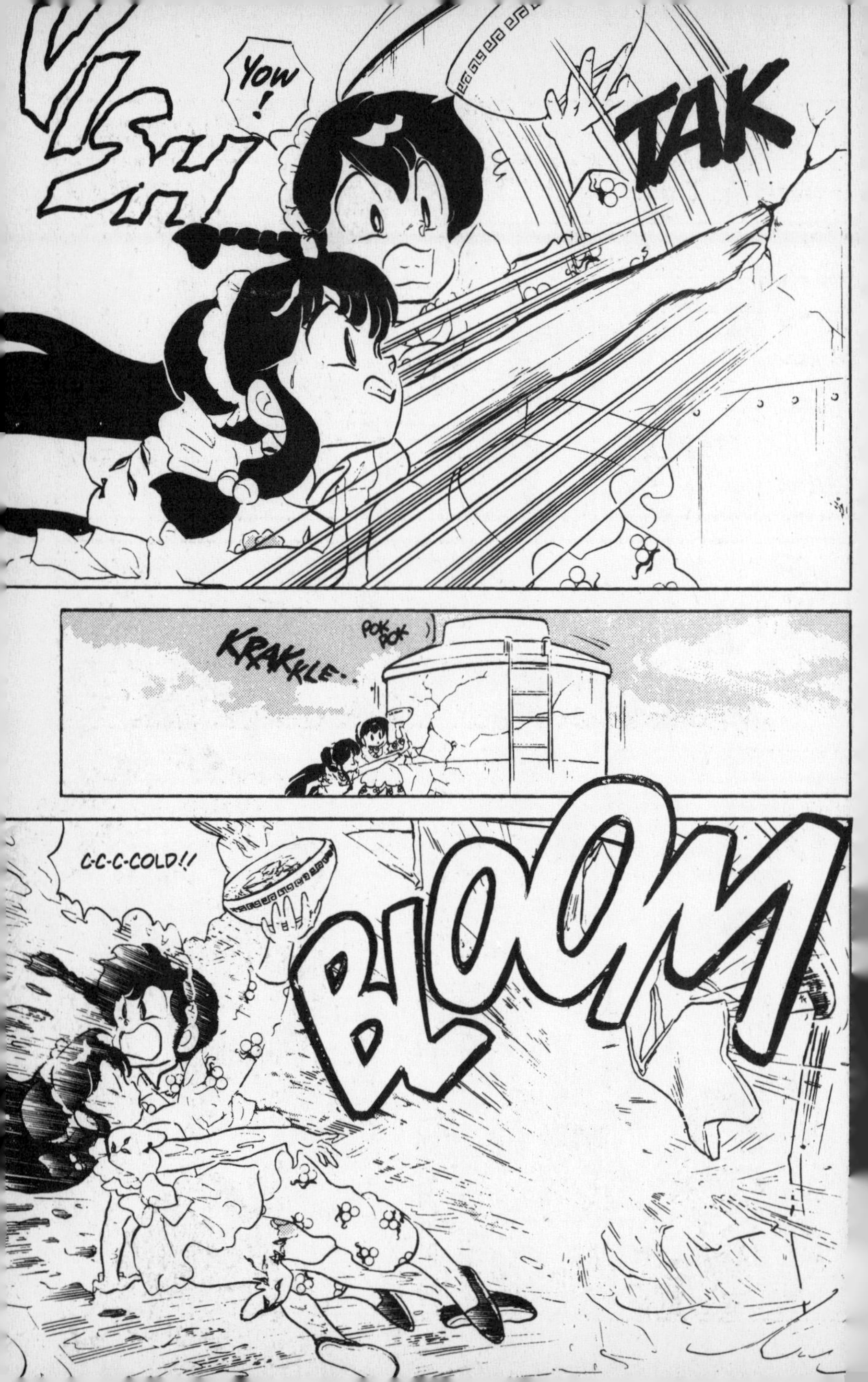
VWSHH!
YOW!
TAK
KRAKKLE..
POK POK
C-C-C-COLD!!
BLOOM

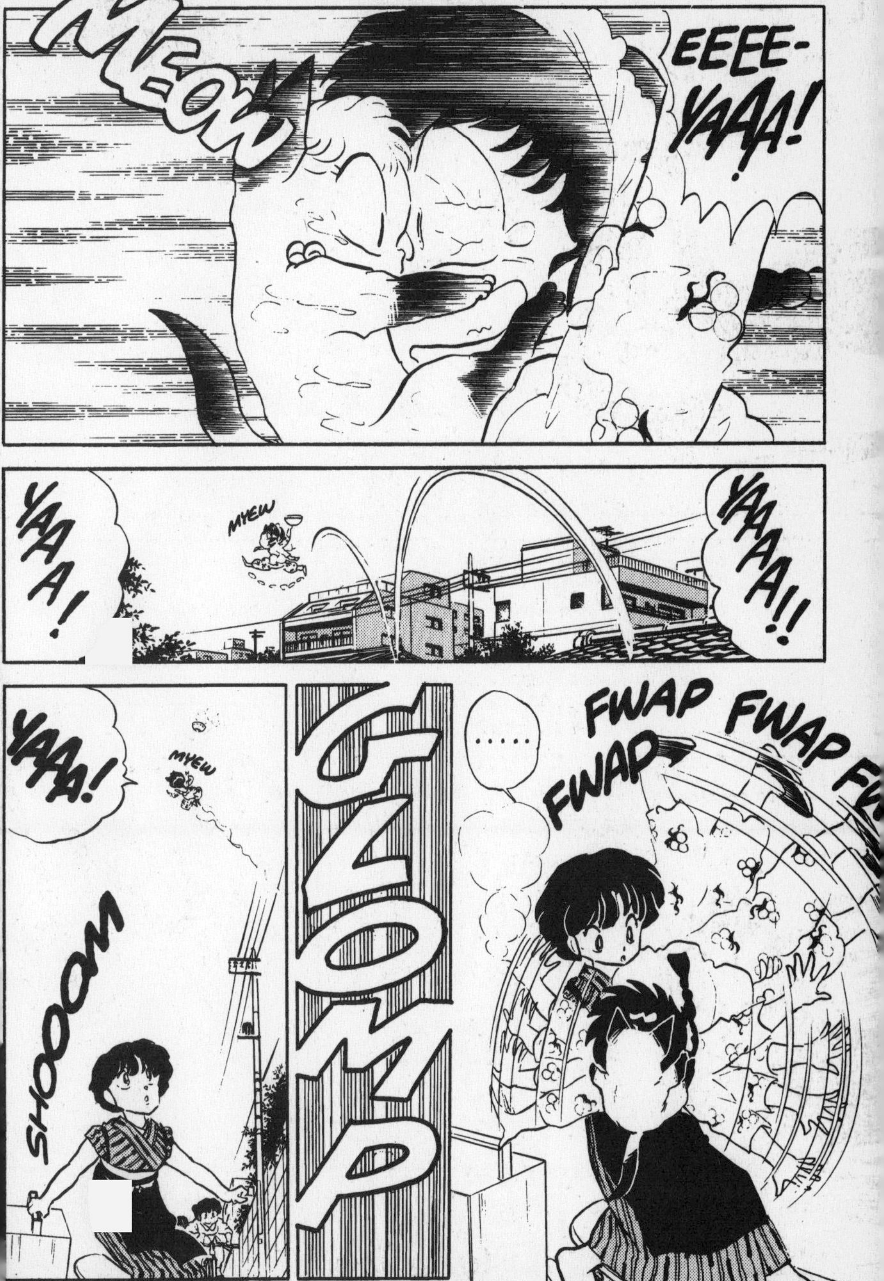
MEOW
EEEE-YAAAA!
YAAA A!
MYEW
YAAAAA!!
YAAAA!
MYEW
SHOOOOM
GLOMP
......
FWAP
FWAP
FWAP
FW

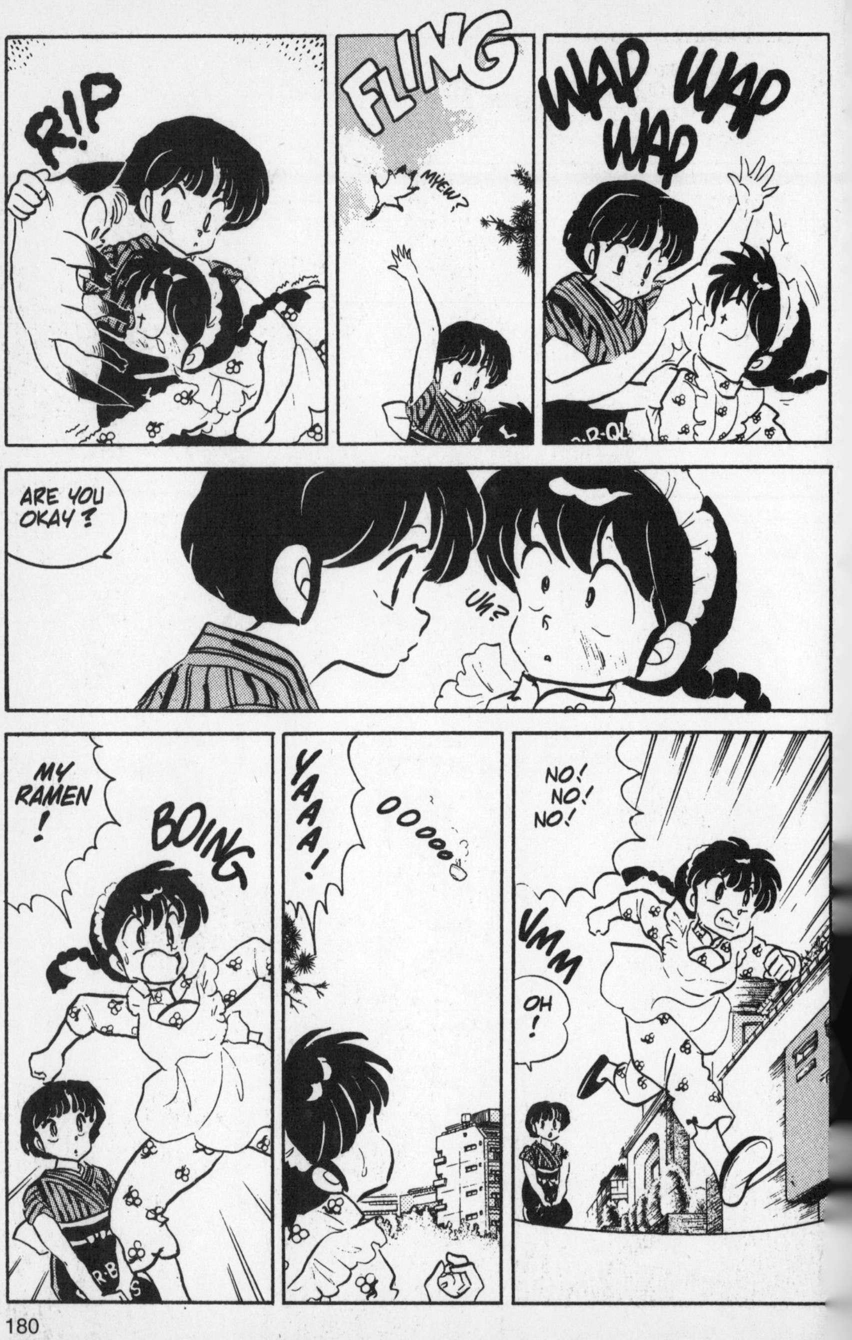
R!P
FLING
MYEW?
WAP WAP WAP
WAP
ARE YOU OKAY?
UH?
MY RAMEN!
BOING
YAAAA!
OOOOOO
NO! NO! NO!
VMM
OH!

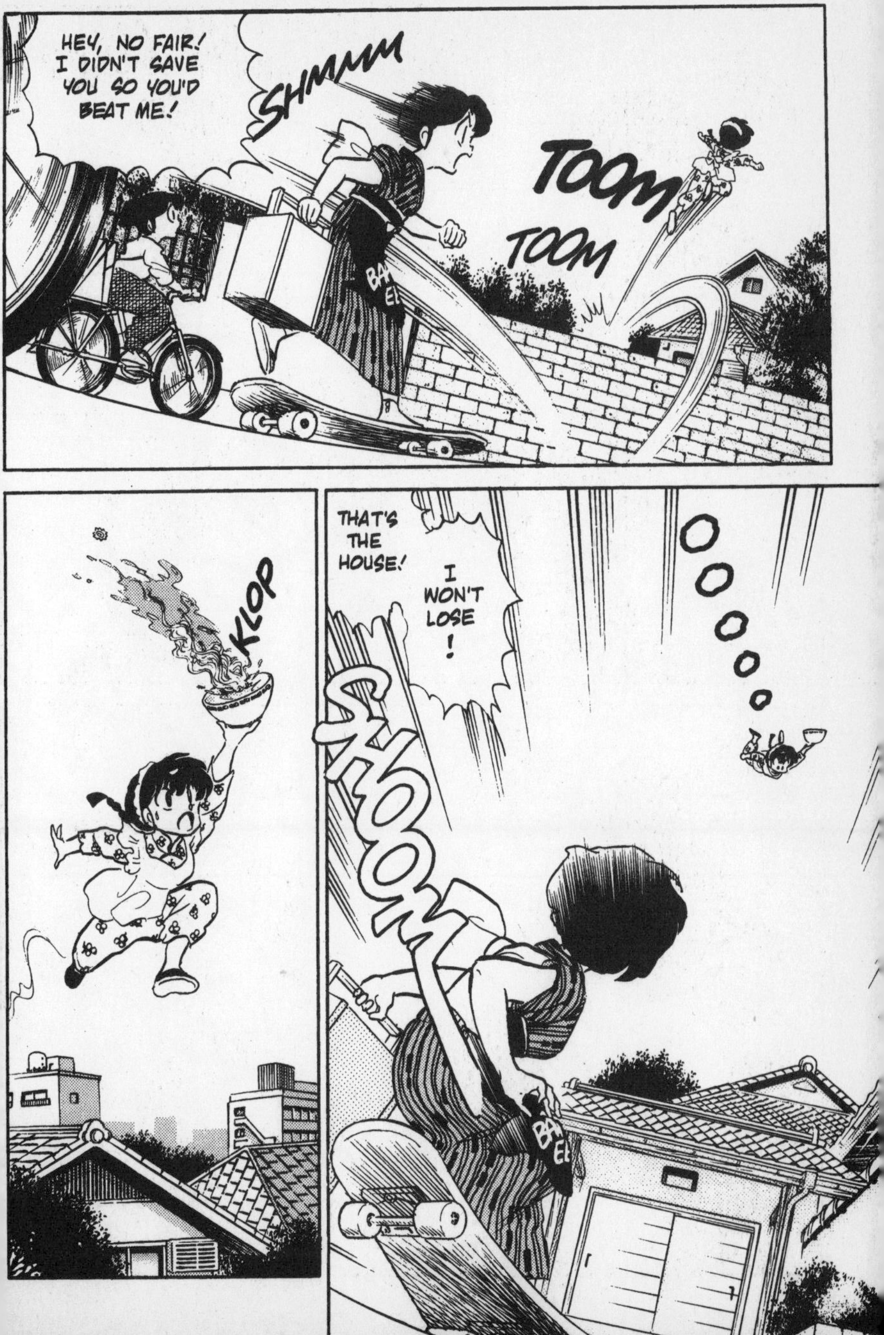
HEY, NO FAIR! I DIDN'T SAVE YOU SO YOU'D BEAT ME!
SHMMM
TOOM
TOOM
KLOP
THAT'S THE HOUSE!
I WON'T LOSE!
SHOOM
OOOOO

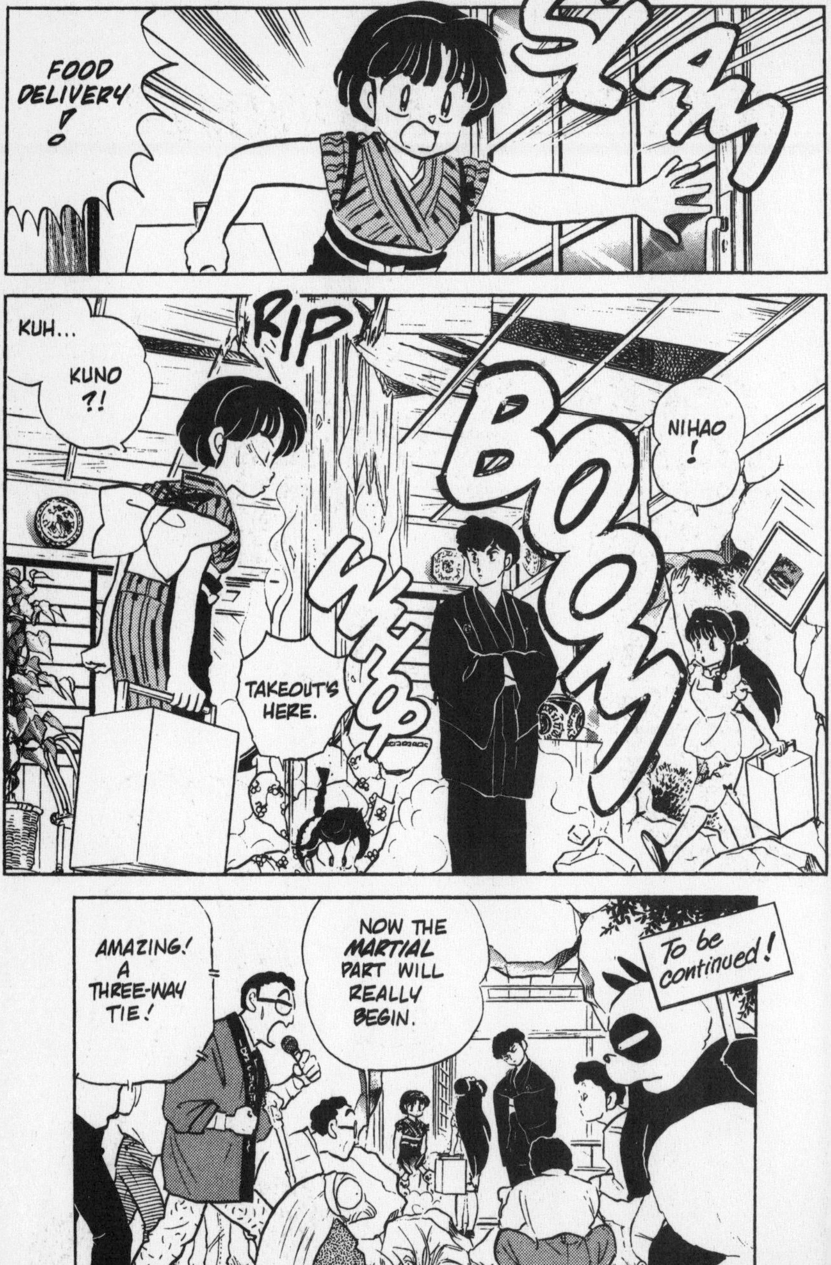
FOOD DELIVERY!
SLAM
KUH... KUNO ?!
RIP
BOOM
NIHAO!
TAKEOUT'S HERE.
WHOP
AMAZING! A THREE-WAY TIE!
NOW THE MARTIAL PART WILL REALLY BEGIN.
To be continued!

Part 12

NOODLES, ANYONE?

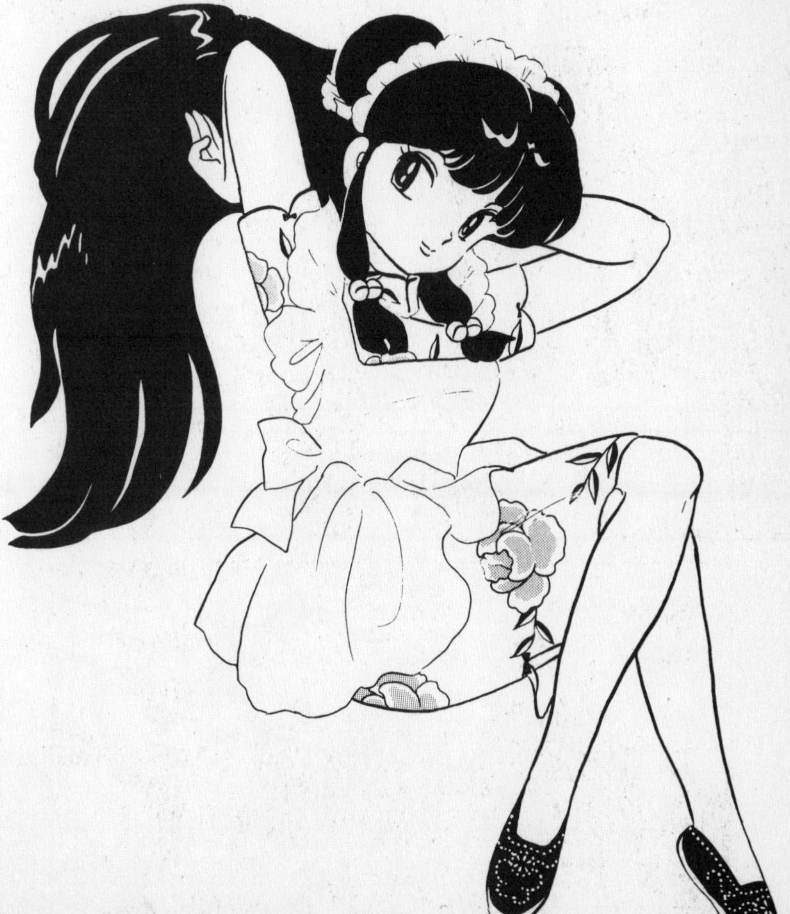

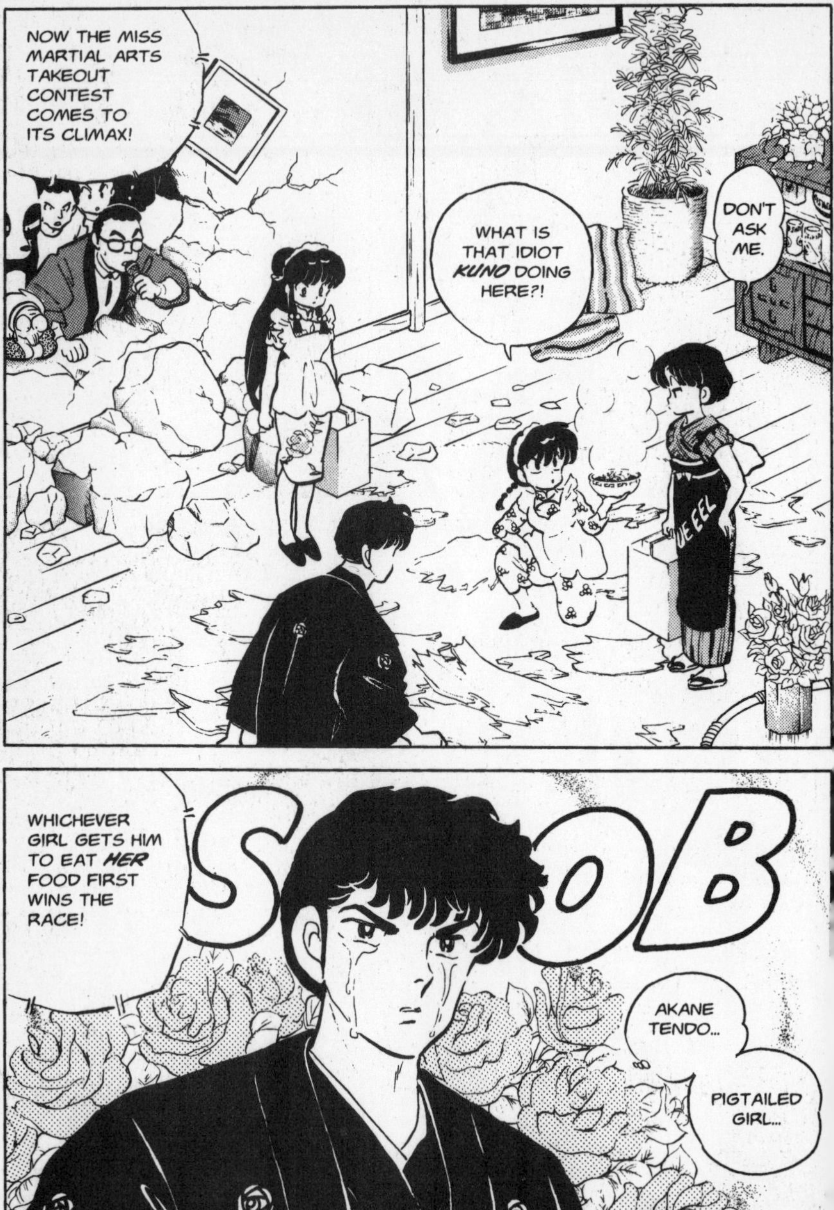
NOW THE MISS MARTIAL ARTS TAKEOUT CONTEST COMES TO ITS CLIMAX!
WHAT IS THAT IDIOT KUNO DOING HERE?!
DON'T ASK ME.
UE EEL
WHICHEVER GIRL GETS HIM TO EAT HER FOOD FIRST WINS THE RACE!
SOB
AKANE TENDO...
PIGTAILED GIRL...

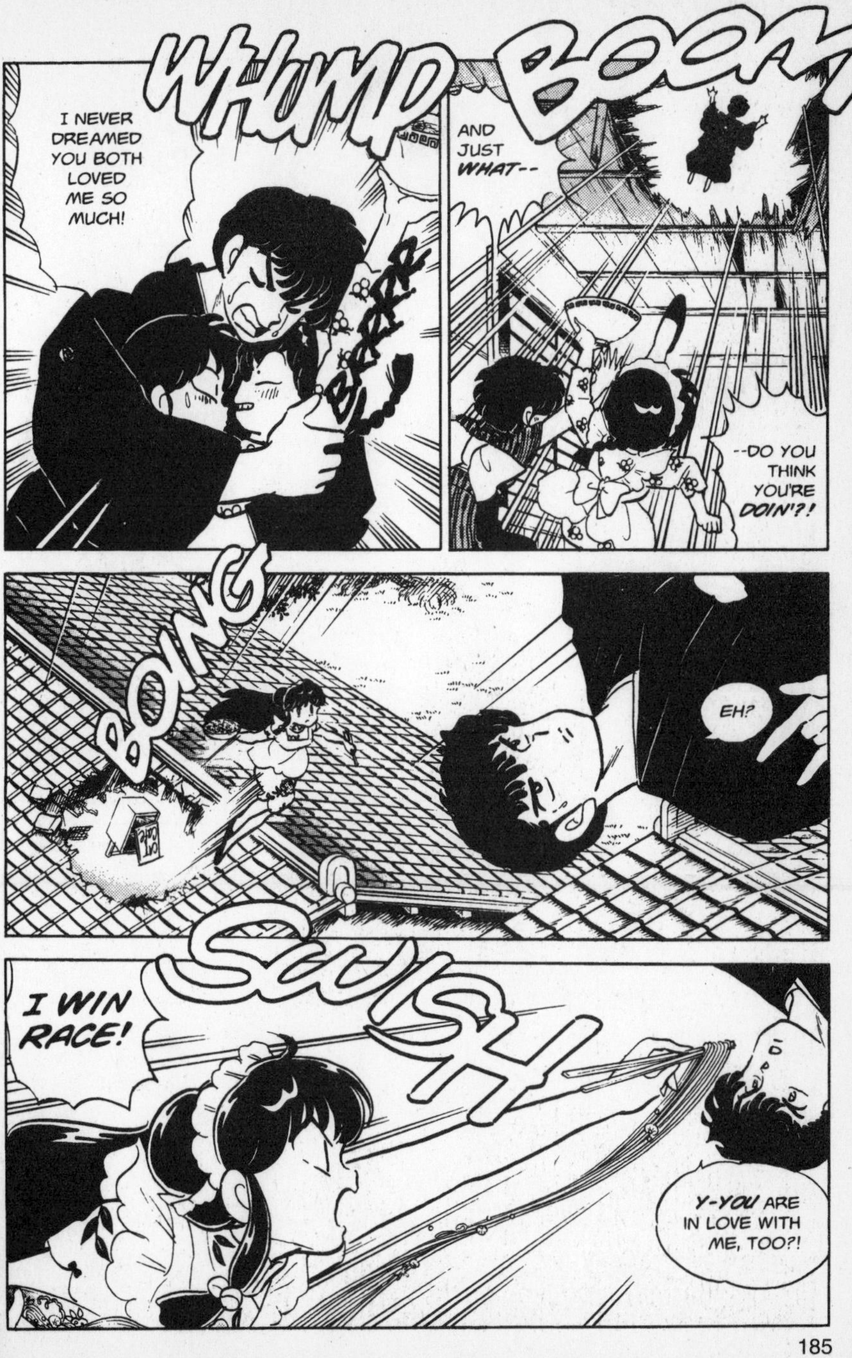
WHUMP
I NEVER DREAMED YOU BOTH LOVED ME SO MUCH!
BOOM
AND JUST WHAT--
--DO YOU THINK YOU'RE DOIN'?!
BOING
EH?
SWISH
I WIN RACE!
Y-YOU ARE IN LOVE WITH ME, TOO?!

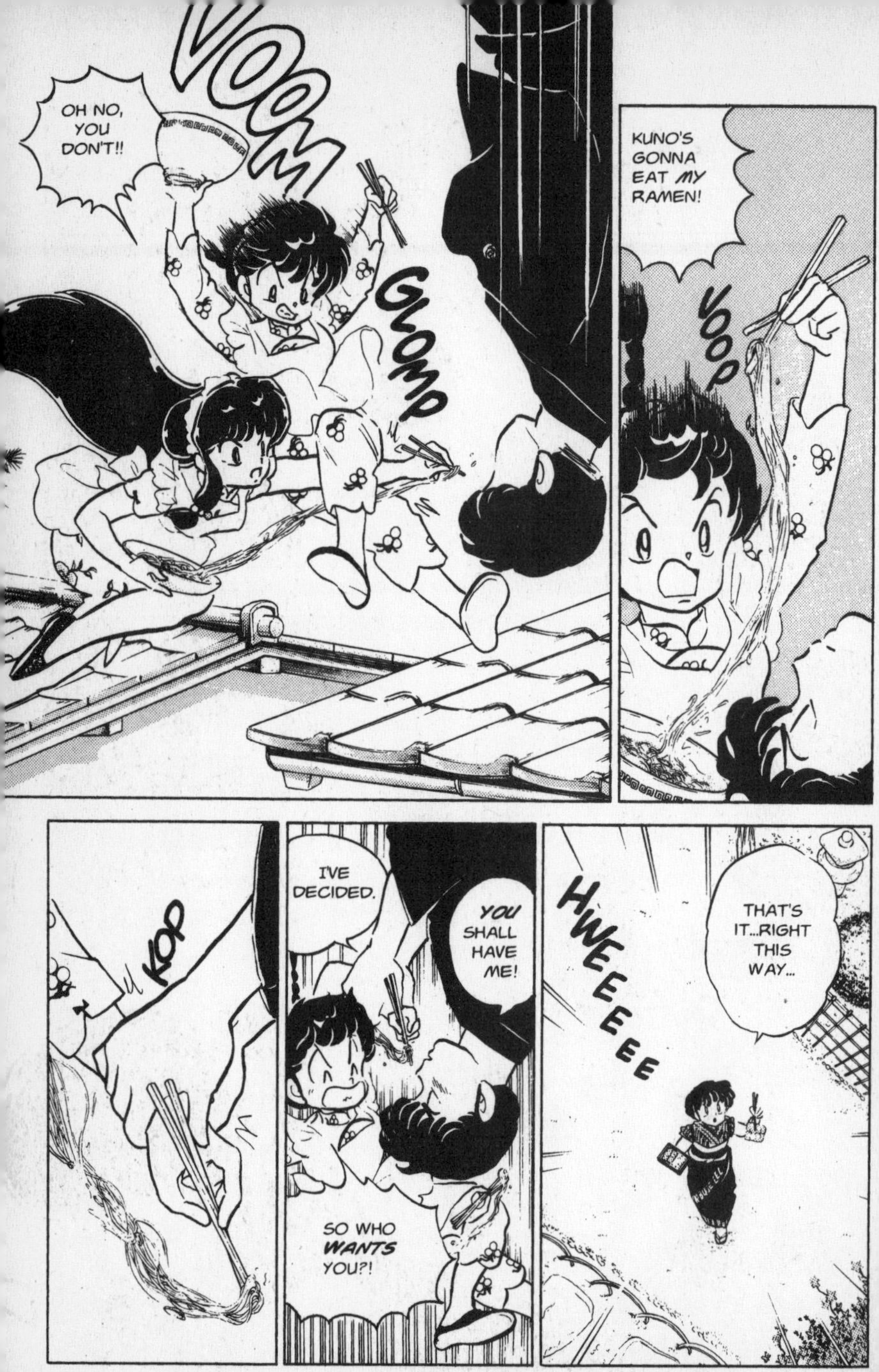
VOOM
OH NO, YOU DON'T!!
GLOMP
KUNO'S GONNA EAT MY RAMEN!
VOOP
KOP
I'VE DECIDED.
YOU SHALL HAVE ME!
SO WHO WANTS YOU?!
HWEEEEEE
THAT'S IT...RIGHT THIS WAY...

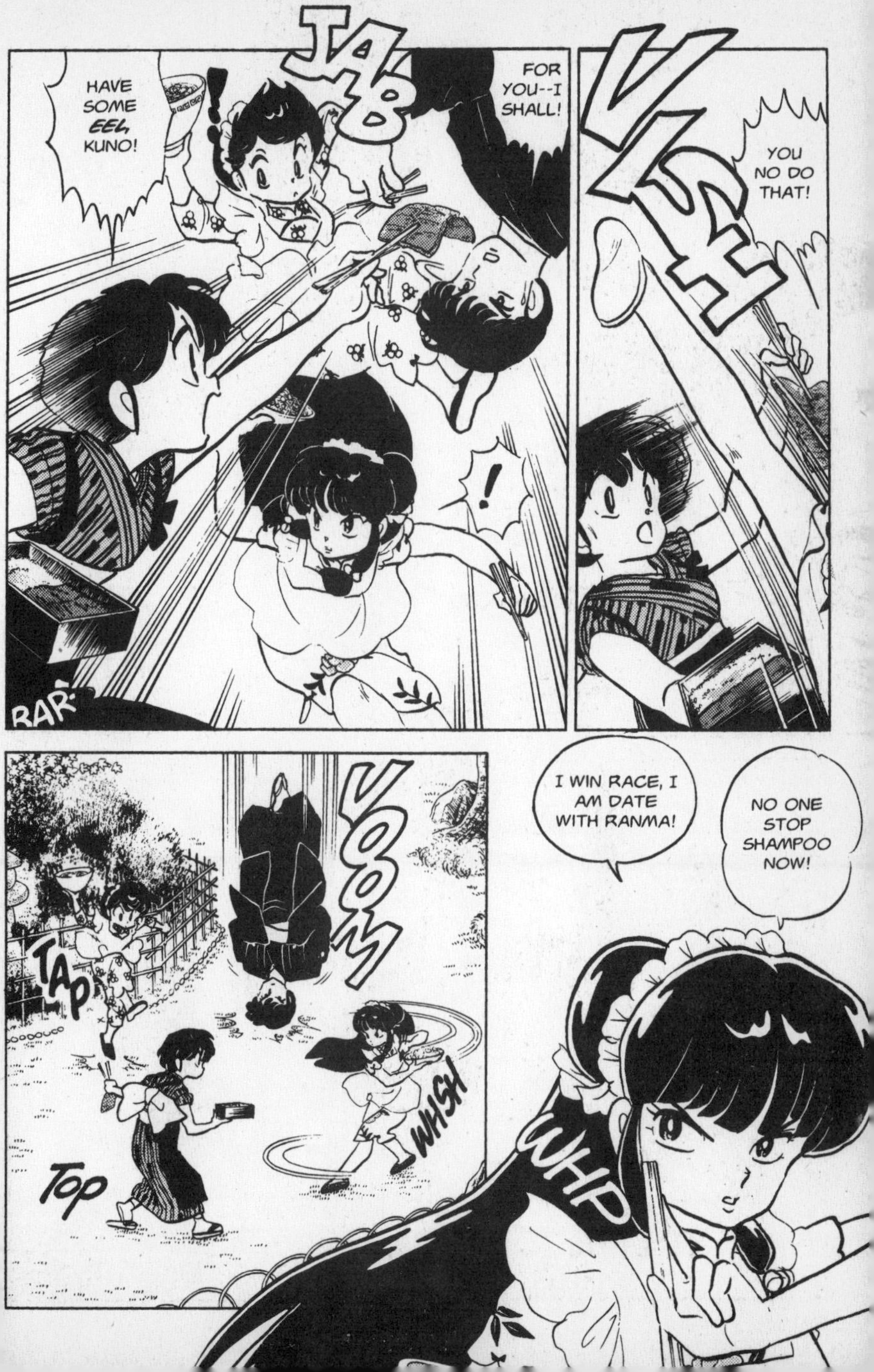
JAB
HAVE SOME EEL, KUNO!
!
FOR YOU--I SHALL!
!
RAR
VISH
YOU NO DO THAT!
VOOM
TAP
WHSH
Top
I WIN RACE, I AM DATE WITH RANMA!
NO ONE STOP SHAMPOO NOW!
WHP

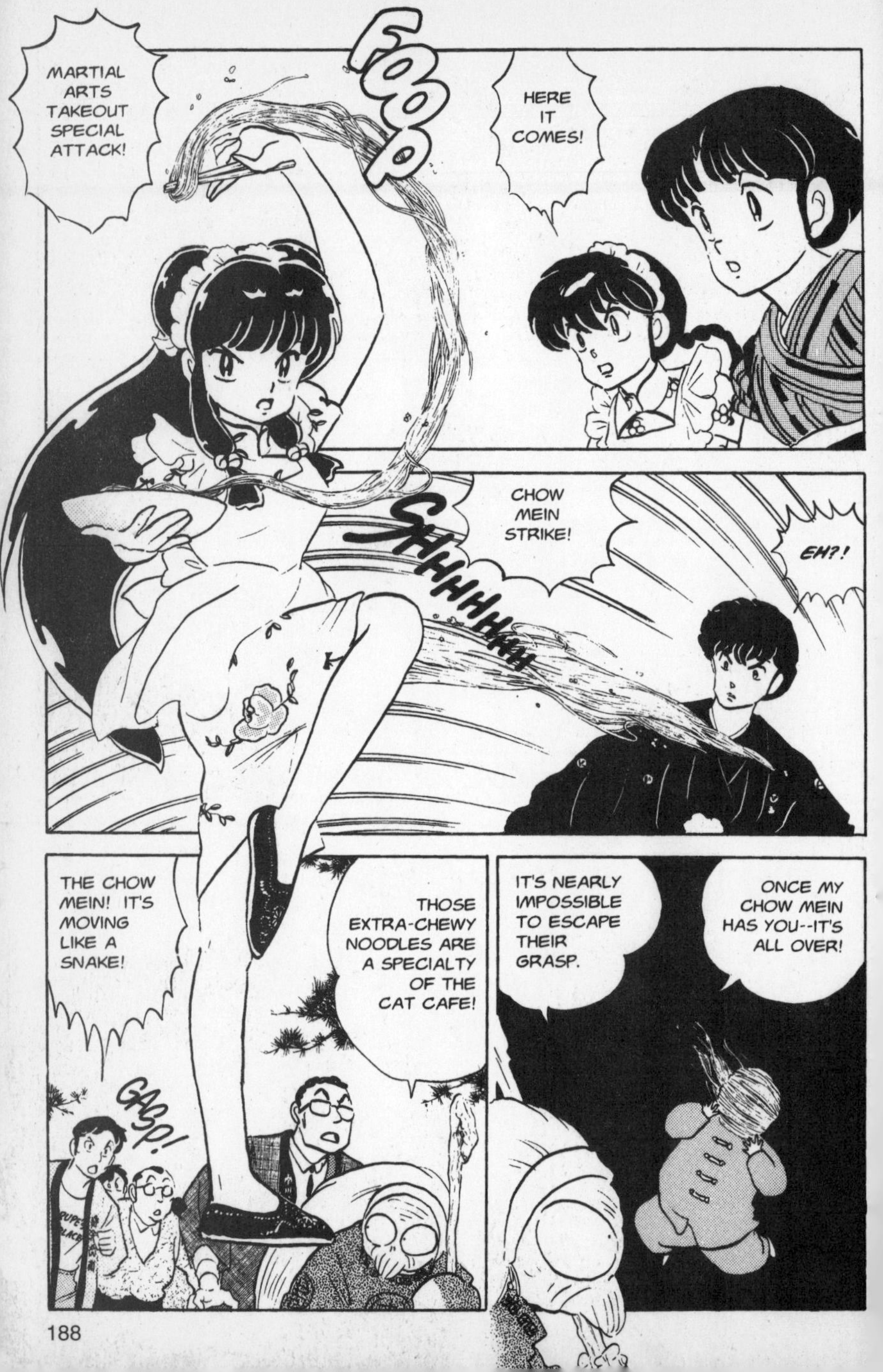
MARTIAL ARTS TAKEOUT SPECIAL ATTACK!
FOOOP
HERE IT COMES!
CHOW MEIN STRIKE!
GSHHHHHHHH
EH?!
THE CHOW MEIN! IT'S MOVING LIKE A SNAKE!
GASP!
THOSE EXTRA-CHEWY NOODLES ARE A SPECIALTY OF THE CAT CAFE!
IT'S NEARLY IMPOSSIBLE TO ESCAPE THEIR GRASP.
ONCE MY CHOW MEIN HAS YOU--IT'S ALL OVER!

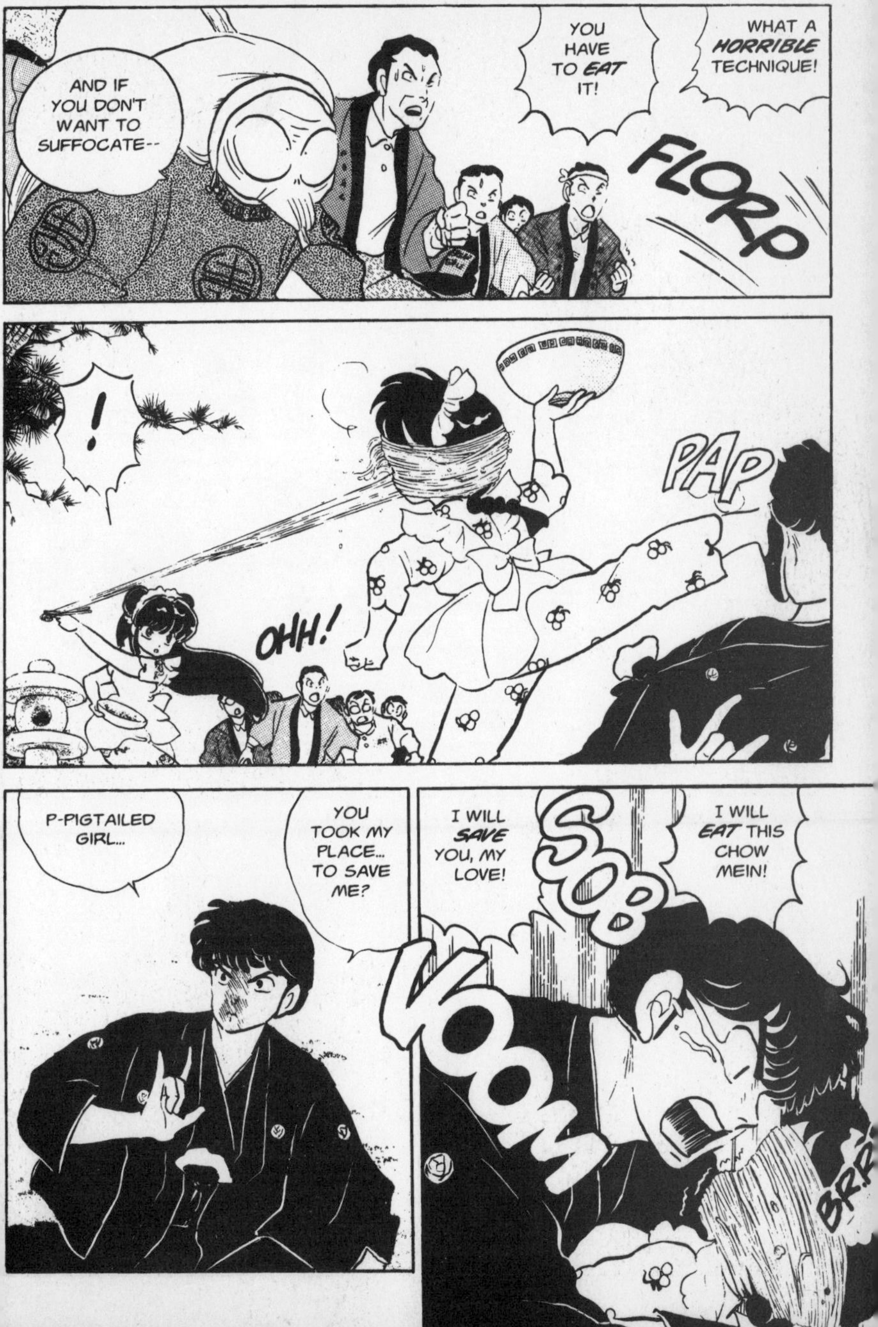
AND IF YOU DON'T WANT TO SUFFOCATE--
YOU HAVE TO EAT IT!
WHAT A HORRIBLE TECHNIQUE!
FLORP
!
PAP
OHH!
P-PIGTAILED GIRL...
YOU TOOK MY PLACE... TO SAVE ME?
I WILL SAVE YOU, MY LOVE!
SOB
I WILL EAT THIS CHOW MEIN!
VOOM
BRR

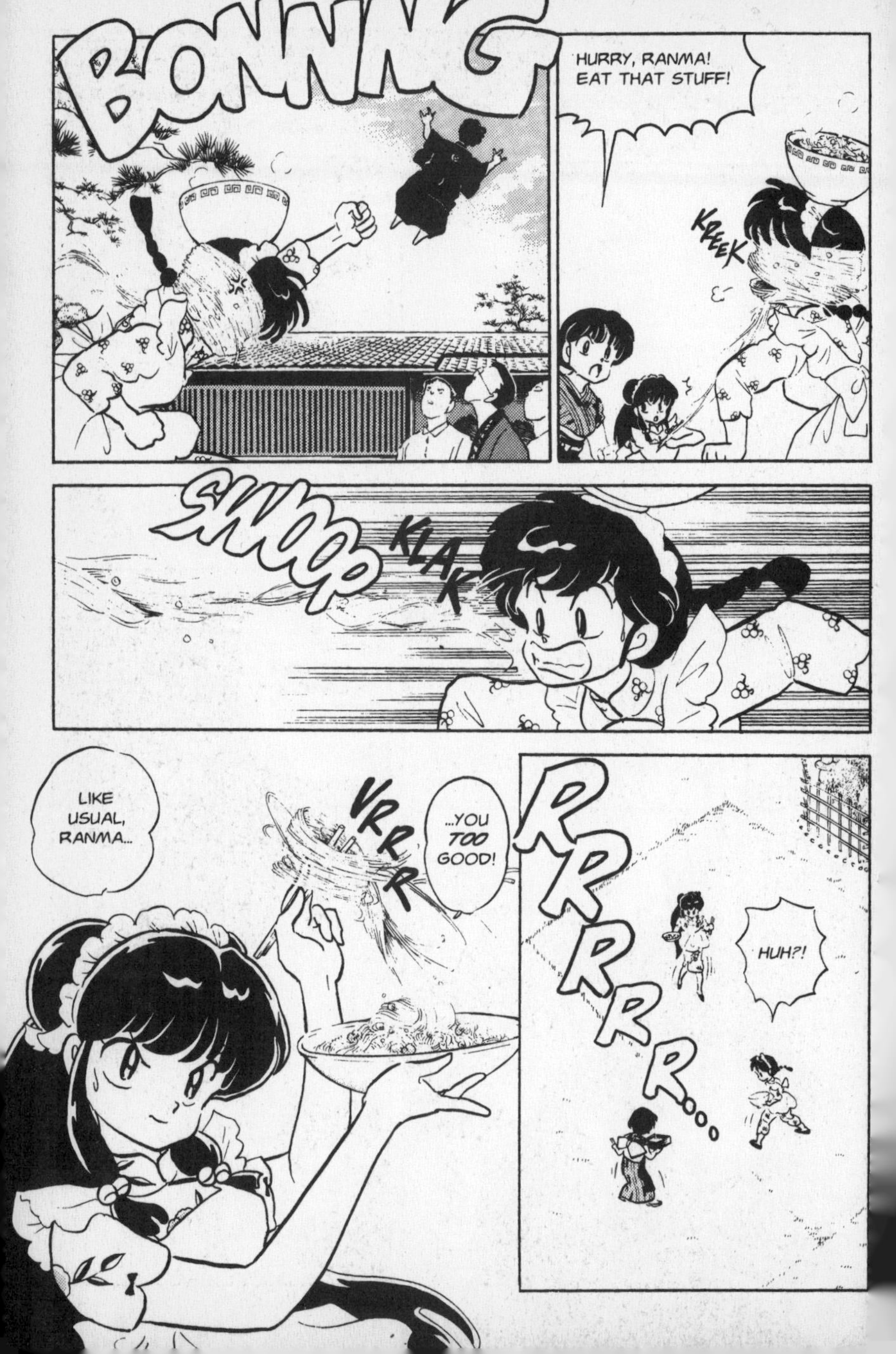
BONNNG
HURRY, RANMA! EAT THAT STUFF!
KREEK
SHLOOP
KLAK
LIKE USUAL, RANMA...
VRRRR
...YOU TOO GOOD!
RRRRRRR...
HUH?!

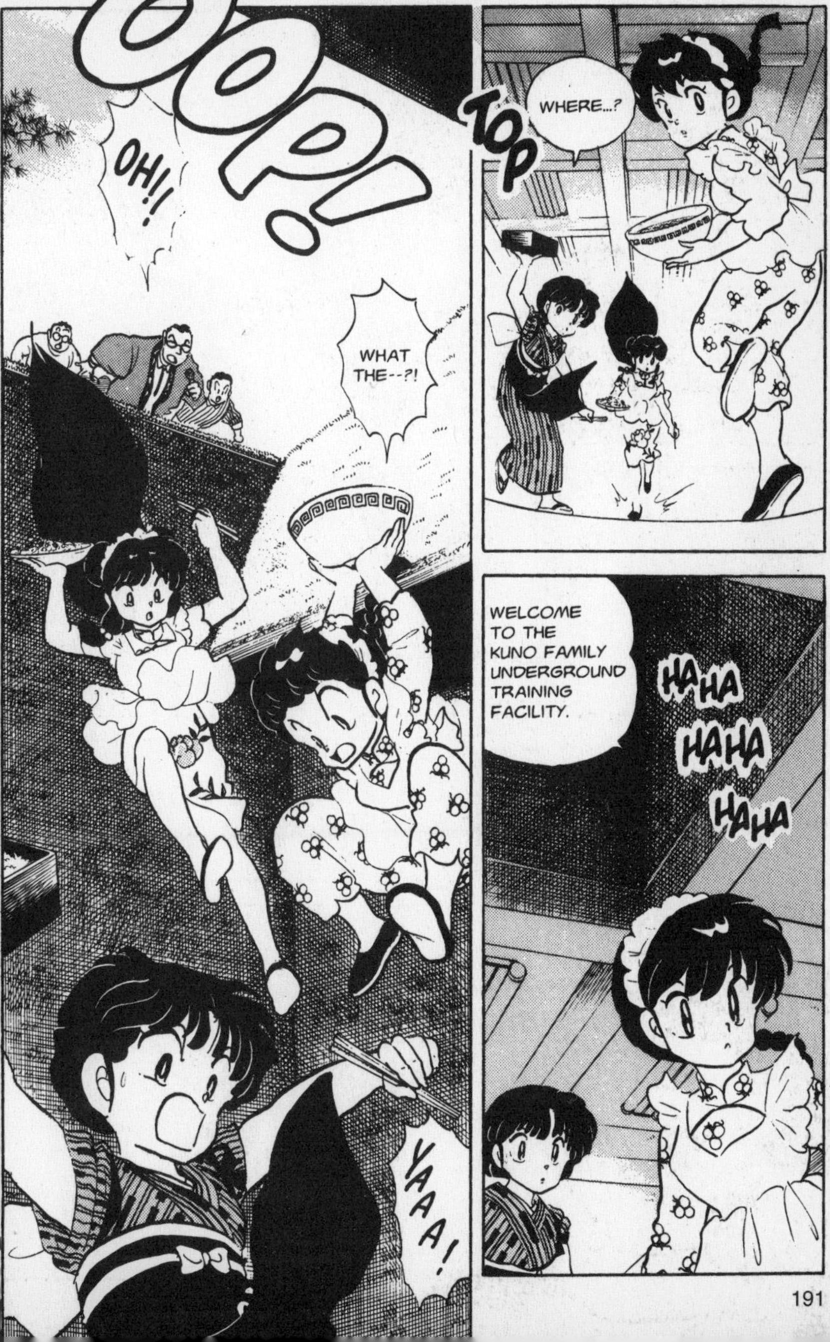

OOOP!
OH!!
WHAT THE--?!
YAAAA!
TOP
WHERE...?
WELCOME TO THE KUNO FAMILY UNDERGROUND TRAINING FACILITY.
HAHA
HAHA
HAHA

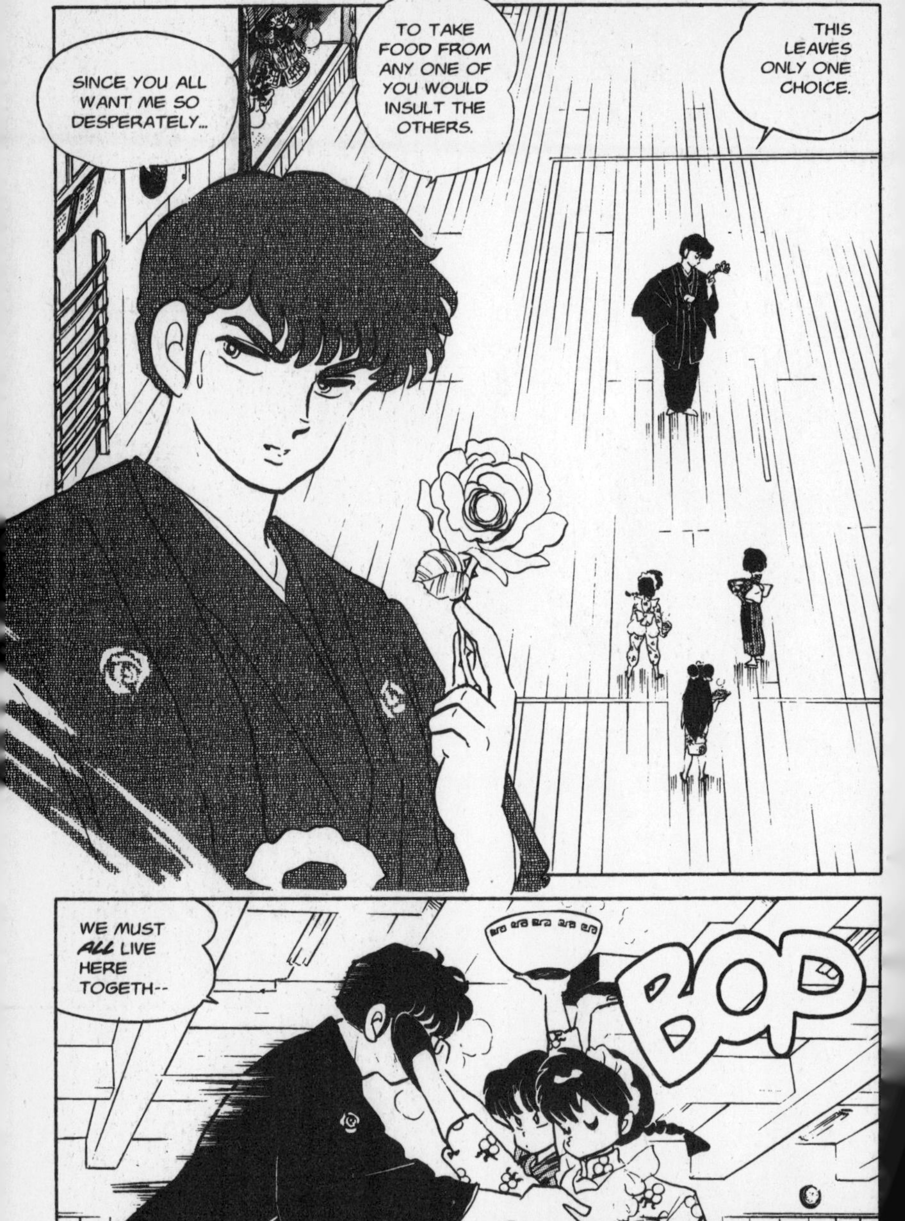
SINCE YOU ALL WANT ME SO DESPERATELY...
TO TAKE FOOD FROM ANY ONE OF YOU WOULD INSULT THE OTHERS.
THIS LEAVES ONLY ONE CHOICE.
WE MUST *ALL* LIVE HERE TOGETH--
BOP

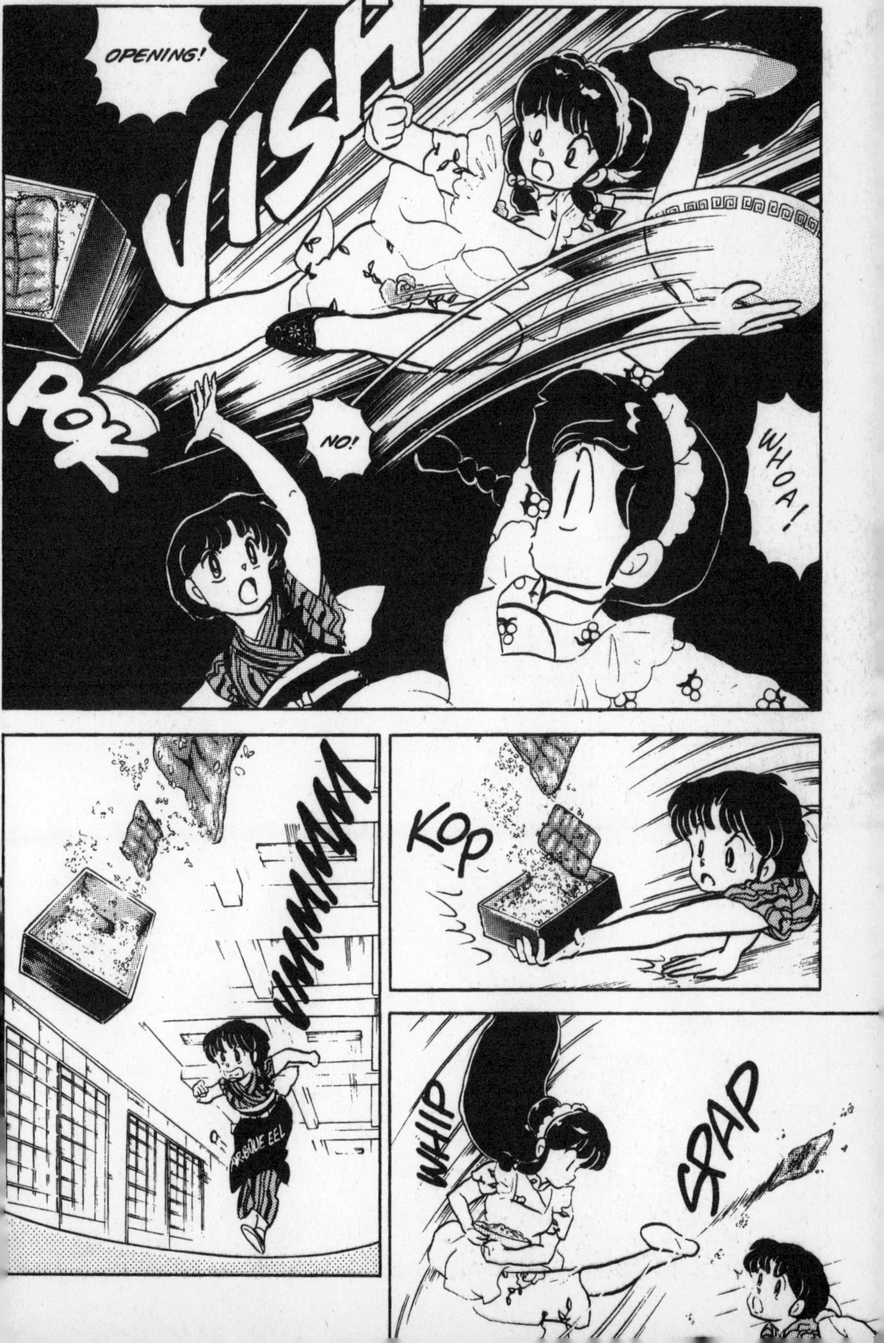
OPENING!
VISH
POK
NO!
WHOA!
VMMMM
KOP
WHIP
SPAP

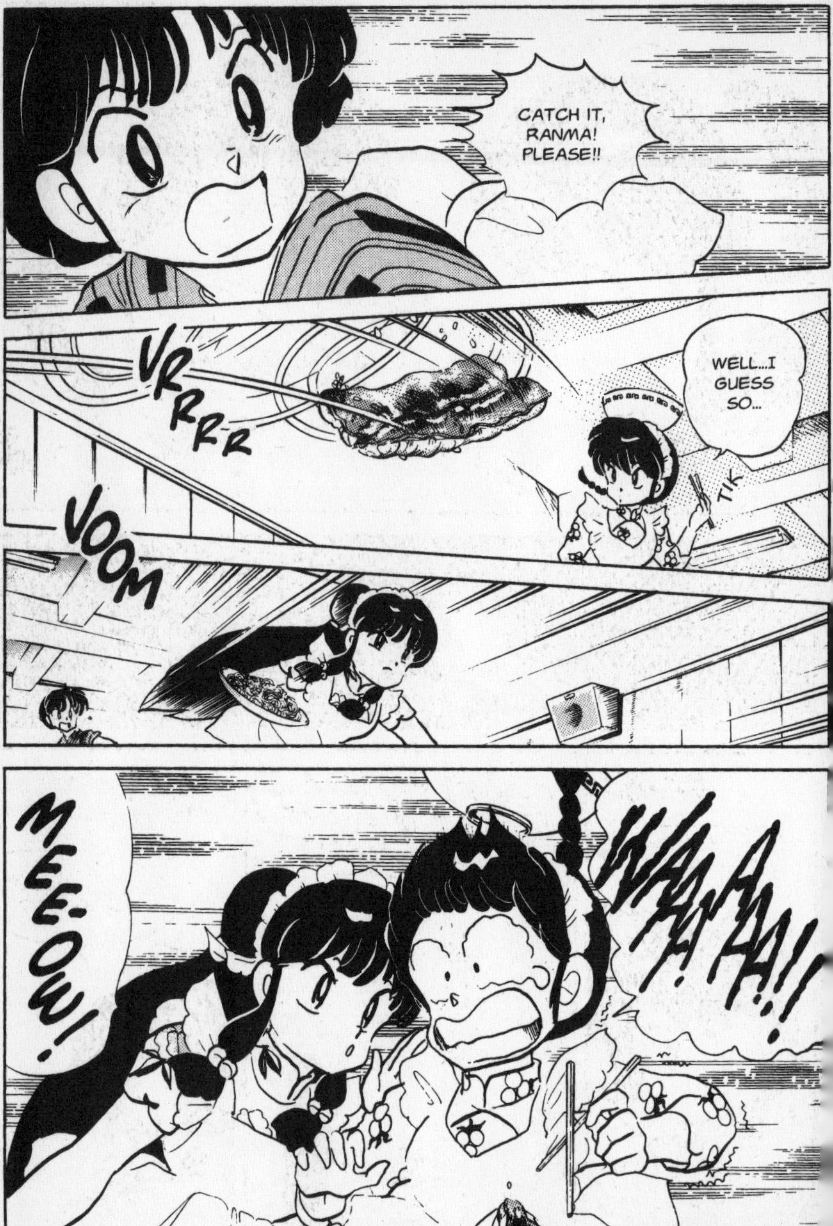
CATCH IT, RANMA! PLEASE!!
VRRRRR
WELL...I GUESS SO...
TIK
VOOM
MEE-OW!
WAAAAA!!

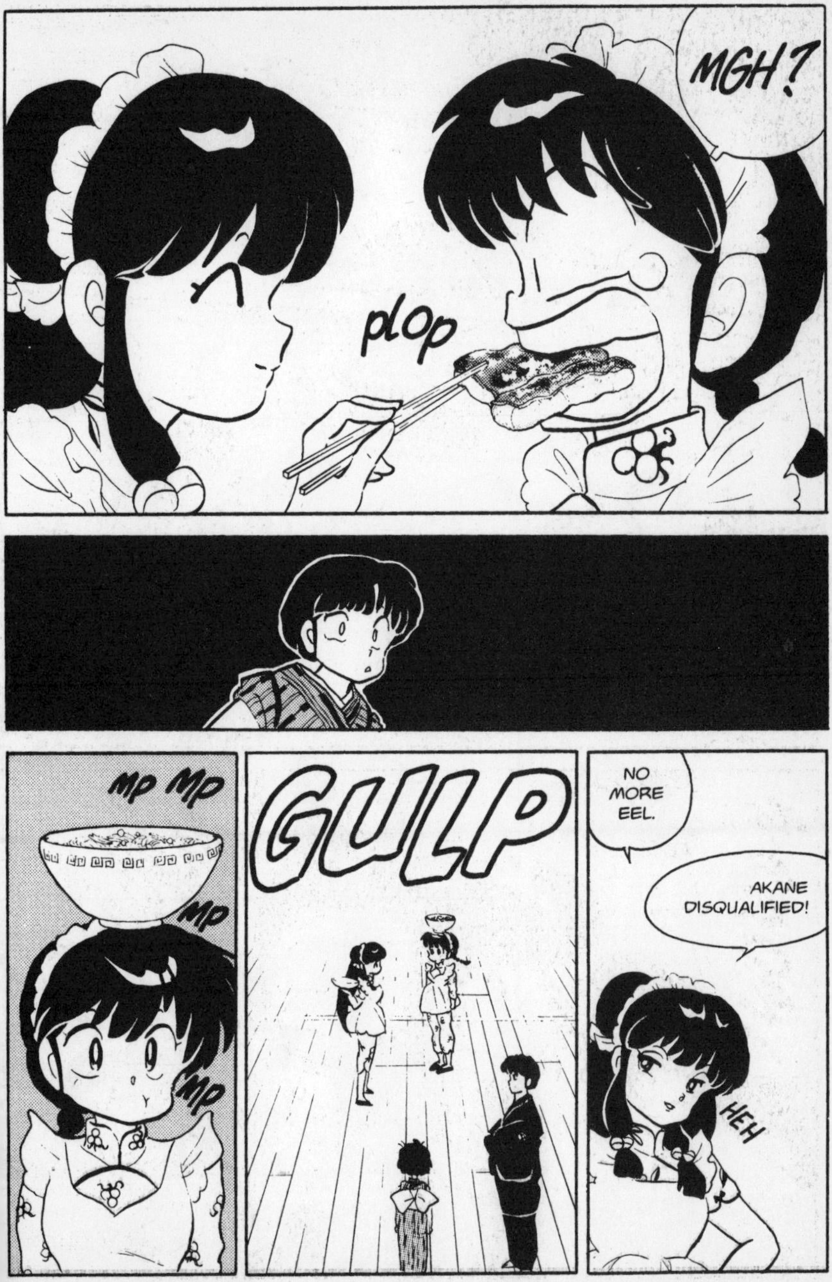

MGH?
plop
MP MP
MP
MP
GULP
NO MORE EEL.
AKANE DISQUALIFIED!
HEH

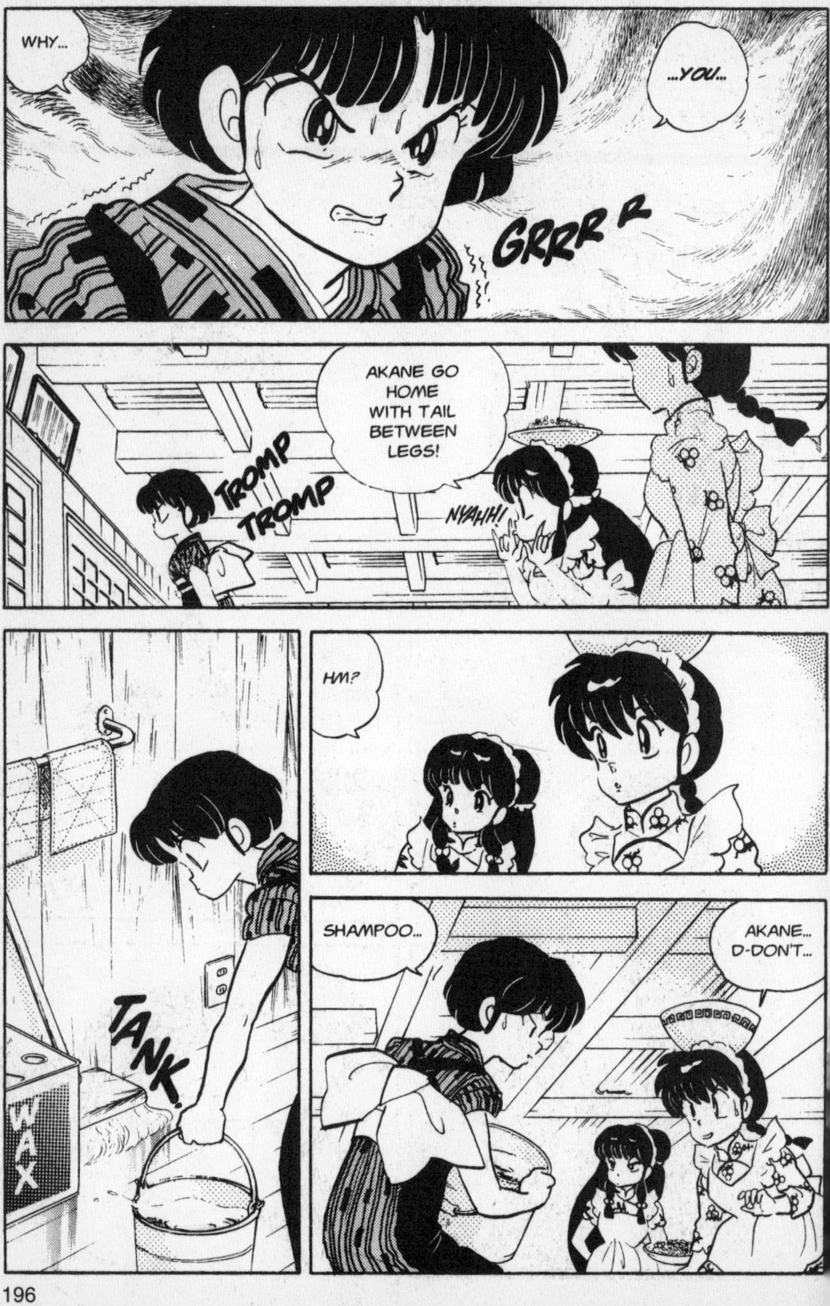
WHY...
...YOU...
GRRRR
AKANE GO HOME WITH TAIL BETWEEN LEGS!
TROMP TROMP
NYAHH!
TANK!
HM?
SHAMPOO...
AKANE... D-DON'T...

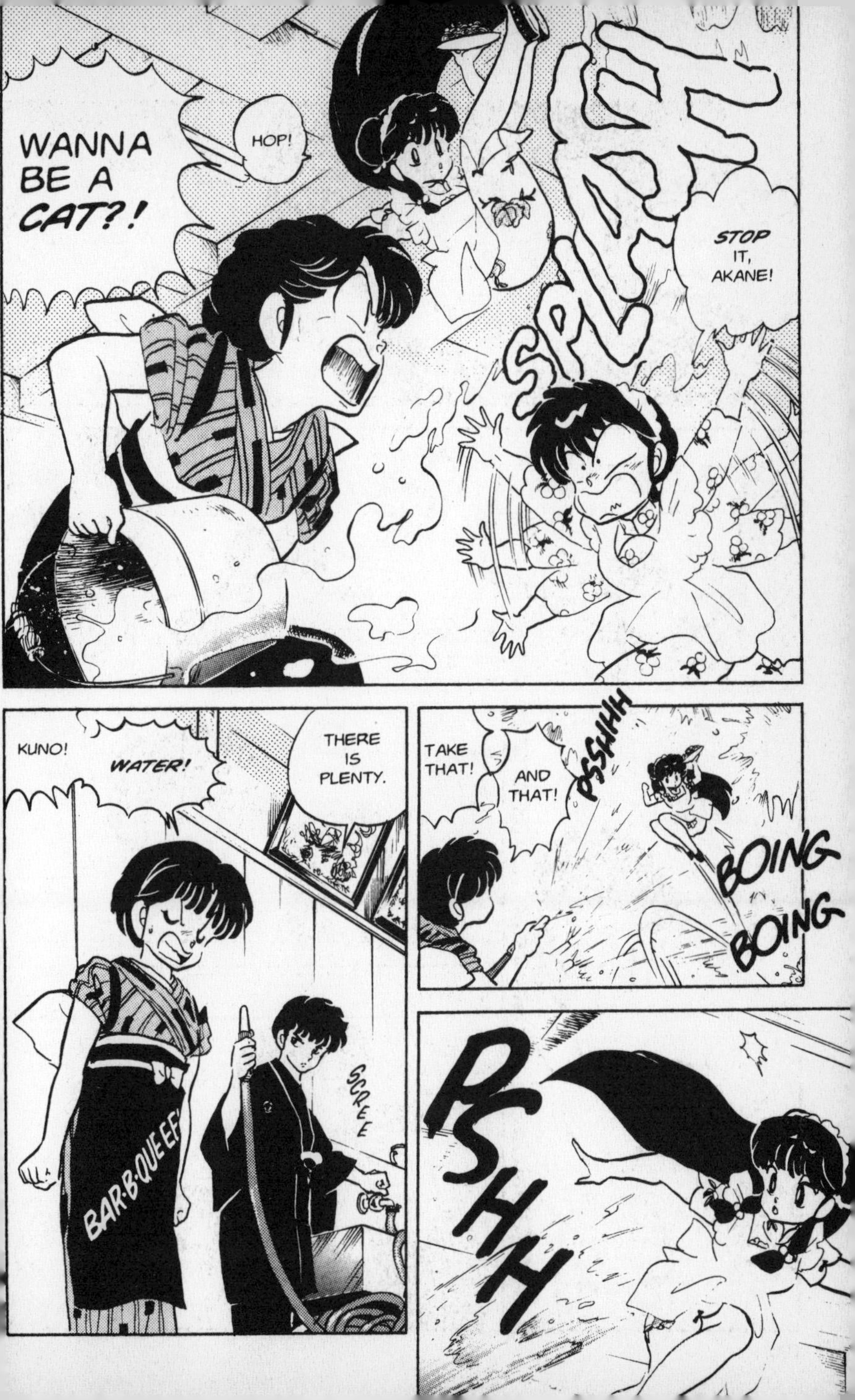
WANNA BE A CAT?!
HOP!
SPLASH
STOP IT, AKANE!
KUNO!
WATER!
THERE IS PLENTY.
BAR-B-QUE EF
SCREE
TAKE THAT!
AND THAT!
PSSHHH
BOING
BOING
PSHH

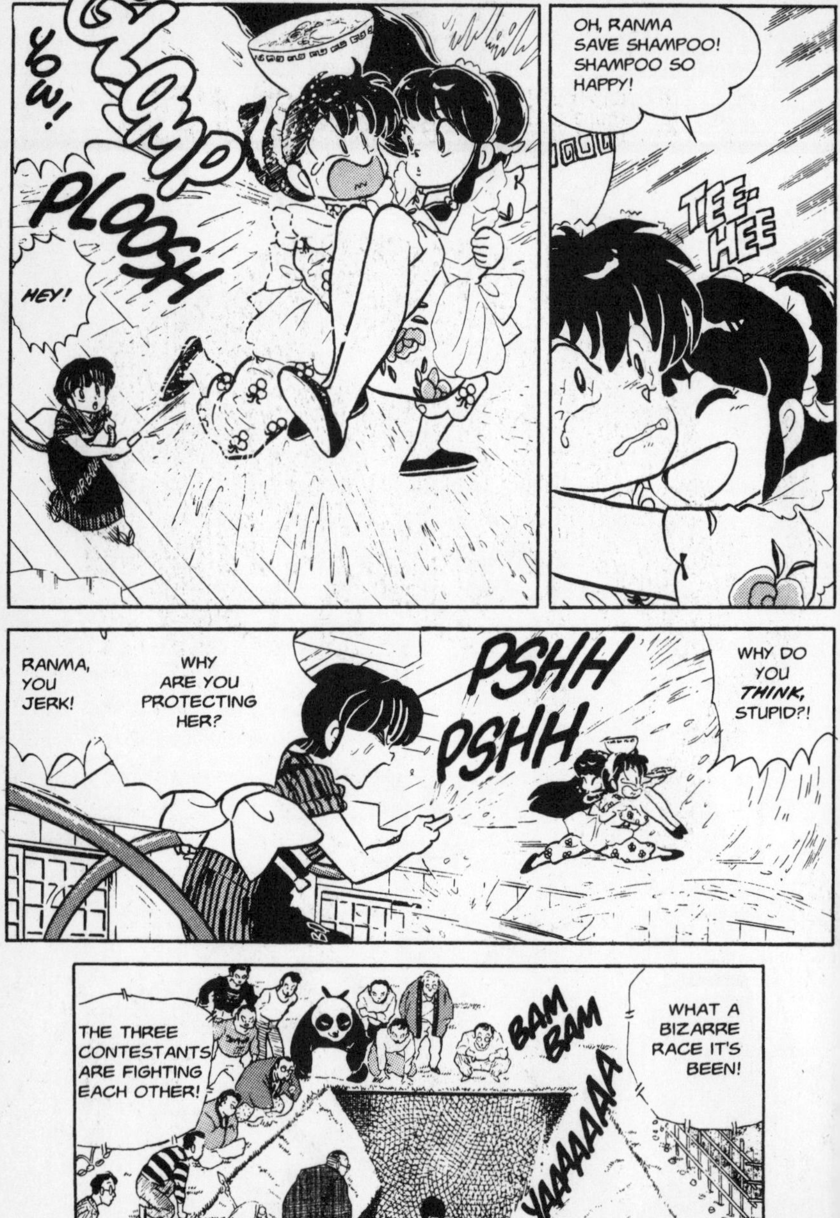
GLOMP
YOW!
PLOOSH
HEY!
OH, RANMA SAVE SHAMPOO! SHAMPOO SO HAPPY!
TEE-HEE
RANMA, YOU JERK!
WHY ARE YOU PROTECTING HER?
PSHH PSHH
WHY DO YOU *THINK*, STUPID?!
THE THREE CONTESTANTS ARE FIGHTING EACH OTHER!
BAM BAM
YAAAAAAA
WHAT A BIZARRE RACE IT'S BEEN!

Part 13

I WON'T EAT IT!

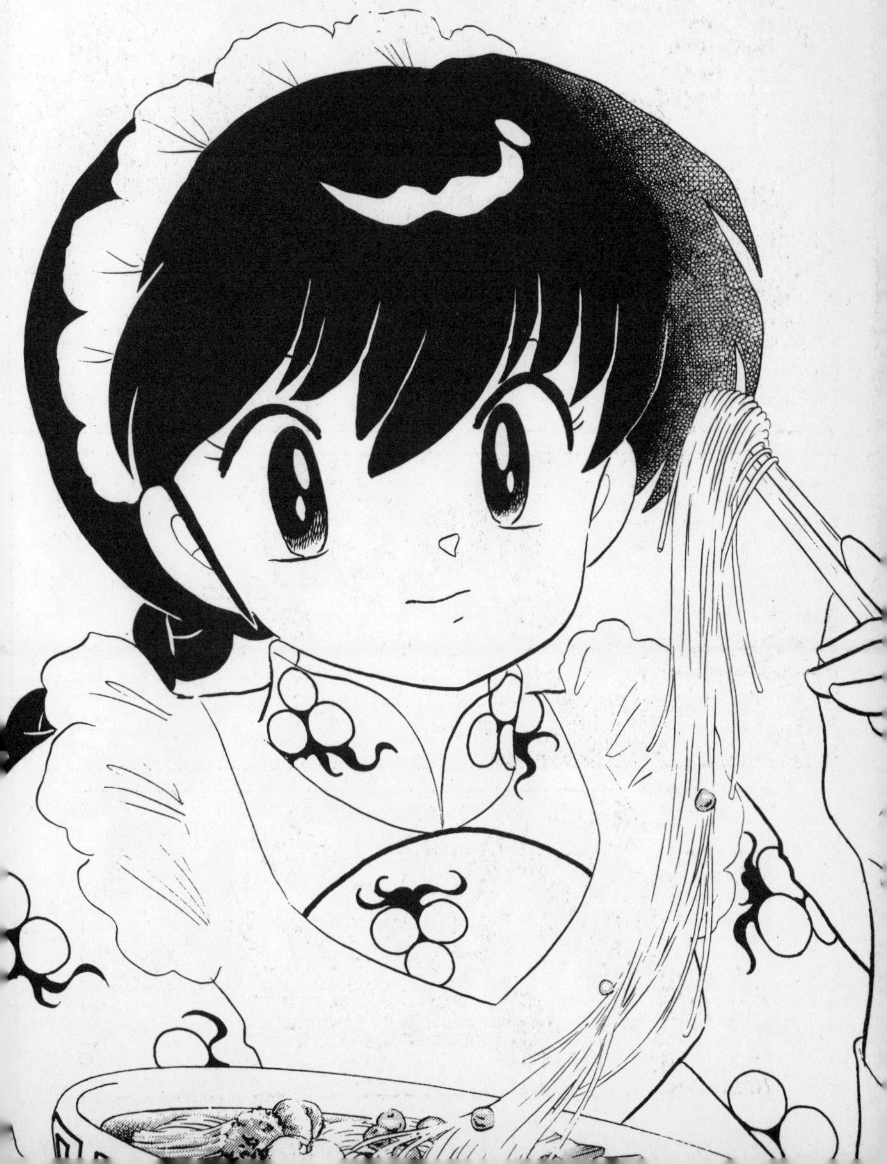

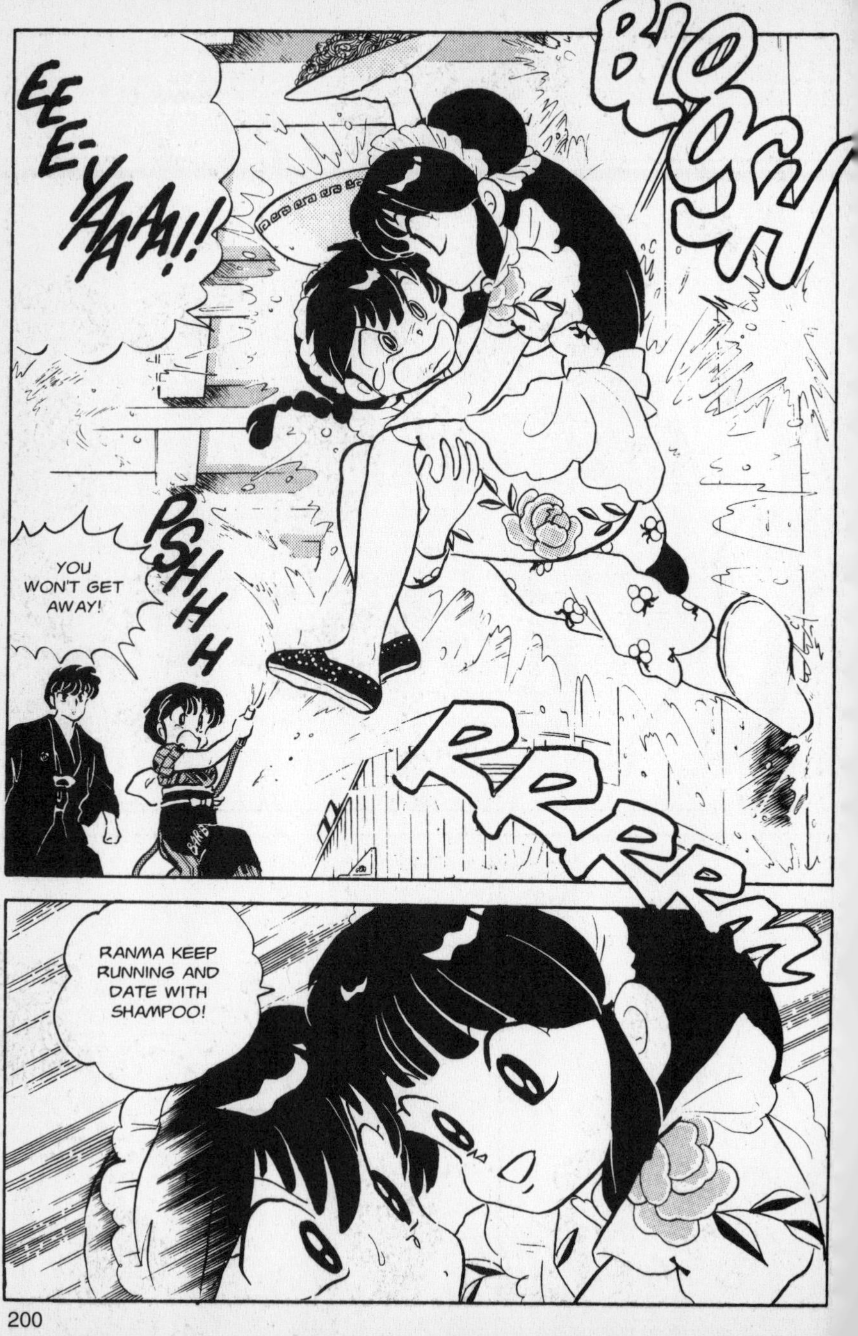
EEE-YAAA!!
BLOOGH!
PSHHHH
YOU WON'T GET AWAY!
RREEEM
RANMA KEEP RUNNING AND DATE WITH SHAMPOO!

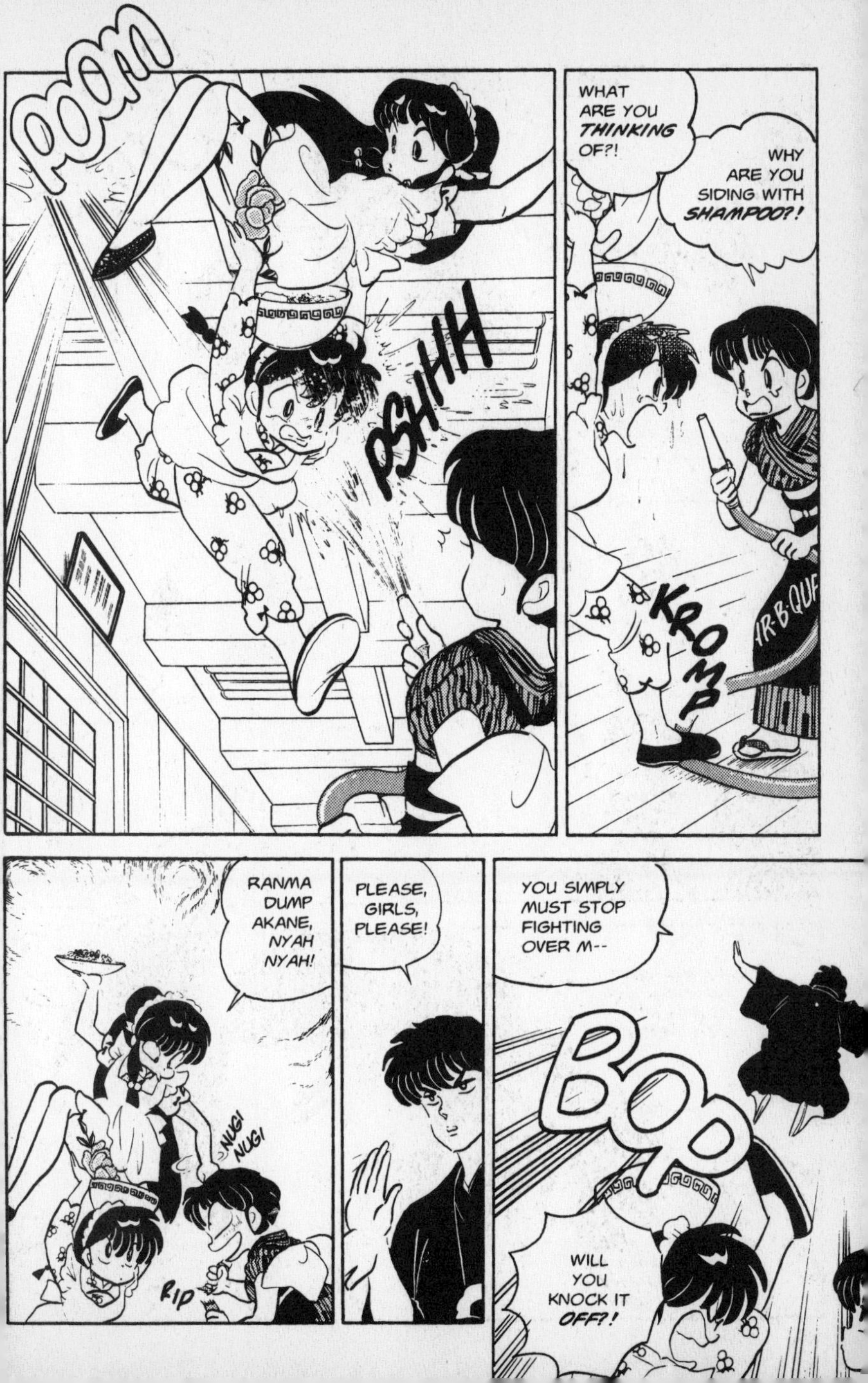
POOM
PSHHH
WHAT ARE YOU THINKING OF?!
WHY ARE YOU SIDING WITH SHAMPOO?!
KROMP
HR-B-QUE
RANMA DUMP AKANE, NYAH NYAH!
NUGI NUGI
RIP
PLEASE, GIRLS, PLEASE!
YOU SIMPLY MUST STOP FIGHTING OVER M--
BOP
WILL YOU KNOCK IT OFF?!

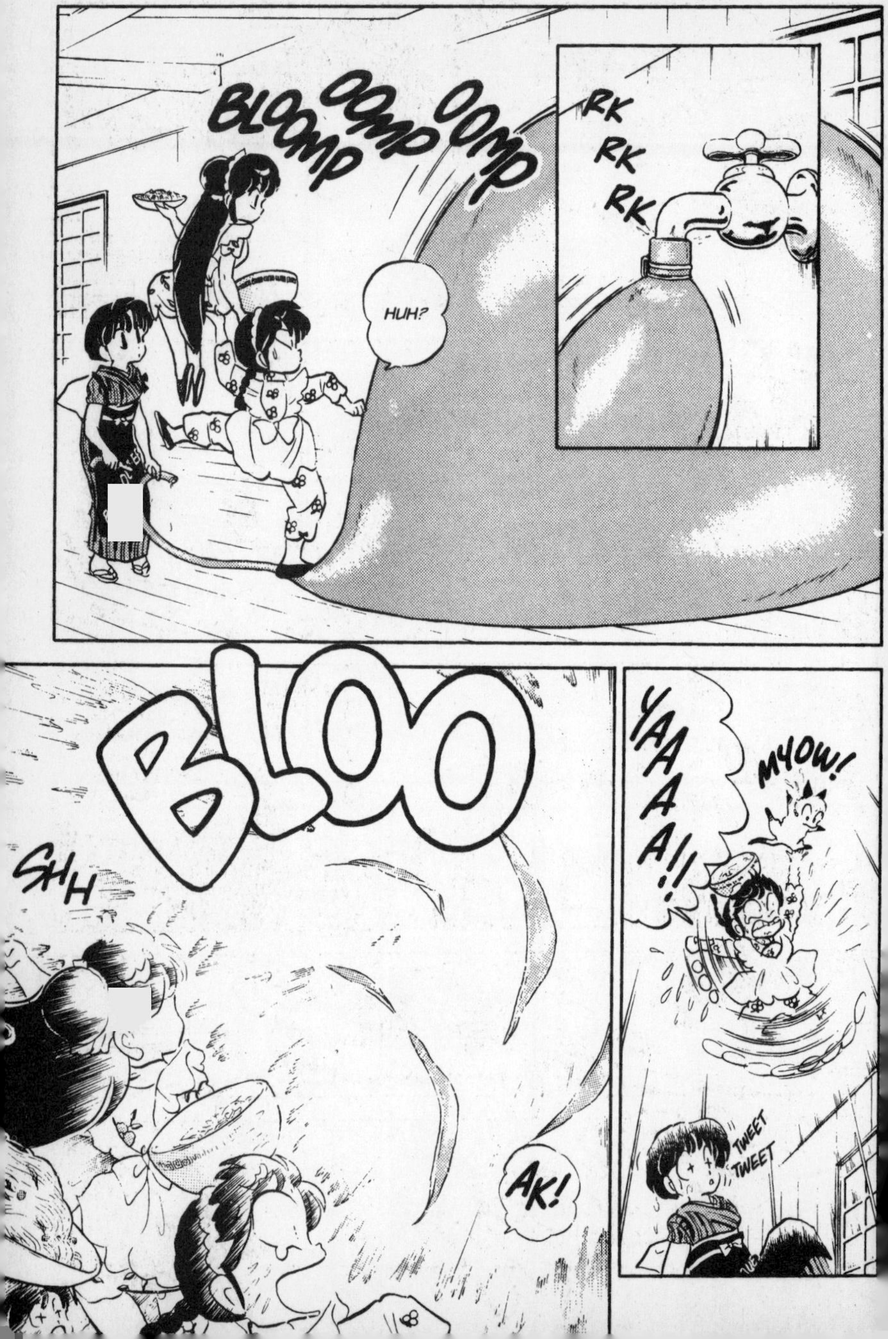
BLOOMP OOMP OOMP
HUH?
RK RK RK
BLOO
SHH
AK!
YAAAA!!
MYOW!
TWEET TWEET

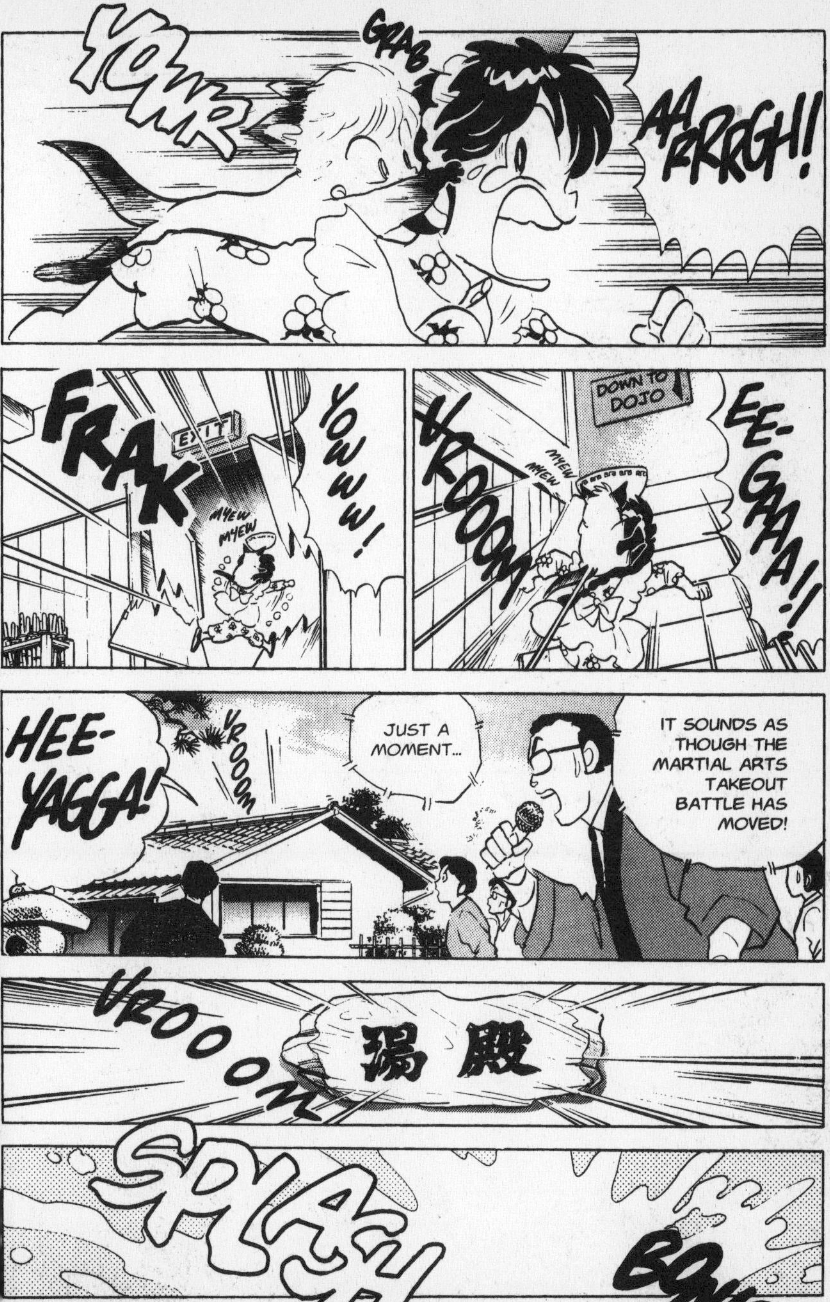
YOWR
GRAB
AARRRGH!!
FRAK
EXIT
MYEW MYEW
YOWWWW!
DOWN TO DOJO
VROOOOM
MYEW MYEW
EE-GAAAA!!
HEE-YAGGA!
VROOOOM
JUST A MOMENT...
IT SOUNDS AS THOUGH THE MARTIAL ARTS TAKEOUT BATTLE HAS MOVED!
VROOOOM
湯殿
SPLASH
BONK

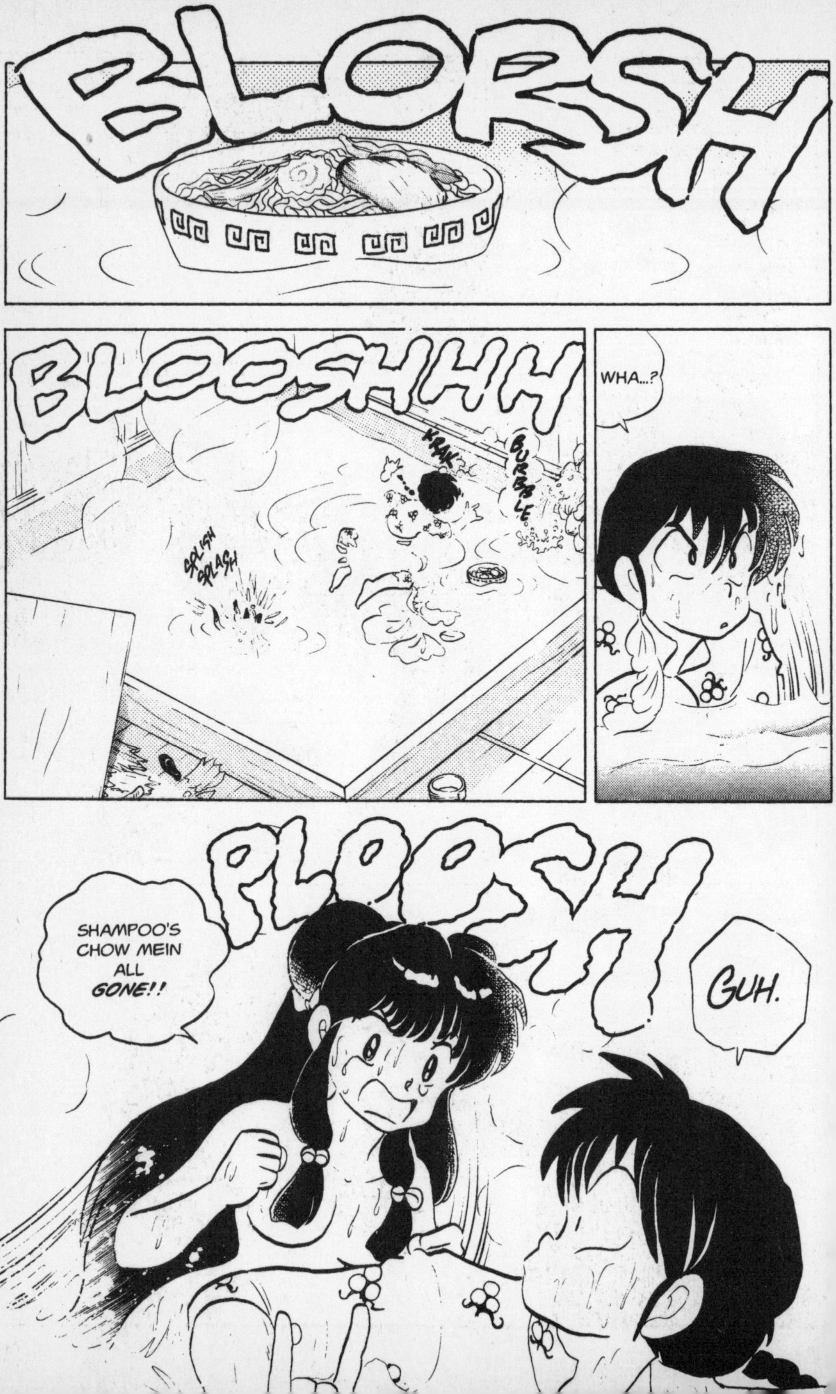
BLORSH
BLOOSHHH
KRAK
BURBBLE
SPLISH SPLASH
WHA...?
PLOOSH!
SHAMPOO'S CHOW MEIN ALL GONE!!
GUH.

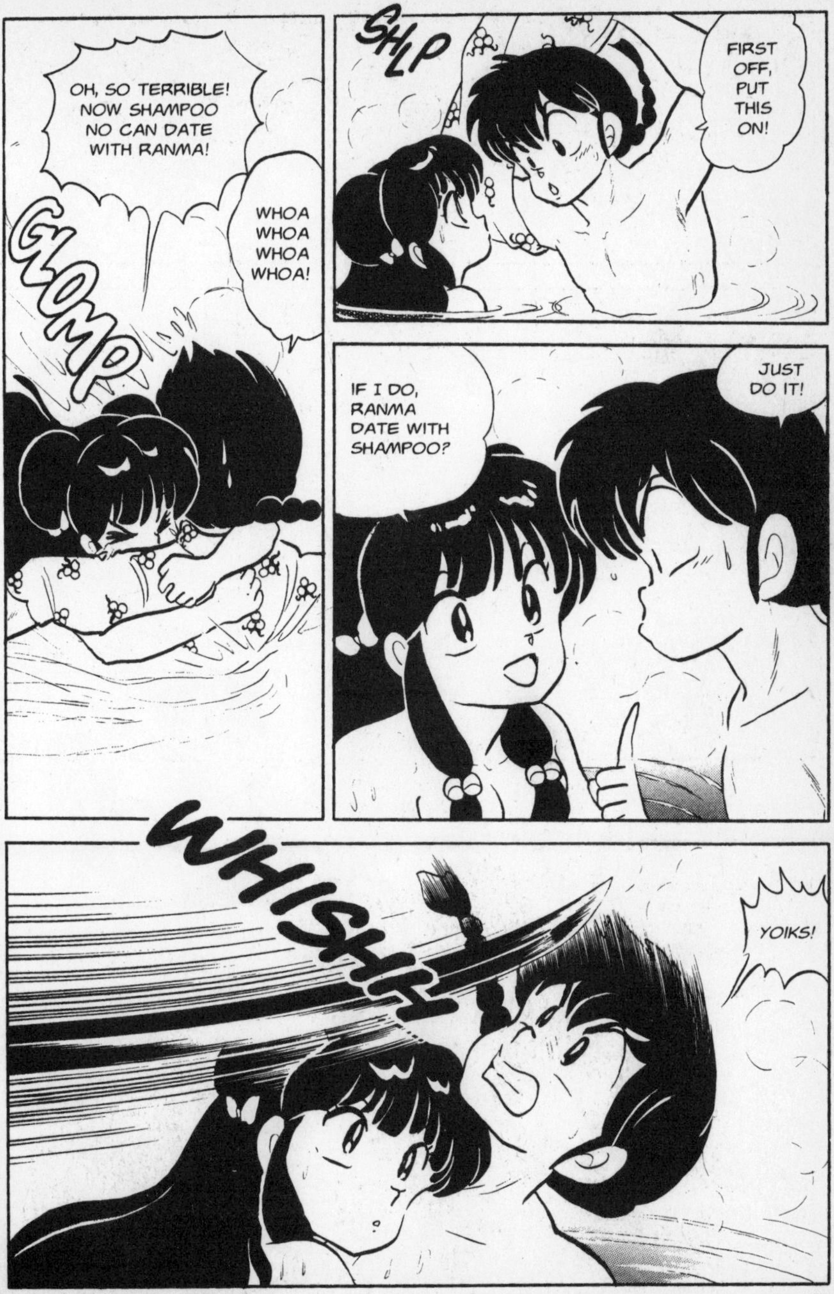
OH, SO TERRIBLE! NOW SHAMPOO NO CAN DATE WITH RANMA!
WHOA WHOA WHOA WHOA!
GLOMP
SHLP
FIRST OFF, PUT THIS ON!
IF I DO, RANMA DATE WITH SHAMPOO?
JUST DO IT!
WHISHH
YOIKS!

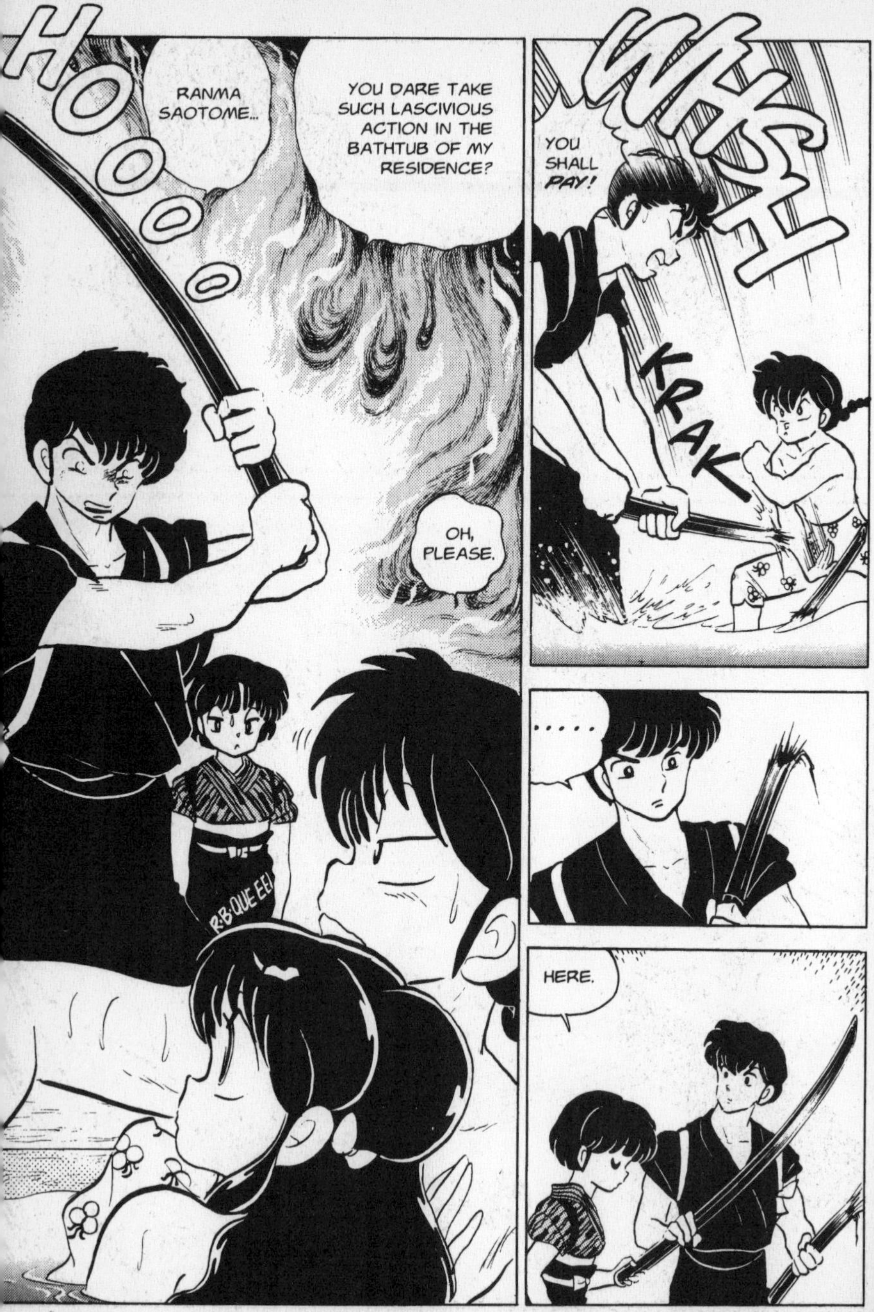
HOOOOOO
RANMA SAOTOME...
YOU DARE TAKE SUCH LASCIVIOUS ACTION IN THE BATHTUB OF MY RESIDENCE?
OH, PLEASE.
WHSSH
YOU SHALL PAY!
KRAK
.....
HERE.

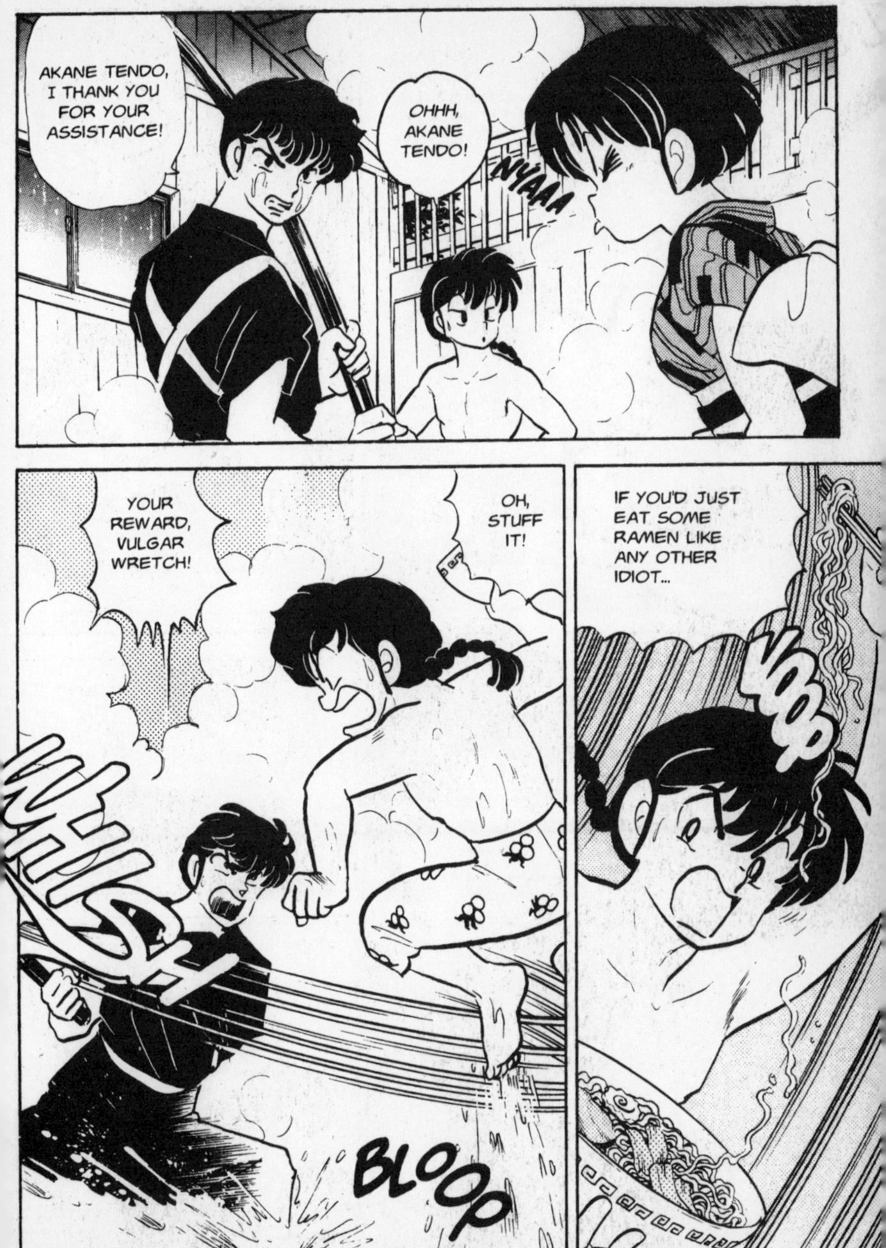
AKANE TENDO, I THANK YOU FOR YOUR ASSISTANCE!
OHHH, AKANE TENDO!
NYAAA
YOUR REWARD, VULGAR WRETCH!
OH, STUFF IT!
WHISH
BLOOP
IF YOU'D JUST EAT SOME RAMEN LIKE ANY OTHER IDIOT...
VOOP

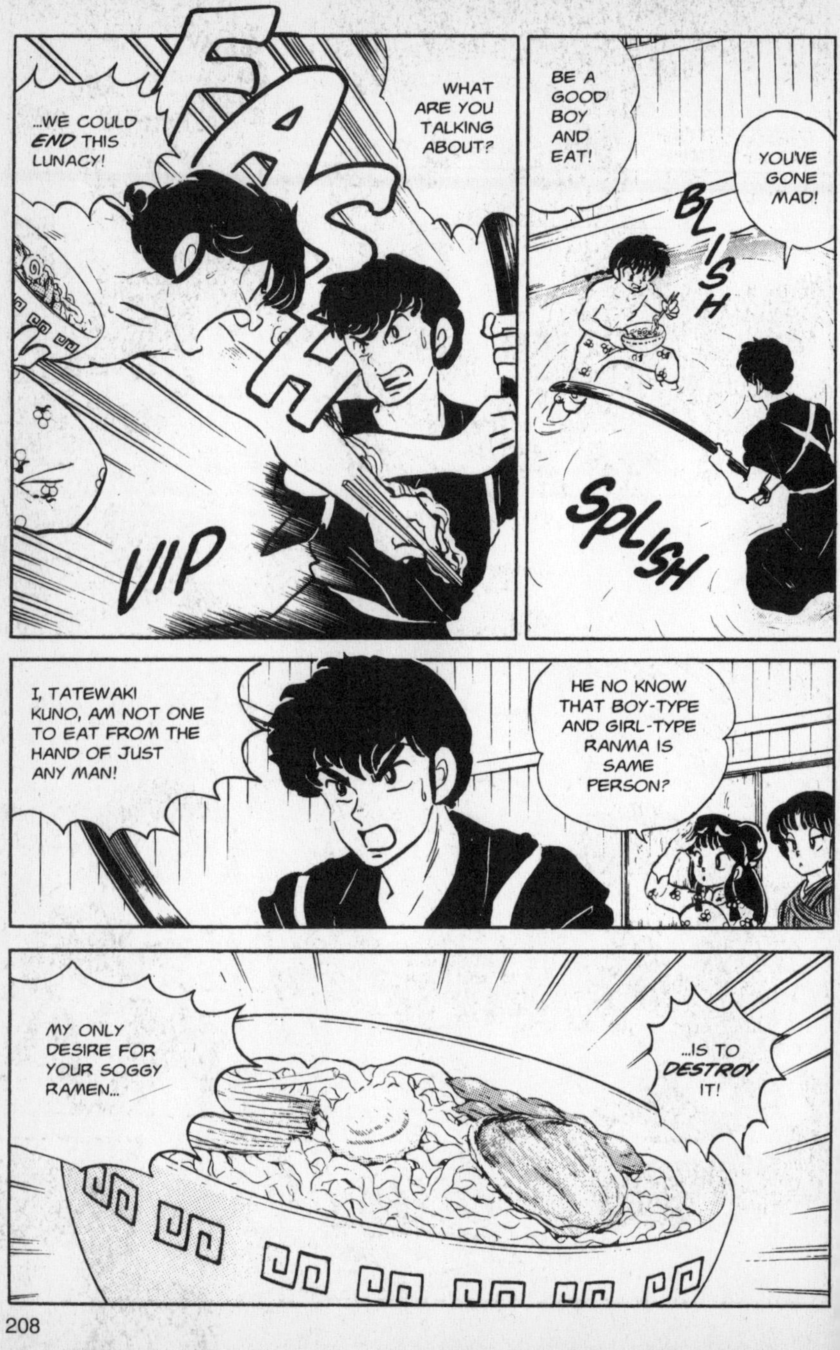
FASH
...WE COULD *END* THIS LUNACY!
WHAT ARE YOU TALKING ABOUT?
VIP
BE A GOOD BOY AND EAT!
YOU'VE GONE MAD!
BLISH
SPLISH
I, TATEWAKI KUNO, AM NOT ONE TO EAT FROM THE HAND OF JUST ANY MAN!
HE NO KNOW THAT BOY-TYPE AND GIRL-TYPE RANMA IS SAME PERSON?
MY ONLY DESIRE FOR YOUR SOGGY RAMEN...
...IS TO *DESTROY* IT!

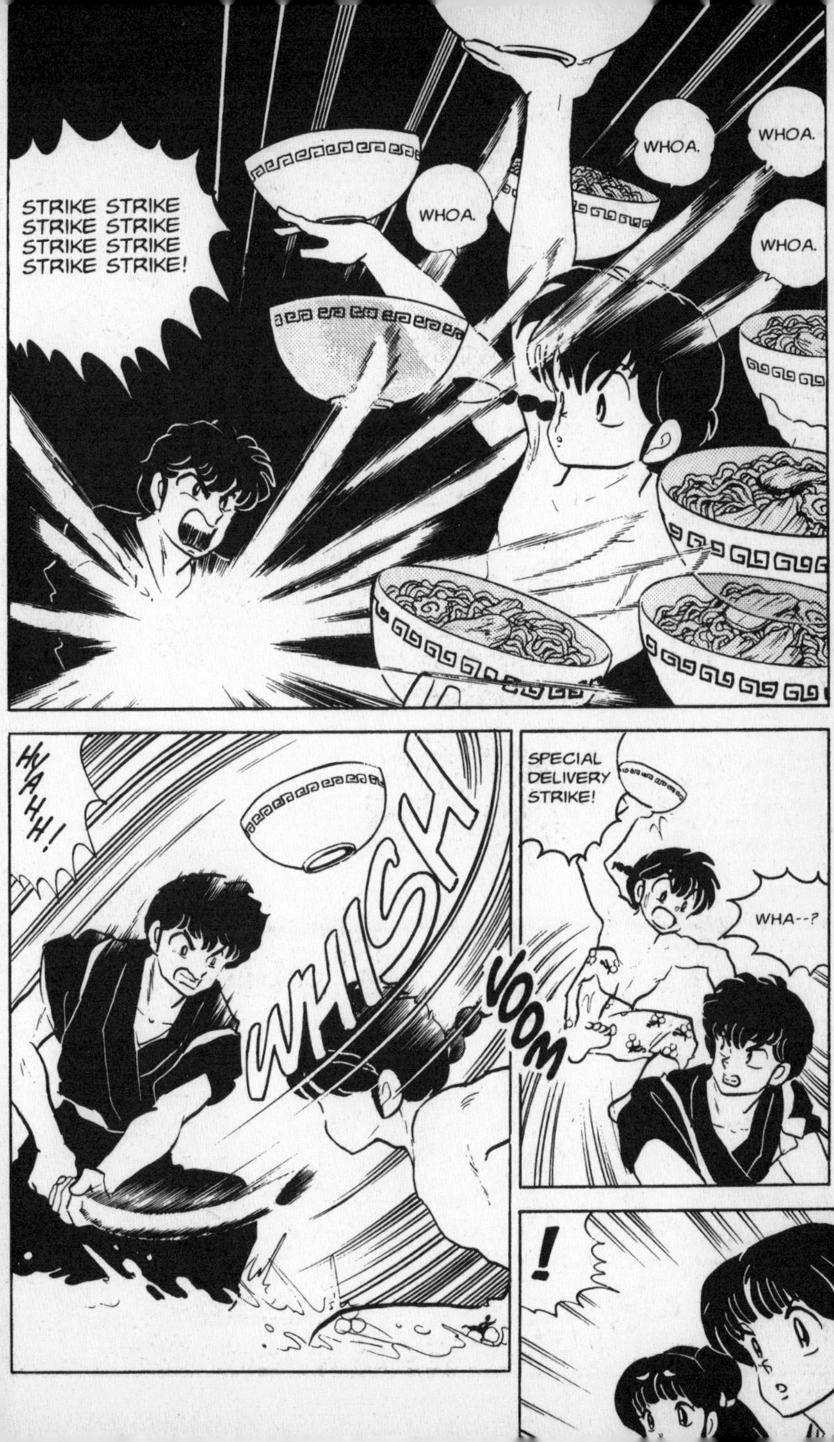
STRIKE STRIKE
STRIKE STRIKE
STRIKE STRIKE
STRIKE STRIKE!
WHOA.
WHOA.
WHOA.
WHOA.
HYAHH!
WHISH
VOOM
SPECIAL
DELIVERY
STRIKE!
WHA--?
!

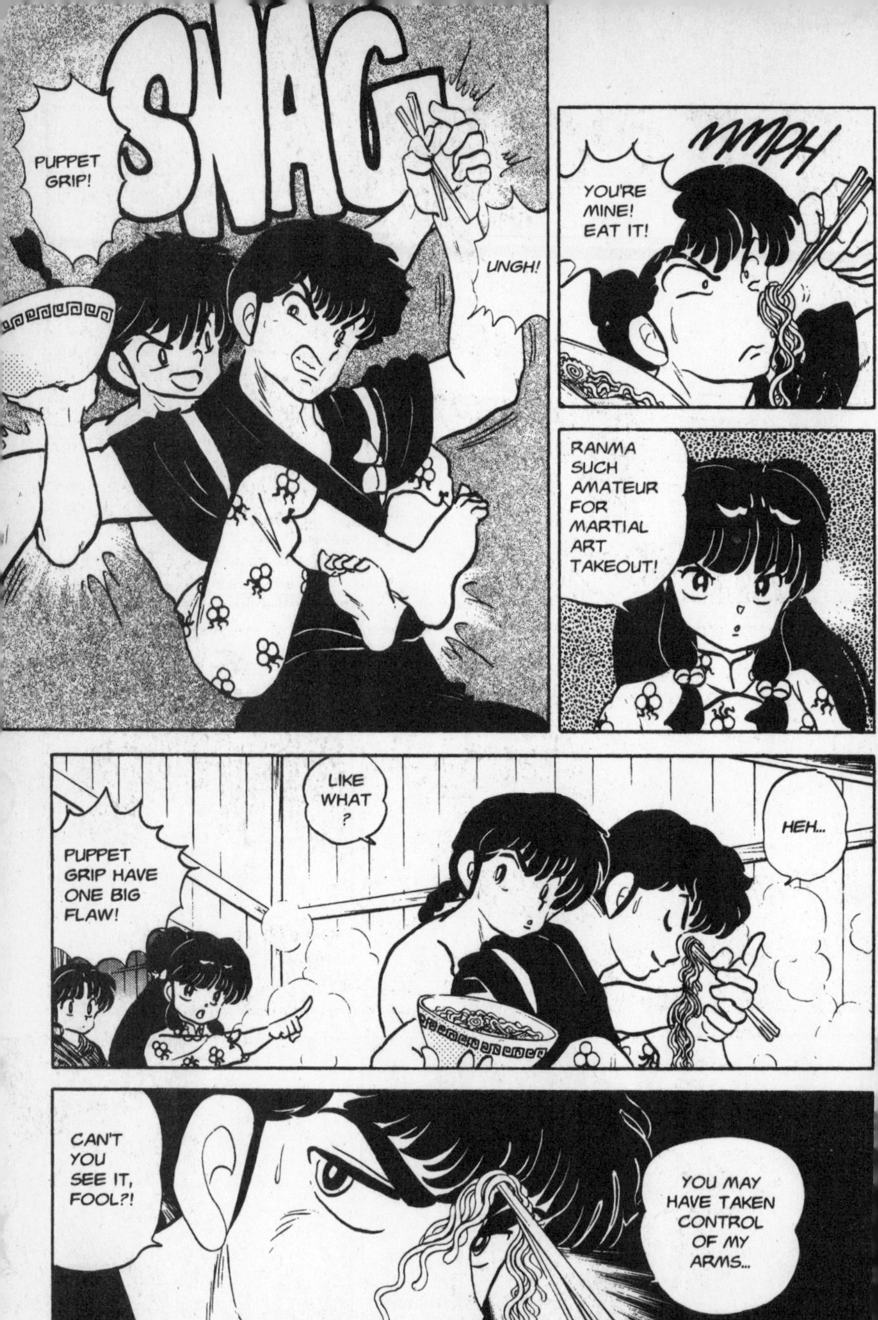
SNAG
PUPPET GRIP!
UNGH!
MMPH
YOU'RE MINE! EAT IT!
RANMA SUCH AMATEUR FOR MARTIAL ART TAKEOUT!
PUPPET GRIP HAVE ONE BIG FLAW!
LIKE WHAT ?
HEH...
CAN'T YOU SEE IT, FOOL?!
YOU MAY HAVE TAKEN CONTROL OF MY ARMS...

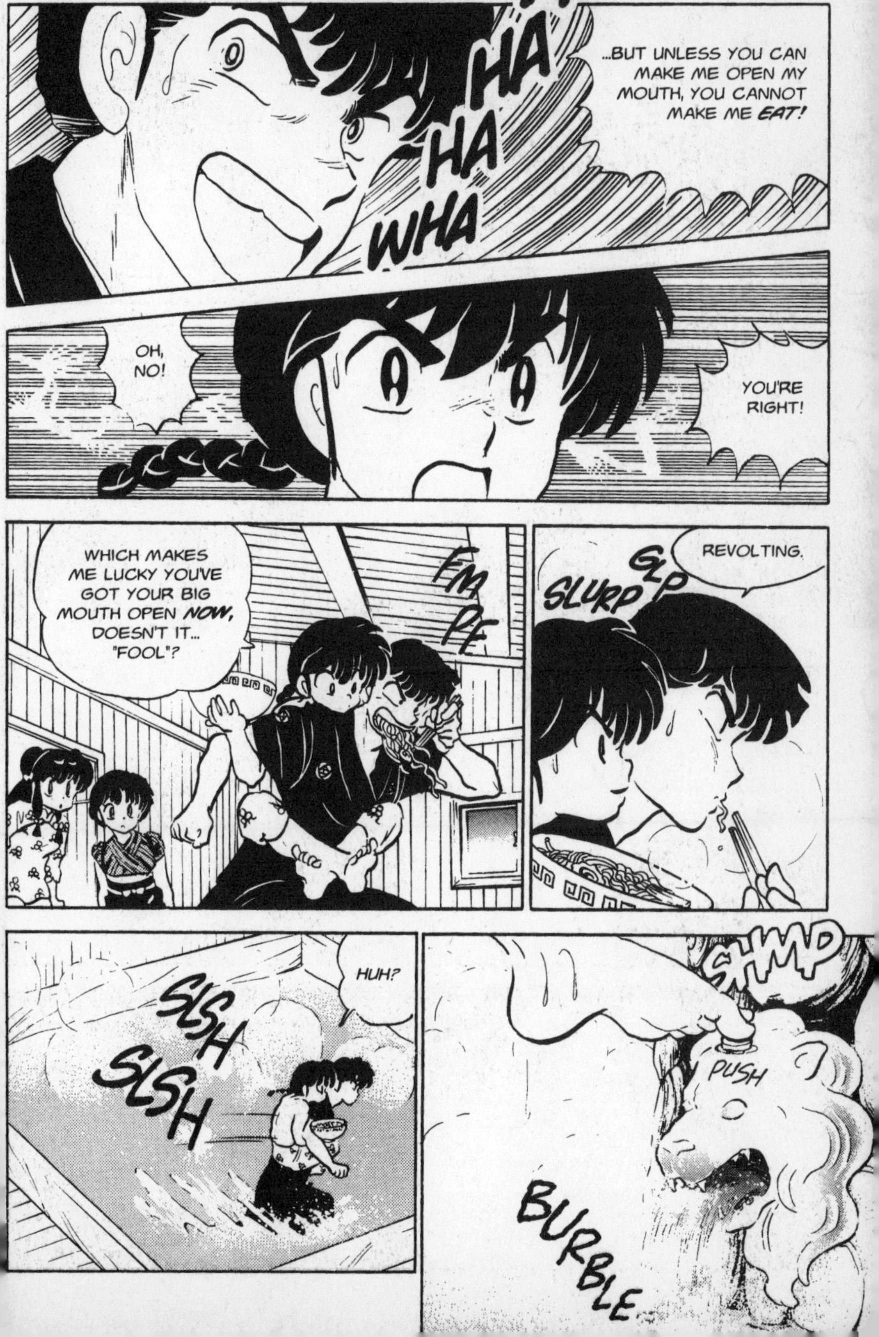
HA
HA
HA
WHA
...BUT UNLESS YOU CAN MAKE ME OPEN MY MOUTH, YOU CANNOT MAKE ME *EAT!*
OH, NO!
YOU'RE RIGHT!
WHICH MAKES ME LUCKY YOU'VE GOT YOUR BIG MOUTH OPEN *NOW*, DOESN'T IT... "FOOL"?
FMPE
SLURP
GLP
REVOLTING.
SLSH
SLSH
HUH?
SHMP
PUSH
BURBLE

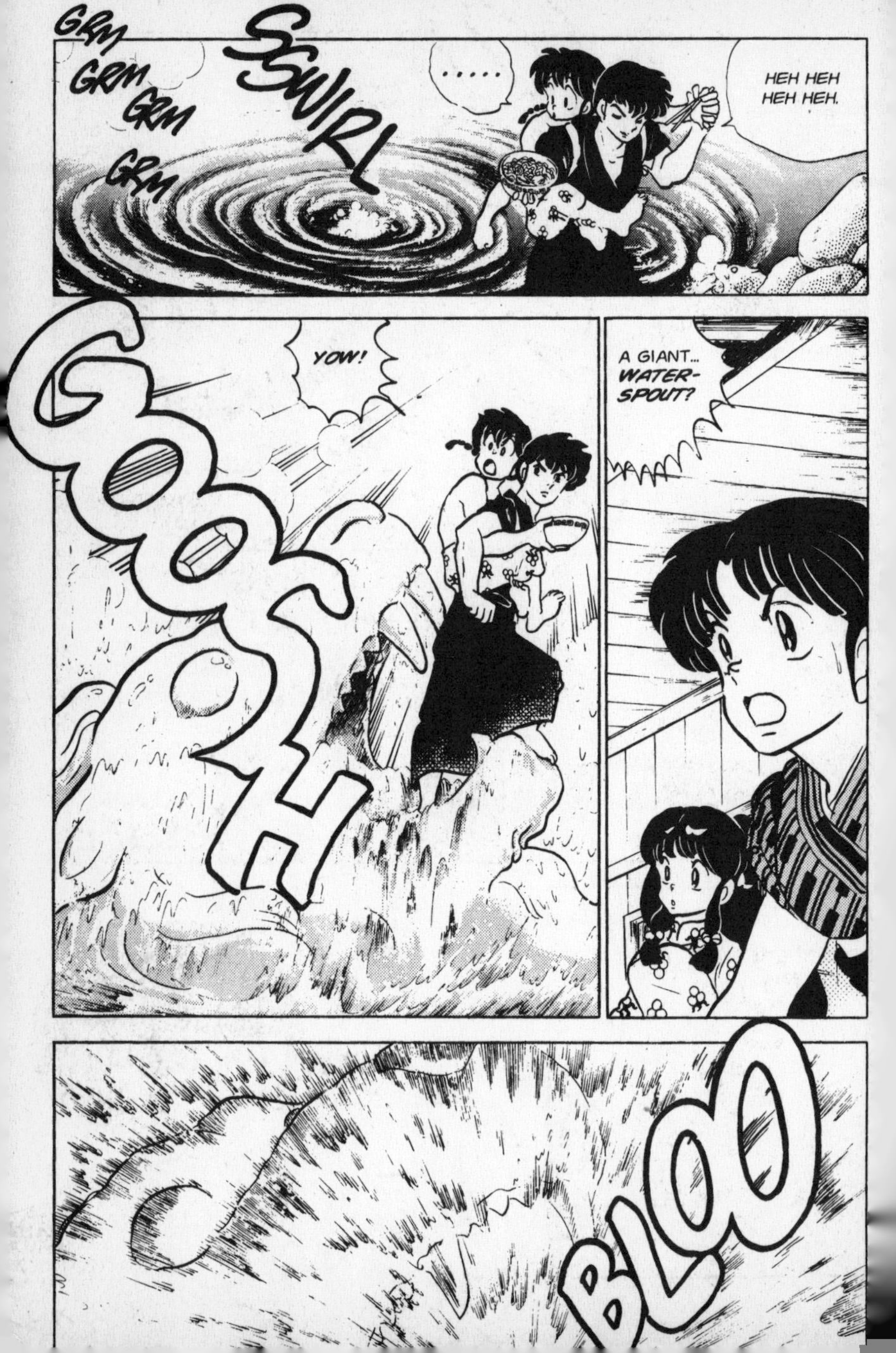
GRM GRM GRM GRM
SSWIRL
.....
HEH HEH HEH HEH.
GOOOSH
YOW!
A GIANT... WATER-SPOUT?
BLOO

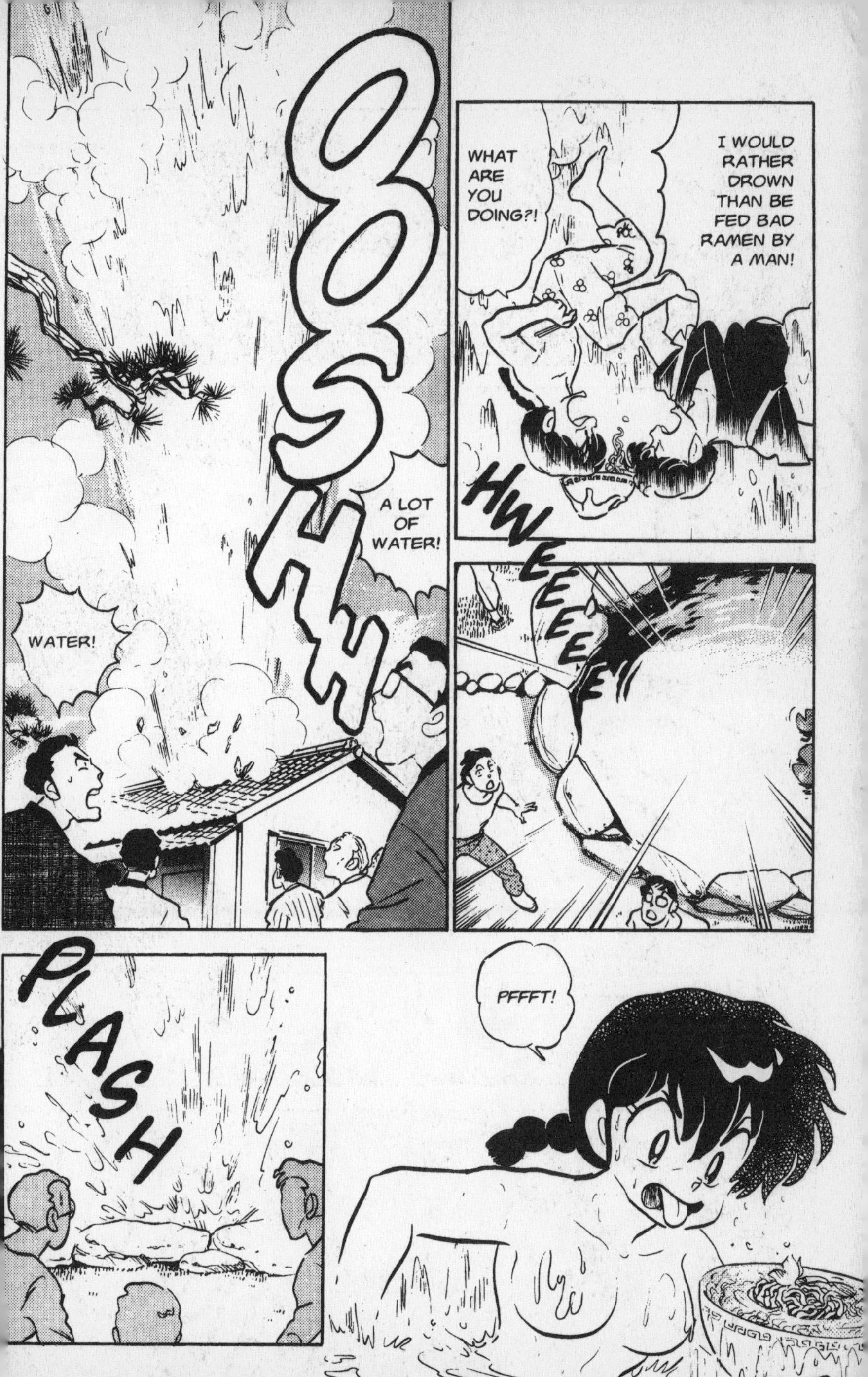
OOSHH
A LOT OF WATER!
WATER!
WHAT ARE YOU DOING?!
I WOULD RATHER DROWN THAN BE FED BAD RAMEN BY A MAN!
HWEEEEEE
PLASH
PFFFT!

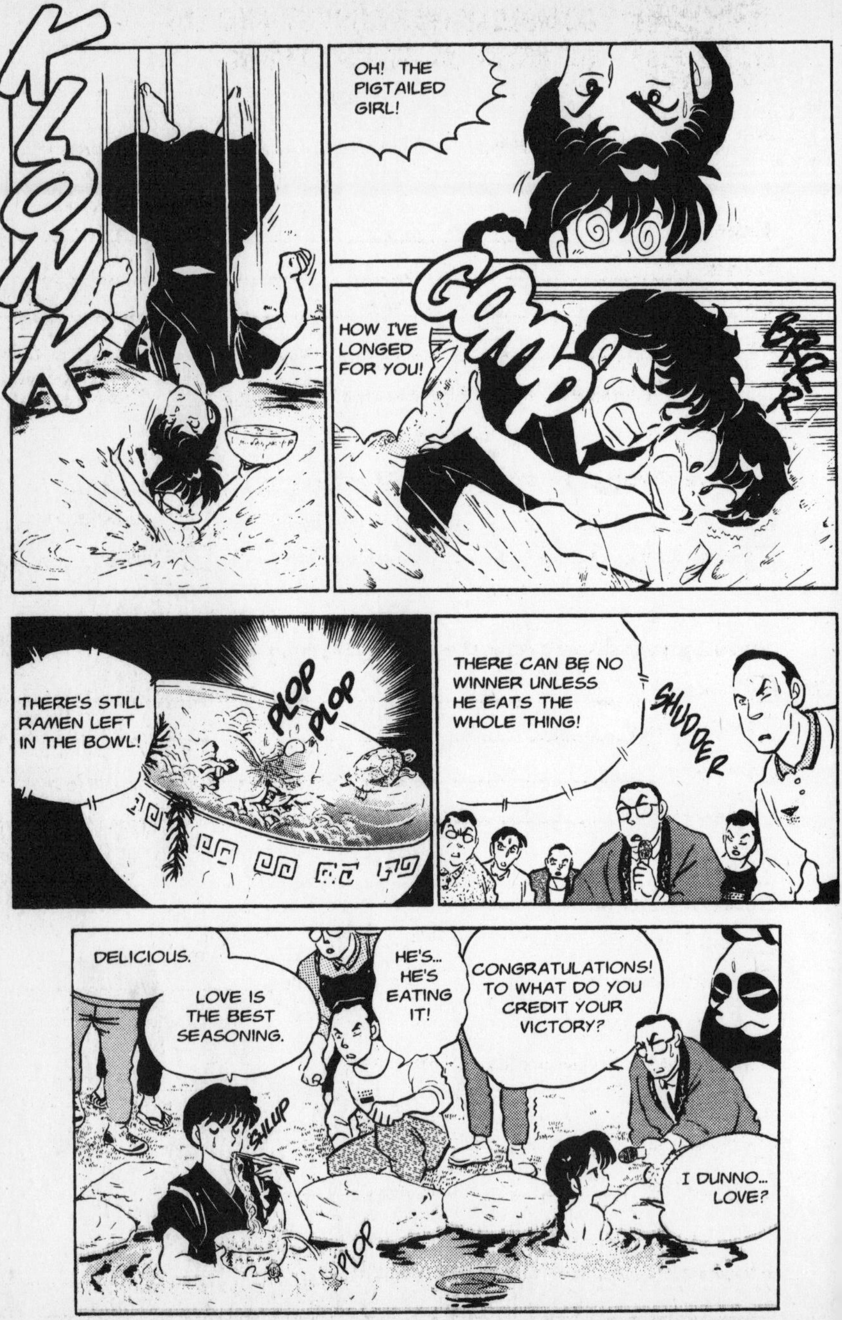
KLONK
OH! THE PIGTAILED GIRL!
GOMP
HOW I'VE LONGED FOR YOU!
BRRR
THERE'S STILL RAMEN LEFT IN THE BOWL!
PLOP PLOP
THERE CAN BE NO WINNER UNLESS HE EATS THE WHOLE THING!
SHUDDER
DELICIOUS.
LOVE IS THE BEST SEASONING.
SHLUP
PLOP
HE'S... HE'S EATING IT!
CONGRATULATIONS! TO WHAT DO YOU CREDIT YOUR VICTORY?
I DUNNO... LOVE?

TO BE CONTINUED

COMPLETE OUR SURVEY AND LET US KNOW WHAT YOU THINK!

☐ Please check here if you DO NOT wish to receive information or future offers from VIZ

Name: _____

Address: _____

City: _____ State: _____ Zip: _____

E-mail: _____

☐ Male ☐ Female Date of Birth (mm/dd/yyyy): ___/___/_____ (Under 13? Parental consent required)

What race/ethnicity do you consider yourself? (please check one)

☐ Asian/Pacific Islander   ☐ Black/African American   ☐ Hispanic/Latino

☐ Native American/Alaskan Native   ☐ White/Caucasian   ☐ Other: _____

What VIZ product did you purchase? (check all that apply and indicate title purchased)

☐ DVD/VHS _____

☐ Graphic Novel _____

☐ Magazines _____

☐ Merchandise _____

Reason for purchase: (check all that apply)

☐ Special offer   ☐ Favorite title   ☐ Gift

☐ Recommendation   ☐ Other _____

Where did you make your purchase? (please check one)

☐ Comic store   ☐ Bookstore   ☐ Mass/Grocery Store

☐ Newsstand   ☐ Video/Video Game Store   ☐ Other: _____

☐ Online (site: _____)

What other VIZ properties have you purchased/own? _____

_____

How many anime and/or manga titles have you purchased in the last year? How many were VIZ titles? (please check one from each column)

ANIME
- ☐ None
- ☐ 1-4
- ☐ 5-10
- ☐ 11+

MANGA
- ☐ None
- ☐ 1-4
- ☐ 5-10
- ☐ 11+

VIZ
- ☐ None
- ☐ 1-4
- ☐ 5-10
- ☐ 11+

I find the pricing of VIZ products to be: (please check one)
- ☐ Cheap
- ☐ Reasonable
- ☐ Expensive

What genre of manga and anime would you like to see from VIZ? (please check two)
- ☐ Adventure
- ☐ Comic Strip
- ☐ Science Fiction
- ☐ Fighting
- ☐ Horror
- ☐ Romance
- ☐ Fantasy
- ☐ Sports

What do you think of VIZ's new look?
- ☐ Love It
- ☐ It's OK
- ☐ Hate It
- ☐ Didn't Notice
- ☐ No Opinion

Which do you prefer? (please check one)
- ☐ Reading right-to-left
- ☐ Reading left-to-right

Which do you prefer? (please check one)
- ☐ Sound effects in English
- ☐ Sound effects in Japanese with English captions
- ☐ Sound effects in Japanese only with a glossary at the back

THANK YOU! Please send the completed form to:

NJW Research
42 Catharine St.
Poughkeepsie, NY 12601

All information provided will be used for internal purposes only. We promise not to sell or otherwise divulge your information.

NO PURCHASE NECESSARY. Requests not in compliance with all terms of this form will not be acknowledged or returned. All submissions are subject to verification and become the property of VIZ, LLC. Fraudulent submission, including use of multiple addresses or P.O. boxes to obtain additional VIZ information or offers may result in prosecution. VIZ reserves the right to withdraw or modify any terms of this form. Void where prohibited, taxed, or restricted by law. VIZ will not be liable for lost, misdirected, mutilated, illegible, incomplete or postage-due mail. © 2003 VIZ, LLC. All Rights Reserved. VIZ, LLC, property titles, characters, names and plots therein under license to VIZ, LLC. All Rights Reserved.